8/6

Sc2

Provincial Power in
the Inka Empire

Provincial Power in the INKA EMPIRE

Terence N. D'Altroy

SMITHSONIAN INSTITUTION PRESS

Washington and London

Rosemary Sheffield edited the complete text of this book,
updated the disk files, coordinated the preparation of
the illustrations and tables, and produced the index.

Printed in the United States of America

01 00 99 98 97 96 95 94 93 92
10 9 8 7 6 5 4 3 2 1

Library of Congress Cataloging-in-Publication Data

D'Altroy, Terence N.
Provincial power in the Inka empire / Terence N. D'Altroy.
p.   cm.
Includes bibliographical references and index.
ISBN 1-56098-115-6
1. Incas—Politics and government.
2. Incas—Social conditions.
3. Incas—Economic conditions.
I. Title.
F3429.3.P65D35   1992
985'.01—dc20   91-17476

British Library Cataloging-in-Publication Data available

Cover: Illustration, dated 1614, by Felipe Guaman Poma de Ayala (Figure
5.2, *infra*).

Contents

v

List of Figures and Tables

Figures

Tables

Preface

The gestation of this book lay in the challenge of addressing a set of issues far narrower than the provincial organization of the Inka empire. Following my dissertation fieldwork on the Inka occupation of the Upper Mantaro Valley of the central sierra of Peru (1977–79), and collaboration in a subsequent project (1982–83) on the impacts of the Inka conquest on the region's domestic economy, I found it increasingly difficult to explain what happened in the Mantaro without considering the broader scope of the imperial formation. I also was discomfited by many elements of the standard explanations for the development of the Inka polity, especially their focus on the empire's distinctively Andean character and their frequent lack of reference to anthropological models of sociopolitical organization. Almost a century of careful scholarship on the peoples of the Andes has made great strides in bringing us closer to an understanding of the formation of the empire, but most of the literature still relies heavily on particularistic or structural approaches, neither of which I have found very satisfactory in providing general explanations. My goal in writing this book was therefore twofold: first, to sketch out a general model for the Inka empire, drawing comparatively from considerations of other archaic empires, and second, in the context of this model, to essay an explanation for Inka provincial strategy in the central sierra of Peru, a region that was incorporated relatively intensively into the state.

In preparing this work, I owe a considerable debt of gratitude to numerous people in the United States, Peru, and Argentina. Because so many participated in the research, some individuals are assuredly missing from my acknowledgments, for which I ask pardon in anticipation of their plaints. I also apologize for occasionally writing in the first-person plural here, but the fieldwork described here was embedded in a much larger project and the ties have been too close for surgical removal of my work from that of my colleagues and friends.

The greatest debt in the United States is to my project colleagues, Timothy Earle, Catherine Scott, and Christine Hastorf. It has been a great stimulus and pleasure to work with them since the inception in 1977 of the Upper Mantaro Archaeological Research Project (UMARP), from which this work is an outgrowth. Tim made the transition from doctoral adviser to friend and colleague with grace and uncommon subordination of his own interests in publication; his commentary on this manuscript was of inestimable value. Although the intellectual and personal origins of this work are diverse, Jeffrey Parsons also deserves particular mention. He introduced me to the pleasures of Latin American field archaeology in Mexico and generously granted our project access to his unpublished survey data from the Peruvian central highlands. Both he and Tom Dillehay provided incisive comments on this study, forcing reconsideration of a variety of issues I had mistakenly thought were put to bed. I also thank Terry LeVine, Glenn Russell, Cathy Costin, Elsie Sandefur, and Melissa Hagstrum, whose codirection or association with the Upper Mantaro field research contributed directly to its success. Some of the data presented here derive from their studies, and I thank them for providing access. More important, many of the ideas in the text stemmed or benefited from their insightful observations.

A number of individuals graciously provided unpublished information gained from their research. Although these persons are cited where appropriate in the text, I would like to thank in particular Deborah Caro, Charles Hastings, John Hyslop, Tom Leatherman, Craig Morris, Brooke Thomas, and Jane Wheeler for their generosity. I would additionally like to express my gratitude to Dr. James Corter (Teachers College, Columbia University) for writing the program to perform the spatial autocorrelation analyses described in Chapter 9 and for providing advice about the use of multidimensional scaling in Chapters 4 and 9. I owe a special thanks to Rosemary Sheffield, the volume editor, who contributed greatly to clarifying the text and caught more errors and inconsistencies than I would like to admit. It has been a pleasure to collaborate with her in the production of the book.

In Peru, Ramiro Matos Mendieta and Jorge Silva Sifuentes were conspicuously generous in assisting our field research. UMARP was organized in conjunction with the studies conducted under Dr. Matos's Proyecto de Investigaciones Arqueológicas de Junín, codirected in 1975–76 by Dr. Parsons. Ramiro introduced us to the Upper Mantaro Valley, provided invaluable advice on the archaeology of the Andes, and gave of his friendship, time, and laboratory facilities. Jorge helped enormously in the field and in the interminable administrative elements of conducting fieldwork.

Quite a number of students and colleagues worked for months in the field and the laboratory with little financial support. Peruvian students included Cristina Baltazar, Enrique Bragayrac, Antonio Cornejo, Carlos Elera, Manuel Escobedo, Rubén García, Beatriz Miyashiro, Virginia Peláez, Carmen Thays, Humberto Vega, and Moisés Vergara. Colleagues and students from the United States, England, and Australia included David Bulbeck, Andrew Christensen, Bruce Crespin, Jim Fenton, Anabel Ford, Patricia Gilman, Elizabeth Hart, David Hearst, Lisa LeCount, Banks Leonard, Sarah Massey, Marilyn Norconk, Bruce Owen, and Elzbieta Zechenter. Many of the illustrations were drafted by Victor A. Buchli, Robert Keller, Joanne Pillsbury, and Kevin Pratt. Their contributions are greatly appreciated.

The people of the Mantaro Valley made us feel welcome in their communities, especially Sr. Miguel Martinez and his family, our hosts in Jauja from 1978 to 1986. The citizens of Jauja, Ataura, Sausa, Pancan, Marco, Concho, Tragadero, and Yanamarca are to be thanked for allowing extended fieldwork on their lands. Ataura contributed many field assistants, in particular Cirlio Arelleno, Martín Casas, Alex Castro, Juan de la Cruz, Victor Esteban, Grimaldo Flores, Carlos Guerra, Zósimo Llanto, Teodoro Marticoreno, Miguel Mateo, Hector Moya, Jorge Neyra, and César Soto.

In Peru, institutional permission and supervision for the project came from the Instituto Nacional de Cultura, Lima; the exceptional support lent by Dra. Isabel Flores is very much appreciated. The principal sources of funding were the National Science Foundation (BNS-820373); the Department of Anthropology and the Friends of Archaeology at the University of California, Los Angeles; and the Columbia University Council for the Social Sciences. I would also like to acknowledge a generous gift from Philip and Ruth Hettleman, via the Columbia University School of General Studies.

On a personal basis, my deepest thanks must go to the family of Sr. Andrés Moya Castro of Ataura. Andrés supervised fieldwork with great intelligence and commitment for 10 years, while doña Faustina Moya contributed mightily to seeing that the house and lab ran smoothly. Their eldest son, José, became an accomplished excavator, and all the family are friends of the highest order. It is to them, in a time of great travails in the Peruvian sierra, that I dedicate this book.

I

Introduction

Research on the evolution of complex society holds a central place in modern anthropology. The pristine states have held special interest, because their appearance represented a fundamental step in the transition from simple kin-based societies to complex, class-based polities. These states' theoretical importance lies primarily in the autonomous formation of specialized, hierarchical institutions of rule, in association with class-based society and economic differentiation. Explaining this transformation, which occurred perhaps five times, remains one of the most challenging areas of research into social change (see, e.g., Fried 1967; Carneiro 1970; Flannery 1972; Service 1975; Wright 1977, 1978, 1984; R. N. Adams 1978; Cohen and Service 1978; Friedman and Rowlands 1978; R. McC. Adams 1981; Haas 1982).

Despite their frequent treatment as the last major stage of autochthonous evolution, pristine states were not remotely the most complex archaic societies. They were vastly exceeded in size, complexity, and diversity by an array of secondary states and empires. Among the more prominent of these polities were the Roman, Chinese, Mongol, Aztec, Parthian, Sasanian, and Inka empires. The evolutionary significance of the expansionist polities, in contrast to that of the pristine states, may be found in the changes that resulted from the integration of diverse societies into single entities. Unfortunately, the internal diversity of the early empires makes them analytically less tractable than simpler societies. Held together by administrative and military overlays, these polities bound their subject populations with varying degrees of intensity (see, e.g., Larsen 1979a). This characteristic provides a partial contrast to the earliest states, which have often been modeled as though they were well integrated. In the early empires, societies with dissimilar capacities and cultural forms were brought under unified rule, creating a need for new types of sociopolitical and economic interaction. The specialized and centralized strategies that worked to control the core polities were likely to be ineffective in ruling simpler groups, such as ranked societies or chiefdoms. Conversely, the more generalized political forms of simple societies were ineffective for relations between local leaders and the rulers of an imperial state. This situation required accommodation on the part of both the core and the subject societies, resulting in the development of new organizational features.

This book examines how the Inkas established control over the societies brought under their rule in the fifteenth century A.D. The meteoric rise of Inka power was one of the most remarkable developments in the indigenous New World. At the end of its century of rule, Tawantinsuyu—the Land of the Four Quarters—was the largest and in some ways the most complex polity in the Americas. During the first decades of their imperial reign, the Inkas gained sovereignty over more than 12 million people, controlling a territory that stretched from modern Ecuador to central Chile (Fig. 1.1). They created a vast bureaucracy and taxation system, resettled much of their subject population, and spread a language of diplomacy among widely disparate peoples. The Inka achievement appears even more extraordinary when we consider the limitations imposed by the lack of a written language and the difficulties of transport in the Andes.

The core territory of this most extensive of native American empires was notably circumscribed, and the people who could properly be called Inkas comprised at most a few score thousand. A substantial proportion of the sites exhibiting imperial Inka architecture, the known royal estates, the sacred places, and the more elegant agricultural and irrigation works were concentrated within a relatively short distance of Cuzco, the sacred imperial capital. Although this territory significantly exceeded that controlled by the pre-imperial Inka polity, it extended no more than 150 to 200 km around Cuzco, primarily in the Huatanay, Vilcanota, and Urubamba drainages. The remainder of the empire—extending about 4,000 km from north to south—was populated by scores of ethnic groups. If we are to believe the oral histories recorded shortly after the Spanish conquest, most Inka subject groups were conquered in a few decades by the armies led by the emperor Pachacutec and his son Thupa Inka Yupanki and were subsequently drawn into the empire with varying degrees of intensity.

The means by which the Inkas established dominion over societies ranging from simple tribes to competitor states has fascinated scholars since the Spanish conquest. Early chroniclers marveled at the ordered government and favorably compared the infrastructure of administrative centers, way stations, roads, and storage facilities with that of contemporaneous Europe. Later Andeanists cast Inka rule as a despotic monarchy, an enlightened dictatorship, and a feudal, utopian, Asiatic, or socialist state. More-recent treatments have tempered conceptions of a highly controlled, standardized society with the recognition that Inka rule varied notably among regions and that life at the local level may not have changed radically in many areas.

In broad scope, Inka success was engineered by an administration built upon extant political systems. It was backed by military force and underwritten by an increasingly centralized political economy. A state religion both legitimized domination and provided a rationale for expansion. As the sketchy history of the empire shows, outright conquest and diplomacy won territories and suppressed revolts, but the Inkas appreciated that power is most effective when it is not expended through use as force.[1] Instead, political and economic power were the most efficient tools used in maintaining control. Part of the mastery the Inkas demonstrated in controlling their holdings also lay in their flexible rule. The patron-client relations established with the small-scale chiefdoms of highland Ecuador (Salomon 1986), for example, differed substantially from the more direct assimilation of the complex polities of the Lake Titicaca basin (Julien 1982, 1983, 1988) or the central coast of Peru (Rostworowski 1978, 1981, 1983). These approaches, in turn, contrasted with the destructuration of the Chimu empire of Peru's north coast (Dillehay 1977b; Netherly 1978; Ramirez 1990).

Despite their accomplishments, the Inkas did not mold their empire out of raw clay. Tawantinsuyu was only the last of a sequence of indigenous expansionist Andean states. Earlier polities in the southern highlands at Wari, in the Bolivian altiplano at Tiwanaku, and on the north coast of Peru, such as the Moche, Sicán, and Chimu states, all appear to have employed organizational approaches later adopted by the Inkas. Administratively, for instance, the Inkas may have adopted the notion of a decimal hierarchy from the Chimu (Rowe 1948; although see Ramirez 1990). There is also evidence that the north coast polities may have relied heavily on corvée as the principal means of mobilizing state economic support, at the same time that economic specialization in sumptuary craft production was directly underwritten by the nobility (Moseley 1975; Moseley and Day 1982; Topic 1982). Several authors have further argued that networks of new regional administrative centers, tied together by road systems, characterized the Chimu, Wari, and Tiwanaku states (Isbell and Schreiber 1978; Kolata 1986; Schreiber 1987, n.d.; Mackey and Klymyshyn n.d.). The Moche, Chimu, and Tiwanaku polities appear to have undertaken extensive land and water improvement projects, as did the Inka state. Inka imperial architectural design also appears to have borrowed extensively from earlier styles (Gasparini and Margolies 1980).

The Inkas thus clearly drew from centuries of Ande-

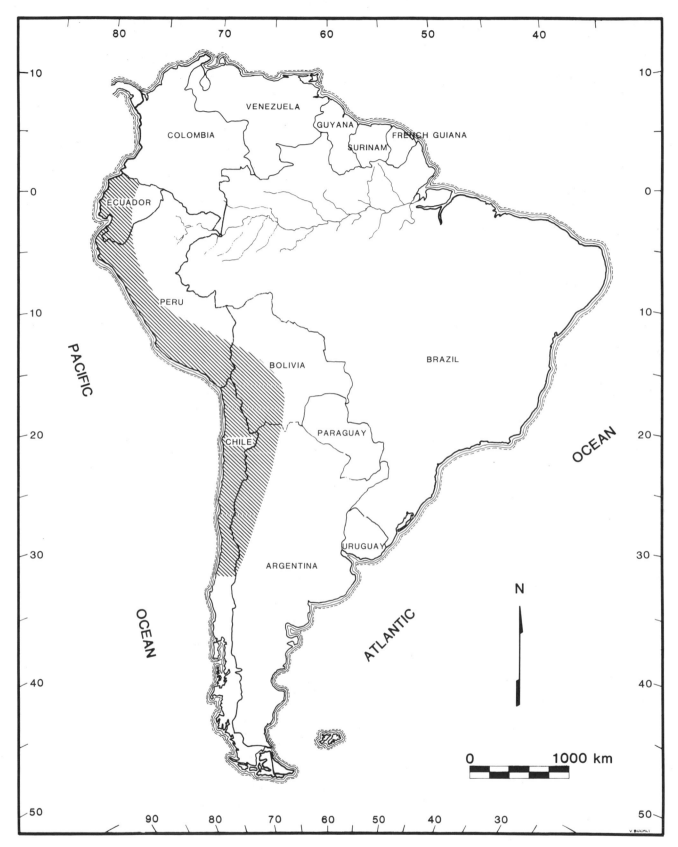

Fig. 1.1. Map showing the Inka empire, along the western edge of South America.

an statecraft in creating their new polity. Nonetheless, Tawantinsuyu was markedly distinct from preceding polities in combined scale, degree of integration, and reorganization of subject societies. No preceding state encompassed a remotely comparable territory, population, diversity of ethnic groups or languages, or range of political and economic formations. The nature of these regional variations in provincial territories and their relationships to broad imperial strategies provides the context for the present study.

The broad intent of this volume is to examine Inka imperial strategy. More specifically, the work explores relations between the Inkas and the indigenous Xauxa and Wanka populations of the central Peruvian sierra

(Fig. 1.2), based on a hegemonic-territorial model of imperial rule. Because the discussion ranges widely—covering military, logistical, political, economic, and settlement problems—it is useful to sketch out the theoretical approach and line of argument here, to provide the reader with a skeletal understanding of the main conclusions.

The approach used to analyze these issues draws from several theoretical premises, detailed in Chapter 2. A central assumption is that the first priority of any polity is to provide for its material support and physical security. For the ruling elites of an empire, the most essential concerns are maintaining control over subject territories and sustaining the administrative system,

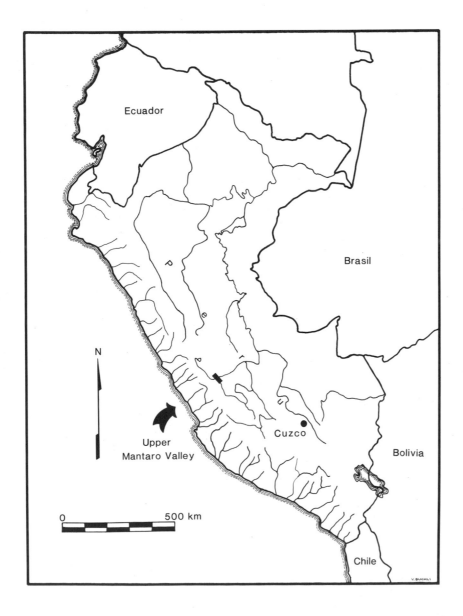

Fig. 1.2. Location of the Upper Mantaro Valley research zone, in the central Peruvian sierra.

so that resources may be extracted. It therefore seems most effective to focus a strategic analysis initially on energetics, material support, and decision-making. This perspective is not intended to deny a pivotal role to ideas or social conventions in organizing imperial rule. Certainly the impetus to conquer may be ideological, material, or both. Nonetheless, if the rulers of an expansionist state are to avert rapid collapse, they must establish an effective system to satisfy energetic and material needs and to secure a modicum of administrative control. A central goal of this book is therefore to assess the kinds of cost-benefit problems the Inkas encountered and how particular strategies were implemented to address them.

The approach taken to evaluating these issues here is basically energetic and materialistic. Theoretical interest in the evolutionary relationships between energetics and sociopolitical forms is well established in anthropology (Steward 1955; Adams 1976; Price 1978, 1982). Based in part on principles worked out over the last century or so, this concern underlies materialist approaches from Marx to Harris (Adams 1978). White (1959), for instance, has argued that the emergence of social elites, governmental bureaucrats, craft specialists, and other non-food-producers depended on the capacity of society to capture and channel energy in a systematic way. Later authors have modified that argument by observing that an increase in the amount of energy brought into a system, whether human or natural, could have resulted in an expansion in its size, its complexity, or both. The energy procured, however, is not solely a consequence of basic economic needs but often results from sociopolitical demands. It follows that the success of early polities depended on both the amount of energy at their disposal and the nature of their organization. For the early empires, this becomes an especially intriguing concern, given that establishing control over broad areas entailed the formation of new institutions of rule and long-distance transportation of personnel and key goods.

A second assumption is that imperial strategies can be most effectively analyzed as a continuum from *hegemonic* (indirect) to *territorial* (direct) control (Luttwak 1976; Hassig 1985:100). The frequent classification of imperial regions into core and periphery tends to obscure continuous, but systematic, variation that is key to understanding imperial development and collapse. For analytic purposes, the hegemonic and territorial strategies can be treated as a mix of three of the four kinds of power recognized by Mann (1986:2)— military, political, and economic. The fourth major

source of power—ideology—was critical in organizing Inka imperial rule, but it always had to operate within the limits set by energetic constraints and material needs. As will be argued in subsequent chapters, the constant interplay between ideology and the requirements of gaining control and extracting resources is visible in the relationship between the form of state facilities and the strategic roles that they were assigned.

A third assumption is that the expansionist states that are usually at the core of empires are limited in their strategic options. Imperial policy is, to a great degree, a consequence of accommodations between the demands of the state and the capacities of the local societies. Perhaps the most important constraints are the nature of the existing societal organizations (e.g., forms of labor mobilization, degree of economic specialization, degree of political centralization) and the material conditions of the subject regions (e.g., demography, resources, geography). The options pursued by the Inkas—patron-client relations, direct incorporation, alliance, and destructuration—can be understood best if these accommodations are treated systematically.

Fourth, because the viability of the early empires depended largely on their ability to extract resources from subject groups, analysis should examine the effects of imperial expansion on levels of society from the household up to the state. In the Inka empire, the heavy dependence of the state on peasant production, especially early on, makes assessment of the domestic economy significant in understanding the directions taken by imperial organization. Conversely, because imperial policies had direct effects on household activities, such as domestic production and consumption, assessment of the nature of community life provides a window into the consequences of imperial rule for the general populace.

In Chapter 3 the specific goals and methods of the research are presented. The research reported here has been conducted as an integral part of the Upper Mantaro Archaeological Research Project (hereafter UMARP), which has focused fieldwork on the Xauxa and Wanka societies of the Upper Mantaro region, in the central Peruvian highlands. Initiated in 1977, UMARP was designed to study the evolutionary relationship between politics and economics in complex, late prehistoric Andean society. Our interest in this problem was stimulated by models of cultural evolution that argue for systematic and causal relationships between political and economic development in prehistory (e.g., Sanders and Price 1968; Engels 1972;

Friedman and Rowlands 1978; Gilman 1981; Earle et al. 1987). The intimacy of the relationship may be seen in the arguments of two standards of evolutionary theory, one of which emphasizes competitive relations and the other, integrative relations. The first of these, Fried's (1967) influential work entitled *The Evolution of Political Society,* is more clearly an evaluation of the role of economics in the formation of complex society than it is a study of political change. In Fried's book, for example, the critical transformation to stratified society is seen to revolve around differential access to strategic resources, notably subsistence. Similarly, Service's (1975) *Origins of the State and Civilization* defines a key political formation by the postulated character of its economic exchange mechanism. Service's chiefdom is a society in which a political leader derives his position from mediating exchange among economically specialized communities through redistribution—the central accumulation and reallocation of society's products.

Regardless of the degree to which we accepted any particular argument, it was apparent that the complexities of political and economic relationships required development of detailed models and extensive testing. UMARP's overarching intent has been to evaluate certain posited relationships through study of the development of indigenous society prior to the Inka conquest (Wanka I–II: A.D. 1000–1460) and the changes that occurred with its incorporation into the empire (Wanka III: 1460–1533). The research objectives included assessment of (1) indigenous Wanka sociopolitical development, (2) settlement and associated land-use patterns, (3) the domestic economy, (4) the nature of Inka rule, and (5) transformations of indigenous society as a consequence of imperial conquest (see Chapter 3 for a more detailed outline).

The Upper Mantaro Valley is an appropriate region for research of this nature because of the rapid political transformations that occurred in the last few centuries before the Spanish conquest and because of the available data base and prior research in the region. Archaeological preservation is often excellent, for hundreds of late prehistoric sites have been recorded, some with thousands of buildings still standing on the ground surface. Historical documents pertinent to the study are also available, and a fairly refined regional chronology has now been developed.

To help assess Inka strategy in the central sierra, Chapter 4 provides the background on pre-imperial society. As was observed above, effective imperial policies are largely limited by the nature of target and subject societies. In the central highlands, the local societies were forming increasingly complex polities during the fourteenth and fifteenth centuries, within a context of endemic warfare. Sierra societies nucleated their members in defensive hilltop settlements and focused subsistence production locally on highland crops and camelid herding. Neither sociopolitical differences nor economic specialization was well developed, although some community-level specialization in local resources resulted in local exchange networks. Most households, whether elite or commoner, produced most of their own tools and processed their own food; neither markets nor monetary systems existed. These societies thus comprised a wealth of potential human and natural resources for exploitation, while regional strife rendered them simultaneously susceptible to conquest and difficult to pacify.

Chapter 5 examines the military and logistical aspects of the Inka expansion and securing of control. In that chapter, Inka military activity is treated as comprising two general phases: conquest and consolidation. The geographic obstacles of the Andes, an inefficient transportation technology, and a reliance on peasant armies challenged Inka control during both phases. As the empire shifted from taking to holding territories, military supply had to switch from exploiting the target populations to developing reliable state resources. Mobilizing manpower and matériel became critical problems in the face of putting down revolts and securing the empire's limits. A principal solution to these problems, discussed in Chapter 6, was the creation of a vast infrastructure of administrative facilities, way stations, roads, state lands, and storage facilities. In the Upper Mantaro, for instance, the Inkas built a provincial center at Hatun Xauxa and a series of support facilities, including what may be the largest set of storage complexes in the empire. In the latter decades of imperial rule, the Inkas also began to elaborate an independent supply system that was less reliant on the productivity of peasant farmers, but for most of the empire's duration, the Inkas depended heavily on the corvée of their subjects.

The historical context of the conquest and incorporation of the central sierra was fairly straightforward. When local societies were faced with the Inka armies circa 1460, regional politics and rivalries undercut their capacities to resist conquest. The general and soon-to-be emperor, Thupa Inka Yupanki, swept through the central highlands, conquering the Xauxas, the Wankas, and their neighbors. With a population of 200,000 or so, the Upper Mantaro constituted a major source of human and natural resources in a highly productive territory. Because of its position at the juncture of the main route along the spine of the Andes and major passes to the coast and jungle, the broad Upper Mantaro Valley served as a natural conduit and breadbasket for the empire. Securing military control over the region was therefore a critical issue. It was accomplished by resettling the indigenous populace from their hilltop communities into many smaller villages and towns at lower elevations, by deporting entire communities to locations as far away as Ecuador, and by importing garrisons of internal colonists whose loyalty lay primarily with the state.

The political incorporation of the Upper Mantaro polities, described in Chapter 7, provides a clear example of the Inkas' territorial strategy in the central Peruvian sierra. The region's large population and agricultural productivity made direct administration the most appropriate strategic option. Many local elites served as state officials, holding positions as high as paramount leaders of the three major provincial subdivisions, while retaining positions of authority within the indigenous hierarchies. In the process of drawing local elites into administration, the Inkas centralized and stabilized regional politics. This approach ultimately backfired, for the Wankas proved capable of coordinating assistance to the Spaniards in helping to overthrow the empire. Given the impacts of Inka domination on native society, it is surprising to recall that imperial rule in the region lasted only about 70 years, with a Spanish foray into the Mantaro Valley in late 1533 effectively ending Inka rule.

The development of the imperial political system was paralleled by the creation of a political economy, discussed in Chapter 8. It is argued here that this system can be modeled most effectively as a dendritic hierarchy, in which most ties and flows of goods and services were vertically oriented (cf. Schaedel 1978). Although couched in terms of reciprocity and redistribution and reinforced through ceremonial ties, the imperial political economy was essentially a means of extracting resources upward. As Murra (1980 [1956]) has argued, natural resources were mobilized from resources alienated from the local communities, whereas labor was initially derived from rotating service applied to households. Over time, the state began to emphasize independent production, creating state farms and specialized labor categories. In the Upper Mantaro region, the populace was drawn into this economy as generalized and specialized labor and as manage-

ment. Lands within about 5 km of the provincial center were set aside for state farms, and their produce was stored in the vast storage complexes. The state appears to have controlled the production and distribution of certain types of goods, notably metals and ceramics produced in the imperial style. Access to these status goods was defined by political ties, and the local elites came to rely upon state largess for sumptuary items and for the goods used in the ceremonial hospitality that fueled political relations.

The effects of imperial rule on subject communities are treated in Chapter 9. One of the most dramatic consequences of the Inka conquest was a shift of the populace out of the nucleated hilltop settlements of the pre-Inka era into a series of towns and villages in the lower maize-growing zone. Coupled with this change was a radical reduction of the largest settlements in the region, from about 14,000 to 4,500 individuals. Despite the loss of autonomy and the onerous burdens of service to the state, life under Inka rule improved in some ways, in particular because of the reduction of local hostilities and an improved access to food. Household production and consumption changed in ways that reflect the use of resources in the immediate vicinity of the new communities. Surprisingly, however, specialization and exchange did not increase, and certain material differences between the elite and commoner strata of society were reduced.

Chapter 10 returns to broader questions of imperial organization. The discussion summarizes the place of the Upper Mantaro region in the Inka empire and evaluates the utility of the general model. In the process, I draw some comparisons between the Inka and other early empires, recognizing that in a book of this nature the comparative material is more exemplary than comprehensive. It would be inappropriate to use Inka rule in the Upper Mantaro as a model for all other imperial provinces, because of the internal diversity of the polities subsumed within Tawantinsuyu. Similarly, the Inka empire differed in significant ways from other early empires. It is equally true, however, that provincial relations in the Upper Mantaro are explicable only in a broader context of imperial development. In an analogous fashion, emphasizing the distinctions between the Inka and other empires at the expense of assessing strategic commonalities undercuts the anthropological commitment to cross-cultural analysis. It is hoped that this study will provide insight into these issues and, by extension, insight into the evolution of complex societies.

2

The
Study
of
Early
Empires

Empires are expansionist states that assume effective control over other polities of varying scope and complexity. Among the premodern empires, the Macedonian, Roman, Chinese, Mongol, Parthian, Sasanian, Aztec, and Inka polities stand out in their scale, their duration, or both. Despite the coercive means that frequently underlay their continuity, these empires could be resilient, some spanning several centuries. Others, like Alexander's Macedonian realm, collapsed with the death of the initial paramount leader. Their diversity notwithstanding, the central authorities of these polities shared two overriding strategic concerns: maintaining the security of the core polity and extracting resources from the expanded territory to benefit a limited segment of the population (Adams 1979a). To achieve these ends, imperial rule employed combinations of coercive and persuasive controls that took military, political, economic, and ideological forms. Military strength was typically used to establish dominion, but political and economic power proved to be more enduring and efficient means of consolidating control. State ideology provided rationales for expansion, means of reducing the costs of maintaining jurisdiction, and methods of assimilating subject groups into increasingly unified polities.

Although historical circumstances were significant in the trajectories of these polities, the polities are also clearly amenable to comparative analysis as complex sociopolitical systems. This chapter begins by exploring the key forms of societal power that provided the underpinnings of imperial polities. This will set the stage for an evaluation of analytical models of empires, the most prominent of which are the core-periphery, the tributary-capitalist, the metrocentric-pericentric-systemic, and the hegemonic-territorial approaches. The use of models affords several advantages critical to comparative study of the Inkas, despite the existence of distinctively Andean features, outlined below. Among the benefits are the properties that make any sort of modeling useful: abstraction, simplification, and extraction of the essential relationships of complex systems (Levins 1966:427–30). Each model of empires described subsequently provides a conceptual vocabulary, highlights assumptions underlying notions of sociopolitical change, directs our attention to issues key to the formation and nature of the polities, and provides a foundation for assessing case-specific explanations for imperial development and organization.

Few authors have considered the Inka empire in light of these or other comparative models; most writers have preferred to focus on particular or historical elements (e.g., Rowe 1946 and Murra 1980 [1956]; although see Katz 1972, Carrasco 1982, and Wolf 1982:59–65). Prior research on the Inkas has emphasized that historical circumstances and the nature of existing Andean societies set conditions for imperial expansion and constrained the options of rule that could be employed. The empire has therefore been justly treated as unusual in critical ways. For example, the means by which the Inkas could underwrite their activities in the Andean sierra were limited by the generalized nature of the highland farming and herding economies and by the virtual absence of markets and money. The small ethnic Inka population and the need to develop an administrative structure at a time of rapid expansion obliged the rulers to rely unusually heavily on subject elites to effect their plans. With respect to transport, reliance on human bearers and llamas limited the effective range of many goods. Similarly, the mnemonic system of imperial accounting and communication restricted and directed administrative options. Andean views of cosmology, kinship, and social organization further contributed to the distinctive character of the empire.

Viewed from a strategic perspective, however, the formation and consolidation of Tawantinsuyu were consistent with paths taken by other archaic empires. Counterparts for most of the essential developmental features of Inka rule can be found cross-culturally. Militarily, for example, the Inka and other empires (e.g., Macedonian, Roman, Mongol) relied on armies of conquest mobilized from vanquished opponents and a peasant populace; strategically located imperial stores were built at key locations to sustain military ventures. A feature common to early empires, among them the Inka, was the construction of a physical infrastructure to facilitate administration, including the upgrading of transport and communications networks. Political relations typically tended toward clientage near imperial perimeters and in the early stages of development and tended toward bureaucracy near the core and in later stages. The chronic factional competition for power among the royal Inka kin that undermined provincial control was also hardly an Andean monopoly. Economically, the heavy Inka reliance on corvée for imperial subsistence needs was not unparalleled, although it was somewhat unusual. Similarly, the creation of imperial economic resources and labor cadres, coupled with restrictions on local independent exchange, was not uncommon. Forced population resettlement for protective and economic reasons also typ-

ified early empires, as did promulgation of imperial culture, religion, and language.

Granted that some parallels existed between the Inka and other early empires, we must still ask if the similarities were largely superficial or were systematic consequences of the opportunities, interests, and constraints common to the early empires. Similarly, we may ask whether the Inka development can be understood as a systemic outcome, given the costs and benefits of differing solutions to the problems of expanding and controlling the empire. Although the balance of the present book is weighted in favor of investigating the second issue, the use of an overarching model provides a means of considering the first problem, especially in the concluding chapter.

To provide the context for addressing these issues, the remainder of this chapter is devoted to examining two related issues: (1) the forms of power that underlay imperial rule and (2) some of the dominant models of imperial polities. Although the archaeological correlates of the various kinds of imperial strategy are central to this volume, the present chapter is concerned explicitly with the theoretical issues pertaining to these models. The succeeding chapters explore problems of archaeological assessment, both for the Inka polity in general and for the Upper Mantaro region in detail. The closing chapter returns to a consideration of the broader questions and essays a comparison of some key elements of the Inka polity with other early empires.

Forms and Domains of Power in Early Empires

Because the early empires were formed by extending control over a range of polities, it is worthwhile to consider the nature of power in societal relations, a topic with appeal for a wide range of disciplines. Power in this context is treated here as the capacity of one party to pursue and achieve goals by eliciting a desired response, whether through coercion, persuasion, reward, or some combination thereof (cf. Skinner and Winckler 1969; Dahl 1972; Service 1975:11–12; Haas 1982:157; Mann 1986:6). This partially conflates the venerated distinction between *power* (the capacity to force) and *authority* (the capacity to induce by virtue of status or office). However, the attainment of sociopolitical goals in a context of ongoing relations, especially those relations that coalesce into regular links, seldom results solely from coercion without positive sanction or from inducement without implied or explicit threat. A balance is generally struck among differing kinds of power in any relations above those of the most personal nature. Even warfare almost invariably couples diplomacy and coercion. In analysis of polities within which rule depended on attaining an effective balance of suasion and force under diverse circumstances, it makes sense to consider both aspects simultaneously. This approach is especially important when evaluating strategies on the basis of energetic considerations, because considered use of persuasion is the most effective means available to reduce the costs expended in coercion.

For analytic purposes, it is useful to follow Mann (1986:2) in examining four kinds of power that operate within social relations: political, economic, military, and ideological (see also Dahl 1972; Haas 1982: 155–71; Earle 1989:87). *Political power* derives from one entity's ability to dominate the processes of managing consent, judging, and decision-making (Service 1975:12). These activities, of course, vary from consensual and generalized to codified and specialized as society becomes increasingly complex (see, e.g., Flannery 1972). The early empires characteristically encompassed societies that ranged in complexity from simple, relatively undifferentiated groups to full-fledged states. The ethnographic and historical records show that, within the highly diverse chiefdom societies, even the most elite sectors do not maintain a consistent ability to enforce decisions coercively. Instead, political capabilities stem more from a combination of social legitimacy, kin relations, and religious sanctions (Wright 1977, 1984; Earle 1978). States, conversely, have an enhanced ability to process information, make decisions, and compel the implementation of those decisions, in part because states are more internally specialized and hierarchically ordered (Johnson 1973; Wright and Johnson 1975). State hierarchies are formally divided into positions, ranks, or subunits (Hodge 1984:3; see also Flannery 1972), whereas various kinds of authority within chiefdoms are typically vested in the same office. As a consequence, the political activities conducted within the heterogeneous early empires cannot be treated as uniform either (1) between the imperial core and subject groups or (2) within and among the subject groups themselves.

The variety of internal political formations, coupled with the often fragile nature of the central structure, required that imperial elites apply a series of flexible options within a broad strategy of rule. Among the many consequences of this situation, two are especially germane here. First, with imperial rule, the source of most political power among subordinate polities shifts from the subject society to the imperial core. In essence, political power becomes delegated from above, not allocated from below (Adams 1976). This shift reduces the ability of polities to interact freely with one another, changes the rules of succession to office and the criteria of decision-making, and removes from the hands of local elites the right to settle many internal disputes. Second, because subject polities often vary radically in their political organizations, the application of imperial political power has to be tailored to meet particular circumstances. The nature of imperial-provincial politics will therefore vary systematically from the simpler to the more complex societies drawn into the empire.

The decision-making aspect of politics raises a key issue in the development of imperial administration. Johnson (1977, 1982) observes that although the scale of polities and their decision-making complexity tend to be directly related, increases in political complexity do not result trivially from expanding the size of the polity. The redundancy or specialization of decision-making, the spatial array of administrative units, and changes in the number of units under one official's purview combine to favor modification of the structure of governance. For example, citing Skinner's (1977: 321, 336) work, Johnson (1982:412) notes that the number of units subsumed under a particular official in late imperial China varied inversely with the range of activities for which he was responsible. In the Inka empire, which developed a state administration as conquest required it, resolving these kinds of trade-offs between control and cost would have required considerable trial and error, especially given that the outcomes of particular strategies would have been dissimilar among societies of differing complexities.[1]

Economic power derives from control over access to natural resources, materially productive labor, goods, and services. In assessing the role of economics in cultural evolution, a number of authors give subsistence and utilitarian needs theoretical primacy, because these needs provide the basis for the existence of inequality in society (Fried 1967), because they compose the most energetically significant aspect of human behavior (Price 1982), or because classes are seen as having been formed around subsistence tasks (Friedman and Rowlands 1978; Mann 1986:24). An additional reason for focusing attention on energetics in analysis of empires stems from the critical role of logistical support in military conquest and maintenance of provincial control (Hassig 1985, 1988). Other authors place greater emphasis on production and circulation of wealth or sumptuary goods, noting their importance in underwriting positions of status as symbolic paraphernalia or as political currency (e.g., Murra 1962; Peebles and Kus 1977; Schneider 1977; McGuire 1989). In a complementary manner, the analytic emphasis in studies of empires is most frequently placed on how the imperial core extracted key resources from the subject groups, with a particular focus on elite-elite ties. A broad-based assessment of imperial economics, however, requires consideration of the full range of goods and services found within domestic and political economies among the core and subordinate populations. It should be apparent that a clear understanding of the Inka economy must treat both the formation of the state economy and the stability and transformation in subject economics.

Generally speaking, the *political economy* was concerned with the production of goods and the rendering of services involved in societal integration above the level of the household (see Johnson and Earle 1987). In early empires, its two principal elements were (1) subsistence support of elite institutions, such as administration, religious sectors, nobility, and the military, and (2) provision of sumptuary goods for political relations, ceremonial activity, and status validation. As with politics, the principal concern of most investigators has been elite-elite ties, in this case the formation of an organization to extract and transfer resources to the core elites by the subject elites. In this process, the regional political economies of the subject polities are viewed largely in the context of imperial transformations. To understand the dynamics of empires, however, we need also to consider the continuities and adaptations of subject political economies in the context of ongoing systems within the subordinate regions.

The *domestic economy* was concerned with the production and distribution of goods and the organization of labor at the household or other minimal corporate level. As was the case with political organization, the imperial core and each subject polity not only likely manifested differing forms of the domestic economy but also varied internally in terms of production, distribution, and exchange. Generally speaking, some features of subject domestic economies under imperial

rule should have remained relatively stable, because households and other basic corporate groups should have continued to function as the fundamental economic units. Moreover, the domestic economy formed the basis of production that supported the activities of the early empires and constituted the bulk of production within imperial territories. Subject self-sufficiency was therefore strongly in the state interest.

There are sound reasons, however, to expect transitions in the domestic economies of the polities subsumed within imperial territory, even when the populace retained substantial control over the means of production. Settlement shifts, intensification of production by households, co-option of disposable labor through corvée levies, development of specialized production enclaves or statuses, expansion of potential trade and market relationships, and alienation of resources would all have potentially contributed to changes in the domestic economy. Access to goods previously obtained through dyadic, market, or other forms of exchange may also have been curtailed, as the state sought to limit alliance-creating activities that could undermine regional security. Conversely, the relative peace often enforced by central authorities had the potential of increasing the intensity of regional exchange within secure territory.

In assessing the nature of economic power within empires, therefore, we must recognize that economic formations, like political relations, were not simply a function of imperial edict. Their evaluation requires consideration of a complex array of distribution of human and natural resources, the structure of labor and exchange systems, and transportation and other technologies—within both the core state territory and the expanded regions brought under some degree of imperial control.

Shifting attention to a third area of societal relations, I treat *military power* as the capacity to elicit a desired response through a combination of force and diplomatic persuasion. Luttwak's (1976:195–200) discussion of the nature of power and its relation to force provides useful refinements to this initial conception (see also Hassig 1988:18–19). In the context of analyzing systems of security, Luttwak treats power as "output"—that is, as "the aggregate of external action capabilities." He observes that the efficiency of systems of security is defined by the relationship between power and the costs of operating the system. Force is treated as an element of the input, proportional to men and material. Because the efficiency of systems of security is inversely proportional to the degree of reliance on force, these systems will be efficient to the degree that force can be held inactive. Luttwak acknowledges that force can permit attainment of goals through coercive persuasion, and he recognizes that under these circumstances it is more properly a political phenomenon than a physical one. Nonetheless, he considers "indirect suasion" to be of narrow tactical, not strategic, importance.

An important point in this argument is that force is consumed in use but power is not. Power partially depends on the knowledge and judgment of the populace being acted upon, so political relations, official propaganda, and disinformation are central to the effective use of military power. Luttwak (1976:198) asserts, however, that "in virtually all conceivable circumstances deployed military force will be the central ingredient of the overall power of states." This argument appears to overstate the relative importance of military force vis-à-vis political and economic power. Coercion indisputably was key to the formation and consolidation of early empires, but the successful implementation of military power in imperial systems was fundamentally contingent on political and economic organization that economized the use of force.

The fourth source of power in society—*ideology*—raises some thorny issues in explaining the development of archaic empires. Because I address the ideology of the Inkas and their subjects only tangentially in this book, my tack needs some justification. This is especially true because the role of ideology in the constitution of prehistoric society is actively debated and because numerous authors assign religion a causal role in the formation of the early empires (e.g., Conrad and Demarest 1984).

My choice not to accentuate ideology stems from theoretical and methodological concerns. At a theoretical level, a materialist and energetic approach is more satisfactory for strategic analysis than an approach that relies on ideological rationales, because the former directly addresses the most basic requirements of conquest, consolidation of control, and extraction of resources and labor. This view contrasts with much of the literature on prehistoric and contemporary Andean societies, in which precedence is given to shared ideas in organizing social relations (Zuidema 1964; Isbell 1978; Rostworowski 1988; Urton 1990). Studies of the spatial organization of architecture and activities at planned Inka settlements, for instance, suggest a strong relationship between notions of cosmic order and the spatial and temporal orderings of state activities (Urton 1981; Hyslop 1985, 1990; Niles

1987; Morris 1990). Several authors extend this argument to contend that widespread structural features of Andean social organization determined social, economic, and political relations far back into prehistory (Wachtel 1977; Netherly 1978; Conrad and Demarest 1984). Among the most important of these features are the parallel dual natures of the political and kin organizations and the reciprocal exchange among hierarchical levels in the sociopolitical organization.

The authors employing this approach have gained insight into Andean cultures, but this view has led to a radical relativism in much of the literature, whereby the Inka empire becomes explicable only in terms of cultural conceptions teased out of the documentary record. The unusual is often emphasized to the virtual exclusion of meaningful cross-cultural comparison and is justified on the basis of the distinctive nature of the Andean worldview. In part, this Andean contextual position stems from the notion that the energetic and material costs and benefits of various political and economic strategies are misapplied modern Western concepts. These costs and benefits are considered to be either less significant than cultural convention, shared beliefs, or historical conditions in explaining behavior or completely inappropriate. In contrast to this view is the certainty that military strategy and tactics, population distribution, labor organization, subsistence strategy, and administrative structure, for example, are subject to spatial and energetic constraints, regardless of concepts of social relations (Smith 1976; Johnson 1977; Skinner 1977; Hassig 1985). Conceptual models of the organization of society may define initial options and constrain the direction of change, but they do not remove energetics from consideration in imperial development.

This draws attention to the disjunction between the benevolence of imperial ideology and the actuality of relations between elites and subjects. In few places is this more marked than in the efforts of the privileged sectors of society to justify their right to their position and to obtain the acquiescence of the majority. How this is effected remains one of the most intriguing questions of the development of complex society. In this regard, Fried's (1967) argument is persuasive that elite ideology largely constitutes an effort to legitimize inequality established on the basis of other criteria (see also Adams 1984; cf. Shanks and Tilley 1982). Jacobsen (cited in Mann 1986:5) offers some insight here by pointing out that the transformation of ideology to serve political purposes may reflect a lack of participation in the ideology by the general populace. The adoption of subject pantheons into the official imperial religion of early empires can be seen here most readily as an effort by the state to reduce costs of compliance with state policy; it does not imply an acceptance of state ideology by the subject population. Unfortunately, what is most frequently preserved for us is precisely this elite conceptualization and not the alternative or complementary views that likely characterized much of the subject population. The contextual approach[2] that emphasizes a unified Andean worldview, however, revives many of the tenets of normative anthropology (Earle and Preucel 1987:509), without paying heed to the point that individuals participate in ideology differentially. Belief systems are not unitary phenomena across space, socioeconomic group, class, gender, or any other division of society. The documentary sources that provide the most secure evidence for ideologies in early empires provide insight most directly into the ideology of the elite sectors. To attribute a cohesive ideology to Andean societies—drawn to a great extent from an imperial point of view—glosses over important variations in the content and use of idea systems.

The second fundamental reason for downplaying ideology in my discussion of the rise of the Inka empire is methodological. Despite considerable recent effort to address the role of ideology in the development of prehistoric society (Tilley 1981, 1984; Hodder 1982a,b, 1986; Leone 1982; Shanks and Tilley 1982, 1984; Miller and Tilley 1984), there are serious problems in assessing the meaningful content of ideological systems through archaeological research. The explanations proffered consistently run aground on the problems of establishing verifiable analogies for meaning and of making meaning tractable in data analysis.[3] Contextual archaeology has been successful, for example, in assessing spatial structure in Inka sites that can be explained as a consequence of social conceptions (Hyslop 1984; Niles 1988; Morris 1990), but what is recognized here archaeologically is an organizing structure and its constituent elements, not the meaningful content of an ideology. For the latter, the authors consistently rely upon documentary sources. Where the documentary and archaeological records are fully complementary, contextual archaeology provides insight. Where the subject of interest potentially complements, contradicts, or is not covered by written records, meaning is elusive. The spatial analysis results obtained in Andean archaeology thus far have important consequences for interpretation of some patterning in the archaeological record, but they provide few, if any, direct insights into strategic behavior.

Despite my reservations about assessing meaning archaeologically, I wish to emphasize that my work should be seen as a complement to the contextual work on the Inkas and not as a substitute. My argument neither denies that ideology was central to the character of the Inka or other early empires nor suggests that belief systems were unimportant in conceiving human relations. Concepts of social relations were critical, for example, in determining preferential paths to power among the Inkas, based on kin and class relationships. Where appropriate, these issues will be raised in the discussion. My point here is that if archaeological and documentary sources are to be treated as independent lines of evidence, we cannot assign meaning to archaeological data from historical sources and then treat the archaeology as verification of ethnohistory.

In sum, I do not see the components of overall power as having been equal in their capacities to elicit desired responses at the level of imperial strategy. Political, economic, and military powers have more-direct effects on imperial control and strategy. Ideology works most importantly as a means of justifying and reducing the costs of compliance incurred in the implementation of other forms of power and less importantly as the cause of imperial organization and change. This does not deny importance to ideology in Inka rule but suggests that we will gain insight into the overall nature of the empire best if we look first to the energetic and material and second to socially shared concepts designed to fit "images of the world to the real flows of energy and material" (Adams 1978:299).

Models of Imperial Organization

Core and Periphery

Most of the recent literature that employs explicit models considers ancient empires in terms of *core* and *periphery*. This heuristic construct gained currency with the influential work of Wallerstein on world systems (esp. Wallerstein 1974). His analysis was intended most specifically to describe the development of western Europe since the sixteenth century, but many of the premises central to his work have also been widely applied to modern Western–Third World relations (e.g., Frank 1966). Recently, appraisals of the early empires have found it a useful approach, especially in the Near East and the Mediterranean (Ekholm and Friedman 1979, 1982; Larsen 1979b; Kohl 1987a,b; Rowlands et al. 1987; Champion 1989a; Chase-Dunn and Hall 1991).

This model concentrates on exploitation of subordinate polities (periphery) by a central, elite polity (core). The core is an advantaged area with a strong state machinery and a national culture, whereas peripheral areas are politically constituted either by weak indigenous states or by societies without state organizations (Wallerstein 1974:349; see also Schortman and Urban 1987:56 and Champion 1989b:13–16). The latter are exploited for low-wage, low-profit, and low-capital labor-intensive goods. Between these two areas are the semi-peripheries, which are intermediate formations in terms of economic activities, strength of the state, and cultural integrity. They serve purposes useful to the core by deflecting political pressures and by aggregating vital skills that are often politically unpopular (Wallerstein 1974:349). For reasons that remain unclear, the notion of a semi-periphery has been underused in archaeological applications (Champion 1989b:16).

Although the model has a spatial component, the most important links in core-periphery interaction occur along political or economic lines, with various authors emphasizing one over the other. Among those sharing the economic focus are Ekholm and Friedman (1979, 1982), who argue that core-periphery relations are defined according to the accumulation of capital, which they describe as a form of wealth that can be transformed into metal, money, land, labor, or other products. A central point of their position is that elite accumulation of economic capital provides a common element to archaic and modern empires. Citing early Mesopotamian empires as examples, they argue that maintenance of the archaic centers depended on the domination of a supralocal resource base, so that the core elites' increasing ability to control capital was key to the centers' emergence as imperial powers.

The cores were generally not dependent upon peripheral regions for basic goods, however, for the simple reason that the available transport technology could not move them regularly (Adams 1974, 1979a). Except in areas of effective water transport, most goods that were moved long distances were prestige items, the procurement of which often underlay expansionist tendencies in the first place (Schneider 1977). Partially in an effort to counter this point, Rowlands (1987:5) has suggested that what mattered was not

what was consumed but *how* the elites extracted and consumed the goods. The essential point in this view is that ruling elites became net consumers of resources from other polities, extracted by a variety of relations. In Rowlands's view, the periphery comprised those areas that were forced to meet demands for surplus production (cf. McGuire 1989). Wallerstein (1974) has argued that this process generally results in the simultaneous development of the core and underdevelopment of the periphery, because the organization of labor and extraction of products in the periphery are intended to meet central demand. Wolf's (1982) incisive study of European-world relations since 1400 provides striking documentation of this transformation. The collusion, co-option, or alliance of peripheral elites with core elites is central to this process. Peripheral elites restructure the organization of production—often focused around one or two critical resources—for the effective transferral of wealth to the core. In this relationship, they have less choice in formation of alliances than do the core elites, but they clearly benefit from it (Rowlands 1987:5). The costs of the intensified production are largely borne by the periphery, however, which receives technology, organization, and some sumptuary goods in exchange (McGuire 1989).

Wallerstein (1974) has further argued that the early empires were primarily political in nature, in contrast to the modern world economies. Few investigators completely share this view with respect to ancient empires (although see Larsen 1979b:91; Doyle 1986), but many view politics as being at least equal in importance to economics as an organizing feature, and as being spatially broader in extent. As was just noted, Adams (1974, 1979a,b) argues that the transportation problems entailed in archaic technologies would have required that the cores be essentially self-sufficient economically, so that the real extension of imperial power would have been primarily military or political (see also Hassig 1985). The elements of economic control that extended beyond the core lay in the procurement of luxury goods and raw materials for the political economy. The core areas would also have been the loci of greatest administrative control, but interactions with peripheral regions would have been increasingly a function of military control as distance increased from the core. This position, expressed specifically by Adams for the Aztecs, partially echoes that of Lattimore (1962:480–91, 542–51), who treated the empires of China and central Asia (see also Mann

1986:9; Morgan 1986). Lattimore conceived of three radii of social integration, determined in large part by organizational and technological constraints. The most extensive of these was the military, followed by civil integration and, ultimately, economic integration.

Many authors have recognized that substantial variation occurred within areas treated as core or periphery (e.g., Adams 1974, 1981; Larsen 1979b; Yoffee 1979; McGuire 1989:44), even though the model lends itself to dichotomized characterizations. This variation has been overlooked in other works, notably in Eisenstadt's (1963) classic study of the political systems of the early empires, which treats institutions as if they were unitary phenomena. More-recent reviews see differing forms of production and distribution of goods as intertwined in varied patterns in distinct social settings (Rowlands 1987:8). Some authors have also emphasized spatial and temporal variation, suggesting that peripheries often became centers of new polities with the waning of power in the antecedent cores (Friedman and Rowlands 1978:269).[4] Such shifts in power are often seen as part of long-term cycles of development and collapse. Similarly, Larsen (1979b:94–95) and others (e.g., Champion 1989b: 17–18; Randsborg 1989) have underscored the spatial dynamics of empires, noting the formation of new peripheries beyond the newly established cores.

Although the model has been exceedingly influential and provides useful insights into the nature of early empires, drawbacks in its application limit its explanatory value. Many of these weaknesses derive from the qualitative breakdown, into two or three distinct types, of relationships that are better conceived as continuous.[5] In fairness, it must be noted that most authors who see significant value in the model are well aware of variations in each kind of territory. Adams (1979b, 1984), who considers core and periphery to be useful heuristic devices, has underscored the critical point that even the heartlands of empires were often highly varied. Similarly, Nash (1987:98) describes the Roman provinces as heterogeneous territories punctuated by regions of allied areas and citizen colonies (see also Bartel 1989). Wallerstein (1974) noted the fluidity of borders for these types but provided no means of readily distinguishing them in practice, as Kohl (1987b:2) points out. Even with the concept of semiperiphery, however, it is difficult to envision graded statuses between core and periphery that permitted differential congeries of political, military, and economic relations.

A related problem derives from the politically charged terminology sometimes used to define *core* and *periphery*. Ekholm and Friedman (1979:46), for instance, define imperialism as a characteristic of a core-periphery process "that tends to reproduce simultaneous development and underdevelopment in a single system." They continue, " 'Empire' is a political mechanism, the control over a larger multi-society region by a single state. Empire, as a function, is a political machine for the maintenance and/or direct organisation of imperialist economic processes." I contend that this is what we ought to be investigating, not assuming. To assert that the dominance of one polity over a series of others necessarily results in development and underdevelopment presumes a conclusion, rather than setting out a problem. Ekholm and Friedman's starting point for analysis unnecessarily constrains the potential forms of interaction and outcomes that we can investigate.

Another related problem focuses on the balance of power between the core and peripheral polities. As Wallerstein (1974) conceived it, and as a number of archaeologists have applied it (e.g., Ekholm and Friedman 1979), the core polity thoroughly dominated the relationship. The terms of interaction and the options of terminating or intensifying it lay solely within the purview of the core. Kohl (1987b:20) has observed that, to the contrary, peripheries were not helpless in dictating terms of exchange. They could often choose to develop or discontinue exchange, depending on their views of its utility for their purposes. As is argued throughout the present work, the interaction between the core and subject societies was constantly negotiated. To be sure, the core powers had by far the upper hand, because of their coercive capacities, but they were not the only players in the game.

Tributary and Capitalist Polities

In an effort to redress these and related problems, Wolf (1982) has reassessed the issue of post-1400 European relations with the rest of the world, using an explicitly Marxist approach. Among the deficiencies he sees in prior explanations is the tendency of researchers to reify sociopolitical and ethnic entities as impervious billiard balls, with no significant contacts among them. He argues that, in contrast, extensive contact across borders had crucial impacts on world development and that our analysis ought to focus on active relationships within and across borders, not on self-contained polities.

Wolf (1982:74) proposes examining development using Marx's notion of mode of production, which describes a set of relations among nature, work, social labor, and social organization. Wolf divides modes of production into three basic sets: kinship-ordered, tributary, and capitalist. He then applies the tributary mode, which combines both the Asiatic and feudal modes of production, to some of the early empires, among them China, the Sasanians, and the Inkas. Wolf argues that in these kinds of systems the central elites are maintained by mobilizing the products of labor of an independently producing populace. Among the key assertions of the argument is that social labor in the tributary mode is controlled primarily through a political process. Such systems may become centralized or fragmented or may fluctuate between situations of power centers and powerful regional elites (Wolf 1982:82). Wolf emphasizes that these oscillations depend fundamentally on both the internal features of the polities in question and their interactions with neighboring groups. The volatile contacts between pastoralists and agriculturalists, for instance, are cited as having been particularly important in shaping tributary-mode polities in North Africa and Asia.

Although receiving accolades, Wolf's approach has not yet been employed widely in archaeological analyses. One effort in this regard may be found in McGuire's (1989) assessment of the North American Southwest as a periphery of Mesoamerica. In this argument, McGuire focuses on the development of a prestige-goods economy among the elites of the Southwest as key to their attainment and maintenance of power. The high status attained by certain descent groups within the periphery as a consequence of differential access to paraphernalia obtained from Mesoamerica is argued to have been transformed into real differences in access to the means of production (McGuire 1989:50).

Wolf's conception, far too comprehensive to do justice to here, provides great insight into the effects of long-distance interaction among Europe and peoples throughout the remainder of the world over the last half millennium. Wolf delineates transformations in labor organization, production and exchange of goods, and social relations that resulted from these contacts. Nonetheless, the analysis evinces two curious lapses. First, although the effects of technological change on transportation are discussed, the study conveys little systematic sense of the energetic effects of the spatial distributions of populations, activities, and resources that provide the essence of much geographic analysis. The analysis of modes of production does not assess the differential costs, effectiveness, or security of

each formation. The social relations of production do not operate in an energetic vacuum, and the outcomes of organizational shifts have definite costs. As Skinner (e.g., 1977) shows for late imperial China, as Hassig (1985, 1988) demonstrates for the Aztec empire and Spanish colonial occupation of central Mexico, and as Van Creveld (1977) and Engels (1978) show for military actions from ancient times to the present, transportation and communications capabilities have provided very real spatial limitations to the potential forms and intensities of interaction. An organization will therefore be pressured to restructure if the changes that occur are ineffective at maintaining the system or if the costs are excessive in material, labor, or maintenance of order. Any treatment of imperial polities or interaction on a grand scale must take these issues into account systematically. To be fair to Wolf, his treatment of the more modern systems does take transportation and other costs into account, but the evaluation of antecedent polities does not do so systematically.

Second, the premodern polities are generally described in normative, homogeneous terms in Wolf's work. It may be unreasonable to expect a book of the scale of his volume to assess variation in the numerous regions that it treats. I suggest, however, that it is precisely the interaction of more or less orderly imperial policy with variation among subject groups over time and space that contributes to the development of imperial organization. To emphasize either variation or cultural conformity, to the exclusion of the other, misses much of what I see as the dynamic nature of imperial development.

Metrocentric, Pericentric, and Systemic Models

Doyle (1986) has suggested an alternative, political science approach, whereby theories of empire may be understood according to the posited sources of imperial development and motivations of the core polity. He divides these theories into three broad sets: the metrocentric, the pericentric, and the systemic. Theories of metrocentric imperial development place the principal causes of expansion within the central polity. Most of this literature is concerned with the development of dependency relationships between the modern capitalist societies of the Western Hemisphere and the peripheral societies of the Third World. According to these arguments, the drive for expansion may lie in the economic, military, or political motivations of those in power in the core polity. Marxist and world systems explanations of imperialism are best understood as metrocentric theories, even though it is generally argued that elites in the periphery play a critical role in the implementation of imperial policies of extraction (Frank 1966; Wallerstein 1974).[6]

Doyle points out an example of the metrocentric view applied to an ancient empire in Harris's (1989 [1979]) evaluation of the formation of the Roman empire from Republican Rome. Harris, who sees a central role for the military in imperial development, argues that the impetus for expansion lay in the need for Roman elites to demonstrate military prowess as a prerequisite for attaining high office. According to this reasoning, the war against the Gauls served as much as a forum for personal advancement as it did for imperial expansion (Doyle 1986; Nash 1987). Luttwak's (1976) examination of the Roman empire in the first three centuries A.D. calls this position into question, however, by observing the disconformity between the irregularity of the glorified campaigns of the emperors and the systematic development and retrenchment of boundaries and provincial control. The key point here is that the imperial system functioned in a manner inconsistent with the stated rationales of the principals.

An alternative, pericentric view of imperial development can be found in arguments that look to the periphery for the catalysts of expansion. This approach assumes that the leadership of the core has established or wishes to establish economic relations with foreign polities that are critical to or useful for the core's well-being. The expansion of a state may therefore turn out to be the result of a defensive strategy under circumstances in which securing borders is a consistent problem (Doyle 1986:26). As is the case with the metrocentric approach, insights may be gained into the empires of both the present and antiquity through this kind of analysis. Badian (1967:62–75), for instance, asserts that the Roman extension of domestic client relations over Greek cities in the third century B.C. resulted from a perceived need to stabilize the volatile political climate of the region to Rome's greater security. A comparable argument may be made for the transformation of increasingly powerful and threatening client polities into annexed provinces in the second century A.D. (Luttwak 1976). Similarly, Lichtheim (cited in Larsen 1979b:92) has argued that the Holy Roman Empire was established in response to the threat of expanding Islamic polities.

A recent approach to explaining the existence of empires integrates some of the two preceding views into a systemic model. In this perspective, developed from modern power politics, catalysts for expansion are found in the core and in the periphery (Doyle 1986:26). At the base of this position is the assumption that competition over international power lies at the center of imperial expansion. Where relatively impermeable states compete with one another, polities will expand to counterbalance or supersede the power of their competitors. Colonial peripheries are assimilated to provide needed resources in the broader competition. The essence of this argument is that the powerful will rule the weak because that is a legitimate and predictable result of the defense of the powerful polity's interests. Doyle (1986) cites De Romilly's (1947) analysis of Athenian power politics in conquering Melos and the repeated partitioning of Poland as examples supporting this position.

These approaches provide some worthwhile ways of conceiving the causes for imperialism, but they do not afford particularly useful means of analyzing flexible strategies of integration and extraction. Among the key problems—also present in the core-periphery model—is a tendency for some authors to treat the elites of the core polity as a homogeneous set of individuals or groups with common values and a common motivation for expansion. Similarly, subordinate polities are often viewed as differing among themselves but being internally homogeneous (see, e.g., the discussion of Sparta and Athens in Doyle 1986:55–81). Yet interests are not uniform within societies. They vary widely according to the status or composition of the individual or the group. Particularly in polities as diverse as the Inka empire, it makes sense to examine the nature and potential interests of the various parties in any relationship before accepting commonality of interest as an explanation for behavior.

In addition, these models often do not distinguish between the political and domestic elements of the economies of the core and subject populations. In part, this situation derives from the scale of analysis to which imperial studies lend themselves. It is difficult to maintain a broad spatial and temporal perspective while examining economic activity from the household level to the state. Nonetheless, economic behavior in the subject economies did not revolve entirely around supplying the needs of the core, nor did economic activity in the core depend solely on resources extracted from subject territories. The domestic economies of both subject and core polities most likely functioned largely independently of one another, but the activities pursued within the imperial political economy assuredly affected patterns of production, consumption, and exchange within both. To understand the balance between subject and imperial power, we need to address the relative importance of and interaction among these economic components.

Most of these approaches make an additional assumption of advanced urbanism for the core polity (e.g., Hodge 1984:2–4). This may be a reasonable empirical generalization, even for archaic empires, but it is not a necessary condition. It is true that the economic and military power associated with high population density and the organizational capacities associated with interdependent populations can contribute directly to the various components of imperial power. This does not mean that a high degree of urbanism is a prerequisite for the expansion of control by the central polity. The Mongols and the Inkas provide prime examples of empires that developed without large-scale antecedent urbanism within the core society.

A further associated assumption is that the core polity is initially more highly developed than the subordinate polities that it brings under its aegis. This assumption also is an empirical generalization, not a necessary feature, of empires. In comparison with their subject polities of the central and northern Peruvian coast, for example, the Inkas were economically and politically simpler. The balance of complexity between the dominant and subordinate societies has direct implications for the way that subject polities were integrated into the empire and for the disposition of resources by the core. Decisions must be made as to the costs and benefits of varying degrees of control—direct and intensive on one end and indirect and extensive on the other (Hassig 1985:100–101). Under conditions in which the imperial polity was initially less organizationally complex than in the subordinated societies, resolution of this problem required a greater centralization of the core polity, a reduction in the complexity of the subordinated polities, or both.

The Territorial-Hegemonic Model
The difficulties entailed in some of these theories of empire suggest that a more flexible model would be appropriate in explaining the diversity of strategies employed in ruling subject territories, particularly where the motivations and stated policies of archaic societies are not readily recoverable or are in conflict with the apparent rationales. This section, therefore, considers the territorial-hegemonic model, as applied to the study of early empires. This discussion derives from the work of Luttwak (1976) and Hassig (1985, 1988), whose studies of the Romans and Aztecs emphasize the strengths of the approach and provide comparative cases for the Inkas.

The territorial-hegemonic model attempts to account for general trends and variations in terms of degrees of control exerted throughout imperial holdings. Hassig (1985:100) suggests that imperial strategies can best be envisioned along a continuum, with differing balances among the sources of power and the nature of extraction providing a complex array of imperial options. At one end is the hegemonic system, which entails a core polity (usually a state) and client polities that are responsible, with varying degrees of autonomy, for implementing imperial policy, extracting resources for imperial consumption, and providing security out of their own resources. At the other end, territorial control entails more-direct occupation and governing of subject territories, with the central state being responsible for underwriting security and administration. Hegemonic and territorial strategies grade into each other and may be differentially applied in different parts of the empire and at different times, as circumstances change. In general, the range of strategies depends on the central polity's own organization, the organization of the subjects, the spatial distribution of resources, and the imperial goals.

A key element of the model is a focus on the costs, benefits, and effectiveness of various strategies, ranging from clientage and provincial annexation to retrenchment. Because conditions vary spatially and temporally, differing combinations of military, political, and economic power become more or less secure and cost-effective. Imperial strategies can therefore be assessed partially as calculated plans and partially as ad hoc responses to changing circumstances, given the participants' incomplete information and often hazy understanding of the consequences of many actions.

In contrast to the core-periphery approach, which has tended to move away from spatial analysis, the territorial-hegemonic model requires consideration of the effects of space on organization. A number of authors, not all subscribing to the latter model, observe that spatial variation in imperial rule is systematic (Skinner 1977; Hassig 1985; Crumley et al. 1987; Dowdle 1987; MacKendrick 1987). Most analysts recognize that control in empires varies in part as a function of distance from the imperial core, although some authors are more explicit about incorporating spatial variation into regional analysis. Skinner's (1977) treatment of late imperial China is by far the most elegant in this regard. Skinner details the intersection of economic (retail marketing), administrative, and defensive organizations in regional urban-rural hierarchies in the late-nineteenth-century territorial empire. Three essential points may be drawn from his argument. First, both microregional and macroregional conditions contribute directly to the spatial organization of imperial activities. Second, distance, under these circumstances, is best conceived in terms of transport costs and communications capabilities, because they translate into logistical support of the military and into ease of economic and political integration (see also Van Creveld 1977; Engels 1978; Hassig 1985, 1988). Third, military, political, and economic power are not locked together in fixed spatial patterns (Mann 1986). Their relationships should be a matter for investigation, not an assumed condition. Lattimore's (1962) notion of military, administrative, and economic radii of control seems too simple a view, but it is equally clear that spatial variation is neither haphazard nor solely a product of historical circumstance.

At this point, it will be useful to return to the forms of power outlined earlier in the chapter, to see how they may be implemented along the territorial-hegemonic continuum.

MILITARY POWER   Luttwak (1976) argues that the military goal of a hegemonic system is to enhance the security of the central polity's territory rather than the security of the entire imperial territory and its populations. Imperial security outside the core area is vested in client polities. This strategy is typically pursued during expansion and in territories where direct control is not feasible or desirable, such as in the marginal provinces of the Aztec empire (Hassig 1985, 1988). Clients are maintained by the subvention of elites and unexpended military force of the central state, and the brunt of the manpower and resources expended in security is carried by the clients themselves. A key element of this strategy is to keep client polities internally stable while reinforcing perceptions of core power (Luttwak 1976:192). As Hassig (1985:100) points out, military forces can be used to address both endemic and sporadic threats, because armies can either serve for extended periods in the field or be used to retake rebellious areas. Hegemonic control is therefore notably economic in its use of force, because its limits are defined by the range within which others see the central state as being capable of compelling obedience. The reach of power and its costs do not have to be proportional (Luttwak 1976:192), but there is significant strategic cost in the loss of security toward the territorial limits of the empire.

Under territorial control, Luttwak argues, the military strength of an empire and its effective power are rigidly proportional, because this strength is now used directly, not as a tool of political suasion. As he observes in describing the Roman situation, client polities still remain useful to the core, although in a reduced fashion. Strong clients cannot be tolerated, because their strength may exceed that of the imperial forces (Luttwak 1976:192). This requires that certain clients be transformed into provinces, with a new set of client polities being established outside the new territorial limits whenever possible.

Luttwak notes that the cost of this shift in policy is dramatic, for three reasons. First, the territorial limits of the empire now have to be secured more firmly than before, because provincial residents can make greater demands for security than could the client populace. Second, the significantly greater costs of securing the harder borders now have to be maintained directly by the core, instead of being passed off to the client leadership. Third, the mobile, disposable forces that had underwritten the military power of the empire when clients were supplying most personnel and matériel now have to be more permanently fixed along the borders. This is not an economical way to use force, because it spreads imperial resources very thin. As a consequence, the power that the state can bring to bear at any given point is seen as markedly reduced, because of the more fixed nature of military resources along an imperial perimeter. The net is greater security of the provincial regions, but at great cost and inefficient use of resources.

Two aspects of the combination of force and diplomacy underscore the ties among military, political, and economic power. First, the expenditure of force diminishes military power, because that which is expended at one location is lost in potential application at all other locations (Luttwak 1976). Thus military power is most efficiently employed when force is held in abeyance. The Inkas clearly appreciated the concept of economy of force, preferring to amass an apparently invincible army and obtain surrender diplomatically (see Chapter 5). When targets capitulated only after prolonged resistance, the Inkas on occasion annihilated the defenders, thereby increasing power for subsequent campaigns. Second, the force that could be brought to bear at any point depended directly on logistics, which were contingent upon economic and transport capabilities (van Creveld 1977). Thus, military power was critically dependent on the capacities of the territories from which support was to be drawn during military expansion and consolidation of control.

ECONOMIC POWER   Hassig (1985:101) contrasts hegemonic with territorial empires by observing that the former are low-control, low-extraction systems. He points out that the limited extraction of resources, such as through tribute, permits a concomitantly low investment in administration by the central authority. This relationship is accomplished primarily through intensification of production, reorganization of labor, and control of certain kinds of exchange within the subject populations. The main purpose is to produce a surplus that can be tapped for the core's purposes. Production can be intensified either (1) indirectly, through taxing the raw or finished material products or the transactions in those goods, or (2) directly, through labor taxes or establishment of state production enclaves.

Indirect strategies characteristic of hegemonic rule intensify production by the expedient of extracting a portion of the products previously consumed by the subordinate populations. Although these are essentially hands-off approaches, in that the means by which the intensification or reorganization is implemented are left in the hands of the subordinate elites, they may cause reorganization of labor in the subordinate polities. More-direct strategies of intensification in a system of hegemonic control result from direct state intervention in the production of key resources. Speaking of the European establishment of control over colonies since the seventeenth century, Wallerstein (1974) argues that direct intervention resulted in development of free wage labor in the core and serfdom or forced cash-crop labor in the periphery. Although this argument is most appropriate to capitalist economies, it may be noted that extraction of materials that had previously been under the control of native elites could result in an increase in attached specialized production in the subject polities. Wolf (1982) argues that the intrusion of mercantile activities into non-Western societies had much farther-reaching consequences for political and social formations.

An alternative result, in a market-oriented subject economy, is intensification of the production of goods that can be exchanged for the raw materials required in tribute by the core. This may have been the case with the intensified production of cotton, gold dust, feathers, and cacao in peripheral areas of the Aztec empire (Brumfiel 1987; Smith 1987b). The structure of labor relations between subject elites and subordinates may have remained relatively stable under these circumstances, even though the elites were now serving essentially as management for the extraction of resources from their people. As will be discussed below, the extent to which the subject populations became attached to regional elites or simply increased their productivity within previously established institutions may have depended on the nature of the commodities required in tribute.

Territorial control is a high-control, high-extraction strategy (Hassig 1985:100). Although this approach to rule reduces the threat of over-strong client polities and increases the security of the periphery, it is markedly more expensive to the core. Territorial control also entails both direct and indirect means of intensification. Direct intensification is likely to produce more marked changes in the organization of labor—for instance, in the development of new institutions of production attached to the central polity. Among these were the specialized agricultural and craft enclaves created within the Inka empire. They yielded new socioeconomic statuses whose existence was entirely dependent on the state political economy. This kind of strategy is also most likely to produce changes in land tenure systems, as competition over the means of production increases within subject polities because of the co-option of resources by the state (see La Lone and La Lone 1987 for a discussion of this change in the Inka economy). Forms of indirect intensification under territorial rule may result from processes similar to those employed in the hegemonic approach, such as taxing mercantile activity or extracting staple goods from the general populace.

Both direct and indirect intensification of production should result in an increase in specialization, because of the economies of large-scale production and the kinds of goods demanded by the central polity. Numerous authors have observed that the intensification of production in subject territories is generally focused on two sorts of resources: raw materials and products specific to their environmental location. The control of certain kinds of raw materials, notably metals and other materials used in the production of sumptuaries, is associated with the core polity's assumption of the right to produce and distribute those goods validating state-affiliated status. It can also be a result of the state interest in controlling media of exchange, such as was the case in nineteenth-century Dahomey (Polanyi 1966).

The kinds of goods extracted and the loci of their consumption are also directly related to the overall strategy of integration. Because the cost of transporting goods depends on the weight and volume of the goods and on the efficiency of the transportation system, subsistence goods will tend to be extracted from territories relatively near their points of consumption (Hassig 1985:24). It is a commonplace principle in economic geography that high-value, low-bulk goods, such as sumptuary items, consume less of their value in transport and thus tend to be moved greater distances. In a hegemonic system, a high proportion of the high-bulk matériel extracted is produced and consumed in the core part of the empire. In a territorial system, a much higher fraction is produced and consumed in the peripheral regions, because of the greater need for investment in administration and security. Thus, the proportions of imperial resources invested in the core and surrounding territories differ significantly between the hegemonic and the territorial strategies.

POLITICAL POWER   Analysis of the hegemonic-territorial variations in the political arena requires consideration of the nature and depth of imperial politics. As Wright (1978:56) observes in discussing state formation, an increasing number of offices generally develops in complex political systems as one set becomes overloaded with administrative or other political tasks (see also Johnson 1982, 1987). This phenomenon is generally coupled with increasing specialization of offices at all levels. Either kind of differentiation increases the need for manpower in the hierarchy. The structure of the decision-making subsystem becomes further defined as decision makers compete or collude to maintain their part of the hierarchy in the face of a chronic excessive demand for limited resources.

In an imperial system facing an increasing administrative load, a single strategy of rule would have been inadequate to the complexities of political transition, because the varying natures of subject societies would have created problems in application of political power. Expansionist state polities typically encounter problems in integrating subject societies with fluid or volatile political structures, whose elites cannot easily command the allegiance of the populace. Difficulties would have arisen, for example, where a core state attempted to apply coercively based political methods to subject societies within which politics were consensual or negotiated between elites and the broader populace. Often enough, subject elites or representatives recognized or appointed by the state would have been unable to exact broad compliance. The expansion of the Europeans onto the American Great Plains and their repeated failure to understand the nature of indige-

nous political decision-making exemplify this situation. As will be argued below, the lack of congruence between the organizational demands of the imperial state and the capacities of subject groups often required early imperial states to adopt patron-client relations with local elites, leaving the subject political organization essentially intact. As is the case with military power, which may act through threat or through deferred application of force, effective political strategy does not entail constant control over subordinate political processes, which would be impossible in any event. It simply requires that the most important decisions ultimately be enacted in the empire's interest. Indeed, even in the most complex states, many local groups exercise control at lower levels and over activities that are not the concern of the central authorities (Yoffee 1979:16; Adams 1984).

Particular kinds of problems would have arisen where the expanding imperial polity was ill-equipped to administer societies politically more complex than itself. Here the Inka conquest of the north coast of Peru and the Mongol conquests of China and Persia may be cited. In these cases, the capacities of the conquest polity were inadequate to manage the regular business of the subordinate society. To have done so would have required dismantling the subject organization, radically increasing the complexity of the conquering polity's political system, or relying on control of key positions in an overarching state structure that maintained the subject system otherwise intact.

The variety of political capacities of subject polities, coupled with the often fragile nature of the central structure, accordingly required that a series of flexible options be applied within a broad imperial strategy of rule. Imperial decisions about the nature of political integration can therefore be treated as cost-benefit choices. Overall, the greater the congruence of core and subject hierarchies, the greater the degree of political control that can be effected with a given investment of favor, manpower, and economic support. The hegemonic-territorial gradient can be seen in the degree of continuity between the core and subject political hierarchies. A major component of this continuity lies in the direct or indirect incorporation of subject elites into the imperial bureaucracy and the associated degree of state penetration into subordinate affairs (Luttwak 1976; Hassig 1988:19–25). A variety of options is available, among them clientage of neighboring paramounts or provincial elites, alliance formation, and establishment of a civil service.

Patron-client political relations between the core polity and subject societies are likely to be implemented in the less complex societies, such as chiefdoms or segmented societies, because they constitute less of a threat than do states and they are less capable of carrying out the management tasks in the specialized manner that states have established. They are also to be expected among polities of virtually any form at the perimeters of state control, where they serve a useful defensive purpose for the core, at minimal expense. In terms of security, patron-client relations are useful during times of imperial expansion, such as the first century A.D. in the Roman empire (Luttwak 1976; Harris 1989 [1979]) or the Aztec expansion out of the Basin of Mexico (Hassig 1985, 1988), because they are cost-effective. In locations where security may be an issue, such as along the periphery between the core and potential enemies or buffers, the core polity may have insufficient resources to invest in integrated control. By coercion and subvention of client paramounts, the core can reserve force but maintain friendly interests and a modicum of control. Because of the forced or bribed nature of client support, however, the allegiance of the provincial hierarchy will be divided. The paramounts will be caught in a position of exploiting their own populations for the benefit of the external authorities and themselves, which is likely to undermine their power with their own people and to promote internal factions. Moreover, the potential threat of client polities is directly proportional to their usefulness. Because of this, it may ultimately be seen as beneficial for the core to invest more heavily in client polities over time and convert them to integrated provinces.

Whereas the hegemonic strategy leaves local decisions relatively untouched, imperial authorities in a territorial strategy attempt to control both interregional and intraregional sociopolitical matters. An example of the former may be found in the central Roman provinces of the second century A.D., where a great deal of continuity existed between the imperial and prior regional authority systems. We would expect this kind of rule to be implemented where there was a pressing interest in defusing potential threats from powerful allies or clients or in exploiting the regional resources. It is also expected to be effective where the political organizations of the central and subject territories were substantially similar, providing a high return of control for investment. Spatially, direct integration is likely to occur in territories immediately adjacent to the core or in key productive or security areas, such as agricultural zones or along transport routes.

Alliance relationships can also be incorporated as part of both hegemonic and territorial strategies. Within early empires, they were likely transitional, occurring early in imperial development. The classic case was the Aztec Triple Alliance, which became increasingly weighted in favor of Tenochtitlán. An additional instance may be seen in the joint ventures of the Inkas, the Quechuas, and the Lupaqas early in the Inka expansion. The advantages of this type of relationship lie in the alliance's ability to mobilize greater manpower and other resources than any one member could individually and in the ostensible removal of allies from immediate competition. A major disadvantage occurs in the constant potential of a member to subvert the relationship. Alliances would generally be expected under conditions of competition among essentially equivalent polities. The security of each polity may have been threatened, but none of the principals had sufficient power to establish control over the others. This condition permeated the Andean highlands in the last couple of centuries before to the Inka conquests. As will be described in Chapter 4, a cyclical pattern of alliance formation and conflict not only characterized the home region of the Inkas but was endemic in the central and north highlands as well.

Assessing the formation of imperial political relations draws our attention to the changing sources of allegiance of elites within subject polities. The core elites of early empires devised a variety of techniques to emphasize central relations and undermine elites' local allegiances. Among the most widely used were economic subvention, forced resettlement, cultural instruction, and granting of wives. Under any circumstances, the provincial paramount elites owed their positions to the grace of the imperium. To the extent that decisions concerning implementation of imperial policy were left in the hands of regional paramounts, however, the political allegiance of intraregional subordinates should have remained with the regional paramount or other internal factions. Conversely, to the extent that the positions of power within a given subject territory were granted directly from outside (i.e., through installation of foreigners as regional paramounts or through development of a central civil service), the provincial elites should have commanded proportionally less allegiance from their subordinates. This is the sort of problem that characteristically arose in the European colonial civil services, in which the various avenues to power, such as nepotism and merit, came into conflict (Burling 1974).

Conclusion

This discussion has suggested that strategies of rule in the early empires are understandable as flexible combinations of military, political, and economic power, legitimized by elite ideology. These approaches were not simply a function of a blanket policy but depended on a set of intersecting considerations, such as core interests in subject territories; the spatial distribution of security threats, population, and resources; core and subject political and economic organizations; transportation and communications capabilities; and historical circumstances. A coherent analysis of these issues will therefore be central to explanation of imperial policy in any given subject region.

I have suggested that the territorial-hegemonic model provides analytic concepts that embrace both systematic patterns and variations over time and space. Although clearly analogous to the more widely used core-periphery model, the territorial-hegemonic model differs in application in at least three ways that are useful for my analysis. First, imperial organization is treated less as a dichotomized system composed of core elites and exploited, dominated polities than as a series of interrelated strategies. The frequent transformation of clients into provinces and the subsequent investment of resources by core elites, for instance, tend to underscore the temporal and spatial shifts that have

played such an important role in the dynamics of imperial rule (see Smith 1987a). Second, the territorial-hegemonic model places greater emphasis on input and output of resources, which accords well with a materialist approach. The key issues become the strategies of decision-making, the disposition of imperial resources, and their relationship to extraction of subject resources. This emphasis provides a more balanced view of the interaction among various sources of imperial and subject power than does the literature on core-periphery, much of which focuses on the sensitive issue of imperial exploitation. The core-periphery emphasis on extraction also tends to obscure important developments in noncore territories resulting from imperial investment. Third, many elements of the core-periphery model are most appropriate to colonial situations, in which the peripheries were spatially removed and in which the core elites often invested little in colonial development. The spatial continuity of many early empires renders them more amenable to analysis in terms of gradations of integration.

In sum, imperial strategies depend upon a complex mix of different sources of power, which in turn depend upon the organizational capabilities and resources of the core and varied subordinate polities. Broadly speaking, we would expect each kind of polity to respond both to internal pressures and to the demands of the other polities. How these relations were worked out in practice for the Inkas in the central highlands of Peru is the subject of detailed study in the remainder of this volume.

3

The Setting and Research Design

The complexity of the models described in Chapter 2 emphasizes that inquiry into imperial organization requires study of a range of issues from a broad spatial perspective. Optimally, it would be desirable to have detailed regional studies across a wide range of provincial territories. That is not possible for the Inka empire at present, because of the breadth of the polity and the lack of intensive fieldwork in more than a few areas. As was outlined in Chapter 1, the analytic approach adopted here is to couple the hegemonic-territorial model of the empire with a detailed analysis of Inka policies in one province of the central Peruvian sierra—Wanka Wamaní (Valley of the Wankas), or the Upper Mantaro Valley. This method is intended to provide a means of conceiving both the general nature of the empire and its concrete implications on the ground in an important highland valley.

The province of Wanka Wamaní lay north of the Cuzco heartland, along the main sierra highway to Quito (Fig. 1.2). One of the more densely populated regions of the Andean highlands, the valley was home to several ethnic groups, known principally as the Hatunxauxa, the Lurinwanka, and the Ananwanka in the Late Horizon and early Colonial Period. Collectively, these groups are generally referred to as the Wankas. The region has proved to be an excellent location for studying indigenous cultural developments and the impacts of Inka rule. Initially, the umbrella Upper Mantaro Archaeological Research Project (UMARP) selected the area because of the extensive archaeological research, described below, that had already been conducted. A second advantage was that Inka rule had an extensive impact on the archaeological record of the region. The Inkas built a major provincial center called Hatun Xauxa, smaller support facilities, and immense storage complexes throughout the valley. In the study of an empire in which the material residues of imperial rule can be sporadic, the advantages of a clearly visible Inka presence are considerable. A third benefit derived from the collaborative efforts of the members of UMARP. Addressing the question of Inka rule within the context of a large project has made a broader data base available for analysis than would have been possible had this been an independent enterprise.

By focusing on a single region, this study has been able to examine the changes within the subject population that resulted from imperial incorporation. A parallel series of issues concerns how the region's extant organization and resources affected the development of imperial strategy. Given the focus on a single province, of course, the detailed data presented here can be used only partially to address the latter problem.

As the preceding chapter described theoretical issues concerned with imperial organization, the present chapter outlines the nature of my research on the ground. Succeeding chapters examine the relationship between general military, logistical, political, and economic aspects of Inka rule and life in the Upper Mantaro. As might be expected, the quality of available information varies among these issues at the imperial and provincial levels, so that the balance here between broad-scale and detailed study also varies somewhat. The general trend of the argument, however, is to examine each issue from top (imperial) to bottom (provincial and local), to see how the Inkas accommodated to and affected their provincial subjects.

The Environmental Setting

Tawantinsuyu encompassed a narrow strip of land, covering about 1 million km² along the western edge of South America. Its borders were set largely by environmental limits. The Pacific Ocean bordered the west, and the Amazonian jungles set the frontier for much of the eastern edge. On the north, the boundaries lay at the present border of Ecuador and Colombia; the southern limits of effective imperial control lay near Santiago, Chile, although the Inka armies penetrated as far south as the Río Maule. The lands inhabited by the Wanka populations, who are the focus of this study, lay somewhat north of the center of the empire, in the central highlands of Peru (Fig. 1.2).

The often harsh environment of the Andes results from rapid altitudinal changes and from the juxtaposition of the cold Peruvian coastal current with the relatively warm land, which rises rapidly to altitudes exceeding 6,000 m (Fig. 3.1). As a consequence of these physiographic conditions, the west coast of South America is largely desert, interrupted only by a series of rivers that drain the inland rainfall. Because the Andes rise so sheerly from the narrow coastal plain, the continental divide lies little more than 100 km from the Pacific coast in central Peru, although farther south, in Bolivia, the divide is found farther to the east.

At the northern end of the empire lay the highlands of Ecuador. The temperate highland valleys were the only part of that region that was ruled by the Inkas, for they failed to take control of the wooded hillslopes and lower jungles to the west and east. To the south of the Peruvian sierra, the focus of the present work, lies the

Bolivian altiplano, home to some of the densest populations of the Andes. This high windswept plain provides a marked contrast to the rugged Andean terrain to the north and south. The principal sources of subsistence for native peoples here were the Andean tubers and camelid herding. The vertical compactness of the contrasting environmental zones in the Andean sierra, extending down to Chile and Argentina, provided an exceptional opportunity for societies to produce a wide variety of resources within a relatively restricted territory. Within a day or two's walk of a central settlement on the eastern slopes, for example, community members might have access to the high puna grasslands for camelid herding, the upper agricultural lands for tuber-complex crops, the lower highlands for maize-complex crops, and the warmer, moister lands to the east for coca, aji, fruits, and other tropical products. The Inkas took notable advantage of this situation, assigning local residents and forcibly resettled colonists to cultivate or collect products of these varied resource zones.

On the Peruvian coast, subsistence depended on the rich oceanic resources and agriculture. Because rainfall is so light and infrequent on the coast, populations relied on complex, valley-wide irrigation systems to provide the water for production of agricultural and industrial crops. The success of the indigenous peoples in devising irrigation systems is reflected in the dense populations of the central and north coasts of Peru, an area of early cultural development and urbanism.

The lands occupied by the prehistoric Wankas fall within the modern Department of Junín, Peru, in the vicinity of Jauja and Huancayo. This territory covers an area of striking environmental variability in the central highlands (Fig. 3.2). Travelers ascending from the irrigated valleys of the coastal desert would have climbed through terraced hillslopes and alpine terrain to the pass of Ticlio (4,500 m above mean sea level), which provides access through the Cordillera Occidental. To the east lie a series of valleys and the Cordillera Oriental ranges, before the land descends rapidly into the montaña, a semitropical forest above the Amazonian jungles.

The research area lies at the northern end of the Mantaro Valley, the major intermontane valley in the central highlands (Fig. 3.3). The main archaeological study region comprises only a fraction of the lands occupied by the Wankas: an area of about 25 km (northwest to southeast) by 43 km (northeast to southwest). The area is bounded generally by Apata on the south, the Huaricolca puna on the north,

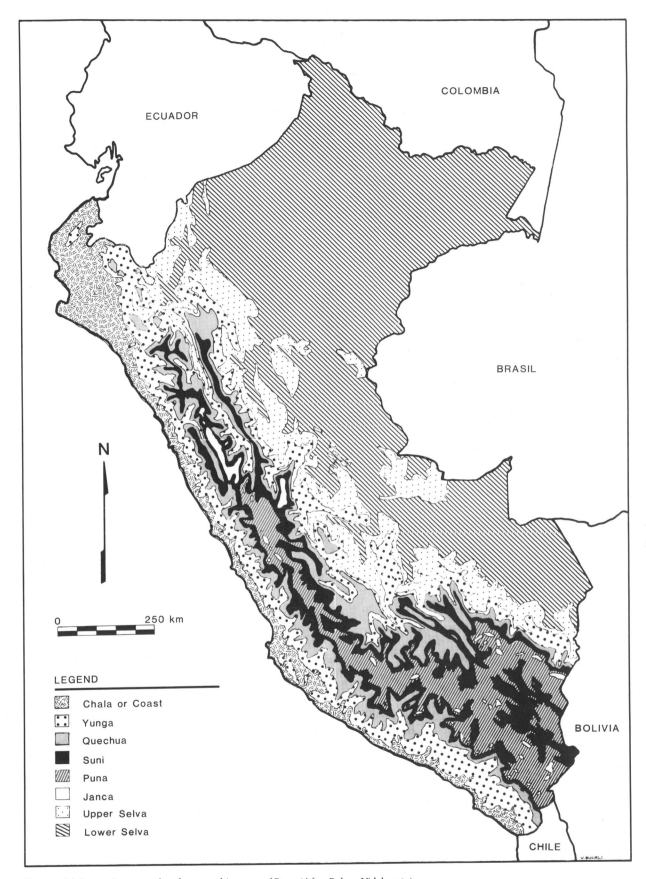

ECUADOR

COLOMBIA

BRASIL

N

0   250 km

BOLIVIA

LEGEND

	Chala or Coast
	Yunga
	Quechua
	Suni
	Puna
	Janca
	Upper Selva
	Lower Selva

CHILE

V. BUCHLI

Fig. 3.1. Major environmental and geographic zones of Peru. (After Pulgar Vidal 1964)

Provincial Power in the Inka Empire

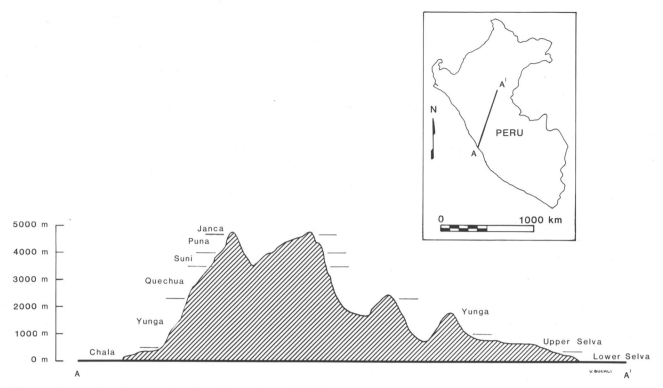

Fig. 3.2. Cross section of topography and environmental zones trending west to east across the central Peruvian Andes, from Lima, through Cerro de Pasco and Huánuco, to the selva.

Masma Chicche on the east, and Tajana on the west. It extends north from the Mantaro Valley floodplain itself onto the Huaricolca puna. East and west, it passes over the first range of foothills of the Cordilleras Oriental and Occidental, whose severe topography is punctuated by glacial lakes.

The Río Mantaro is the principal drainage in the region, arising in Lake Junín, flowing south through the mountains, and emerging from a narrow gorge just south of modern Jauja (Fig. 3.4). The river then courses through the main Mantaro Valley, an intensively cultivated floodplain that varies in width between about 4 and 24 km before narrowing into a gorge once again on its course to the Amazon. Within this 50-km-long valley, the river cuts a braided channel between natural terraces, dropping about 250 m in elevation from Jauja (3,400 m) to Huancayo (3,150 m). North, east, and west of the open valley, the land rises onto the rolling grasslands of the puna (3,800 to 4,800 m).

Tributary and internally drained valleys lie among the surrounding hills. Three of these—the Paca, the Yanamarca, and the Masma valleys—are particularly interesting to UMARP because of their dense late-prehistoric occupations. Paca is a small internally

draining basin at the farthest north end of the main Mantaro Valley. The Masma Valley lies to the southeast of Paca, behind the first range of foothills, and the Yanamarca Valley lies behind a moraine just north of the mouth of the Río Mantaro gorge. The importance of these valleys archaeologically stems largely from the quality of their agricultural soils and the concomitant concentration of prehistoric population. These were the principal zones of prehistoric agricultural intensification, through the construction of drained fields, irrigation systems, and terracing.

Although the study region lies at about 12° south latitude, the potentially tropical climate is moderated by the high altitude. Day length varies only slightly throughout the year, but pronounced differences occur in temperature and precipitation at all altitudes (see Earle et al. 1980:8). In general, the year is marked by two distinct seasons: a cold, dry winter from June to September and a warmer, wet summer from October to March.[1] Along with the highly seasonal rainfall, frosts are a seasonally and altitudinally limiting factor for agriculture. Because delayed inception of the agricultural season can cause problems for crops that are sensitive to low temperatures, irrigation is currently

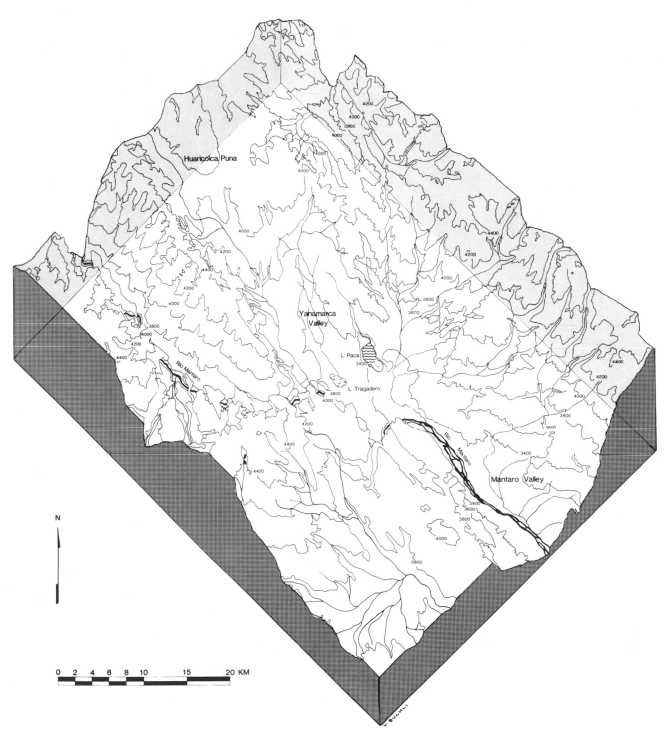

Fig. 3.3. Isometric projection of topography encompassing the UMARP study region.

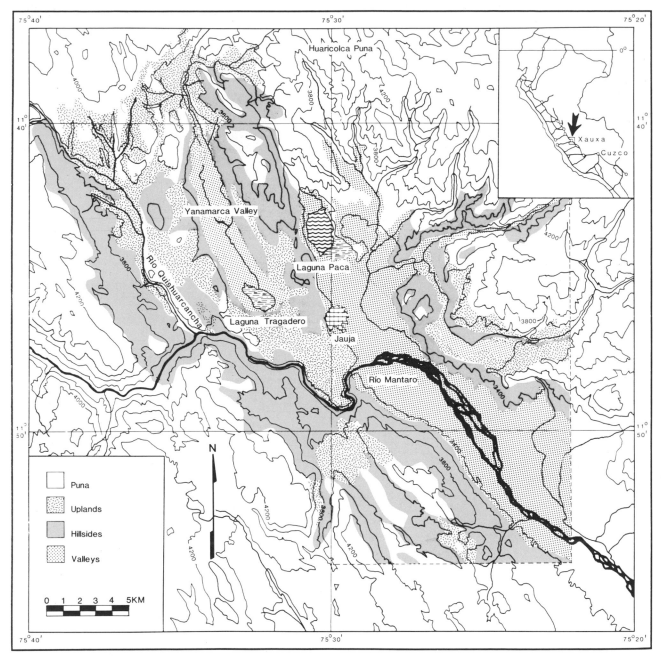

Fig. 3.4. The UMARP study region, divided according to land-use zones. (After Hastorf 1983)

used to start crops in the main valley. Even given these environmental constraints, the Mantaro Valley is highly productive for the indigenous crops of maize (*Zea mays*), quinoa (*Chenopodium quinoa*), potatoes (*Solanum* spp.), other Andean tubers, and the European crops of barley (*Hordeum*), wheat (*Triticum* spp.), and garden vegetables.

Because of the spatially compact changes in altitude, the study area encompasses several environmental

zones (see Tosi 1960; Pulgar Vidal 1964; Hastorf 1983). For the present work, this variation can be summarized as five interdigitated land-use zones: (1) the valley floor, (2) tributary valleys and quebradas; (3) surrounding hillslopes, (4) rolling uplands, and (5) rolling grasslands, or puna (Hastorf and Earle 1985). These zones compose a simplified set of the eight geographic zones defined by Pulgar Vidal (1964) for Peru (see also Figs. 3.1 and 3.2): *chala* (coast; 0–500 m above sea level), *yunga* (warm valleys on both sides of the Andes; on the west, 500–2,300 m; on the east, 1,000–2,300 m), *quechua* (hilly zone cut by valleys and quebradas; 2,300–3,500 m), *suni* (rolling hills and sharply cut ridges and valleys; 3,500–4,000 m), *puna* (high rolling grassland; 400–4,800 m), *janca* (sharp peaks and ridges; 4,800–6,768 m), *selva alta* (upper jungle; 400–1,000 m), and *selva baja* (lower jungle; 80–400 m).

The valley floor (3,150–3,400 m) encompasses an alluvial fan and benches along the river, remnant lake terraces, and side fans from tributary streams (Figs. 3.5 and 3.6). The topography is quite flat, with some knolls rising up to 50 m or so above the surrounding terrain. Because the temperate climate here is conducive to cultivation of frost-sensitive crops, traditional dry farming systems produced maize, beans (*Phaseolus vulgaris*), and garden vegetables. Other indigenous cultigens included ulluco (*Ullucus tuberosus*), oca (*Oxalis tuberosa*), mashwa (*Tropaeolum tuberosum*), talwi (*Lupinus mutabilis*), and quinoa. Modern mech-

anized techniques now also produce wheat and barley. There may have been some prehistoric irrigation in the valley, although any evidence has been obliterated by modern land practices.

The adjacent, small tributary valleys and quebradas (3,200–3,500 m; Fig. 3.7) are less hospitable to frost-intolerant plants and so are cultivated primarily with hardy grains, legumes, and tubers. Prehistoric irrigation was more common here than in the main valley, taking advantage of streams and small springs. Along the soggy margins of small lakes and springs, prehistoric farmers also dug drained-field systems to reclaim productive soils. These systems are concentrated at the edges of Lagunas Tragadero and Paca and in the northern Masma Valley.

The steep hillslopes (3,370–3,850 m) surrounding the main and tributary valleys are subject to erosion, which in many places has cut deep quebradas or reduced the soil cover to bedrock. Some form of soil retention is practiced extensively along the slopes, ranging from lynchets with relatively casual supports

Fig. 3.5. The Upper Mantaro Valley (foreground), looking west across Jauja and the Yanamarca Valley (background). (Photo courtesy of Servicio Aerofotográfico Nacional, Lima, Peru [#0-1310])

Fig. 3.6. The northern main Mantaro Valley and surrounding uplands. (Photo courtesy of Servicio Aerofotográfico Nacional, Lima, Peru [#0-15298])

to formal stone-faced terraces. It is likely that much of the terracing occurred late in prehistory, to judge from the association of prehistoric settlements and the integration of prehistoric architecture. They are typically cultivated in Andean tubers, quinoa, lupine (talwi), and the European crops of wheat, barley, oats (*Avena sativa*), and fava beans (Hastorf and Earle 1985).

The rolling uplands (3,600–3,900 m) to the north and west of the valleys have deeper soils than the lands below (Fig. 3.8). The climate is cooler and moister, and frost can be a serious problem. In this area, tubers have been the dominant crops both in prehistory and in modern times. Although mechanized cultivation has disturbed much of the area that was probably used prehistorically for agriculture, two remnant irrigation systems have been found (Parsons and Matos Men-

dieta 1978; Hastorf 1983:54). They probably were constructed and used in the latter part of the Late Intermediate Period, a time of intense occupation. In the upper reaches of the Yanamarca Valley, one system contained at least 15 km of interconnected canal (see Parsons and Matos Mendieta 1978; Hastorf and Earle 1985).

The highest land-use zone in the study region is the puna (4,000–4,650 m), a gently undulating grassy plain interrupted by rock outcrops and occasional peaks and valleys (Figs. 3.9 and 3.10). The weather is cold and often damp, with heavy fogs and violent storms rolling over the ground during the wet season. Although the puna is marginal for agriculture, some hardy indigenous and European crops for both human consumption and animal forage can be cultivated suc-

Fig. 3.7. The Yanamarca Valley, with the Huaricolca puna in the background, looking north-northwest. The Wanka II–IV settlement of Hatunmarca lies on the ridge just west of internally draining Laguna Tragadero. (Photo courtesy of Servicio Aerofotográfico Nacional, Lima, Peru [#0-1308])

Fig. 3.8. Rolling uplands zone west of the Mantaro Valley. (Photo courtesy of Glenn Russell)

Fig. 3.9. View looking west up the Río Mantaro as it cuts through the hills and puna adjacent to the main Upper Mantaro Valley. The Inka subsidiary site Cutocuto (J63) is in the lower left corner. (Photo courtesy of Servicio Aerofotográfico Nacional, Lima, Peru [#0-1306])

cessfully. Among them are frost-resistant tubers, such as bitter potatoes (*Solanum juzepezukii* Buk and *S. curtilobum* Juz and Buk), the root crop maca (*Lepidium meyenii*), mashwa, and ulluco (Hastorf 1983: 55). The dominant economic use of the zone in prehistory and at present is as pasturage. Llama and alpaca herds were critically important elements of the highland economy until sheep and cattle replaced them during the European occupation. Highland communities often established small settlements in these higher reaches to tend their flocks effectively in the late prehispanic periods, a strategy used in the Upper Mantaro Valley in prehistory and today.

At a two or three days' walk east across the Andes—about 75 km—lie the moist uplands of the montaña, an area of rugged terrain covered by a dense tropical forest. This environmental zone is the source of crops consumed by highland peoples, notably coca (*Erythroxylon coca*), fruits, and vegetables. Although the region has been relatively sparsely populated since its initial occupation, the Wankas inhabited some small settlements throughout the region under the Inkas and perhaps before. Some crops from the zone, such as coca, tobacco, and lucuma, have been recovered from archaeological sites in the study area (see Earle et al. 1987).

The compactness of the many environmental zones means that the native populations could potentially have gained access to a wide range of highland and tropical resources. A pattern of exploitation of multiple zones by single communities or polities—a pattern known as *verticality*—has become a focal point of interest for students of human ecology in prehistory and at the present. Whether or how the Wankas established such land-use practices is an empirical question that will be considered later in this study. For the moment,

Fig. 3.10. Puna to the north of the Mantaro Valley. Note the late prehistoric settlements and corrals near the center and center right of the figure.

it is sufficient to note that multiple resource zones were available and that strategies to exploit them may have played a major role in the development of human occupation of the region.

Archaeology in the Upper Mantaro Valley

As early as a century ago, travelers and archaeologists were taking an interest in the prehistory of the Upper Mantaro Valley. Wiener's (1880:242–43) travelogue, for example, described and illustrated architecture at the region's major Inka site, Hatun Xauxa. Kroeber (1944), Rowe (1944:54), Horkheimer (1951), Lumbreras (1957, 1959), Flores (1959), Fung (1959), and Lavallée (1967) have all published ceramic chronologies that incorporate the region's materials. Not until the 1950s, however, did archaeologists make a concerted effort to survey the area and to determine changes in settlement patterns. This work began under the auspices of the Junín Project, directed by Ramiro Matos Mendieta (Universidad Nacional Mayor de San

Marcos), who was among the first to investigate prehistoric human ecology in the Andean highlands. Although his detailed studies and excavations have focused on Formative Period occupations (Matos Mendieta 1959, 1971, 1972, 1975), Matos Mendieta's reconnaissance survey has outlined the development of prehistoric occupation from the Mantaro Valley to the Junín puna. David Browman's independent survey in 1969–70 covered an area from the northern end of the main Mantaro Valley to its southern end, some 50 km away (e.g., Browman 1970, 1975, 1976). This research provides a complementary settlement-pattern description and refined-ceramic chronology, focusing on pastoralism and the effects of the Wari presence in the valley.

The Junín Project's extensive surveys in the central sierra have been most useful to UMARP's research. The survey of 1975–76, codirected by Jeffrey Parsons (University of Michigan) and Matos Mendieta, recorded virtually all ceramic period sites in four major sectors of the central highlands. These sectors include the Jauja region (major intermontane valley), the Junín puna (high grasslands), the Huasahuasi region (uplands forest), and the Tarma region (warm eastern valley). Covering more than 1,000 km², the survey subsumed the present research area within the Jauja survey sector. The data collected include site location, site size, environmental setting, basic architectural data, and chronological position based on surface ceramic collections (Parsons and Hastings 1977; Parsons and Matos Mendieta 1978; Matos Mendieta and Parsons 1979; Hastings 1985; Parsons and Earle n.d.). Intended to detail major settlement changes throughout the prehistoric occupation, this survey provides the best data available for understanding the sequence of sociopolitical and economic developments in the central highlands.

Other works by UMARP members treat elements of the region's prehistory complementary to those examined here. Three major phases of fieldwork have been conducted as of the time of this writing: the first in 1977–80, the second in 1982–83, and the last in 1986. These studies have been extensive regional projects, with an overarching goal of examining the relationship between the changes in sociopolitical organization and economic specialization (Earle et al. 1980, 1987; Hastorf et al. 1989).[2] The principal research problems addressed during this work include the following.

Indigenous Wanka Sociopolitical Development

A major concern was to determine the nature of Wanka sociopolitical organization during the Late Intermediate Period, that is, in the last three to four centuries before the Inka conquest. Parsons's survey indicated that a markedly differentiated settlement hierarchy had developed during this period. This information pointed to the emergence of a centralized political system among the inhabitants of the region. It was unclear whether this change had taken place within the Late Intermediate Period and, if so, under what circumstances. A major research goal was therefore to determine what had precipitated the development and what settlement changes were associated with it.

Research into this problem formed the basis of the dissertation study by Catherine LeBlanc (1981). The principal question of theoretical interest concerned the role of population growth and warfare in the sociopolitical development of the Wankas before the Inka conquest. LeBlanc's work entailed excavations to refine the settlement chronology, detailed mapping at selected Late Intermediate Period sites with standing architecture, and surface collecting at all sites within the Yanamarca Valley, described below. The refined

ceramic chronology permitted division of the Late Intermediate into two periods: Wanka I (A.D. 1000–1350) and Wanka II (1350–1460) and the partial definition of a Late Horizon component separate from the prior occupations (Wanka III: 1460–1533). This division permitted reevaluation of the demographic trends in the region and analysis of the development of settlement and sociopolitical hierarchies. The results of LeBlanc's work are summarized in Chapter 4; specific data collection practices are mentioned where pertinent.

Changes in Land-Use Patterns

The distribution of habitation sites and agricultural features, recorded throughout the region by the Junín survey, indicated significant shifts in the use of lands for agriculture over time. The doctoral research conducted by Christine Hastorf was intended to investigate the relationships among land use, changes in settlement organization, population growth, and the developing sociopolitical hierarchy. The research entailed evaluation of a least-cost model for land-use intensification associated with political development (Hastorf 1983, n.d.; Hastorf and Earle 1985; see also Hastorf 1985, 1986). The fieldwork for the study included a modern land-use survey, the analysis of prehistoric agricultural practices, and the study of botanical remains recovered from archaeological contexts.

Organization of the Inka Administration of the Region

The Junín Project survey data indicated no significant reorganization of the Wanka population under Inka rule. Parsons and Hastings (1977:59–60) concluded that the principal archaeologically recognizable impact on the region was the establishment of an administrative overlay, visible in the form of the provincial capital, the road network, and the storage system. The Inka occupation was visible primarily in the newly established state sites and in a limited distribution of pottery in the state style at some of the Wanka communities. Research into the nature of these Inka-Wanka relations formed the basis of the present study.

Changes in the Wanka Domestic Economy under Inka Rule

The second major phase of UMARP fieldwork was conducted in 1982–83. The goals of the research were to determine the organization of the pre-Inka Wanka domestic economy (Wanka I and II) and to describe and explain the transformations that occurred as a consequence of the Inka conquest (Wanka III). We wished to determine if the development of the chiefdoms of Wanka II and the intrusion of the Inka empire in Wanka III resulted in shifts in the organization of labor and exchange. More specifically, we were interested in determining if attached specialization and bulk specialization for exchange increased because of the indigenous development of political hierarchies and the intrusion of imperial political and economic demands. The principal results of this work are reported elsewhere (e.g., Costin 1986; D'Altroy 1986; Hastorf 1986; Earle et al. 1987), but a brief summary of the major research questions is in order here because some of the results will be summarized later.

Four principal areas of study were defined. The first concerned consumption of subsistence and craft goods by the members of households before the Inka conquest and the changes that occurred in these patterns after the conquest. The questions of interest included defining the Wanka II and III diets and use of craft items. The second area entailed defining the organization of production by households for their own use. We were interested in determining the nature of subsistence and food procurement activities and of cottage-level craft production for the members of the residential compounds. The third area of study concerned specialized craft production within Wanka communities. The questions of interest here were whether attached specialists produced special goods (e.g., decorative metal objects) for the elite members of communities and whether the amount of bulk specialization (e.g., in pottery manufacture) for exchange increased from Wanka II to III. The fourth area of interest concerned changes in systems of exchange resulting from incorporation of the region by the Inkas, specifically whether the amount of exchange changed from Wanka II to III, whether the residents of elite compounds had preferred access to exchanged goods in Wanka II and III, and whether the concentration of exotics in elite compounds increased from Wanka II to III. A more thorough discussion of these areas of study, the research strategy used to address them, and a summary of results will be presented throughout this book.

The Regional Chronological Sequence

The research described above shows that the first significant occupation of the Mantaro Valley occurred in the latter part of the Early Intermediate Period (200

B.C.–A.D. 600; Table 3.1). In contrast to coastal societies, which constituted the first states in South America at this time, the societies inhabiting the Jauja area were relatively simple. Only a hint of a site-size hierarchy exists, and no clear evidence of monumental construction has been found. Judging from the valley-flank location of the settlements, Parsons and Hastings (1977:53) infer that proximity to prime agricultural land played a major role in determining settlement location among highland populations.

The Middle Horizon occupation (A.D. 600–1000) is problematic, largely because the period has not been well defined in the ceramic chronology. Parsons and Hastings (1977:31) suggest that the occupation continued essentially in the same pattern as in the preceding period. Browman (1970, 1975), in contrast, argues that the Middle Horizon witnessed radical shifts in economy, settlement patterns, and political organization, resulting from an invasion by the Wari empire. Basing his conclusions on survey data from somewhat farther south in the Mantaro Valley, he contends that the Wari conquest (ca. A.D. 600) resulted in a regional shift from a highland pastoral economy to a valley-based agricultural economy. That view is not consonant with the our current understanding of the occupation of the Jauja area, where virtually no impacts of a Wari presence are visible (Parsons and Earle n.d.).

The Late Intermediate Period occupation (A.D. 1000–1460) witnessed marked changes. Chronological studies conducted by UMARP in the Yanamarca Valley have permitted the definition of two subphases, termed Wanka I (A.D. 1000–1350) and Wanka II (1350–1460) (Earle et al. 1980, 1987; LeBlanc 1981). The nonhierarchical settlement distribution for the early phase suggests that the political structure was decentralized and that population density was much lower than it was subsequently. Radical changes occurred in the demography, the settlement distribution, and the sociopolitical organization of native society during Wanka II. During a little more than a century, the population grew rapidly and became concentrated in incipiently urbanized communities that formed centers for hierarchical polities. That transformation is explored in Chapter 4.

The Late Horizon (1460–1533) in the region began with the Inka occupation and ended with the Spanish conquest. This book is primarily concerned with the effects of the Inka presence. To evaluate the strategy of Inka rule within this territory, the problem has been broken down into a series of related questions that can be addressed directly, as was noted in Chapter 1: (1)

Table 3.1. Chronology of Upper Mantaro Valley Occupations

Estimated absolute date (A.D.)	Andean period	Mantaro Valley period	Inka emperor	Major ceramic type(s)	Period, as per Parsons and Matos Mendieta (1978)	Ceramic type, as per Browman (1970)
1532	Late Horizon	Wanka III	Atawalpa, Wascar	Inka	Inca	Arhuaturo Inca
1527				Wanka Reds, Base Roja, Base Clara		
1493			Wayna Qhapaq			
1471			Thupa Inka Yupanki			
1463						
1460			Pachacutec			
1438	Late Intermediate Period	Wanka II		Base Roja, Base Clara, Wanka Reds	Yanamarca	Arhuaturo
1350		Wanka I		Base Clara		Matapuquio
1000						
	Middle Horizon			Huacrapuquio	Wariwillca I	Quinsahuanca
600						Calpish
	Early Intermediate Period			Usupuquio	Patankoto Jauja	Huacrapuquio
						Usupuquio

Note: Bracketing dates for the Late Intermediate Period and the Late Horizon in the Upper Mantaro were determined by radiocarbon dates (Earle et al. 1987:79–82) and documentary evidence on Inka and Spanish conquests (esp. Cabello Valboa 1951 [1586]; see Rowe 1946). Wanka III refers specifically to the regional period coinciding with the Inka occupation (1460–1533 in the Upper Mantaro), generally known throughout the Andes as the Late Horizon.

the social context of the region at the time of Inka conquest; (2) the impacts of military, logistical, and administrative demands on the physical infrastructure of imperial rule; (3) the imperial political economy; (4) political organization under Inka dominion; and (5) the effects of Inka rule on native society.

In the remainder of this chapter, the research procedures used to address these issues are sketched out, including a description of the settlement typology used to classify the sites described throughout the text.

Research Methods

Documentary Sources

The data used in this study were collected from both archaeological and documentary sources. Although documentary sources contain information not recoverable archaeologically that could have helped refine the fieldwork strategies, I did not undertake independent archival research. Instead, I have relied on published documents, because the project was conceived primarily as an archaeological study, and independent archival research would have been prohibitively time-consuming, despite its benefits.

The documentary sources belong to three major categories: (1) chronicles, normally firsthand accounts of the conquest of Peru, the organization of the Inka empire, and the physical character of the Andes and its people; (2) legal documents, particularly petitions to the Spanish authorities for rights and privileges of office, return of lands, and restitution for services and goods rendered to the Spaniards; and (3) Spanish inspections (*visitas* and *relaciones*), which often contain census information. Each type of source provides a set of information complementary to the others, but each has its own drawbacks.

Because the chronicles have been discussed in detail by numerous Andeanists, I will provide only brief comments on the major sources used (see Means 1928, Rowe 1946, and Porras Barrenechea 1986; cf. Pease 1977). Among the best early accounts of the Upper Mantaro area were the official diaries kept by Estete (1917 [1532–33]), Xérez (1917 [1532–33]), and Sancho de la Hoz (1917 [1532–33]). All of these men were members of Francisco and Hernando Pizarro's military contingents who saw the Inka empire in the earliest days of the conquest. Their reports are most useful here for their descriptions of the physical characteristics of the Mantaro Valley and its towns. They provide much less information on the organizational side of the society. Hernando Pizarro's (1959 [1553]) letter to the Spanish authorities is also useful for descriptive data, as are Pedro Pizarro's (1986 [1571]) reminiscences, written about 40 years after the conquest.

The clear, detailed reporting of Pedro de Cieza de León (1967 [1553], 1984 [1551]) provides a generally objective, balanced perspective. Unfortunately, he visited the area about 15 years after the conquest, as did the Lic. Polo (1917 [1567], 1940 [1561]), so much of their information must have been drawn from oral accounts given by Wankas and previous Spanish visitors. Cieza's detailed description of the Inka administrative center Hatun Xauxa, presented later, must therefore be viewed critically. Perhaps the most widely praised chronicle is that of Bernabé Cobo (1956 [1653]), who wrote his volumes more than 100 years after the Inka demise and who relied on other chronicles to a great extent (Rowe 1946:196). Despite their temporal removal from the functioning Inka system, the chronicles by Cieza and Cobo provide the most thorough and useful accounts of state political and economic organization of any sources applicable to the area.

The second class of documents—legal papers—has been most useful in reconstructing specific features of the political organization of the region under the Inkas. These documents provide almost no information on the organization of the Inka state system itself but focus on Wanka disputes with one another or with the Spanish. I have relied especially on two sets of papers. The first is series of petitions filed with the Audiencia Real (Royal Court) in Lima from 1558 to 1561 by the paramounts of the three provincial political divisions under Inka rule. The Wankas were early Spanish allies in the conquest of the Inkas, providing material and human support from 1533 until 1554 (Espinoza Soriano 1971). During this period, the Wanka lords kept track on *khipu* (mnemonic knot records) of all goods and services provided and began petitioning for limited restitution in 1558. Espinoza Soriano (1971) has published these documents, but his analysis was largely restricted to historical reconstruction. The organization of the khipu records and the accompanying testimony reveal structural aspects of the economic organization of the two northernmost groups (Hatunxauxa and Lurinwanka), while providing insight into the political system used to mobilize goods.[3]

Espinoza Soriano (1969) also published the second set of legal papers used in this study. It consists of a running series of depositions filed with local Spanish authorities over succession to leadership of a local corporate group called the ayllu (see Chapter 4). Because these papers trace the succession of previous leaders and the rights of office, they provide detailed information on the structure of local political organization in the sixteenth century. The documents must be used carefully, however, because they were filed from 1571 to 1602, well after the Spanish conquest, and the two contesting sides differed in matters purported to be fact. Nonetheless, there is enough consistency to provide insight into the lower-level political system in the last two or three decades of the Inka occupation.

The last class of historical sources—Spanish inspections and reports—contributes detailed information on demography, Inka history, political structure of the Inka administration in the Upper Mantaro area, economic resources of the valley and its environs, and pre-Inka political organization. These must also be interpreted conservatively. The visitas of Toledo (1940a [1570], 1940b [1571]) referred to here are two of an extensive series commissioned or undertaken by a zealous administrator, whose goals included demonstrating the despotism of Inka rule and reorganizing the local populations under Spanish rule. The 1570 visita was recorded November 20–24 at Concepción, in the central part of the Mantaro Valley. It includes testimony by six elite witnesses, five of whom were native Wankas and one of whom was the head of three colonist groups installed by the Inkas. The 1571 visita was recorded March 13–18 in Cuzco by Toledan subordinates. It includes information on resettled Wankas in the Cuzco area and a 1563 petition (verbatim) filed on behalf of the son of a Wanka elite in the Mantaro Valley, requesting official sanction of his succession to office.

Some modern authors (e.g., Means 1928:479–97) have vilified Toledo, but the answers to some of his clearly biased questions fill in major gaps in political organization if examined carefully (see Rowe 1946: 195–96). Their greatest strength lies in the provision of detailed answers to the same questions by multiple witnesses. Repetitive phrasing in the first visita suggests that a scribe or translator was standardizing responses or that Wanka informants were aware of one another's answers and were coordinating testimony. Enough differences exist in the details of the answers, however, to permit some of the basic features of the pre-Inka and Inka political organizations to be extracted.

The other report on the Mantaro Valley itself—a relación of 1582 (Vega 1965)—is a synthesis of the testimony of numerous witnesses, precluding comparison of statements for variation or corroboration. Because this relación, like the Toledan visitas, was recorded several decades after the Spanish conquest, the information includes oral history and personal memories from a society that had already lost about 50 percent of its 1533 population. The Vega report nonetheless provides the best historical information available on territorial organization, environmental conditions, and province-wide demography.

Although these are not the only sixteenth-century sources used in this study, none of the other documents cited is nearly so important to the arguments presented. For these other documents and for the documents just discussed, qualifying comments are made in the text where applicable, so that the context of information can be taken into account in its interpretation.

A final note concerns the ongoing debate over how literally to take the oral accounts recorded in early documents (see Bauer 1990:2–11). Considerable disagreement exists over the degree to which the histories recounted to the Spaniards were mythologized reconstructions (e.g., Zuidema 1964, 1977, 1983, 1990; Urton 1990:1–17) or codified renderings of historical occurrences (e.g., Rowe 1944; Niles 1987; Rostworowski 1988). As Bauer (1990) observes, the Inka view of time as cyclical, the dual structure of many Andean societies, and the efforts of the Inkas to glorify their history cloud the accuracy of the early accounts. The issue is not helped by the probably unavoidable conflict among sources on such basic issues as the chronological order of Inka emperors. Even those authors who favor critical, but more literal, acceptance of the documents tend to view much of Inka history as myth.

Although I am not in a position to resolve this debate, my inclination is to accept the argument that the imperial era was largely confined to the last century before the Spanish invasion. As will be described in subsequent chapters, details of the oral histories of the Inka conquest recounted by Wanka informants conform well to histories narrated by residents of the Cuzco area in independent legal documents. Perhaps even more important is the concordance of these histories with radiocarbon dates from the Upper Mantaro that define the transition from the pre-Inka era to the Inka era (Earle et al. 1987:79–82). My preference is therefore to read the sources with a discriminating eye, but not to discount their historical value entirely.

Archaeological Methods

SELECTION OF THE ZONE FOR INTENSIVE STUDY
When UMARP personnel began to work in the study region, the first problem was to choose an area within which to conduct detailed archaeological research. The known political history and environmental variations made the general area appropriate for addressing our theoretical interests, but the Wankas occupied an area of about 100 by 150 km, including mountains, valleys, and montaña. The extent of this domain precluded investigation of more than a restricted sample of the preserved sites, even if the investigation were limited to the areas previously surveyed. Given this problem, several options seemed reasonable: (1) random sampling of the population of sites in a large region, stratifying by site characteristics; (2) random sampling of the region by block or transect, stratifying by environmental characteristics; or (3) intensive study of all sites within a restricted zone considered to be generally representative of the region.

UMARP, as a collective project, chose the last option. We felt that a continuous area would be most effective for studying such problems as local settlement shifts and land-use practices. The territory examined in detail included the northern half of the main Mantaro Valley and some of the tributary valleys beyond the first range of hills flanking the main valley (Fig. 3.4). The Junín Project had surveyed this region systematically in 1975–76, ascertaining the basic settlement patterns prior to UMARP's entry into the field. UMARP conducted an additional survey in 1983 to assess the settlement patterns in the Jisse area, to the west of the Jauja survey zone (D'Altroy n.d.).

Excavations at residential communities were largely restricted to the Yanamarca Valley, an internally draining basin to the northwest of the main Mantaro Valley. Several advantages accrued to studying the occupation here. The Inka provincial capital, Hatun Xauxa, lay in the main Mantaro Valley, just outside the Yanamarca, so a large fraction of the Wanka III population lived within 10 km of the focus of state power in the province. The Yanamarca Valley in fact supported a major population from at least A.D. 1000 well into the Colonial Period (Parsons and Hastings 1977). Numerous sites attributable to this period, including the largest known Wanka settlements, lay in the valley; many were inhabited during the Inka occupation of the region. The presence of Inka polychrome ceramics at sites of various sizes and internal complexities suggested that differential state-local interaction could be evaluated at these communities. The main highland Inka highway also passed through the east side of the valley, providing access north to Tarma and eventually Quito, or south through Hatun Xauxa and Willka Wamán to Cuzco. In addition, the Inkas constructed a series of small administrative and road stations within the region. The local population was accordingly exposed to the range of cosmopolitan traffic passing between Cuzco and most of the northern highland part of the empire. The area also encompassed the basic range of highland environmental zones. It therefore seemed reasonable to assume that a representative range of the agricultural and herding communities would be subsumed within the restricted study area. These characteristics together suggested that the region would be especially amenable to addressing the kinds of questions that concerned the project in general.

SELECTION OF STATE SETTLEMENTS FOR STUDY
Prior research in the region had shown that the Inka occupation in the Upper Mantaro Valley was extensive. Because only a few sites were well-defined state settlements, UMARP studied all of them in the field. The Junín Project's survey had recorded all Late Horizon sites in the area, with the exception of J62 (a small state facility west of Hatun Xauxa), J125 (a storage facility south of Marca, taken to be only the Early Intermediate Period settlement over which an Inka site was built), and J63, J67, and J68, which lay in a tributary valley west of the limits of the survey zone (see Fig. 6.1). J62 was located during the detailed study of the storage complexes above Hatun Xauxa (see Chapter 8), and the last three sites were encountered during an environmental survey. The surface collections taken by the Junín Project identified those sites with a high proportion of Inka ceramics in the rest of the region, and they were assigned a high priority for further work.

Historical sources also alluded to specific state facilities, including Hatun Xauxa, the imperial highway, the storage complexes, and bridges (e.g., Estete 1917 [1532–33]; Sancho 1917 [1532–33]). These references corresponded well in certain instances to sites identified by the Junín survey. The information was combined with the results of other research on the Inkas that had shown the regular placement of state settlements with respect to the road system (e.g., Morris 1967, 1972b; Hyslop 1984).

Apart from the storage facilities, the Junín Project isolated five sites of probable state construction or management: Hatun Xauxa (J5), J6, J45, J58, and J63. Hatun Xauxa was clearly the administrative center, and J63 appeared architecturally to be a small Inka center. Three settlements—J6, J45, and J58—shared the characteristics of small size (2.0 ha or less), proximity to the state highways (within 200 m), predominantly Inka surface ceramic assemblages, and location at strategic points for commanding road traffic. Two other sites with possible religious aspects—J4 and J55—were added to this group, based on information gathered from UMARP fieldwork.

SELECTION OF VILLAGES FOR INTENSIVE STUDY
Although UMARP restricted the study area of subject communities to the Yanamarca Valley, more sites had known late prehistoric components than could be investigated in detail. Fifty-nine of the 68 sites the Junín survey recorded in the Yanamarca area had ceramics attributable to the Late Intermediate Period (Wanka I and II) or Late Horizon (Wanka III). Rather than exclude particular types of sites from our study, UMARP decided to concentrate work on the sites that had more than a trace of ceramics from these periods in the collections recovered by the Junín survey. This strategy

raises the possibility that some sites of interest have been systematically excluded from our sample. Because the sites with trace concentrations of late prehispanic ceramics were distributed throughout the study area, it seems unlikely that any subarea or environmental zone was excluded from consideration. However, it should be kept in mind that very small, or temporary, occupations may be missing from the settlement hierarchy described here (LeBlanc 1981: 127–28).

The results of the 1977–80 fieldwork were used to design the second phase. The intent was to excavate in residential compounds to recover materials that would allow description of the domestic economy in Wanka II elite and commoner contexts and then to compare them with materials recovered from analogous Wanka III residential compounds. The earlier research showed that the residential sites for the periods of interest here (A.D. 1350–1533) included communities ranging from small villages to centers. Six sites were chosen for excavation in or bordering the Yanamarca Valley, along with Pancan (J1), a small multicomponent village adjacent to Laguna Paca in the northern Mantaro Valley. For Wanka II, Tunanmarca (J7) was selected as the only well-preserved single component center in the region. The site of Umpamalca (J41) was chosen as a Wanka II town that we believe was politically dominated by Tunanmarca. None of the suitable Wanka II villages in the region (e.g., Chawín [J40]) was excavated, because their remote locations would have made large-scale work prohibitively expensive.

During Wanka III no centers were present, because such large settlements no longer existed, probably as a result of Inka control, pacification, and deliberate resettlement. The three single-component Wanka III sites excavated were Marca (J54), the only reasonably well-preserved town in the region, and Huancas de la Cruz (J59) and Chucchus (J74), the best-preserved large villages. The site of Hatunmarca (J2) was also chosen for excavation, because its architecture is fairly well preserved and it was continuously occupied from Wanka I through IV. During Wanka II it was a major center, but it decreased to the size of a town during Wanka III.

SURFACE COLLECTION AND EXCAVATION   The details of the techniques used to recover archaeological materials and information are presented elsewhere (esp. Earle et al. 1978, 1980, 1987; D'Altroy 1981; LeBlanc 1981; Hastorf 1983; D'Altroy and Hastorf n.d.; Parsons and Earle n.d.), but a brief review will help the reader understand the nature of the data used for this study. The general UMARP strategy was to move from extensive mapping and surface collection to intensive excavation (see Redman 1973; Earle et al. 1980). The spatial extensiveness of the problems addressed and the practical limitations of fieldwork required that work at many sites of interest be restricted to surface architectural study and artifact collection. The standard technique was to map the surface architectural remains directly onto airphoto blowups of a scale ranging from 1 : 600 to 1 : 5,000. Field crews divided the sites into collection strata, based on visible distinctions in architecture wherever possible. Where such variation was not visible on the surface, the sites were divided arbitrarily (e.g., in quarters). Within each surface collection stratum, field crews collected all surface materials from one or more locations chosen randomly (e.g., by selecting from numbered fields within a stratum, according to a random numbers table).

In general, reliance on surface data should not be a significant drawback for regional analysis, because the principal questions being raised concern variation among sites, not within them. The surface collections were intended to recover only a representative sample of the range of Late Horizon materials on them. Surface collecting was a highly effective technique because of the relatively high proportion of a site's area that could be sampled rapidly, in comparison with excavation. Mixing of sherds from earlier periods was of little consequence at state sites, once the ceramic sequence had been defined, because the Inkas erected their facilities in locations that were not occupied in the immediately preceding phase (Wanka II). In addition, state settlements were apparently abandoned rapidly after the collapse of Inka power in the region in 1533, so that the component of interest is the most easily accessible through surface work. On the other hand, mixing of Wanka III materials with the components immediately preceding (Wanka II) and following (Wanka IV) presented difficulties at some communities (see Chapter 9).

UMARP undertook intrasite analyses of artifact distributions through surface collecting at only three Inka-era sites: the Inka administrative center Hatun Xauxa (J5) and the two largest Wanka III towns in the region, Hatunmarca (J2) and Marca (J54). At Hatunmarca, architectural remains could be used to make an informed stratification for surface collection and to help interpret the remains recovered. At these three sites, the occupations were also so extensive that the spatial variation was analyzed on a gross level. For

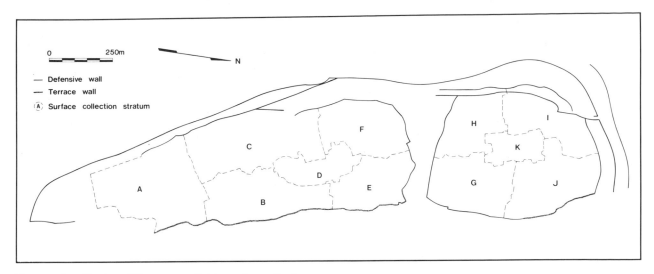

Fig. 3.11. Stratification of Hatunmarca (J2) for surface collection.

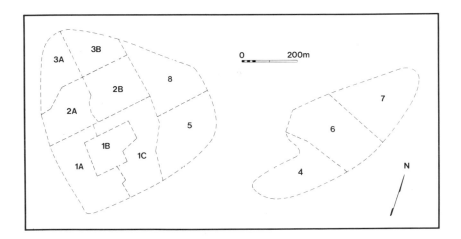

Fig. 3.12. Stratification of Hatun Xauxa (J5) for surface collection. Stratum 8 lay completely underneath modern Sausa and was not surface-collected.

instance, the 76 ha of occupation at Hatunmarca was collected as 11 strata (Fig. 3.11), so that comparisons were drawn among areas encompassing about 7 ha each. Hatun Xauxa (47.4 ha) was divided into 12 strata (Fig. 3.12). Problems of horizontal mixing should therefore be of minimal consequence for the present analysis.

Excavations consisted of two basic types: (1) test pits in stratified deposits and (2) clearing excavations to collect extensive materials from a range of architectural compounds. The first excavations, conducted in 1977–80, were directed primarily toward refining the ceramic chronology (LeBlanc 1981), gathering paleobotanical remains (Hastorf 1983), and testing the nature of the deposits in state storehouses (D'Altroy and

Hastorf 1984). Large-scale clearing excavations began in 1982. As will be described in Chapters 4 and 9, the Wanka sites consisted primarily of architectural compounds that we take to be the residences of households. For purposes of sampling, these compounds were differentiated into elite and commoner statuses on the basis of location, size, and architecture. All together, 29 compounds were excavated either fully or in part (about 25 percent) during the 1982–83 field seasons (Earle et al. 1987:12–13). In selecting compounds for excavation, the strategy was to divide the sites into natural architectural sectors or into arbitrary sectors if no natural sectors were visible. Elite and commoner compounds were chosen randomly for excavation within the sectors, if the quality of the preser-

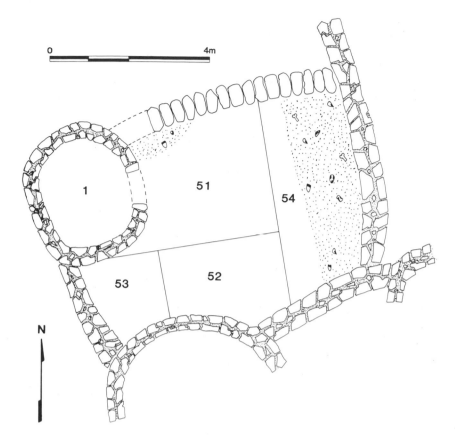

Fig. 3.13. Wanka II commoner residential compound J7=4.

vation permitted a choice. As described in Earle et al. (1987), the degradation of surface architecture or the lack of a suitable number of candidate compounds necessitated the purposive selection of some excavation areas on a number of occasions. The compounds were then divided internally into areas within and outside structures, with those areas being subdivided into excavation units (Figs. 3.13 and 3.14).

SITE TYPES   UMARP has developed a settlement typology, derived from the demographic data and architectural information described in subsequent chapters (see also Earle et al. 1987; D'Altroy and Hastorf n.d.). The typology, used to describe settlements in all periods, can be summarized as follows:

Hamlet: A residential settlement with a population of no more than 100 people, often with dispersed residential architecture. No public or ceremonial architecture was present.

Small village: A residential settlement with a population estimated to be between 100 and 500 people. No public or ceremonial architecture was present.

Large village: A residential settlement with a popu-

lation estimated to be between 500 and 2,000 people. Public or ceremonial architecture was generally not present.

Town: A residential settlement with a population estimated to be between 2,000 and 7,500 people. Public or civic-ceremonial architecture and clearly defined public space were not present in Wanka II but were present in Wanka III. The settlement was often differentiated into areas of high- and low-quality residential architecture.

Center: A residential settlement with a minimum population of about 7,500 people, with civic-ceremonial architecture and public space differentiated from the residential areas. Centers were found only in Wanka II; their political functions within subject society were taken over by towns in Wanka III.

An additional series of site types has been devised to classify those sites that are not remains of indigenous residential communities. The most important of these for the present analysis are, of course, the Inka sites. The remaining site types are as follows:

Small Inka (state) site: A settlement of fewer than 500 people, often with fewer than 100, generally lo-

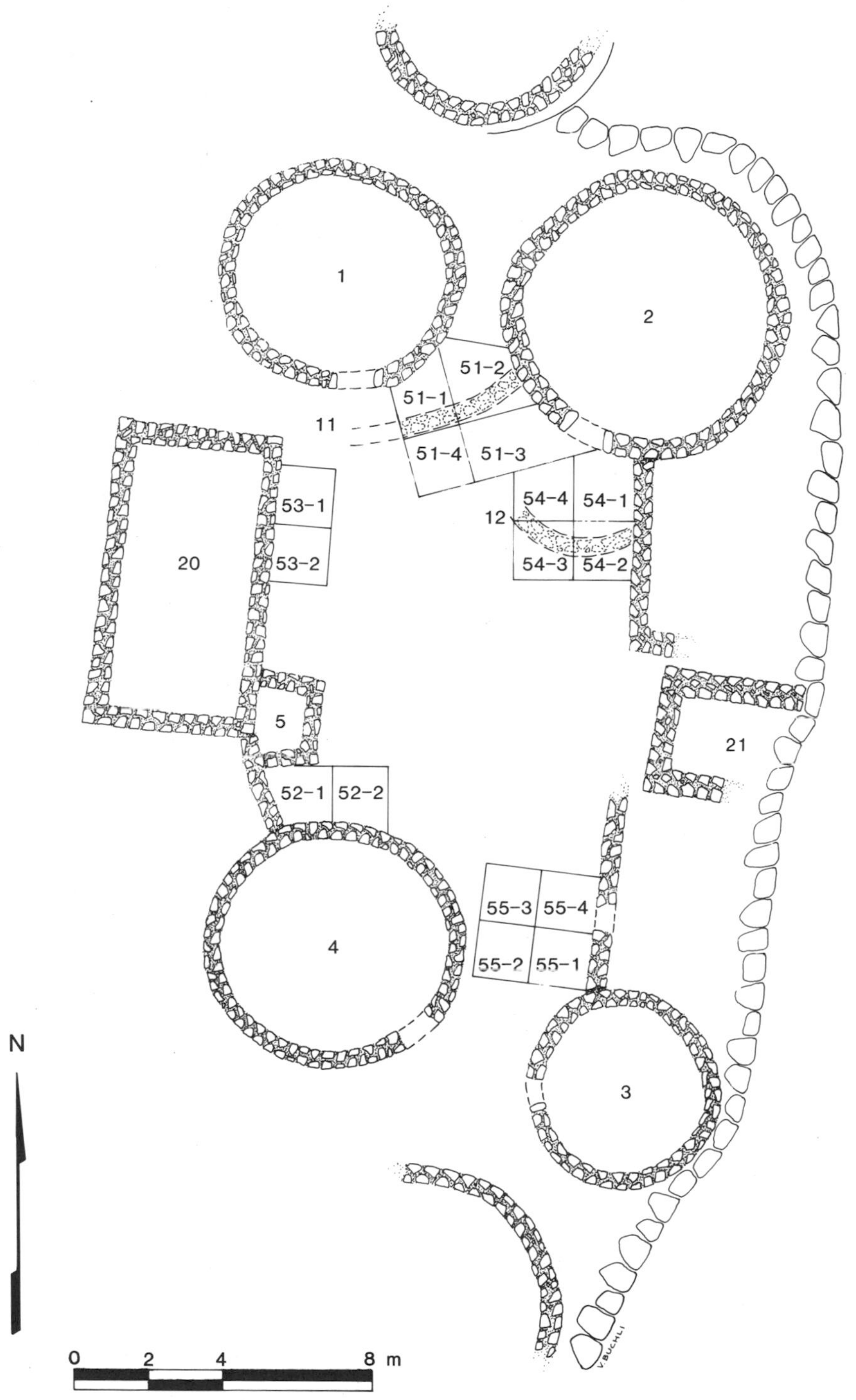

Fig. 3.14. Wanka III elite residential compound J2=1. Numbered areas 1, 2, 20, and 51-*x* delimit excavations.

cated along the Inka road system. Civic-ceremonial architecture was not present or was of minor significance.

Inka provincial center: A settlement capable of housing several thousand people permanently and billeting tens of thousands more temporarily. It was characterized by Inka architecture, a significant pro-

portion of which was buildings intended for public activity.

Inka storage facility: A site comprising single or multiple rows of standardized buildings of either circular or rectangular floor plan, or both. Little or no population was resident.

Agricultural site: Drained fields, irrigation systems,

and other features associated with specialized agricultural practices.

Special-purpose site: A site characterized by no residential, storage, or administrative remains. Among such sites were road, bridge, and quarry sites.

Summary

As laid out at the beginning of the chapter, the general approach taken for the present work has been to study military, political, and economic problems in one sector of the empire in light of the general hegemonic-territorial model of empires. This approach is intended to provide a means of conceiving both the general nature of the empire and its concrete implications on the ground in an important highland region. The UMARP research described here was intended to focus on the latter issue—indigenous development and imperial transformation in the Upper Mantaro Valley. It proceeded through a series of field projects, from extensive mapping and surface collection to extensive clearing excavations that examined the chronological sequence of the entire ceramic period. I would therefore like to stress that, despite the length of the present work, the material presented here has been selected to address a specific set of questions concerned with imperial organization and that the reader should consult the related readings cited throughout for a fuller picture of the Upper Mantaro regional development.

4

Wanka Society before the Inkas

In the last few hundred years before the Spanish invasion, the Upper Mantaro region was occupied primarily by two major ethnic groups known historically as the Xauxas and the Wankas. The Xauxas inhabited the northern part of the valley and surrounding region, and the Wankas occupied the valley and adjacent lands to the south (Fig. 4.1). For convenience' sake and because of historical tradition, these groups will be collectively referred to as the Wankas, except where discrimination is key to understanding a particular situation. With a total population in the neighborhood of 200,000, these societies were among the most populous of the late-prehistoric central Andean highland societies. They appear to have been similar in many ways to their Inka conquerors in social and economic organization and likely resembled the late pre-imperial Inkas politically.

Perhaps because of the indigenous population size and the extent of the region's archaeological remains, most studies have portrayed the pre-Inka society as a kingdom or a state. According to Espinoza Soriano (1971:38), for instance, the two groups were politically centralized under a single paramount (*hatunkuraka*), who presided from the capital of Siquillapucará (see also Matos Mendieta 1958, 1966; Espinoza Soriano 1971, 1973b; Lumbreras 1974; Earls 1981). Reevaluation of published documents and the archaeological research outlined in the preceding chapter yield a picture of a simpler society. Although sometimes acting in concert in early relations with the Spaniards, the Upper Mantaro polities were probably never unified nor developed the sociopolitical complexity of a state, before or after the Inka conquest (Parsons and Matos Mendieta 1978; LeVine 1979; Matos Mendieta and Parsons 1979; Earle et al. 1980, 1987; LeBlanc 1981; D'Altroy 1987). Instead, Wanka society of the eleventh to thirteenth centuries seems to have constituted a series of simple, relatively undifferentiated groups. Not until the fourteenth century did these societies consolidate their population into fewer, more hierarchical polities. Even at the time of the Inka conquest, about 1460, political power was divided among a series of competing political units, the largest of which could boast a population of only a few tens of thousands. The impact of Inka rule was thus not to overwhelm and divide a powerful, unified society but to centralize power within ethnic groups notable more for internal competition and instability than for unity.

The intent of this chapter is to sketch out the nature of Wanka society at the time of the Inka conquest and to place it in the context of its highland neighbors.

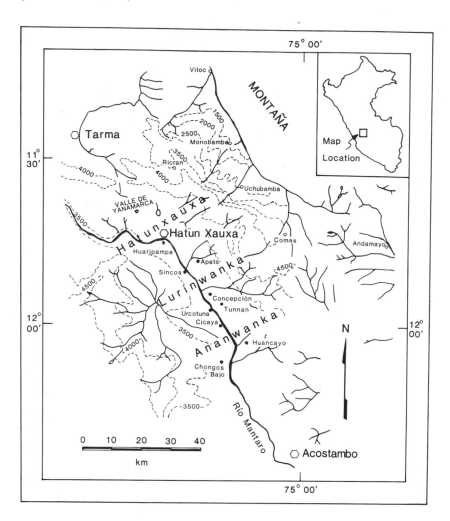

Fig. 4.1. Xauxa and Wanka territory, showing the three *saya* (divisions) of Hatunxauxa, Lurinwanka, and Ananwanka as their territories were constituted under Inka rule. (After LeVine 1979)

Because Inka rule in the region was bound up intimately with subject politics and economics, outlining the organization of the indigenous society will help provide insight into the reasons for Inka policies and the transformations that occurred during the century of imperial power.[1]

Territory and Demography

To characterize the nature of fifteenth-century Wanka society, it will be useful to begin by examining the extent of the province under the Inkas. According to informants testifying in 1582 to Spanish inspector Andrés de Vega (1965:166), the Inkas incorporated all populations of the Upper Mantaro region into a single province named Wanka Wamaní—Valley (or Province) of the Wankas. In keeping with imperial policy throughout the empire, the Inkas reportedly marked off provincial boundaries to conform largely to the lands inhabited by existing social groups. The Inka province covered a continuous territory, including the main Upper Mantaro Valley, the adjacent foothills and mountains to the east and west, the southern section of the Huaricolca puna, and lands into the *ceja de selva* to the east (Fig. 4.1; see Espinoza Soriano 1971: map 1). The population thus had access to the full range of resources available to highland groups: puna lands for herding, uplands for tubers and quinoa, valley lands for maize-complex crops, and montaña lands for coca, fruit, and other warm-weather crops.

Several lines of evidence suggest that the peoples of the Upper Mantaro region formed two or three partially discrete populations before Inka rule. From north to south, the principal named groups were the Xauxas (or Hatunxauxas), the Lurinwankas, and the Ananwankas, the last two being paired subunits of the more inclusive Wanka ethnic group. Within the region, these groups can be separated on the basis of association of named groups with specific territories and on the basis of variations in language, demography, and dress. The groups can also be readily distinguished from neighboring societies on the basis of named-group identities, languages, and characteristic material cultures. Care should be taken, however, not to reify the imperially defined territories of these societies into those of pre-Inka polities. Much of the population was resettled under imperial rule, and the lands of the Inka province and earlier territories may not have coincided precisely. The fourteenth and fifteenth centuries were a particularly volatile era in the highlands, so that territorial boundaries were probably not well fixed for any great length of time. Moreover, imperial policies that were designed to improve security and productivity resulted in the definition of new boundaries between ethnic groups, the transferral of resources, and the transplantation of entire communities.[2]

Even if we take these problems into consideration, it still seems clear that the Wankas and Xauxas encompassed what could broadly be termed ethnic groups with fairly well-defined territories, from perhaps the eleventh century on. One principal line of evidence can be found in early Spanish inspections and legal records, in which it was consistently recorded that the residents of the Mantaro Valley region belonged to three *saya* (divisions) of the Inka province. From north to south, these divisions were called Hatunxauxa, Lurinwanka, and Ananwanka. They became the territorial and demographic bases for establishing Spanish political and doctrinal units and for allocating land and labor grants. In the 1582 relación, for example, inspector Andrés de Vega recorded native testimony to the effect that these divisions corresponded to pre-Inka units (see also Garcilaso 1960 [1609]: vol. 2, bk. 6, ch. 10, p. 206):

[T]here are three centers of three districts in [the province], as has been said, one of which is called Santa Fee de Hatun Xauxa, which was the name given by the Inka; because before the Inka it was called Xauxa, and because he resided there some days, it was called Hatun Xauxa, which means Xauxa the great; and the other center of Lurinwanka was in ancient times the town by the same name, which is now San Jerónimo de Tunnan, and at present is the town of Concepción de Achi . . . and the center of the other division of Ananwanka was the town that is now called Santa Domingo de Cicaya.[3] (Vega 1965 [1582]: 168–69)

Pedro de Cieza de León (1984 [1551]: ch. 84, p. 242), who visited the valley in 1549, cites different names for the divisions: Jauja, Maricabilca, and Laxapalanga.

These names referred not to the divisions themselves but to settlements centrally located within them.

Linguistic patterns recorded in the fifteenth century and at present also imply that the divisions corresponded to pre-Inka sociopolitical entities. The native language of the region is a dialect of Quechua, known as *runasimi* (human speech) by its speakers. Cerrón-Palomino (1976a,b) classes it as Huanca-Quechua or Junín-Wanka Quechua in his regional grammar and dictionary (see also Cerrón-Palomino 1977). It is spoken in the modern provinces of Jauja, Concepción, and Huancayo in the Department of Junín. In an alternative classification of modern Quechua languages (Torero 1964, 1974; Mannheim 1985:489–91), Jauja-Wanka is treated as one of the three principal divisions of the Wankay, or southern set of Central Quechua languages. Both schemes emphasize that the Wanka dialect is not mutually intelligible with the Quechua of the Inkas and the other ethnic groups of southern Peru (Torero 1974:36–51; see also Cerrón-Palomino 1977 and Mannheim 1985:489–91). It is also distinct from the Quechua dialects of the nearby Tarma, Pasco, Bombon, and Lima regions and from the languages of the societies of the Amazon less than 100 km to the east.

Cerrón-Palomino (1972, 1977) distinguishes two main branches of the language spoken in the Mantaro Valley (Fig. 4.2). One of these—Ñuqa-Huanca, or Shausha Wanka—is spoken in a territory that corresponds roughly to the Province of Jauja. The other branch, Yaqa-Huanca, is spoken in the provinces of Concepción and Huancayo; the author breaks this branch into the subbranches Waylla Wanka, to the south, and Waycha Wanka, to the north (Cerrón-Palomino 1972:12, 1977:19–21). He asserts that the "linguistic bifurcation" between Ñuqa-Huanca and Yaqa-Huanca "is straightforwardly correlated with the traditional pre-Inca distinction among the Shaushas and the Huancas" (Cerrón-Palomino 1977:13). This assumes that the Inka administration did not substantially reorder the broad-scale relationships between Wanka and Xauxa territories, a contention that appears to be substantiated by the other evidence cited here.[4]

Early Spanish visitors noted the regional linguistic variations, associating them with pre-Inka ethnic distinctions. In the 1582 relación, Vega (1965:169) recorded that the Wankas spoke two languages—Quechua (runasimi) and Wanka. Although the Wanka-Quechua language was indigenous, Cuzco Quechua was almost assuredly introduced by the Inkas as an

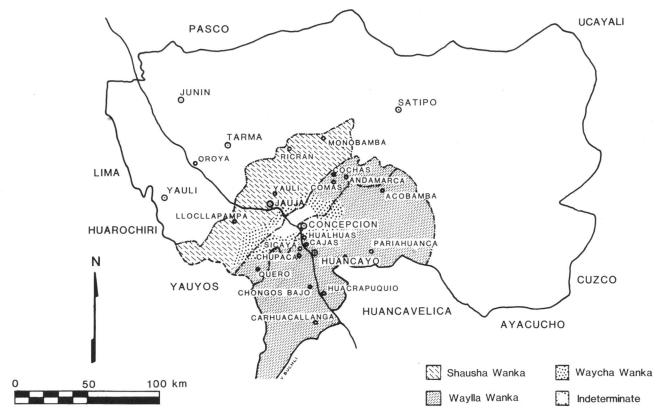

Fig. 4.2. Distribution of modern linguistic groups, showing their relationship to the three saya (Cerrón-Palomino 1977).

administrative language. Pedro Pizarro, some 40 years after the conquest, recalled that the two were quite similar to one another: "The language of the Wankas differed little from the common one: as that of the Portuguese does from that of the Spaniards, I speak of that of these Xauxas and that of the Wankas" (Pizarro 1986 [1571]: ch. 13, p. 75).[5]

Drawing on a more detailed understanding of variations within the Mantaro region, inspector Andrés de Vega recognized the linguistic distinctions among the three provincial divisions: "Each division [saya] of the three of this valley has its own language, each different from the other, although all understand and speak the general language of the Quechuas, which is the first of the three general languages [Quechua, Aymara, and Puquina] of this realm" (Vega 1965 [1582]: 168).[6] Vega's assertion that everyone understood Cuzco Quechua is probably overstated, although it seems likely that all the elites who testified to him were capable in the Inka language, because of their role in managing imperial affairs in the region. The internal variations that Vega noted in the Wanka language almost cer-

tainly antedated the Inka conquest. The implication seems to be that the saya separated groups that culturally were at least partially distinct before Inka rule. The Spanish policy of using native ethnic groups and territories as the basis of land grants has undoubtedly contributed to maintaining the phonological, grammatical, and lexical distinctions that are recognizable between the divisions more than 450 years after the Spanish conquest.

The names of the divisions themselves—Hatunxauxa, Lurinwanka, and Ananwanka—draw attention to the sociopolitical or ethnic distinction between the northernmost group and the central and southern groups. The last two names reflect a "moiety" pairing, excluding Hatunxauxa. This sort of internal pairing of social subgroupings was typical of Andean society throughout the late prehistoric period and continues today; it will be examined further, in discussions of sociopolitical organization. If *Lurin* is taken to be a variant of *Urin*, Lurinwanka would have been the lower, or subordinate, moiety and Ananwanka the upper. Cerrón-Palomino (1977:20) suggests, alternatively, that *Lurin* is a variant of *Lulin,* meaning "inner," in recognition of the central-valley location of the group. In either case, the names appear to indicate that the two southern groups were closely tied to one another, forming matched parts of a larger whole. By implication, they would have stood separate from Hatunxauxa.

In his chronicle, Pedro Pizarro recalled this to have been the case. He describes the Xauxas and Wankas as two separate groups, visually distinguishable by colored headbands:[7] "These natives of Xauxa are of two divisions: some who are called Xauxas, and others Wankas. . . . The Xauxas wear colored [red] bands around their heads, the width of a hand; the Wankas wear black ones. Their language is the general one called Quechua" (Pizarro 1986 [1571]: ch. 13, p. 75).[8] Although Pizarro completed his memoir four decades after the Inka collapse, the distinction he draws seems credible, because he briefly resided in the area in the 1530s and was therefore present before the decimation of the population.

Given that the Xauxas and Wankas were ethnically separate, the implication is that the Inkas combined territories of two ethnic entities into a single province, for ease of administration. A comparable administrative assimilation—and partial loss of ethnic independence—may be cited for a small group who resided in the southwest part of the main Mantaro Valley. Native informants testifying to Vega placed the pre-Incaic Chongos on a par with Hatunxauxa, Lurinwanka, and Ananwanka as a separate, named group (Vega 1965 [1582]: 174). During the Inka occupation, the Chongos were incorporated into the Ananwanka saya. LeVine (1979:26–27) has pointed out that this assimilation raises the possibility that other independent groups were assimilated into the major divisions and their identities subsequently lost. Also consonant with the interpretation is the idea that the Xauxas and Wankas were closely related, but not coterminous, populations in the early fifteenth century.

Cieza de León, in contrast to Pizarro, reported that the people of all three groups considered themselves to be Wankas. Cieza (1984 [1551]: ch. 84, p. 242) stated, "They were all separated into three divisions: although all had and have Wankas for a name."[9] This report implies that the linguistic and material cultural distinctions between the Xauxas and the Wankas may not have differentiated fully discrete ethnic groups. One solution to the apparently conflicting information is that the term *Wanka* may have varied in inclusiveness, depending on the sociopolitical context and on

the party using the term. It seems probable that the name *Wanka* was assumed only by the Lurinwankas and Ananwankas but was assigned to all native residents of the Upper Mantaro region by the Spaniards and perhaps the Inkas. Thus, Xauxas and Chongos were lumped as Wankas in situations in which the overriding issue was to distinguish them from other groups outside the province or region, such as the Yauyos, Astos, or Taramas. Some confusion over place names may also have resulted from a situation in which the regional names used by the local population changed over time, as the dynamics of local politics restructured the relationship between people and territory.

Demographic information from the last decade of the Inka empire substantiates the view that the subdivisions had a basis in pre-imperial times. Several students of the Inka have suggested that Inka provinces were generally divided into two, three, or four saya, such that each section contained about 10,000 heads of household (Rowe 1946:262; Zuidema 1964:221; Wachtel 1977:79). Each saya would have been structured to correspond to the decimal category *hunu*.[10] The concept of a strict decimal structure is an idealized view (Murra 1958; cf. Julien 1982), but the broad principle of internal division of Inka provinces by population size appears to have been applicable to many societies in the central Andean highlands. Review of the data for Wanka Wamaní, however, suggests that population size was not the critical factor in establishing the saya as an intraprovincial political and territorial unit.

Three documentary sources provide estimates for the size of the late prehistoric Upper Mantaro populations. Cieza, unfortunately, provided two different estimates. In his first chronicle, Cieza (1984 [1551]: ch. 84, p. 242) reported that the valley's population at the time of the Spanish conquest was in excess of 30,000— probably Inka tributaries. As census figures were reckoned at the time, the individuals counted were the *hatun runa,* the married adult male heads of household. Cieza's figure should be taken as a rough estimate, because it was probably based on his knowledge that the three divisions should have comprised three hunu with 10,000 tributaries apiece (LeVine 1979: 24). At the time of his highland tour, the population had decreased so much that Cieza doubted that 10,000 lived in the region.[11] In his second chronicle, Cieza (1967 [1553]: ch. 49, p. 163) recalled that the local elites had told him that more than 40,000 men had lived in the region at the time of the Inka conquest. In that version, he doubted that 12,000 remained.

A more precise figure is reported in the 1582 inspection (Vega 1965:167), in which local *kurakas* (elite or leaders) stated that there were about 27,000 "war Indians" when the Spaniards invaded: "[I]n past times of the Inka, [the people] were more plentiful; because the division of Hatunxauxa was counted at that time to have 6,000 war Indians, and the division of Lurinwanka 12,000 war Indians, and the Ananwankas 9,000 war Indians."[12] The kurakas were most likely citing figures recalled from a census conducted in the 1520s by the Inka emperor Wayna Qhapaq (see Espinoza Soriano 1973b:244; Cook 1981:41–54). Setting aside for the moment the problem of the correspondence between war Indians and heads of household, it may be noted that the military populations of the three divisions were not equivalent. Had a balanced structure been applied strictly to the indigenous societies, each saya ought to have boasted about 9,000 war Indians each. Lurinwanka, the most populous of the three saya, had about twice the population (12,000 vs. 6,000 soldiers) of Hatunxauxa, in which the provincial seat of government was situated. The population of the saya therefore did not conform well to a balanced organization, at least in the mid-1520s. If the population or even the ratios among saya had remained static under the Inkas, the balance would have contravened Inka administrative principles. Moreover, the population limit for a saya was ostensibly 10,000 heads of household (Rowe 1946:262), but the Lurinwanka division contained 12,000. Unless the population shifted radically after the initial layout of saya territories, it must be concluded that a significant demographic imbalance existed when the saya were created.

An additional line of documentary evidence may be cited to support the pre-Incaic existence of the three divisions. In the reign of Wayna Qhapaq (1493–1527), the sovereign undertook to resolve a territorial dispute among the three saya: "[Wayna Qhapaq] did not stop until the Valley of Xauxa, where there was some controversy and disagreement over the borders and fields of the valley, among those who were lords. . . . Wayna Qhapaq . . . ordered the leaders Alaya, Cusichaca, and Guacrapáucar to assemble and he divided the fields equitably among them in the manner that they have today" (Cieza 1967 [1553]: ch. 64, p. 215).[13] The territorial reallocation cited here would have given Wayna Qhapaq ample opportunity for shifting the saya boundaries to balance the populations had he so desired. That this relatively late border settlement seems to have left the saya imbalanced fur-

ther suggests that the Inkas respected the major existing ethnic divisions in the area.[14]

To judge from this information, it seems probable that the three saya were not organized with an eye to balancing population evenly among provincial subdivisions. Rather, they reflected pre-Inka ethnic divisions that were maintained during Inka rule despite their demographic imbalance. As will be argued below, the saya exceeded the maximal pre-imperial political entities, however, and were not simply reifications of existing political and economic alliances.

Wanka Sociopolitical Organization

The ayllu, a localized descent group, constituted the foundation of many of the central Andean societies in late prehistory, providing group membership and access to productive resources.[15] Because of variations in and early misunderstandings of its nature, characterizing any late prehistoric ayllu is not readily tractable. Judging from early Spanish inspections (e.g., Miranda 1925 [1583]; Diez de San Miguel 1964 [1567]; Ortiz de Zúñiga 1967 [1562], 1972 [1562]), ayllu populations could number from just a few to thousands of households. Many members of a particular ayllu were generally co-resident, but the practice of setting up extended settlement systems often dispersed ayllu over several discrete locations. Conversely, members of several ayllu could live in a single village or town. This problem makes archaeological recognition of ayllu a particularly thorny issue. The documentary information on Wanka ayllu pertains most directly to the Inka and early Colonial periods, but an introduction to the unit will be useful here to set the context for the Inka conquest of the region.

Authors generally agree on the fundamental role of the ayllu in central Andean society, but they vary substantially in their description of its structural elements. Rowe (1946:254), for instance, describes it broadly as a theoretically endogamous kin group with descent in the male line, holding a communal territory (cf. Moore 1958:22). Access to resources, such as agricultural lands and pastures, was allocated to the households through usufruct (Rowe 1946:254). Murra (1980 [1956]: 191), following the 1608 dictionary of Diego González Holguín (1952), has identified the ayllu as a "subdivision of a social unit, genealogy, lineage or kinship, or caste." With respect to resources, Murra (1980 [1956]: 29) notes that although "a settlement controlling certain fields was a *llacta*," land "was owned and cultivated '*ayllu* by *ayllu*.' " In the view of Zuidema (1964:26–27), the ayllu "was the group of all people who were [bilaterally] descended from one particular ancestor." He contends that it could be viewed as variable in extent to ensure that marriage took place between exogamous divisions of an endogamous unit.

The conflicting opinions on the nature of the ayllu cannot be resolved with Mantaro regional data. Nonetheless, it seems highly probable that the ayllu formed the basic socioeconomic group for the societies of the Upper Mantaro Valley. In general terms, the notion of the ayllu as a localized descent group seems to describe the local unit well. The more particular features of corporateness and discrete territoriality, however, cannot be resolved satisfactorily with present data.[16] As will be described in Chapter 7, membership in and leadership of ayllu seem to have been invested in lineal groups (see Espinoza Soriano 1969). Patrilateral inheritance also appears to be applicable, at least in the early Colonial Period. Over a period of decades, litigating Xauxa kurakas laid claim to ayllu and saya lordship on the basis of direct male succession and other kin relationships. Some of these rights of access based on lineage affiliation ostensibly extended back to the Inka conquest (Toledo 1940a [1570]; Espinoza Soriano 1969, 1971; Alaya 1971 [1558]; Alvaro 1971 [1558]; Cusichaca et al. 1971 [1561]; Guacrapáucar 1971a,b [1558], 1971c [1560]).

In contrast to the ayllu, which historically has been a robust social grouping, Wanka sociopolitical organization at the supralocal level was fluid in the fourteenth and fifteenth centuries. Warfare pervaded the Andean highlands, providing the volatile cultural matrix out of which the Inkas arose as the dominant power. Simultaneously, the development of sociopolitical hierarchies occurred within and among the region's communities. Three broad lines of evidence can be cited to document the transformations taking place at this time. The first and perhaps most tenuous source consists of Wanka oral history recounted to Spanish authorities in the latter half of the sixteenth century. The other two lines draw from archaeological data on changes in settlement organization and the indigenous economy.

The 1570 inspection by Viceroy Toledo (1940a) is the most explicit published source for Wanka testimony on pre-Inka political organization.[17] The 1582 relación of Vega (1965) provides corroborative statements and a few embellishments, which is not surprising considering that some witnesses or immediate rela-

tives were undoubtedly present for both hearings. In these documents, witnesses testified that political office was achieved by males primarily through military prowess. The leaders were called *cinchecona*, or valiant men (the singular is *cinche*). Witnesses said that cinchecona attained their elevated statuses by voluntarily leading their communities in military ventures and were supposed to relinquish power in times of peace (Toledo 1940a [1570]: 18, 22, 27, 30, 33–34). In the 1582 relación of Vega (1965:169), each of the four named groups in the valley recalled its own heroes: "[B]efore the Inka, they were never subject to anyone, other than each of these divisions had and recognized for their lords the most valiant Indians there were; and these were, in *Hatun Xauxa*, Auquiszapari and Yaloparin, valiant Indians; and in *Lurinwanka*, Canchac Huyca and Tacuri and Añana, valiant Indians; and in *Ananwanka*, Patan Llocllachin and Chavin; and among the *Chongos*, Patan Cochache, valiant Indians."[18]

Warfare purportedly arose largely because of population pressure on existing community resources and because of the desire of military leaders to expand their economic bases (Toledo 1940a [1570]: 28). If that is true, the advantages of procuring and maintaining office lay in the benefits realized through successful warfare and coercive diplomacy. The cinchecona and their followers reputedly instigated conflicts to increase their lands, herds, and numbers of women and to gain similar new resources for their communities (Toledo 1940a [1570]: 19, 24, 28, 31, 35). This strategy may have taken on the form of a calculated risk, because the division of lands and other spoils obtained through war or threat favored the cinchecona and their immediate subordinates (Toledo 1940a [1570]: 19, 24, 28, 31).

The archaeological work of Hastorf and Earle on the agriculture and politics of the Wankas, however, suggests that this view of the relationship among warfare, pressure on resources, and sociopolitical development is too simple (Hastorf 1983, n.d.; Hastorf and Earle 1985; Earle et al. 1987:82–84). They have shown that fertile expanses of the lower main Mantaro Valley lands were essentially uncultivated during the latter part of the Late Intermediate Period (A.D. 1350–1460). At the same time, the use of rolling uplands 10 km away was intensified through the construction of irrigation systems associated with large nucleated settlements (see the section "Archaeological Settlement Patterns," below). The pattern of localized use of land resources is supported by the consistent recovery of high-elevation food crops in residential compounds and the relative lack of maize-complex crops. Hastorf and Earle conclude that the intensification of production during Wanka II was essentially a consequence of demand set by the political economy and did not result from the requirements of feeding the rapidly increasing regional population. In that context, warfare over resources may be explained more reasonably as a political process than as a consequence of subsistence pressure.

According to oral tradition, accession and succession to power were allocated by community consensus. Positions were to be yielded once the danger had passed, but some cinchecona were loathe to give up their positions in peacetime. Others assumed power forcibly (Toledo 1940a [1570]: 22–23, 27, 34). In keeping with an ethic of popular rule, the death of a cinche was to result in a new consensual selection. In practice, able sons of cinchecona succeeded preferentially to the office, the justification being that they could be lord unless shown incapable (Toledo 1940a [1570]: 20, 23–24, 28, 35). The contradictory elements in this testimony indicate that the realities of sociopolitical life differed notably from the ideal. The ethic of consensual, temporary leadership was subverted by permanent concentration of power in the hands of restricted kin groups. Such comments may also have been partially self-serving on behalf of the elites testifying to the Spaniards. Given the Spanish regard for patrilateral and lineal passage of power and wealth, any evidence the Wankas could cite in favor of similar passages may have bolstered claims of legitimacy for elite witnesses. Regardless of the motivation, if the testimony was a fair approximation of reality, the process of investing power in a particular kin group was present among the local societies before Inka rule.

Similar testimony was recorded in the Toledan visitas throughout the highlands. The office of cinche and the associated dynamic political structures were seemingly widespread in the last couple of centuries before Inka ascendancy. The pre-imperial Inkas, in fact, may be cited as a comparable case, so that the political climate from which the empire of Tawantinsuyu emerged may not have been much different from that of the Upper Mantaro societies.[19]

The size of the region's largest pre-Inka polities provides additional evidence suggesting moderately complex political organization. Although the populations and territories of the polities undoubtedly varied, both documentary and archaeological data indicate that the polities attained a maximum population in the low

tens of thousands. One witness testified that the largest unit referred to in the sources comprised about half of the Ananwankas, that "each division had a cinche and that in this Valley of Xauxa up to half of the Ananwankas were protected [by one cinche]" (Toledo 1940a [1570]: 18).[20]

Recall that the indigenous kurakas recounted in 1582 that Ananwanka could field 9,000 "war Indians" at the time of the Spanish conquest (Vega 1965: 167). Investigators disagree over the use of this figure to extrapolate an immediate pre-conquest regional population. Assuming that each war Indian represented a tributary, or hatun runa (i.e., a married adult male head of household), Rowe (1946:184) uses a multiplier of 5 to arrive at a total population estimate of 45,000 for the Ananwankas. Smith (1970:459) argues that the war Indians and tributaries were not coterminous and assumes an age range of 17 to 30 for war Indians. This range contrasts with the broader range of 25 to 50 or of 25 to 60 that is often taken to be a rough estimate for men of tributary status.[21] Using population profiles from the 1567 (Diez de San Miguel 1964) and 1940 censuses in Chucuito, he then estimates that men in the category of soldier constituted about one-ninth of the population. Accordingly, he chooses a multiplier of 9, which yields a pre-Columbian estimate of 81,000. Cook (1981:41–54, 201), who takes the 9,000 figure to reflect tributary population, argues that the actual figure lies somewhere between Rowe's and Smith's estimates, but he does not provide a precise figure.

Because military service was one of the major tributary duties, a rough correspondence between the two statuses may be provisionally accepted. The tributary : population ratio may be estimated at about 1 : 6 (Earle et al. 1987:9), and thus the maximal Ananwanka unit may have been about 27,500. If a middle figure between Rowe's and Smith's estimates is accepted, the maximum polity referred to in the available sources may therefore have attained a population of 30,000. Even the highest estimate (Smith's) produces a population of no more than about 40,000.

Testimony on the opponents in warfare reinforces the perception of limited political units, for the oral histories emphasized the local character of conflict. Wars were reportedly fought with nearby communities, although immediate neighbors were often allied (Toledo 1940a [1570]: 35): "[B]efore the Inka, . . . they did not leave this valley to fight, but [fought] within it, those of one bank of the river with those of the other" (Vega 1965 [1582]: 169).[22] Although the

Wankas did not mention it, the Yauyos, their neighbors to the west, disagreed with the implied noncombative relations between adjoining ethnic groups. In a relación of 1586, the Yauyos recalled that their ancestors had fought with several neighbors, among them Yungas, Chocorbos, Wankas, Taramas, and Atavillos (Dávila Brizeño 1965 [1586]: 155). It may be the case here that neighboring communities of different ethnic groups fought across local borders, but that massive conflicts between adjacent ethnic groups occurred rarely or not at all.

The oral history recounted in the early documents thus suggests that the Upper Mantaro societies were in a highly volatile state for several generations before the Inka conquest. According to this tradition, shared widely among other sierra populations, the political systems were being restructured by war leaders, who were subverting an egalitarian ethic in favor of greater status differentiation, inherited within kin groups. The codification or mythmaking involved in oral history should make us wary of the accuracy of these accounts, but the archaeological evidence described below conforms surprisingly well to the expectations that would be derived if the narratives were correct.

Archaeological Settlement Patterns (A.D. 1000–1460)

The occupation of the Upper Mantaro Valley during the Late Intermediate Period is evident in more than 100 well-preserved archaeological sites.[23] Chronological studies conducted by UMARP in the Yanamarca Valley have permitted division of the Late Intermediate occupation into two subphases, termed Wanka I (A.D. 1000–1350) and Wanka II (A.D. 1350–1460) (Earle et al. 1980, 1987; LeBlanc 1981). The Wanka I phase corresponds to a time of relatively simple society, whereas Wanka II shows clear evidence of the conflict and sociopolitical development reported in the oral tradition. Each of these phases is described briefly here.

Wanka I (A.D. 1000–1350)
The populace at this time was dispersed among 8 to 13 small villages. Those settlements that could be measured securely yielded a mean size of about 3.4 ha and a range 0.7 to 11.1 ha (cf. Parsons and Hastings 1977: 41–44, 57–58; Matos Mendieta and Parsons 1979: 167–69; LeBlanc 1981). Sites lay in various microenvironmental zones, ranging from the valley floor

(3,450 m) to the edge of the puna (3,900 m). The Yanamarca villagers were thus afforded access to agricultural land for grains, legumes, and tubers, as well as to grazing land for camelids (LeBlanc 1981:242–49).

Population density for the Wanka I phase was much lower than for the Wanka II and III (Inka) phases. Residents of the villages occupied architectural compounds that consisted of one or two circular buildings and open patio areas. Although the architecture of the time was comparable to that of the immediately succeeding periods, the internal density of communities was substantially lower than in subsequent phases. Measurements of residential density at the well-preserved site J56 produced an estimate of 50 structures per hectare, which works out to about 90 to 150 people per hectare.[24] Given the total estimated residential area (43.7 ha) in the Yanamarca Valley, we currently estimate a total population of about 3,933 to 6,555 for the valley.

The exposed location of most villages and the lack of preserved defensive architecture indicate less fractious relations between neighbors than would be the case in Wanka II. No site-size hierarchy is apparent in the settlements, and no evidence for monumental constructions, such as platform mounds, is preserved in any of the villages. The lack of (1) any disproportionately large settlements, (2) labor investment in large-scale ceremonial architecture, (3) site planning, and (4) elite residential architecture suggests that Yanamarca Valley political power was decentralized at this time. Certainly, there is no outstanding evidence for central authority, as can be seen in the sites of the following phase.[25]

Wanka II (1350–1460)
Radical changes occurred in the demography, settlement distribution, and sociopolitical organization of the region's society during Wanka II. During a century and a half, the population grew rapidly and became concentrated in incipiently urbanized communities. The short length of this period has been established both by radiocarbon dating and by the exceedingly shallow deposits, often less than 0.25 m, at many of the sites. The carbon samples taken from Wanka II deposits in the Yanamarca Valley cluster tightly between the dates A.D. 1320 and 1465 (Earle et al. 1987:80–81), indicating that the pattern of defensively located, nucleated settlements lasted only a brief period before the Inka conquest terminated it.

Thirty-eight sites have been recorded for the population within the entire survey region (main Mantaro

Valley, Yanamarca Valley, and Jisse region; Fig. 4.3). The total population estimated for these settlements fell between 36,517 (at 60 percent occupation) and 60,862 (100 percent).[26] Because of the density of occupation at the well-studied Wanka II settlements, we estimate that the actual population probably fell close to the upper end of this range.

In the Yanamarca Valley, two large communities—

Hatunmarca (J2; 73.7 ha of habitation) and Tunanmarca (J7; 23.1 ha)—dominated the region's population (Figs. 4.4–4.6). Each settlement was surrounded by cordons of defensive walls, as were numerous other contemporary sites in the area. Both communities contained civic-ceremonial sectors associated with elite residential zones (Figs. 4.7 and 4.8). At Hatunmarca the peak population fell in the range of 6,633 to

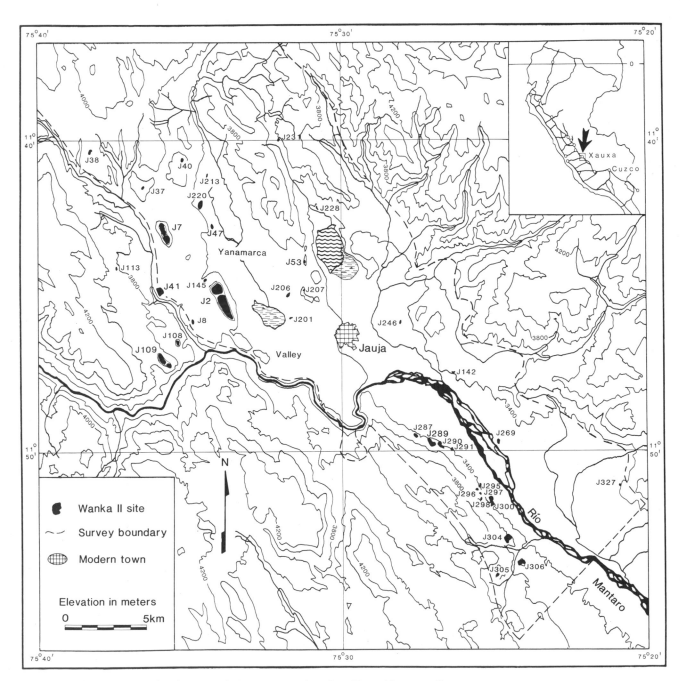

Fig. 4.3. Wanka II settlement distribution in the Yanamarca and northern Upper Mantaro valleys.

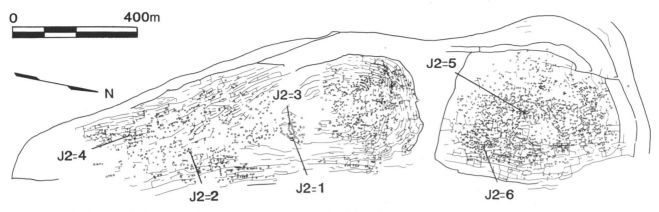

Fig. 4.4. Wanka II center of Hatunmarca. Excavated compounds are labeled (e.g., J2=1).

11,055; Tunanmarca's maximum population attained 7,955 to 13,259. Within the entire Yanamarca Valley, only 10 sites are potentially attributable to this phase, with a total area of 147.4 ha ($\bar{X}$ = 16.4 ha, range = 1.5–73.7 ha). The population is estimated to have attained a size 9.3 times that of the Wanka I population.[27]

The residential population at the two centers is estimated to have been between 14,588 and 24,314—that is, about 67.9 percent of the Yanamarca Valley's population. The third-largest settlement in the study region—Llamap Shillón (J109)—lay in the Jisse area, overlooking the Río Mantaro gorge. It too was defended by up to five concentric walls. With a population of 4,374 to 7,290, this community combined with the other two large settlements to house about 31,604 people, or about 51.9 percent of the estimated maximum of 60,862 inhabitants of the entire survey region (including the Yanamarca Valley, the main Mantaro Valley, and the Jisse area). In contrast, the largest settlement in the main Mantaro Valley potentially occupied at this time (J289) held only about 1,359 to 2,265 inhabitants. The distribution of the region's population is illustrated in Figure 4.9, which displays the heavy concentration of Wanka II population between about 3,750 and 3,900 m. Included in this graph are all settlements in the main Mantaro Valley (25 sites), the Yanamarca Valley (10 sites), and the surveyed sections of the Jisse region (3 sites).

Perhaps surprisingly, little public or ceremonial architecture can be found at even the largest sites. Incipiently stratified complex polities often invest a great deal of labor in ceremonial and monumental constructions (e.g., Peebles and Kus 1977; Sanders et al. 1978;

Moseley 1983; Wright 1984). Why many highland Andean societies of the time did not undertake such efforts is an intriguing question, for which only a few suggestions can be made at present. The most likely reason for a lack of public or ceremonial building is that large-scale mobilizations of group labor were invested primarily in defensive construction and military activity. It is probable, although not demonstrable, that the Wankas' public labor was directed to securing defensible positions for their communities. The Inka investment of subject labor in monumental construction is well documented, and it may be that the peace conducive to channeling labor into public architecture was not readily available to the societies of the Upper Mantaro in the century before the Inka conquest.

The residential sectors of these and smaller contemporary villages comprise hundreds of architectural compounds (Earle et al. 1987). These compounds consist of *pirka* (fieldstone) masonry houses and open patio areas, enclosed by stone walls that set each unit off from its neighbors (Fig. 4.10). Occasionally storehouses and *chullpas* (beehive-shaped surface tombs) were constructed within the bounds of these minimal residential units. The household compounds were accessible through a series of circuitous paths meandering throughout the settlements. In some of the larger settlements, such as Tunanmarca and Llamap Shillón (J109, in the nearby Jisse area), the residential sectors were internally divided by walls that may have distinguished neighborhoods.

The effects of extensive hostilities among the Xauxas are visible archaeologically in a radical shift to a defensive settlement posture at about A.D. 1350. Located primarily on high ridges on the northwest side

Fig. 4.5. Wanka II center of Tunanmarca (J7) on ridgeline (top center of photo), as viewed from Hatunmarca, about 5 km to the south.

of the Yanamarca Valley, the communities were protected by defensive walls on the sides accessible to attack. Access to the residential zones was further restricted through the construction of narrow entrances and circuitous paths. Comparable patterns of population nucleation in apparently contemporary, defensively structured communities are found in the Jisse-Pomacancha area, just to the west of the Yanamarca Valley (D'Altroy 1983), and in the southern Mantaro Valley (Browman 1970). This archaeological evidence implies strongly that sociopolitical complexity in the valley increased substantially from Wanka I to Wanka II and that the native peoples became increasingly concerned with defense (LeBlanc 1981:353–54; cf. Matos Mendieta and Parsons 1979:165–68).

Wanka II Rank-Size Distributions

One means of addressing the sociopolitical structure of the settlements in the region at this time can be found by analyzing the relationship between the logarithm of the size of the settlements and the logarithm of their position on a rank scale. The rank-size relationship

can be viewed as a special, continuous case of the discrete distributions associated with central-place theory (Beckman 1958, cited in Paynter 1983:239). The premise underlying this analysis is that a systematic relationship exists between the size of the settlement and its functional importance in a political or economic hierarchy (Haggett et al. 1977; Johnson 1977). Although the appropriateness of that assumption must be demonstrated independently, analysis of empirical deviations from an expected, theoretical distribution has provided insights into concentration or dispersal of power within an archaeological region (e.g., Johnson 1977, 1987; Blanton 1978; Paynter 1983).

The rank-size relationship structure of a settlement system can be expressed in its general form as $P_i = KR_i^{-q}$, where P_i is the size of settlement i and R_i its rank (Schacht 1987:174). The coefficient K and the exponent q can be estimated by regressing the log of the settlement size against the log of its rank. Typically, archaeologists assume that $q = 1$, which is convenient mathematically and often closely fits empirical distributions within well-integrated regions (Schacht 1987:

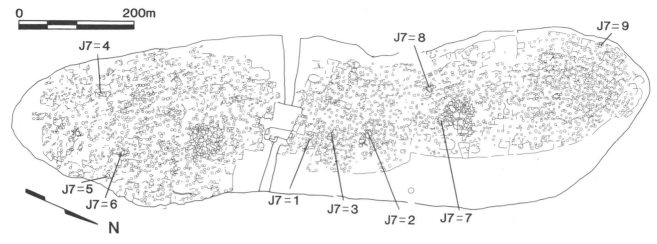

Fig. 4.6. Wanka II center of Tunanmarca. Excavated compounds are labeled (e.g., J7=1).

Fig. 4.7. Dense residential architecture at Tunanmarca. The well-preserved buildings in the center left are in an area of elite habitation.

Fig. 4.8. Residential architecture at Tunanmarca.

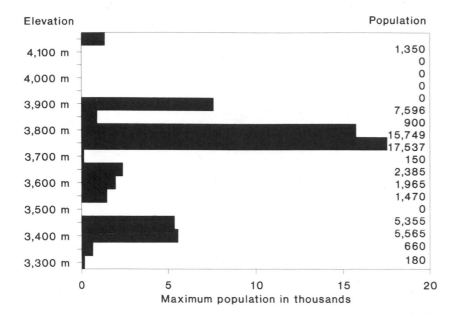

Fig. 4.9. Distribution of Wanka II population, by elevation.

174). The expected size of settlement n in a region is thus determined by dividing the size of the largest settlement in the system by the rank of settlement n (see Paynter 1983:238). On a log-log graph, the expected distribution is represented by a straight line.

Markedly concave deviations from the expected log-log distribution result when the largest settlement is much larger than expected, in comparison with the second-largest settlement. As Schacht (1987:174) observes, such a system, called primate, may indicate either that the largest settlement is larger than expected or that the second-largest is smaller. The literature on rank-size distributions suggests two general explanations for rank-size convexity. Johnson (1980) argues that a curve of this shape may result from the inclusion of multiple well-integrated settlement systems within a single plot. Thus, several centers of essentially equivalent status may have been included in the plot. Paynter (1982, 1983:242) additionally points out that peripheries of larger political economies may also exhibit convex deviations from the expected. Both the pooled and the peripheral situations result from poor integration of settlements encompassed by the region defined for the study (Johnson 1980).

The rank-size hierarchy of Wanka II settlements within the survey zone is exhibited in Figure 4.11. This curve shows an initial marked convex shape (i.e., above the line of expected distribution) and ends with a rapid falloff below the line of expected settlement size. The first four sites are more similar in size to one another than anticipated, and the remaining sites are generally somewhat smaller than expected from the size of the largest settlement in the region. The northern end of the Upper Mantaro region clearly was not a periphery of a major political or economic system before the Inka conquest but instead was a central area in a highly fractionated political landscape. Regional surveys have shown that Hatunmarca and Tunanmarca were almost certainly the largest contemporaneous settlements within a distance of 100 km or more (e.g., Matos Mendieta 1958; Browman 1970; Parsons 1976; Parsons and Hastings 1977; Lavallée and Julien 1983; Hastings 1985). The concentration of population in fortified settlements and oral histories recounting extensive localized conflict have already been described to indicate the highly competitive nature of politics at the time. Similarly, LeBlanc's (1981) identification of multiple spheres of consumption of Wanka II ceramic styles within the Yanamarca Valley indicates the restricted interaction among settlements in proximity. Under these circumstances, the relative comparability in size among the largest sites, especially Tunanmarca and Hatunmarca, is most effectively explained as a consequence of the presence of multiple centers in the survey region. The convexity of the rank-size curve thus likely results from inclusion of two or more settlement systems within the study region.

The break in the curve after the first few settlements should be accepted with great care, because of the assumptions underlying the population estimates made

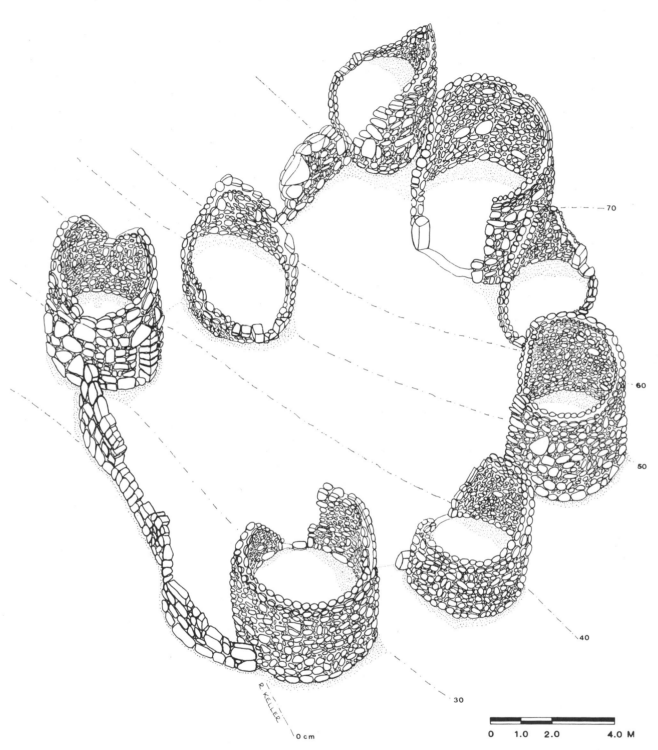

Fig. 4.10. Elite residential compound J7=2 (axonometric view), in the southern part of the northern residential sector of Tunanmarca.

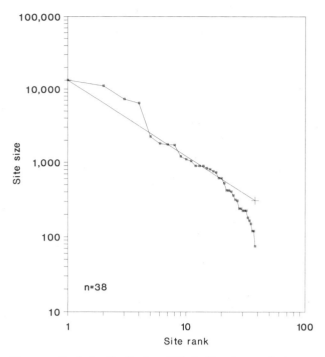

Fig. 4.11. Rank-size distribution of Wanka II settlements in the survey region. Site size refers to estimated population.

here. In general, there is a curvilinear tendency in the concentration of population at Wanka I–III settlements in this region, for those sites for which solid data are available. The largest and smallest sites yielded comparable structure densities, whereas the sites of moderate areal extent were substantially denser. The densities of structures at the small sites (ranging up to about 10 ha) of Wanka I J56, Wanka II J108, and Wanka III J47 all fell very close to about 50 structures/ha. Similar architectural densities were present at Wanka II–III Hatunmarca, in sectors occupied in either or both phases. Between these extremes were Yanamarca and Jisse settlements ranging from 15 to 25 ha, in which the measured structure density reached 146 structures/ha (Umpamalca) and 174 structures/ha (Tunanmarca).

In contrast, the moderately sized settlements of the main Mantaro Valley were substantially less dense than those to the north, exhibiting densities roughly estimated to have been more comparable to the 50 structures/ha at the smaller sites. Because the structure density at Wanka II sites in the main valley has not been established as firmly as that in the more northerly areas, however, the population sizes of the main valley sites are open to revision, probably upward. The break

between the well-measured sites of the Yanamarca and Jisse areas and those of the main valley therefore remains to be investigated more thoroughly in the field.

The question of the relationship between the size of the settlements and their position in their respective political hierarchies still needs to be addressed briefly. Earlier discussions of the two major centers of Tunanmarca and Hatunmarca have described their central civic-ceremonial sectors. Excavations in residential compounds, described elsewhere (Earle et al. 1987; Costin and Earle 1989; D'Altroy and Hastorf n.d.), show that the most elite levels of the society probably lived in these settlements. The combination of elite residence, site size, and public architecture argues persuasively that, at least at the highest echelons, the population sizes of these sites corresponded well to their political and functional sizes by the end of Wanka II. The rank-size graph therefore appears to present a reasonable abstraction of the competitive, fractionated political climate before the Inka conquest.

The archaeological data on settlement patterns and architecture summarized here thus appear to conform well to the Wanka oral history of fractious, increasingly complex sociopolitical relations. Settlements in Wanka II were clearly differentiated internally and among themselves, and the evidence for active conflict is strong. We may now turn to a brief consideration of the economy of the times, to see how the domestic and political economies were contributing to the incipient differentiation of Wanka society.

The Wanka II Economy

In keeping with the approach laid out earlier, the Wanka II economy can be treated as having two components: domestic and political. The domestic economy refers to the production, distribution, and consumption involved in subsistence and utilitarian craft activities of the households. The political economy refers to those activities entailed in maintaining the elite and political institutions of society. In the present study, the complexities of the local economy before and under Inka rule will be treated only briefly. The purpose of the present discussion is to summarize the more salient features of the Wanka II economy as a means of establishing the baseline for comparison with Wanka III.[28]

The Domestic Economy
The general patterns found in UMARP's studies of the Wanka II domestic economy in the Yanamarca Valley

show that the residential compound, which we take to be analytically equivalent to a household, was the fundamental production and consumption unit (Earle et al. 1987). All households produced a basic set of goods for their own consumption, regardless of their status as elites or commoners[29] or their residence in large centers or small villages. Residential compounds shared functionally similar sets of ceramics—including cooking, serving, and storage vessels—and the groundstone tools that indicate household-level food preparation and consumption (Costin et al. 1989). Such activities as casual stone-tool manufacture and spinning also characterized all the residential units excavated. Additionally, all residential units appear to have participated in agricultural activities, as evidenced by consistent recovery of hoes, sickle blades, and digging-stick weights (Russell 1988). As is described below, however, the proportions of these activities varied among households and settlements.

PRODUCTION   Within the domestic economy, production was organized along lines of both generalized household activities and specialized manufacture. Certain materials were casually produced or processed as needed for household consumption, such as simple flake tools (Earle et al. 1987:96; Russell 1988), spindle whorls (Costin 1986), and bone tools for weaving (Sandefur 1988). Goods made by specialists and intended for consumption by a broad population seem to have been produced by communities that were specialized in their manufacture. The most notable of these goods were the fine prismatic blades that were probably used in harvesting grasses (Russell 1988) and ceramics such as the widely used Mantaro Base Clara and Wanka Reds (Costin 1986). During Wanka II, the site of Umpamalca appears to have specialized in the production of both blades and pottery, perhaps because of its relatively marginal agricultural position.[30] A number of goods were also produced for an elite consuming sector. Among them were the finer decorative silver objects, obsidian, and marine shell (Earle 1985).

In situations in which goods were consumed by a relatively wide market, specialization appears to have been organized along community lines. Regardless of elite or commoner social status, member households participated in the manufacture of the goods. Goods made by specialists included the fancier ceramic styles, such as Base Roja, and perhaps the more quotidian styles, such as Micaceous Self-slip, Base Clara, and the Wanka Reds (Costin 1986).

In situations in which the consuming population was restricted to the higher-status households, evidence for production was recovered from every settlement studied, but the production was divided along status lines. In these instances, the residential compounds that yielded a high proportion of the finer goods were the same compounds in which most evidence of manufacture was found. This pattern was especially marked in minor refinishing of imported rare materials, such as marine shell (Earle 1985).

Exemplary evidence for production by residential compound and site at Wanka II communities is presented in Table 4.1 and Figures 4.12a and 4.12b. Excavations were conducted in 17 residential compounds in three Wanka II sites. Two of the sites, Hatunmarca (J2) and Tunanmarca (J7), were major population centers, whereas Umpamalca (J41) was a satellite town affiliated with Tunanmarca. At the last two sites, the residential compounds were tentatively classified as elite or commoner before excavation, based on surface architectural evidence (see Earle et al. 1987:12). Patio group J2=4 at Hatunmarca was classified as a commoner compound, based on its small size, its location at the margins of the settlement, and the presence of only a single house. The other two Wanka II compounds at the site were encountered below Wanka III–IV architecture. They were initially assigned elite status because they occupied a central position in the site and because the superimposed compounds were the most elite in the later occupation.

To evaluate variations in production, four indexes have been calculated for the excavated compounds (Tables 4.1 and 4.2; cf. Earle and D'Altroy 1989). The hoe density index (frequency of hoes/m³) is a rough measure of the intensity of maize agriculture, because hoes were used for cultivation of maize, not of tubers or other highland crops (Russell 1988). The waster index ([frequency of wasters/frequency of total sherds] × 100) measures the intensity of ceramic manufacture (Costin 1986:400). Similarly, the blade production index (frequency of unused blades/frequency of used blades) provides a measure of the relative intensities of fine stone-tool production and use (Russell 1988). Whorl density (frequency of spindle whorls/m³) is a measure of the amount of spinning conducted within the household (Costin n.d.). When applied as a group, these indexes are intended to provide a general measure of the range and intensity of productive activities pursued within the households.

The relationships among households with respect to these measures of production are represented in two

Table 4.1. Production Indexes for Wanka II Residential Compounds

Site	Residential compound	Status	Hoe density[a]	Waster index[b]	Blade production index[c]	Whorl density[d]
Hatunmarca	J2=3II	Elite	0.00	0.16	2.20	11.80
(J2)	J2=4	Commoner	0.18	0.21	0.82	0.70
	J2=5II	Elite	1.59	0.19	0.50	25.40
Tunanmarca	J7=2	Elite	0.11	0.06	0.41	2.40
(J7)	J7=3	Elite	0.11	0.05	0.36	2.28
	J7=4	Commoner	0.00	0.00	0.09	4.22
	J7=5	Commoner	1.17	0.00	1.00	3.15
	J7=6	Commoner	0.00	0.25	0.63	2.58
	J7=7	Elite	0.13	0.09	0.61	6.44
	J7=8	Commoner	0.00	0.18	0.83	2.76
	J7=9	Commoner	0.00	0.00	0.42	1.56
Umpamalca	J41=1	Elite	1.99	0.05	1.10	2.73
(J41)	J41=4	Commoner	0.00	0.50	2.95	0.31
	J41=5	Commoner	0.00	0.00	0.89	0.00
	J41=6	Commoner	0.00	0.24	2.39	1.45
	J41=7	Commoner	0.18	1.14	5.20	2.88
	J41=8	Elite	0.00	0.06	2.42	4.17

[a] Hoe density = frequency of hoes/m^3. *Source:* Russell 1988.
[b] Waster index = (frequency of wasters/frequency of total sherds) × 100. *Source:* Costin 1986:400.
[c] Blade production index = frequency of unused blades/frequency of used blades. *Source:* Russell 1988.
[d] Whorl density = frequency of spindle whorls/m^3. *Source:* Costin n.d.

multidimensional scaling plots (Fig. 4.12).[31] In these solutions, the similarity between compounds is shown by the spatial proximity to one another of the points representing each compound. The more similar the compounds were to one another in production, the closer the corresponding points are on the plots. The dimensions themselves are composite representations of the four production indexes. In the upper solution (Fig. 4.12a; Kruskal's stress 1 = .181, R^2 = .806), the compounds from Umpamalca lie on the right side of the figure, and those from Tunanmarca lie on the left. Two of the Hatunmarca compounds (J2=4, J2=5II) lie in the upper left section of the figure, and the other (J2=3II) is found in the midst of the Umpamalca group.

The sets of points from Umpamalca and Tunanmarca can be separated from one another primarily on the basis of their intensities of blade production (see the raw values in Table 4.1), which accounts for a great deal of dimension 1. The households at Umpamalca tended to have much higher indexes of blade production than those of any other settlement studied in the region, before or after the Inka conquest. This concentration was most likely the result of community specialization in stone tool manufacture. Such special-

ization, in turn, is almost assuredly a consequence of the location of the settlement quite close to the principal chert quarry above Pomacancha, to the northwest of the Yanamarca Valley (see Russell 1988). Household J2=3II (from Hatunmarca) falls in the same area as the Umpamalca households because of its blade production index. Dimension 2 is primarily a representation of the other three production indexes: maize agriculture, ceramic manufacture, and spinning. High index values tend to place compounds in the lower part of the plot, whereas low index values place compounds in the upper section. Placement of residential compounds along dimension 3 appears to be largely a direct function of the density of spindle whorls recovered in the occupational debris. Compounds with high densities of spindle whorls thus have high values for dimension 3, whereas compounds with low densities have low values.

Perhaps surprisingly, the distribution of elite and commoner compounds in the Wanka II production index plots provided only moderate indications of class separation by household labor. The lower solution (Fig. 4.12b; stress 1 = .069, R^2 = .956) has been rotated to maximize the visible differences between the elite and commoner compounds. Here the separation

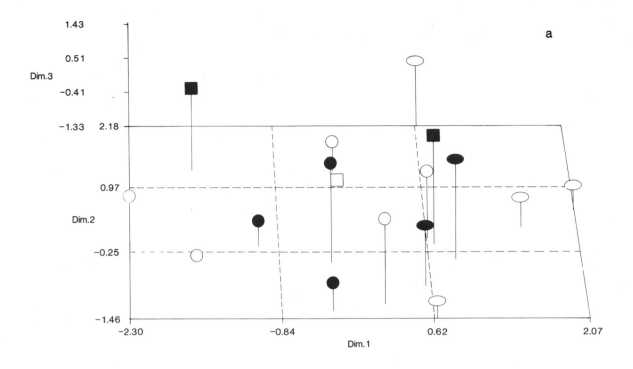

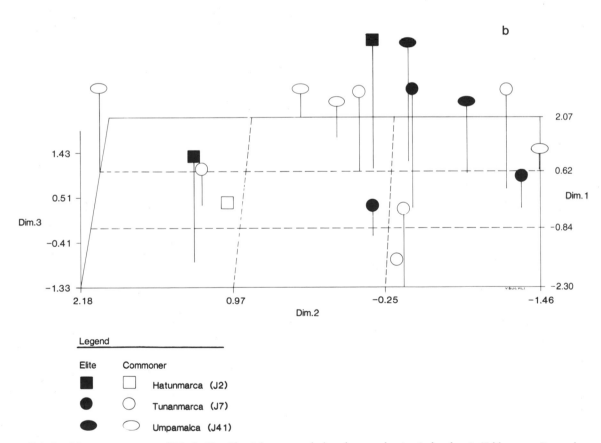

Fig. 4.12. Relationships among excavated Wanka II residential compounds, based on production index data in Table 4.1. *a*, Rotated for visibility of site clustering; *b*, rotated for visibility of status clustering. See text and note 31 for more information.

Table 4.2. Production Index Ranks of Wanka II Residential Compounds

Site	Residential compound	Status	Hoe density	Waster index	Blade production index	Whorl density
Hatunmarca	J2=3II	Elite	5.0	10.0	13.0	16.0
(J2)	J2=4	Commoner	13.5	13.0	8.0	3.0
	J2=5II	Elite	16.0	12.0	5.0	17.0
Tunanmarca	J7=2	Elite	10.5	7.5	3.0	7.0
(J7)	J7=3	Elite	10.5	5.5	2.0	6.0
	J7=4	Commoner	5.0	2.5	1.0	14.0
	J7=5	Commoner	15.0	2.5	11.0	12.0
	J7=6	Commoner	5.0	15.0	7.0	8.0
	J7=7	Elite	12.0	9.0	6.0	15.0
	J7=8	Commoner	5.0	11.5	9.0	10.0
	J7=9	Commoner	5.0	2.5	4.0	5.0
Umpamalca	J41=1	Elite	17.0	5.5	12.0	9.0
(J41)	J41=4	Commoner	5.0	16.0	16.0	2.0
	J41=5	Commoner	5.0	2.5	10.0	1.0
	J41=6	Commoner	5.0	14.0	14.0	4.0
	J41=7	Commoner	13.5	17.0	17.0	11.0
	J41=8	Elite	5.0	7.5	15.0	13.0

Note: Ranks are calculated within each variable (e.g., hoe density).

of Tunanmarca and Umpamalca is again visible, and the Hatunmarca compounds again overlap the other two settlements' compounds. No single dimension or combination of dimensions in the three-dimensional plots separated well-defined clusters of compounds belonging to either status, although there is a trend toward elite clustering in the right half of Figure 4.12b.

Several reasons for this lack of distinction between statuses may be suggested. The most straightforward reason is that the indexes of production used here do not measure the significant variations in labor between statuses. This possibility seems unlikely, however, because agricultural activity, stone tool production, spinning, and ceramic manufacture are represented in this set of indexes. Alternatively, the statuses may have varied systematically in production, but we may have misidentified the statuses of some of the compounds. As will be shown below, however, the architectural variation used to identify residential group status for purposes of sampling is very consistent with measures of consumption of goods.

A third possibility is that status-related variations in production are masked by composite representations such as those shown here. To determine if this explanation was correct, tests were conducted to see if there were significant differences between compounds of the two statuses in terms of individual production activities. Mann-Whitney (Wilcoxon) rank-sum tests for independent samples were carried out (Snedecor and Cochran 1980:144–45), comparing elite and commoner ranks across sites for hoe density, waster index, blade production index, and whorl density (Table 4.3). None of these tests was significant at the .05 level of significance.

The evidence points to a final and most likely explanation for the lack of significant differences between statuses in the production indexes used here. During Wanka II, elite and commoner households simply did not differ significantly in most of the basic manufacturing activities. Despite emerging status differences in the century and a half before Inka rule, the elites had not yet seized control of specialized or intensified labor among the region's communities, as would be the case under imperial rule.

The one exception to this pattern of comparable elite and commoner household labor can be found in textile manufacture. Costin (1986) has shown that the spindle whorl densities from each Wanka II compound show a definite trend toward higher densities in elite compounds. This trend suggests that the elites were beginning to control a disproportionate amount of female labor. Whether the access of elite males to mul-

Table 4.3. Mann-Whitney Rank Sum Tests for Independent Samples, Comparing Elite and Commoner Statuses

---

Hoe density

H_0: The distribution of hoes is the same between the residential compounds assigned to elite and commoner statuses.

Elites: $N_1 = 7$
Commoners: $N_2 = 10$

$T_1 = 5.0 + 16.0 + 10.5 + 10.5 + 12.0 + 17.0 + 5.0 = 76.0$
$T_2 = 7(7 + 10 + 1) - 76 = 50$

$T_{.05} = 42$

The null hypothesis is not rejected.

Waster index

H_0: The distribution of wasters is the same between the residential compounds assigned to elite and commoner statuses.

Elites: $N_1 = 7$
Commoners: $N_2 = 10$

$T_1 = 10.0 + 12.0 + 7.5 + 5.5 + 9.0 + 5.5 + 7.5 = 57.0$
$T_2 = 7(7 + 10 + 1) - 57 = 69$

$T_{.05} = 42$

The null hypothesis is not rejected.

Blade production index

H_0: The distribution of blade production is the same between the residential compounds assigned to elite and commoner statuses.

Elites: $N_1 = 7$
Commoners: $N_2 = 10$

$T_1 = 13.0 + 5.0 + 3.0 + 2.0 + 6.0 + 12.0 + 15.0 = 56.0$
$T_2 = 7(7 + 10 + 1) - 56 = 70$

$T_{.05} = 42$

The null hypothesis is not rejected.

Whorl index

H_0: The distribution of spindle whorls is the same between the residential compounds assigned to elite and commoner statuses.

Elites: $N_1 = 7$
Commoners: $N_2 = 10$

$T_1 = 16.0 + 17.0 + 7.0 + 6.0 + 15.0 + 9.0 + 13.0 = 83.0$
$T_2 = 10(10 + 7 + 1) - 83 = 97$

$T_{.05} = 42$

The null hypothesis is not rejected.

Note: Raw and rank data are presented in Tables 4.1 and 4.2.

tiple wives, the elites' ability to support larger families, or the presence of servants underlay this concentration of labor merits further exploration.

CONSUMPTION   Consumed goods can be separated into three analytic categories: foods, utilitarian goods,

and sumptuary goods. For exemplary purposes, the present discussion will summarize variations in food consumption in this section; consumption of prestige goods will be discussed in the section "The Political Economy," below.

The Wanka II plant diet was based heavily on cultigens that could be produced in the immediate catchments of the communities (Hastorf 1983). The studied Wanka II settlements were located in the higher reaches of the Yanamarca Valley, on ridgetops and knolls at 3,800 m elevation or higher. At these elevations, the dominant crops are the highland grains, such as quinoa, and tubers, such as potatoes, oca, and ulluco; maize cannot be grown. At both Tunanmarca and Umpamalca, the archaeobotanical remains that were recovered corresponded closely to the mix of field production predicted from the lands available to each community. Stable-isotope analyses of human bone collagen also point to a diet heavy in tuber-complex crops and light in maize, as do comparable analyses of food remains recovered from the interiors of cooking vessels (Hastorf and DeNiro 1985).

A principal source of dietary variation within the populace lay in the elites' preferential access to certain kinds of foods, such as maize (DeNiro and Hastorf 1985; DeNiro et al. 1985; Hastorf 1985) and camelid meat (Sandefur 1988). The close correspondence between the productive capacities of the lands near the Wanka II settlements and the foods actually consumed by the populace implies that warfare may have precluded the exploitation of lands no more than a half hour's walk away. The abandonment in Wanka II of prime maize lands, later reoccupied and exploited heavily in Wanka III, underscores the restrictions that warfare placed on subsistence behavior in the last century before the Inka conquest.

The Political Economy

The Wanka II political economy is not as well understood at present as the domestic economy. In general, the political economy of a society of this level of complexity should be involved in two kinds of activities: subsistence support of the elite sector and distribution of prestige goods to a broader populace (see Earle 1978:158–62; Wright 1984:49–51). Both activities are supported primarily through a centripetal flow of labor and subsistence and utilitarian goods from the general populace into the central elite sector. Additional goods, particularly sumptuaries, may be controlled through production subsidized by or attached to the elites. The purpose of this flow and manufacture is to provide a fund from which the paramounts build a political power base. This process is fostered by ceremonial and political disbursement of the goods moving out from the center. The essence of this type of redistribution is political (see Smelser 1959). Contrary to a broadly held concept of redistribution (see Service 1975; Murra 1980 [1956]), it does not provide sustenance to the population as a whole (Earle 1977, 1985).

At the inception of fieldwork in 1982–83, we anticipated that the production or distribution of certain kinds of goods had been controlled by the elite sector of society in Wanka II (Earle et al. 1987:34). In particular, the elites were expected to have had preferential access to sumptuary goods, such as exotics (e.g., feathers from the jungle, *Spondylus* from coastal Ecuador), fine ceramics, textiles, and metals. Goods of this nature would have been of value for their symbolic importance, their scarcity, and the labor invested in their procurement or manufacture. In the late prehistoric political economies of the Andes, cloth played a particularly major role in validating status and cementing political relationships (Murra 1962). A Toledan witness reported such a ceremonial exchange, when his great-grandfather received fine textiles and a drinking cup as validation of his voluntary subjugation to the conquering Inka general Thupa Inka Yupanki (Toledo 1940a [1570]: 19–20).

The expected pattern of preferred elite consumption of prestige goods generally fits the materials recovered from Wanka II contexts. Remains of the higher-status goods concentrated in elite compounds included relatively local consumables, such as maize and camelid meat; exotic consumables, such as coca and capsicum; the finer ceramics, such as Base Roja; metal status goods, such as silver and copper ornaments; and exotic durable objects, such as obsidian and marine shell (Earle et al. 1987). Earle (1985:388) has also shown variations in the distance that the Wankas transported particular kinds of goods to their point of final consumption within the residential areas of Wanka II communities. The bulkier materials, such as subsistence foods, lithics, and ceramics, were produced primarily for local consumption. In contrast, the Wankas obtained some of their higher-status goods, such as metals, shell, and the finer stone objects, from locations as distant as 50 km or more. This pattern is partially a simple affirmation of the commonplace principle that the ratio of value to weight of a good is generally proportional to the distance that the good will be transported. The lower the weight for a good of a given value, the farther people will generally be willing to

transport it. This issue is explored in greater detail elsewhere, in consideration of the Inka political economy (Chapter 8) and logistics (Chapter 5).

Procurement of prestige goods from neighboring regions is also likely to indicate elite-elite ties that transcended ethnic boundaries. Present information does not allow us to determine if marriage or other formally sanctioned ties lay at the base of the exchange relationships. Documentary evidence suggests, however, that in late prehistory, dyadic ties between highland and lowland groups (on the coast and in the montaña) provided the means for obtaining goods from resource zones that were not available within a community's territory (see Burchard 1974; LeVine 1987:29). Not until the imposed Inka peace did the fractious highland societies have adequate opportunity to expand their direct control over productive resources into distant territories (see Chapter 9).

The distribution of metal goods will be examined here briefly to show the lines along which differential access to prestige goods were drawn. The importance of metals in signifying status in Andean societies has been amply demonstrated by both archaeological research and evidence in early documentary records (e.g., Lechtman 1984). Along with fancy textiles, exotics, and labor-intensive goods (e.g., earrings, necklaces, staffs), metal objects were consistently used to denote high status. For example, for many Andean societies, silver was identified with the moon, a major deity in the native pantheon.

In Wanka II, metal forms consisted primarily of silver and copper decorative objects, such as disks, pins, and pendants. Not until the advent of the Inka empire did the Upper Mantaro populations use metals extensively for tools. Access to the various kinds of metal objects consumed within the region should therefore provide a measure of the status of the households from which they were recovered. Before the Inka conquest, both silver and copper were concentrated in elite compounds. The distribution of these goods can be treated in a variety of ways. The ubiquity (the percentage of a given set of proveniences within which a particular kind of material is found) of the two principal metals is a broad measure of the frequency with which a material was used and discarded across a compound. The frequencies and total weights of objects, standardized against excavated volume, measure differential access more directly; they are, however, subject to distortion in that the materials may be heavily concentrated in a very small proportion of the cultural units—in this case, households. The use of the ubiquity measure partially compensates for the bias introduced by this kind of distribution.

All three measures show the concentration of metal goods in households classified as elite on the basis of architectural evidence. The percentage of excavated proveniences in elite compounds in which silver was present was higher than in the commoner compounds, implying greater use, storage, or discard of metal goods among the elites. The difference is pronounced in the use of both silver and copper objects. Of the 421 elite occupation proveniences, 15 (3.6 percent) yielded silver goods and 11 (2.6 percent) yielded copper objects. Of the 267 commoner proveniences excavated, 5 (0.2 percent) yielded silver goods and 3 (0.1 percent) yielded copper. Similarly, elite households contained a much higher proportion of both copper and silver by weight and by frequency of object class. In the elite compounds, silver objects (fragments or finished goods) were recovered at a density of $0.43/m^3$ and copper objects at a density of $0.21/m^3$. In commoner compounds, silver objects were found at a density of $0.07/m^3$ and copper objects at $0.11/m^3$. Analysis by weight densities yielded the same pattern. Silver was recovered at 2.41 g/m^3 and copper at 14.27 g/m^3 in elite compounds; in commoner patio groups, silver was recovered at 0.47 g/m^3 and copper at 2.06 g/m^3.

Put simply, no matter how the data are treated for metals, the elite households of the communities at Tunanmarca, Umpamalca, and Hatunmarca prior to the Inka conquest had preferred access to the material and the labor invested in manufacturing the objects. Because metals were used almost exclusively for goods that were involved in status identification or legitimation, not in utilitarian tasks, the concentration of metals in elite compounds demonstrates a clear distinction between the two emerging classes of indigenous society before the Inka conquest.

Summary of Wanka II Society

The political, economic, demographic, and settlement data of the Wanka I and II phases outline a society in transition from a simple to a more complex organization. Each of the features described in the documentary sources is suspect because the testimony was drawn from oral tradition. Nonetheless, the historical and archaeological data for the end of Wanka II together are consistent with the organization of moderately complex chiefdoms. Wright (1984:49–51) argues that such societies characteristically are not well differentiated politically but exhibit hierarchical ranking of distinct social groups. Political positions tend to be redundantly linked to ritual and extractive activities, so that authority and power are vested in a restricted class of individuals.

Chiefdoms also typically exhibit periodic warfare, shifting alliances, and appropriation of land, all of which were codified in local oral history and recounted by the kurakas. Together, these factors would have contributed to occasional territorial reorganization and provided the opportunity for consolidation of power in an increasingly restricted series of polities. The association of endemic warfare and sociopolitical transformation has led LeBlanc (1981:356–73) to suggest that conflict provided a vehicle for development of sociopolitical complexity. Within the broader context of political consolidation, the dispersal of captured lands and women among the military elite would have promoted a system in which favored individuals or kin groups could control a disproportionate amount of critical resources. That this was to their benefit is underscored by the testimony that cinchecona fomented conflict for their own gain.

It is intriguing to observe that the archaeological evidence appears to show a more rapid increase in differential access to the products of specialized production, such as metals, than in status-based access to the labor that produced the goods. The data cited above indicate clearly that the elites had preferred access to exotics, to a better diet, and to status-associated goods before the Inka conquest. Conversely, the region's elites appear to have only begun to control labor. Because data on consumption are always more direct than data on production, this conclusion should be forwarded tentatively and should be tested further. However, the pattern appears to anticipate the economic changes introduced by the Inkas: Control over resources and the products of their exploitation preceded the development of specialized labor institutions. The general populace was surely used to produce for the elites, but this use occurred primarily in the context of extant labor institutions. It remained for the Inkas to create the new forms of labor employed for imperial production.

At the same time that the economic system was undergoing change, the political system was in a dynamic phase, with power becoming increasingly invested in the hands of a limited few who passed it down to able sons. A mechanism was thus present before the Inka conquest for the merging of polities and for the development of strongly differentiated social groups within them, with unequal access to land and labor.

The available evidence suggests that the Wankas were somewhat more complex and internally differentiated than their neighbors. To judge from population size, settlement size, settlement hierarchies, and architectural differentiation, the Upper Mantaro groups lay at the upper end of sociopolitical complexity in the central Andes immediately preceding the Inka conquests. Reports of comparably organized or simpler societies throughout the central highlands may be found in the Toledan visitas (see Levillier 1940) and in the *Relaciones Geográficas de Indias* (e.g., Dávila Brizeño 1965 [1586]). Similar descriptions are found in the modern documentary and archaeological analyses of the following ethnic groups: Asto (Lavallée and Julien 1983), Tarama and Pilcosuni (Hastings 1985), Huarochirí (Spalding 1985), Guamanga (Stern 1982), Chinchaycocha (Rostworowski 1975; Hastings 1985:162–78), and Yuraccama (Krzanowski 1977). This evidence indicates that the Wankas were more populous and complex than any of their immediate neighbors, but they do not seem radically atypical in organization for sierra ethnic groups of the time.

Contrary to reports of a unified Wanka kingdom, then, the data support a picture of numerous competing polities within the region. It is simply not the case that shared ethnic identity requires political unification. Sociopolitical power in the central sierra in the Late Intermediate was divided among numerous polities, but the region's societies were becoming increasingly centralized and stratified. In one of the paradoxes of history, conquest by the Inkas did not curtail this process but accelerated it.

5

Inka Military Strategy and Logistics

The development of Tawantinsuyu was predicated on the Inkas' abilities to organize effectively on a grand scale. The consequences of this proficiency are most clearly visible archaeologically in the provincial centers, military posts, storehouses, and roads preserved throughout the Andes. Together these facilities provided the skeleton of the system through which the Inkas governed their subjects (Fig. 5.1; see Hyslop 1984:257). Because the evidence for planning extends over the length of the Andes, the underlying principles that impelled the planning merit study, granted that they likely changed during the course of the empire. Other investigators, of course, have considered this problem. In a widely cited observation referring to the south coast of Peru, for example, Menzel (1959:140) has suggested that the Inkas used as their capitals population centers where central authority already existed. Where authority was not centralized, the Inka state built an administrative installation. The road system then connected Inka centers to one another.

Although these points have merit, they beg at least three critical issues: (1) why centers were thought necessary in a number of sparsely inhabited locations, such as Huánuco Pampa and Pumpu, on the Peruvian puna; (2) why some areas of dense population, such as the north coast of Peru and the southern Upper Mantaro Valley, were not the focus of regional administration; and (3) why some densely occupied areas, such as Willka Wamán, were deliberately vacated and resettled. To address these questions, we need to recognize that the distribution of imperial settlements and roads in a given region likely balanced regional needs with the strategic demands of administering an extensive, variegated polity. In Chapter 2, I argued that military, political, and economic issues must be considered concurrently to address this issue. This chapter begins that task by discussing the nature of Inka military activity and logistics and their impacts on the imperial occupation of the Upper Mantaro Valley. Chapter 6 explores the effects of political and economic elements on the layout of the imperial infrastructure in the Upper Mantaro.

It might seem odd to introduce the discussion of the region's Inka facilities by appraising military strategy, given that no Inka fortifications are known in the Upper Mantaro Valley and that there is no history of Wanka rebellion. The continuum from hegemonic and territorial approaches to imperial rule must be assessed on a broad scale, however, because military strategy in one region can be understood only in the context of empire-wide concerns. This idea draws at-

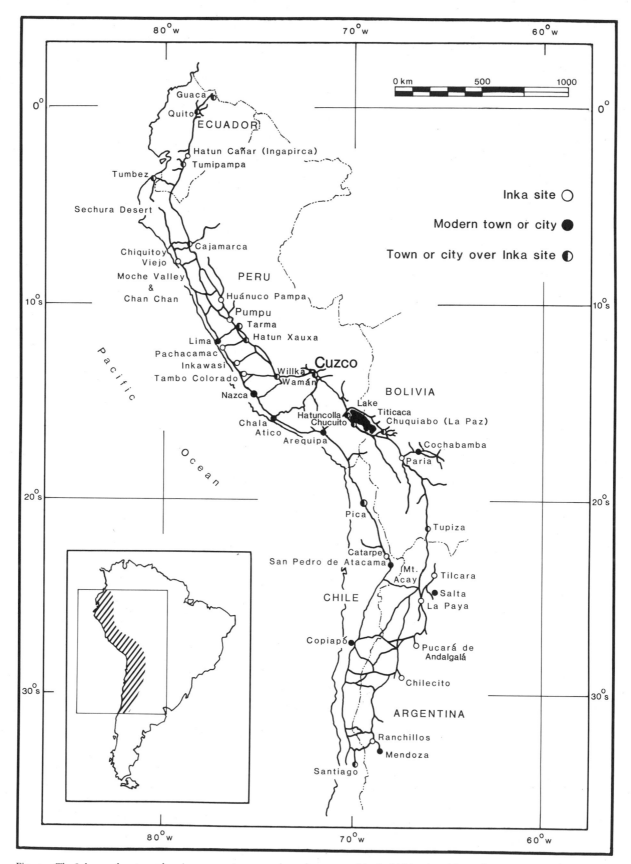

Fig. 5.1. The Inka road system, showing two main routes along the coast and in the highlands, with trunk routes joining them at intervals. (After Hyslop 1984: frontispiece)

tention to one of the paradoxical elements of investigating empires archaeologically. In a sense, we must be able to evaluate both what is there materially and what is not. A lack of known material evidence for imperial occupation at any location may imply any of several situations, among them (1) lack of imperial control, (2) indirect rule under a hegemonic system, (3) short-term imperial occupation, or (4) lack of archaeological investigation. It is therefore worthwhile here to sketch out some of the lines of material evidence that can be correlated with military strategies along the hegemonic-territorial continuum. This information can then be coupled with the documentary evidence to flesh out the Inka military approach.

Generally speaking, the nature and location of military facilities and the logistical infrastructure are likely to provide the greatest archaeological insights into military strategy. Under a hegemonic approach, we would anticipate relatively little imperial investment in military facilities outside the core territory or in the infrastructure that provided support to the imperial frontier (see Luttwak 1976:21–22). The Aztec case may be cited as an example, in that Aztec military control was constantly reasserted through threat and reconquest, rather than through construction of extensive military facilities in subject territories (Hassig 1985, 1988). The Julio-Claudian approach to empire followed a similar strategy in the spatial distribution of military facilities (Luttwak 1976:7–50). Because hegemonic control forms graded margins rather than sharply defined borders, we might anticipate a fairly extensive distribution of goods from the core region well beyond the limits of imperial military architecture (e.g., forts), supply facilities (e.g., storehouses), and engineered support systems (e.g., ports and upgraded road systems). Similarly, because the brunt of military defense along the perimeter zone would be maintained by clients, fortified settlements and other architecture would likely vary according to regional traditions rather than exhibit the stamp of imperial standardization. Those imperial fortifications that were constructed would tend to be few and concentrated at points of special contention.

In contrast, a territorial strategy would result in a more clearly demarcated perimeter of regular military facilities with evidence of imperial construction, beyond which distribution of other imperial-style architecture and imperial products would be quickly curtailed. Because of the need to establish a hardened perimeter to protect provinces surrounding the core territories, we might anticipate a major investment

of resources in imperial military architecture in well-defined alignments. Classic cases of this kind of construction may be found in the cordons of Roman forts through Germany, along the Danube, and along the eastern, Sasanian perimeter (Luttwak 1976; Bartel 1989; Kennedy and Riley 1990). To meet the communication and supply needs of these hardened perimeters, the transport infrastructure (engineered roads, way stations) would tend to be more highly developed than in the hegemonic approach. Similarly, the distribution of imperial storage facilities throughout imperial territory, especially in association with military architecture at the perimeter, can be taken to imply heavy investment in protecting provincial areas. It is important to note here that the presence of a cordon of self-contained forts alone would not imply territorial control, because client polities that provided the military support under a hegemonic regime might also develop hardened defenses. Such defenses, however, would likely be recognizably different in layout and construction from core architecture.

A third military approach, defense-in-depth, provides an intermediate degree of defensive capability between those at the hegemonic and territorial ends of the strategic continuum (Luttwak 1976:127–90). Under this approach, a series of fortified "hard points" is established to limit incursions at key points of transportation, such as passes and constrictions in watercourses. This system is backed up by mobile military forces that are stationed in the interior or can be readily mobilized. The archaeological consequences of such a military approach would thus fall between those of the two options outlined above. We might anticipate imperial frontier defenses that encompassed the distribution of other evidence of imperial construction, but we would not anticipate a great investment in military architecture, such as walled perimeters, designed to foil all low-intensity incursions. Similarly, we might expect the presence of internal fortifications for garrisons with access to large-scale storage facilities and of road systems designed to expedite both access to the perimeter and movement of internal traffic.

Regardless of their eventual uses, therefore, we must consider the likelihood that the layouts of the Inka roads, provincial centers, *tampu* (smaller way stations), and warehouses all had roots in military requirements. To assess the overall role of any given region, such as the Mantaro Valley, in imperial rule, the broad scope of Inka military strategy must be assessed.[1]

Military Strategy

The Inka conquest of almost 1 million km² of territory and more than 12 million people was remarkably rapid, but the campaigns by which it was accomplished were sporadic and laborious. The logistics of mobilizing and maintaining forces of tens of thousands in the field were demanding—so much so that the Inkas appear not to have moved toward permanent military forces until late in the empire's existence. Instead, armies were mobilized for specific campaigns, largely as part of labor tax obligations to the state. Command structures, though elegant for the time, were not well differentiated in comparison with more-modern armies (see Van Creveld 1985). Given these conditions, it is reasonable to ask how the conquests succeeded and, more specifically for the present work, what role the Mantaro played in the process.

At the outset, it will be useful to distinguish strategy from tactics. Although their meanings are often blurred in the literature, the term *military strategy* refers to a plan for the conduct of war or particular campaigns, and the term *tactics* refers to battle plans (see Ferrill 1985:54). In the present discussion, I am most directly concerned with strategy, because that aspect of Inka militarism was the more significant in imperial regional planning.

According to the military history of the Inkas as recounted to the chroniclers, their military scheme shifted over time from an offensive emphasis on conquest to a defensive posture of consolidation. From Pachacutec's possibly apocryphal first victories in the Lake Titicaca Basin to Wayna Qhapaq's final campaigns in the highlands of Ecuador, policy shifted from expansion to assimilation of annexed populations and territories. These shifts are better understood as stages in the incorporation of imperial holdings than as a chronological sequence whose phases occurred concurrently throughout the empire. The Inkas established effective imperial rule in the central highlands, for example, in the last decades of the fifteenth century, well before they dominated the northern reaches of the empire. Even within territories pacified early, control varied widely in intensity and form, depending on logistics and security and on the resources and organizational capacities of the subject populations.

In the first, expansionist phase of Inka military strategy, the leadership was predominantly concerned with extending imperial borders and asserting control over annexed populations. If the oral histories are taken literally, Pachacutec and Thupa Yupanki were primarily responsible for the conquests, including the Wanka territories, which were taken about 1460 (see Rowe 1946:203–9 for a review). The second phase entailed pacifying the new subjects and securing borders against incursions by societies beyond imperial control. Thupa Yupanki, who reigned during most of the imperial conquests, also began to strengthen military control by installing internal garrisons throughout the highlands, resettling much of the population through internal colonization, and establishing fortifications at key points along the frontiers (Fig. 5.2; see Dillehay and Netherly 1988c and Lorandi 1988).[2] Although the details of the early occupations are sketchy, it appears that these actions reflect an early emphasis on a territorial approach to rule in the sierra, coupled with a more hegemonic approach in the north and south and on much of the coast.

Inka military methods entailed coercion, masked as

Fig. 5.2. Illustration of the storming of an Andean fortress (*pucará*), by Guaman Poma (1980 [1614]: /155 [157], p. 134).

diplomacy, and direct assault as the principal means of taking territories, although the armies also conducted campaigns of attrition. Some operations lasted more than 20 years and were directed by professional officers, but armies were generally mobilized from the peasantry for specific campaigns. The Inka military tactics reported in the Spanish sources were relatively unsophisticated, consisting principally of variations on massed attack with troops, such as slingers and archers, who threw projectiles or with shock troops who engaged in hand-to-hand combat (Fig. 5.3). Battles were usually conducted either as melees in the open field or as assaults on hilltop redoubts. Lacking tactical or technical superiority over their opponents, the Inkas spied out the territory and concentrated overwhelming forces at the point of attack. Inka tactical ingenuity should not be underestimated, however, for some major battles were won by coupling feigned

Fig. 5.3. Illustration by Guaman Poma (1980 [1614]: /162 [164], p. 140) of Inka general Chalcuchima leading shock troops in combat. Chalcuchima headed Atawalpa's military forces stationed at Hatun Xauxa when the Spaniards arrived in 1533.

withdrawals with pincers counterattacks (see the section "Imperial Logistics," below). As the support system of the empire was elaborated, the state's ability to mobilize large armies was significantly improved. Nonetheless, armies could not be moved simply at the will of the commanders, because relocating large numbers of soldiers and support personnel was a formidable task. Even in planned campaigns, the resources of the immediate vicinity of the conflicts were occasionally exhausted. As will be described below, the development of roads, storehouses, and way stations was therefore fundamental to Inka military strategy.

Strategies of Conquest

The Inkas understood that the most efficient way to annex new territories was to convince their inhabitants that they should surrender peacefully. The rapidity of imperial expansion owed a great deal to the persuasive combination of threats of destruction for those who resisted and incentives for those who acquiesced. This approach, employed with success by other renowned strategists, such as Alexander the Great (Engels 1978:40–41) and Chingiz Khan (Morgan 1986:55–83), minimized the chances for military defeat. Compliant local elites could expect to retain or enhance their status, and communities were allowed to keep many traditional lands. The success of coercive persuasion depended on the Inkas' willingness and ability to crush recalcitrant adversaries, thereby convincing other foes of the wisdom of capitulation. Stories of Inka cruelties against staunch antagonists are documented for several parts of the empire. The reported massacres of the Huarco and the Caranqui are matched by the killing of thousands of Wankas for their support of the Spanish invasion in the 1530s (Cobo 1956 [1653]: vol. 2, bk. 2, ch. 17, p. 91; Sarmiento 1960 [1572]: ch. 60, pp. 262–63; Cieza 1967 [1553]: ch. 60, pp. 198–202; Cieza 1984 [1551]: ch. 73, pp. 218–20; Espinoza Soriano 1971; Hyslop 1984:8–13). Although the information available is largely anecdotal and often embellished, it appears that the Inkas may have followed a policy whereby those who capitulated most readily were afforded the greatest courtesies, whereas those who resisted were punished to a degree commensurate with their obduracy.[3]

Many regions, including much of the Mantaro Valley, were thus occupied relatively peacefully. Several benefits accrued in this approach to conquest, apart from the obvious conservation of manpower and time. An immediate gain lay in the Inkas' ability to follow the honored military dictum of living off the enemy's resources. An associated benefit derived from keeping intact the subsistence base in the region; a captured province that is immediately productive is far more valuable than one that has been destroyed while being subdued. In addition, because the Inkas depended heavily on existing political systems to rule on their behalf, it was often in their best interest to minimize disruption of indigenous sociopolitical organizations.

Where diplomacy failed, Inka armies overwhelmed defenses with sheer numbers (e.g., Toledo 1940a [1570]: 18–36; Cobo 1956 [1653]: vol. 2, bk. 2, ch. 14, p. 85; Sarmiento 1960 [1572]: chs. 34–61, pp. 238–63; Murúa 1962: vol. 1, ch. 21, p. 51). Reliable estimates of the sizes of Inka armies are hard to obtain, especially because the estimates seem often to have been exaggerated considerably. Reports on the sizes of major armies of conquest range from the 10,000 Thupa Yupanki used to take the Mantaro Valley (Toledo 1940a [1570]: 19) to the less credible 200,000 reported by Cobo (1956 [1653]: vol. 2, bk. 2, ch. 14, p. 85) for the conquest of Chile and the 250,000 reported by Sarmiento (1960 [1572]: ch. 46, p. 250) for Thupa Yupanki's first campaigns against the Cañares and Quitos.[4]

For the armies seen firsthand by the Spaniards, estimates of scores of thousands are common. Cristóbal de Mena, for instance, reported 80,000 effectives among Atawalpa's forces at Cajamarca, although Hernando de Soto and Hernando Pizarro put the figure at half that, perhaps to allay their men's fears (Anónimo Sevillano 1930:238; Hemming 1970:36). The author of the *Relación del sitio de Cuzco,* probably Diego de Silva, estimated 100,000 soldiers and 80,000 auxiliaries at the siege of Cuzco (Hemming 1970:190). Pedro Pizarro (1986 [1571]: ch. 8, p. 34) recalled that Atawalpa dispatched 20,000 soldiers under Rumiñahui to meet the first major Spanish contingent ascending the mountains to Cajamarca. His brother, Hernando Pizarro (1959 [1533]: 89), also reported that the *khipu kamayoq* (keepers of the mnemonic knot records) counted 35,000 soldiers in the army stationed at Hatun Xauxa under Chalcuchima in 1533. Regardless of the precise numbers involved, the sizes of these forces represented a considerable step upward from any highland military aggregates before the Inka expansion.

The Inkas mounted a number of notable sieges, but they appear to have had more difficulty with protracted investments than with diplomacy, frontal assault on a stronghold, or pitched battle in the field. In general, the capacity of the state to maintain a siege was high at the core of the empire but increasingly restricted away from magazines and productive lands directly under state control. The preferred practice appears to have been to mount a series of assaults, punctuated by retreats to strongholds for replenishment of supplies if the attacks did not attain the goal immediately. Once a territory was taken, the invading army on occasion built fortifications to house garrisons in the midst of potentially fractious populations. An early instance may be found in the detachment that Pachacutec left at Hatuncolla to preserve the successes of his campaigns in the Titicaca Basin (Sarmiento 1960 [1572]: ch. 37, p. 241). Thupa Yupanki applied a similar approach by installing a garrison of Cuzqueñans in the town of Quilcay, near Huánuco, to forestall rebellion among the Chupachu and to guard the bridges (Ortiz de Zúñiga 1972 [1562]: 187).

The Inka strategy in Ecuador may be instructive here, if we keep in mind that the area surrounding Incaic Quito was subdued late in the empire's existence; it is likely that the methods applied at the end of a century of conquests had been refined in the practice. Salomon (1986:147) suggests that the "importance of Quito derived more from its strategic location than from its demographic or political status" (see also Meyers 1976). Quito lies at a natural crossroads for north-south traffic along the Andean cordilleras and for trans-sierran traffic of precious exotics from both the Ecuadorian coast and the eastern jungles. The Inka occupation consisted of a garrison at Quito, ringed by two cordons of heavily fortified installations, forming a hardened perimeter around the imperial center. Placed along key natural lines of transit, these forts stood guard over the suspect peoples of the basin and the routes from which other groups could threaten state control (see Oberem 1968; Plaza Schuller 1980; Hyslop 1990). At times when campaigns were not faring well, the army retreated to Tumipampa to regroup for subsequent ventures (Salomon 1986:144–51; Idrovo 1988:100).

The deployment of Inka military forces and the construction of fortified settlements or forts raise issues concerning the nature of the Inka frontier. Recent assessments of this problem have documented the diversity of Inka policy at the often fuzzy limits of imperial control (esp. Dillehay and Netherly 1988b; Hyslop 1988). A key point is that virtually all areas of the empire were at some time at or near state frontiers (Dillehay and Netherly 1988a:274). The erection of state forts throughout northern Chile, for example, may therefore have been partially a consequence of the Inkas' early fortification of an expanding frontier and a later hardening of a more stable perimeter (see Raffino 1983; Niemayer and Schiappacasse 1988; Stehberg and Carvajal 1988). Morris (1988) makes the related point that some of the internal relations that the Inka state maintained with subject groups suggest administrative internal frontiers, maintained after the state had established control. The downward shifting of the border between coastal and highland groups on the north coast of Peru suggests the formation of such internal frontiers (Netherly 1988).

A second issue involving Inka frontiers concerns the nature of interaction across them. Salomon (1986: 217) has suggested that the expanding imperial borders in Ecuador were permeable fringes across which the Inkas encouraged economic and cultural interaction, apparently to facilitate acceptance of their coming rule. In support of this argument, Salomon notes that the Inkas seem to have promoted contacts into Pasto territory, across moving borders in the north of Ecuador. He also shows that the degree to which Inka cultural institutions were introduced into an area correlated well with the length of time that the area had been under imperial control. Thus, the more southerly regions of Ecuador were more fully assimilated into Inka culture than were the Pasto (see also Idrovo 1988). Similar fluid relations between groups under direct Inka rule and groups outside imperial control but with active interaction have been posited for the southern limits of Tawantinsuyu (Dillehay and Gordon 1988).

These models of frontier relations seem cogent when applied to the extremities of the empire, principally because of the sometimes halting pace with which new territories were brought under imperial sway. In the central sierra, the more-rapid conquests could have been preceded only by brief introductions to the prospective benefits of Inka rule. In the Mantaro region, for example, two major Wanka II communities—Tunanmarca and Umpamalca—show no evidence of Inka goods, implying rapid abandonment (Earle et al. 1987). Little time seems to have been allotted to the residents of the central sierra region to accept Inka culture across a moving, permeable border before military occupation.

The Inka Conquest of the Upper Mantaro Region

We may use the conquest of the Upper Mantaro Valley to illustrate basic Inka military strategy in action. The chroniclers conflict with one another in details of the sequence of conquests, but they agree that the region was among the first to fall to the Inka armies.[5] Pachacutec, who ruled from 1438 to 1471, and Thupa Yupanki, who ruled from 1471 to 1493, are consistently credited with conquering the highlands between Cuzco and Tumipampa and with subsequently developing the empire's physical infrastructure. The accounts of the conquest of the central sierra conflict with one another over timing and military leadership (Rowe 1946:206, n. 2). A central issue concerns whether Pachacutec's general, Qhapaq Yupanki, conquered the Mantaro Valley in a sweep north in pursuit of the deserting Chanca, as Sarmiento (1960 [1572]: ch. 38, p. 243) and Cieza (1967 [1553]: ch. 49, pp. 162–64) state. Other accounts contend that his military successor, Thupa Yupanki, accomplished the task following his father's cession of control of the armies about 1463 (e.g., Cabello Valboa 1951 [1586]: ch. 16, p. 319). Among those taking the latter view were the individual Wanka witnesses testifying to Toledo (1940a [1570]: 19–36) and the Cuzqueñan descendants of Thupa Yupanki (Rowe 1985:208), who independently corroborated one another in ascribing the conquest to Thupa Yupanki's early campaigns.

The available testimony does not permit firm resolution of the problem, in part because the Wanka informants conceivably gave conflicting statements to Cieza in 1549 and to Toledo in 1570. In testimony before Viceroy Toledo at Concepción in 1570, all five native witnesses recalled that they had heard from their fathers, grandfathers, and other ancestors that Thupa Yupanki had subdued the inhabitants of the region (Toledo 1940a [1570]: 19, 24, 28, 32, 35–36). Four of the five were local Wanka lords, and the last, don Diego Lucana, was the *principal* of the *mitmaq* (colonist) community of La Purificación de Guacho. With one exception, all witnesses stated that, on orders from his father, Thupa Inka Yupanki had killed Qhapaq Yupanki because he had traversed beyond Vilcas, the limit set by Pachacutec. Thupa Yupanki then continued the conquests north, taking the Upper Mantaro Valley in a subsequent campaign. This account differs from that of Cieza (1967 [1553]: ch. 49, pp. 162–64), who commented that Qhapaq Yupanki had gone as far as Cajamarca; presumably, Cieza obtained some of his detailed information from the Xauxas or the Wankas themselves, raising questions about the reliability of each of the conflicting stories.

The year 1460, a date late in the reign of Pachacutec, is provisionally accepted for the conquest here. The date represents something of a compromise between the documentary accounts and corresponds well to the radiocarbon dates taken from Wanka II settlements (Earle et al. 1987:80–81). Seven of the 10 acceptable dates clustered tightly in the fifteenth century, with 4 dates falling between 1440 and 1465. Because the settlements from which these samples were taken—Umpamalca and Tunanmarca—were abandoned under Inka rule, Rowe's (1946:203) chronology seems to be supported. Thus, the Inkas would have had little more than 70 years in which to consolidate imperial political and economic control.

The accounts of the conquest of the Upper Mantaro Valley differ in detail but illustrate the Inkas' effective combination of coercive suasion and outright military victory. As the quotation presented below describes, a first show of strength was combined with offers of honors and peaceful occupation. Those who resisted, notably in the north, were overrun and resettled or destroyed. The Wankas' unwillingness or inability to put up a united resistance reflects tellingly on the fractious state of affairs at the time:

[T]o the eleventh question, this witness said that he had heard said to his father and grandfather that when said Inka [Thupa Inka Yupanki] came to conquer and rule this land he positioned himself on a hill in this division [Lurinwanka] with the people whom he brought who were ten thousand soldiers called an *hunu* in his language and that his great-grandfather named Apoguala went there and pledged obedience and bowed down and that he took with him ten soldiers because he was one of the cinchecona of this valley and he said to the Indians that they should respect him because he was a cinche [and] that they were hidden because they wanted to see if the Inka did any harm to or killed [the envoys] and thus he heard said to those whom he had [led] that said great-grandfather arrived to speak with said Inka and to subject himself and that the other Indians that he took with him arrived with him and the others remained hidden and said Thupa Inka, this witness heard, had given to his great-grandfather some elegant shirts and blankets and some drinking cups they called *aquilla* and that with this they returned to the Indians who were hidden and who took delight in seeing that which said Inka had given to his great-grandfather and when they saw him returning they thought that it was the Inka who had come to kill them and when they recognized that it was their cinche they delighted much and as he found them eating [fearful?] he told them not to fear and that they should go with him to give obedience to the Inka because he had asked for them and thus said cinche, the great-grandfather of this witness, took all his Indians to said Inka and he said that he wanted to make them [subjects?] and said Inka told him that they were to go with him to Quito and that he heard said that there they gave him obedience and that he made war and subjected those who did not obey him nor came to bow down, killing some and taking their lands, and he received others who came to give him obedience and that this is what this witness has heard said about this question.[6] (Toledo 1940a [1570]: 19–20)

This and the other Toledan testimony suggest that the Wankas were divided in the face of the Inka approach, as might have been expected given the infighting that plagued the region in the preceding century. At least some of the Lurinwanka population capitulated without resistance and were rewarded with gifts and positions of status in the new regime. Other accounts recalled that some regional polities put up steadfast resistance. The descendants of Thupa Inka Yupanki stated in their 1569 *probanza* that their ancestor conquered the province of Xauxa, taking the fortress of Siquillapucará (Rowe 1985:224). Cabello Valboa (1951 [1586]: ch. 16, p. 319), Sarmiento (1960 [1572]: ch. 44, p. 249), and Murúa (1962: vol. 1, ch. 21, p. 51) echo this document, perhaps drawing directly from it for their accounts (Rowe 1985:208). Apparently relying on native testimony, Cieza (1967 [1553]: ch. 49, pp. 163–64) provides greater detail on the futile resistance:

Those of the Valley of Xauxa, knowing of the coming of the enemies, exhibited fear and sought assistance from their relatives and friends and in their temple of Wari Willka made grand sacrifices to the demon who responded there. The allies having arrived, there being many of them, because it is said that there were more than forty thousand men where today I do not know if there are twelve thousand, the captains of the Inka arrived and positioned themselves above the valley, wanting to win the graces of the Wankas without war and to have them go to Cuzco to recognize the king as their lord; and thus, it is common knowledge that they sent messengers. Moreover, gaining nothing [from this stratagem], they came to hand-to-hand combat and fought a great battle in which it is said many died from both sides, and those from Cuzco prevailed; and being of great wisdom, Lloque [Qhapaq] Yupanki did not consent to wreaking destruction in the valley, sparing the pillaging, ordering that the captives be freed; thus, the Wankas, knowing the[ir] favor and with the clemency shown them as the vanquished, came to speak and promise to live from then on according to the orders of the kings of Cuzco and to pay tribute with that which they had in their valley; and moving their settlements onto the slopes, they grew their crops, without dividing up the lands, until the king Wayna Qhapaq assigned to each division what they ought to have.[7]

Espinoza Soriano (1971:38) has identified Siquilla-pucará with the archaeological site of Tunanmarca, without specifying the basis for the relationship. His map, unfortunately, is only generally accurate with respect to the locations of archaeological sites and seems to have conflated the two major centers, Hatunmarca and Tunanmarca. Citing unpublished documents, he states that the settlement held out against the invaders until hunger and thirst caused them to capitulate. Following the Inka victory, some of the vanquished Wankas were forcibly resettled in Chachapoyas, on the eastern slopes of far northern Peru.

Although the details of this story may be apocryphal, archaeological and documentary evidence lends credence to the resettlement referred to by Cieza and embellished in Espinoza Soriano's documents (see Chapter 9). In brief, the populace shifted downward radically from their hilltop redoubts to a more dispersed pattern along the valley flanks in Wanka III. The Wanka II settlements of Tunanmarca, Umpamalca, and the associated communities of the upper Yanamarca Valley were all abandoned. Litigation in Spanish courts in the latter half of the sixteenth century refers to the use of Wanka soldiers in Wayna Qhapaq's Ecuadorian campaigns (Espinoza Soriano 1969:23), and documents from highland Ecuador confirm the presence of "Guanca" *mitmaqkuna* in the region (Salomon 1986:163).[8]

From a military perspective, the most significant aspect of the settlement shift was a reduction in the potential threat posed by a native population inhabiting nucleated, residential fortresses. Considering the Inkas' repeated problems with internal rebellions, dispersal of the populace into smaller, vulnerable settlements would have been an important step in asserting control over the newly subjugated populations. Equally significant was the decision to retain many local elites in positions of local authority and not to pillage the new holdings. This strategy was a break with sierra military traditions, in which sacking the settlements of the defeated was apparently an honored principle. The benefits of this choice, aside from gaining the gratitude of the vanquished, lay in the preservation of important resource bases and the makings of an administration with which to exploit them (see Patterson 1985, 1986).

Strategies of Consolidation

With the conquest of the central highlands accomplished, the Inkas undertook the longer-term process of integrating the subject peoples into the nascent empire. Militarily, strategy shifted from an emphasis on offense to defense, as the early, quick conquests were replaced by fortification of frontiers and suppression of rebellions. By the late fifteenth century, the Inkas were retooling for a military strategy that fits a defense-in-depth model (see chapter introduction, above), because of threats along the eastern perimeter (Rawls 1979:146). In his analysis of Roman military strategy, Luttwak (1976:130–32) suggests that a defense has two broad alternatives when faced with a mobile enemy strong enough to penetrate a defensive perimeter. In an elastic defense, the border is abandoned and the defense relies on forces that should be as mobile as those of the offense. A strategy of defense-in-depth depends on a combination of self-contained strongholds and mobile forces deployed between or behind them. Such a strategy employs fortifications as "hard points" in a line of defense against threats from outside the borders of the empire, the goal being to deny passage into the territory. The logistical infrastructure, which previously had served in part as a front line of offense, now shifts more heavily to a supporting role of communications and transportation. The advantages that defense-in-depth offers in terms of greater security for the borderlands are countered by reduced flexibility in the disposition of military resources and by a need for greater investment in fortifications and end-depot supply facilities.

If we can accept the documentary sources, Thupa Inka Yupanki initiated a strategy of defense-in-depth fairly early in the imperial era. His successor, Wayna Qhapaq, continued to consolidate the border and extended Inka rule into previously unpacified areas in Ecuador. As part of the military strategy to subdue new territories, the Inkas built fortifications among the conquered populations in some regions. Manned by imported garrisons, they provided direct control over refractory subjects. The problem of rebellion plagued the Inkas from the beginning, for Pachacutec had to put down the first of several uprisings in the Titicaca Basin (Rowe 1946:206). Perhaps surprisingly, considering the size of the population, there is no record of Wanka rebellion against Inka rule. It is likely that deportation of part of the population, abandonment of fortified settlements, and incorporation of indigenous elites into the state bureaucracy combined to discourage open revolt.

Rebellions elsewhere continued to threaten imperial control throughout Inka rule, however, leading to several changes in military strategy and use of support facilities. With respect to personnel, a late shift in staffing policy entailed a move away from an army of peasants impressed on a rotating basis to a more professional force composed of militarily specialized ethnic groups (see Murra 1986:56). Among these groups were the Cañare and the Chachapoya, who formed internal garrisons throughout the empire in the last decade of Inka rule. One garrison in Lurinwanka contained members of both of these groups and the Llaguas (Toledo 1940a [1570]: 22); the size of the mitmaqkuna settlement is unfortunately not recorded in published sources.

In contrast to the fortresses that were positioned to serve specifically military functions, the major provincial centers between Cuzco and Quito were founded in locations that facilitated efficient movement of goods, people, and messages between regions. Linked by the principal highways, they were sometimes constructed in places removed from the densest concentrations of local populace (e.g., Pumpu, Huánuco Pampa), although some centers were constructed at the location of subject communities (Tumipampa, Quito). At other times, the populace was removed from the immediate vicinity (Willka Wamán). All these centers lay adjacent to open valleys or plains, which would have facilitated bivouacking an army, and they were usually at the juncture of natural conduits of travel. Because the assertion of control over conquered territories was an ongoing activity, the positioning of major centers may well have been part of a series of tactics to reduce the threat of internal attack and to support reprisals when insurrections did occur.

The fortifications in the valleys along the edges of the empire formed a line of hard-point defenses in the overall strategy, complementing the internal garrisons, which were intended to maintain tranquility within territorially ruled imperial territories and to respond to incursions. Cieza (1967 [1553]: ch. 64, p. 216) recounted that Wayna Qhapaq, after subduing an uprising by the Chachapoya, "installed the normal garrisons with mitmaq soldiers, so that they would be by the [eastern] frontier."[9] Farther south, in the Huánuco region, indigenous Chupachu and Yacha and mitmaqkuna from Cuzco were posted in a series of Inka fortifications along the eastern slopes, such as the previously mentioned Quilcay. Other fortified sites, such as Angar, Ocollupagua, Catapayza, and Colpagua, were later established in the *ceja de la montaña* to repel external attacks (Ortiz de Zúñiga 1972 [1562]: 34; Rawls 1979:128). As Hyslop (1990:159) points out, however, these sites have yet to be identified or studied archaeologically. Another, similar line of hard-point

fortifications may have been established down the Río Urubamba from Cuzco, to protect the heartland against incursions by eastern tribes (Rawls 1979:150–56; see also Kendall 1974, 1976). Among the fortifications in the eastern Bolivian altiplano were Incallacta, Batanes, and Incahuasi—established by Thupa Yupanki and rebuilt by Wayna Qhapaq, reportedly to repulse invasions by the Chiriguano (Nordenskiöld 1924; Rawls 1979:146–50; Hyslop 1990: ch. 6). In northwest Argentina, where the Inkas often occupied previously existing forts, Pucará de Andalgalá stands out as a notable Inka fortification, but other smaller forts, such as Cortaderas (Calchaquí Valley), were also established (Hyslop 1984, 1990; see also Fock 1961 and Lorandi 1988). Similar hard-point roles may be reasonably assigned to the cordons of forts around Quito (Plaza Schuller 1980) and to the Chilean forts at Chena and Angostura, for example (Dillehay and Gordon 1988:220; Stehberg and Carvajal 1988: 182, 201–4).

In the Wanka region, neither published documents nor archaeological surveys have recorded Inka fortifications along the eastern periphery, perhaps because the thin occupation of the jungles to the east posed no serious threat to the security of the central highlands. Because little archaeological research has been conducted in the area, however, any Inka forts that were erected would likely still not be recorded. Forts were constructed in the Huánuco area to control the Chupachu and later to secure the frontier, so it seems possible that some modest facilities of this nature were erected to the east of the Upper Mantaro but remain to be discovered. The aforementioned presence of Cañare, Chachapoya, and Llaguas mitmaqkuna in the region lends additional support to the notion that at least some Inka forts were built in the Mantaro.

In the general process of consolidation of military control, the military functions of many support facilities would have shifted from offense to defense, except in regions in which protracted engagements were still under way. The shift to defense-in-depth was only partially completed by the Inkas, because it works most effectively when imperial territory is internally secure. Even at the end of Inka sovereignty, however, the support system was needed to keep internal peace throughout the unwieldy length of the empire. Without a large, permanent military and secure internal control, the Inkas opted for a hardened perimeter in active areas, such as Ecuador and eastern Bolivia, and a well-provisioned support system that could be mobilized to quell internal uprisings and to repel incursions that penetrated the frontier defenses. In this strategy, the provincial centers, tampu, storage facilities, and road network provided the defensive infrastructure for multiple kinds of threats. It would therefore be a mistake to conclude that Inka centers lacking fortifications—such as Hatun Xauxa—were not an integral part of state military strategy. A lack of obvious defenses at a provincial center more likely implies that there was no serious expectation of investment by an invading force than it implies a lack of participation in military campaigns.

For the Wanka role in military activity, we may turn to some of the early sources. Most soldiers in the Inka military were peasant conscripts with relatively rudimentary training in the tactics of battle, until the movement toward a more professional army late in the empire's existence (see Bram 1941; Rowe 1946:278; Rawls 1979:118–21). According to Xauxa and Wanka witnesses testifying in 1582 to inspector Andrés de Vega (1965:167), the Lurinwanka populace could field 12,000 soldiers in the mid-1520s, the Ananwanka boasted 9,000, and the Xauxa 6,000, for a total of 27,000. Murra (1975:246) has noted that the number 266 and its multiples (e.g., 133, 532) appear several times in the local mobilizations of personnel in early support of the Spaniards (Espinoza Soriano 1971). This figure is suspiciously close to 1 percent of the total manpower in the valley, according to the Inka census, and may have been a basic proportion of mobilization. There is, however, enough diversity in the numbers of individuals mobilized that additional information would be needed to confirm this supposition.[10]

Litigating over succession to a local lordship in 1597, Xauxa claimants testified that a number of kurakas of Hatunxauxa had accompanied Wayna Qhapaq to Quito and Tumipampa, never to return (Espinoza Soriano 1969: doc. 3, p. 63; see also Cieza 1967 [1553]: ch. 64, p. 215). The size of the units at issue is not clear from the litigation. Because the minimal unit of military duty was likely 100 households, it seems probable that several hundred households were involved. Additional evidence of Wanka military duty away from home may be found in the Wanka presence as mitmaqkuna in the garrison at Willka Wamán (Carbajal 1965 [1586]: 218), but again numbers of personnel are not available.

More-notable participation in Inka warfare by residents of the Upper Mantaro can be found in the civil war between Wascar and Atawalpa, in which the Wankas sided with the losing Cuzqueñan armies. The significance of the commitment can be seen in part by the role of Guanca Auqui, son of Wayna Qhapaq and a Xauxa wife, as general of Wascar's armies. Guanca Auqui had the misfortune of commanding the losing forces in a series of Atawalpa's army's greatest victories, including Tumipampa, Cajamarca, Pumpu, and Vilcas. A particularly bloody encounter took place in the Yanamarca Valley, just north of Hatun Xauxa. Reinforced by Soras, Chanca, Rucana, Aymara, Quichua, Wanka, and Yauyos recruits, Guanca Auqui's remnant army of Chachapoya and other northern ethnic groups were routed by Quisquis and Chalcuchima (Cabello Valboa 1951 [1586]: ch. 30, p. 449–50; Cobo 1956 [1653]: vol. 2, bk. 2, ch. 18, p. 96; Murúa 1962: vol. 1, ch. 52, p. 153). Guanca Auqui fled south, leaving Mayca Yupanki to lead the tattered losers to Willka Wamán. Atawalpa's army re-formed and supplied itself at Hatun Xauxa before continuing south for its ultimate victory over Wascar and the end of the civil war. The effects of these defeats at the hands of the Quiteñans must have devastated the residents of the Mantaro. As the unhappy hosts of Chalcuchima's army at Hatun Xauxa on its return from Cuzco, they were only too willing to side with the Spaniards when the latter unexpectedly appeared.

In sum, if we take into account the issues of strategy sketched out here, we may see that the military importance of any given imperial region cannot be assessed simply in terms of fortifications or proximity to areas of active combat. Instead, the dominant military role for areas in the central sierra, such as the Upper Mantaro Valley, lay in mobilizing and sustaining forces in the field. This conclusion directs our attention to the second principal issue to be treated in this chapter: military logistics.

Imperial Logistics

Supplying the Inka armies in the field was a daunting problem, and the logistical system set up to meet the demand ranked among the most astounding marvels of the New World. A road network exceeding 30,000 km, perhaps 2,000 way stations spaced along the way, and voluminous storage complexes awed the Spaniards with the empire's organizational capabilities. In our continued admiration for this achievement, a pivotal issue has often become obscured. Inka logistics did not reflect efficient movement of goods so much as the limitations of traditional transport. The technology available so constrained the transport of goods that state supply facilities had to be replicated regionally throughout the empire. Given the demanding terrain, the lack of boats and carts, and the light loads that llamas and humans can pack relative to the loads transported by draft animals, it seems reasonable to ask how logistical problems affected Inka conquests and integration of subject territories.

Analysts of military logistics consistently observe that mobilizing and supplying an army in the field are often critical to the success of a campaign. Alexander the Great's brilliant conquests, for example, were demonstrably influenced by the constant need to procure supplies. Engels (1978:20) estimates that the soldiers, camp followers, and animals of that army could have packed supplies to last only two and a half days. Hassig (1988:63) similarly notes that, on at least one occasion, Aztec soldiers were issued a three-day supply of cacao as part of normal war supplies. He calculates eight days to be the limit of travel for the Aztec forces without replenishment, based on a ratio of one porter to two soldiers. Even armies possessing markedly superior technological capabilities and operating in regions more productive than the Andes encountered serious logistical obstacles. For instance, comparably sized western European armies of the sixteenth and seventeenth centuries had access to water-based and wheeled transport and pack animals far superior to those of the Inkas. Nonetheless, they were repeatedly forced to abandon or radically modify military ventures because they were unable to maintain field support (van Creveld 1977).

Logistical Options

In the field, an army with transport capabilities similar to those of the Inkas had five basic options available for provisioning itself. Among the key issues affecting choice among these options were whether the military strategy was offensively or defensively oriented, whether most military actions were to be undertaken within or outside home territory, whether support was to be mobilized from the home resources or from the enemy's resources, whether the military forces were mobile or sedentary, how large was the force to be supplied, how far the goods had to be transported, and what means of transportation were available.[11]

The first three options are appropriate for hegemonic empires or for expansionist phases of imperial growth, because they are designed to use the resources of client, tributary, or target populations. The first method—allowing soldiers to forage for themselves—undermines discipline and destroys productive resources in the wake of the army. Although its destruc-

tiveness generally makes foraging an undesirable choice, it may be an effective instrument of attack, because a foraging army can decimate an enemy's ability to support itself (van Creveld 1977:23). Such an approach, however, too often ravages the homeland and contains the seeds of disaster for retreating forces. A second method provides purchasing power through monetary levies and makes anticipatory arrangements for supplies in the projected path of the army, through sutlers or other agents. This approach was substituted for foraging in European warfare in the late sixteenth century. Although a disaster in practice, this procedure was intended to be a humane solution to the problem of military pillaging (van Creveld 1977:8).

A third general alternative is to make formal arrangements for orderly provisioning within client or tributary territories and within territories targeted for conquest. The Inkas employed this tactic widely, stationing an overwhelming force at the borders of the territory and offering to accept surrender on favorable terms (e.g., Toledo 1940a [1570]). Using a similar approach, Alexander interpreted an adversary's failure to surrender before the Macedonian army's occupation as a hostile action (Engels 1978:41). Aztec logistical strategy entailed a combination of transport by porters from the Basin of Mexico and mobilizations exacted from towns along the march route (Hassig 1988:63–65). The costs of the latter were the responsibility of the local lord, which placed a heavy and not always predictable burden on tributary resources. The principal advantages to this kind of occupation are minimization of personnel losses and maintenance of the army without significant core investments in transport of supplies.

The last two logistical methods, based on mobilizing resources from the polity's own territory, are more appropriate for a territorial imperial strategy. In contrast to the first three approaches, which emphasize the offensive element of military action, these two methods are suitable for external ventures, defense, and consolidation of new holdings. One approach under these circumstances is to mobilize support as needed from the general populace or from state resources, such as agricultural lands or herds. This approach, however, is subject to temporal fluctuations in productivity and to local resistance to state levies. A final, preferable alternative is for the leadership to establish regularly stocked, strategically situated magazines so that provisions can be drawn as required. Implementing this scheme in the seventeenth century, Louvois developed the use of storehouses in western Europe as both a defensive strategy and an offensive one. Even with this major step forward, the French could not sustain themselves in the field without depending on local supply for practically all fodder and much of their provisions (van Creveld 1977:20–21, 25). As Van Creveld puts it, "The most difficult logistic problem facing Louvois, his contemporaries and his successors was much less to feed an army on the move than to prevent one that was stationary from starving" (p. 25).

The problem for mobile offensive forces with premodern transport abilities was thus to keep moving to new resources. A siege could be sustained only if efficient transport was available (e.g., over water) or if the army could bring in provisions from magazines near the conflict. In contrast to the required mobility of many offensive forces, a defensively oriented military was more concerned with concentrating provisions for a more stationary army or for moving armies around internally to put down rebellions or repel invasions.

The question arises as to how the Inkas addressed these logistical problems and what impelled them early on to invest such remarkable effort in their supply infrastructure. As might be expected, Inka methods varied over time and space, as the military concerns changed from conquest to consolidation and from core to perimeter. Broadly speaking, the Inka solution was to shift from a hegemonic dependence on client and target resources to a territorial reliance on resources specifically developed to sustain state personnel. The establishment of state lands, herds, and raw resources and the storage of many goods in state warehouses can be seen as part of a territorial strategy intended to mobilize vast quantities of matériel with minimal internal resistance.

The need for regular supplies may be appreciated if we look at the documentary evidence on Inka sieges. The histories of the conquests suggest that Inka armies found it difficult to maintain protracted sieges, for both logistical and agricultural reasons. For example, supply problems beset Wayna Qhapaq's efforts to take a Caranqui stronghold in Ecuador (Cobo 1956 [1653]: vol. 2, bk. 2, ch. 17, p. 91; Sarmiento 1960 [1572]: ch. 60, pp. 262–63; see Rawls 1979:136). According to the sometimes unreliable Murúa (1962: vol. 1, ch. 34, p. 90), Wayna Qhapaq withdrew to Tumipampa following an abortive series of frontal attacks but failed to supply the forces left to invest the fortress. Unable to live off the land in the vicinity, some part of the forces left the field to petition the emperor for support. With the Inka army thus depleted, the Caranqui broke the siege and resupplied themselves.

Ultimately, Wayna Qhapaq returned to the fray, drew the Caranqui out of their redoubt with a feigned withdrawal, and slaughtered them. The Inka conquest of the Huarco of the Cañete Valley also suffered from supply problems (see Cieza 1967 [1553]: ch. 60, pp. 198–202; Cieza 1984 [1551]: ch. 73, pp. 217–18). At Inkawasi, built to sustain the conquest, the Inkas erected blocks of rooms that are thought to have been storehouses; no coastal Inka site has more storage units (Hyslop 1985: 8–13). Nonetheless, the Inkas withdrew to the highlands between annual investments of the valley, the rationale being that the soldiers suffered from the heat. It seems possible, however, that the difficulties of besieging the coastal fortifications resulted partially from the problems of importing logistical support, compounded by inadequate local resources and a need for the peasant farmers to till their fields.

A similar problem occurred during the Spanish conquest, when Manco Inka invested the Spanish, Cañare, and Chachapoya forces in Cuzco with an army generally estimated to have comprised between 100,000 and 200,000 individuals (Hemming 1970: 190, 572–73).[12] After four months, the peasant troops largely disbanded for the duration of the planting season and had to be reassembled. Pedro Pizarro (1986 [1571]: ch. 20, p. 142) commented that the soldiers lifted the siege for want of food and returned to their lands to cultivate their crops. Cristóbal de Mena (Anónimo Sevillano 1937 [1534]: 31, 37) further reported that mounted forays by the Spaniards discouraged native women from supplying the investing forces (see Murra 1980 [1956]: 129–30).

Assessment of Traditional Transport Capacities

The accounts cited above provide anecdotal insight into the limitations on the Inkas' ability to support a large army in the field, but it will be instructive to consider logistical capacities more concretely. Two kinds of transportation were available to the Inka armies: llama caravan and human porter (Fig. 5.4). Humans appear to have been more extensively used than llamas (Murra 1980 [1956]: 48), although the proportions of loads carried by humans or animals cannot be determined from the data available at present. Once state control and the support infrastructure were established, the standard technique appears to have been to use local porters to carry goods from one border of their territory to the opposite. Soldiers or other personnel en route were supplied from state storehouses

Fig. 5.4. Llama caravan descending the misty eastern slopes of the Andes above Comas. (Photo courtesy of Catherine Scott)

constructed about 20 km apart along the road. Although this seems to have been a very effective system, largely unconstrained by energetic limitations, the logistics bear closer examination.

The Inkas were faced with three basic military supply problems: maintaining a force at the ends of imperial supply lines, sustaining an internally bivouacked force, and supporting a force on the move. The second situation was addressed largely through establishment of a well-stocked, regionally sustained storage system. Because the details of this situation are described in Chapter 8, the present discussion will address the other two problems, both of which entailed movement of large amounts of goods, personnel, or both.

Earlier discussion observed that the Inkas successfully took over numerous territories without pitched battle and could thus live off the resources of the conquered populace, at least for the short term. When they met with concerted resistance or when battles occurred at great distances from the locations from which forces were mobilized, supply became a key issue. The down-the-line transport system could be effective at supplying personnel close to the sources of production. At the end of Inka supply lines (e.g., beyond the borders of imperial control) or where local resources were otherwise unavailable, the support of military forces became difficult (see Rowe 1946:280).

Spanish eyewitness accounts concurred on the principal use of llama caravans to transport goods for the army (see Murra 1980 [1956]: 48–54 for a review), but few solid estimates of the size of these herds are available. Probably the best-known is the potentially exaggerated account given by Zárate (1862 [1555]: bk. 2, ch. 12, p. 483) of Quisquis's abandonment of more than 15,000 animals, along with more than 4,000 male and female prisoners, following a battle with Almagro. A Cañare kuraka estimated the size of Quisquis's army to be in excess of 12,000. Zárate himself put the figures at an advance guard of 2,000, with 3,000 on the left flank and 3,000 to 4,000 more in the rear; he did not estimate the size of the main body of the army.[13]

Another estimate is available from the Upper Mantaro region. At the inception of the Spanish conquest, when Pizarro was in Cajamarca, the Wankas began to provide food, goods, and portage. In late 1533 the native elites provided large quantities of supplies and herds to the governor upon his arrival in Hatun Xauxa. In testimony to the Audiencia Real in Lima in 1558, the Lurinwankas recounted that, according to khipu records, they had turned over 514,656 mature and 20,386 young camelids (Guacrapáucar 1971a [1558]: 202). The Xauxas stated that they had given 13,320 mature camelids (Cusichaca et al. 1971 [1561]: 279). Later prestations consistently fell below 1,000 apiece. Whether these remarkably high initial figures were accounts of native stock or state herds abandoned by the Inkas in their precipitous retreat is not clear from the sources, nor are the uses to which the stock was put.

Despite the vast herds, the abilities of llamas to move goods had limits, because they can carry only relatively small loads and they need frequent rest. For simplicity of calculation, transport figures for the typical castrated male of 3 to 8 years have been rounded as follows: 30 kg for an average load for long treks, 20 km per day of travel, and 6 days of active work per week (West 1981; J. Wheeler and D. Caro, pers. com. 1987). Two additional factors must be considered for a simple estimation of the effectiveness of caravans carrying loads: the need to rotate loaded llamas with relief animals and the dietary needs of the drovers. Even with relatively light loads, short days, and a day off a week, only about two-thirds of a llama caravan can carry loads at any given time (J. Wheeler, pers. com. 1987; see Murra 1980 [1956]: 48). The other third is partially rested by traveling without a load. No firm numbers of animals controlled by each drover are available from the early documents, so contemporary figures will be used here. West (1981:66) reports 2 drovers, each with an assistant, herding a total of 55 llamas and 3 burros. Wheeler (pers. com. 1987) estimates about 20 llamas per drover. In the prehistoric situation, it is not clear if drovers were accompanied by assistants or their wives, as soldiers generally were, so an estimate of 20 llamas per drover seems to be generous and an assistant has been added for some of the calculations. The estimations of llama transport capabilities are presented in Table 5.3 and Figure 5.5. Because of the combined use of human and llama transport, discussion of the significance of these estimates will be deferred until the procedures for estimating the capabilities of human porters have been presented.

Despite the apparent utility of llamas as pack animals, human porters played the major role in transportation for the Inka military. It is difficult to estimate the size that these supporting groups attained, but camp followings in early organized warfare often were of a size approaching that of the combatants. Engels (1978:13) estimates 1 follower for each 2 to 3 soldiers in Alexander's army, and Hassig (1988:64) uses a ratio of 1 follower to 2 soldiers for the Aztecs. Given that the wives of Inka soldiers often accompanied them to provide care and that women were often used as bearers, it seems reasonable to assume that these support groups would have been substantial. One estimate of the proportions of supporting personnel can be found in the 1558–61 Wanka petitions to the Audiencia Real in Lima. Over the first decades of Xauxa and Wanka support to the Spaniards, the indigenous populations committed more than 12,000 individuals explicitly to the Europeans' purposes. In 1533, in the first provisioning, 589 men, 437 women, 311 porters, and 110 servants were put at Spanish disposal, the last two groups being committed at the time of departure. This proportion of noncombatants to men (soldiers?) approached 1.5 to 1. A total of 3,465 men (not counting porters), 1,915 women (not counting porters), and 7,131 porters were mobilized from 1533 through 1548 (Murra 1975:252, insert). The combined women and porters thus outnumbered the men committed to the Spaniards by 2.6 to 1.

Some Spaniards were appalled at the burdens carried by the highland bearers, but reliable estimates for typical loads and distances in late prehistory are unfortunately not readily accessible. In his 1543 report, *Ordenanzas de Tambos*, Vaca de Castro (1908:468) stipulated that porters could be forced to carry a load of no more than 30 libras (13.8 kg).[14] Such a limit is less a specification of real loads than a confirmation of the overwork to which the Spaniards subjected native bearers. As early as 1535, Francisco Pizarro complained that one of the reasons for moving the capital from Jauja to Lima was that all the local people had moved away to avoid being drafted for transport service (Cobo 1956 [1653]: vol. 2, bk. 1, p. 284). Dismayed by the excessive burdens carried by porters, Lope de Atienza (1931 [1575?], cited in Salomon 1986:153) reported transport of cargoes weighing 2 to 3 arrobas for distances of 4 to 6 leagues at a stretch, or 34.5 kg transported about 25 km per day. Murra (1980 [1956]: 106) notes the transport of Atawalpa's ransom almost 1,000 km from Cuzco to Cajamarca in 15 days, for an average of about 65 km day, but this seems to have been an extreme case, far outstripping the norm.

Historical and modern references to human transport of goods vary widely (Hyslop 1984:294–98). Systematic studies of modern professional porters[15] in La Paz, Bolivia, provide measurements useful for present purposes (Greksa et al. 1982:2; Leatherman et al. 1983; see also Leonard 1987). The authors report that although it is not uncommon for a porter to carry a load equivalent to his body weight for relatively long distances and up steep slopes, 81 percent of the loads measured fell between 21 and 34 kg (Greksa et al. 1982:7). The average length of time spent carrying cargo per day was about 2.4 hours; 4.6 additional hours were spent looking for work. It seems reasonable, from these data, to set a working upper limit of about 30 kg for long treks, while recognizing that loads likely varied somewhat.

A normal day's travel will be assumed here to be about 20 km, for three reasons. First, as was noted above, llamas will normally travel this distance without breaking down or refusing to move. Second, the chroniclers consistently recorded that tampu were spaced a day's travel apart, but they differed in what they considered to be a day's travel. After an extensive review of the literature, Hyslop (1984:294–96) concludes that most estimates fall in the range of 3 to 5 leagues, which may be roughly translated to 15 to 25 km.[16] Third, constriction points on the road system that would have caused little inconvenience to small groups of travelers would have been major obstacles for large forces on the move. In the Upper Mantaro, for example, bridges or gorges would have restricted travel along the main highway to single file to the east, west, and south within about 75 km of Hatun Xauxa (cf. Hyslop 1984:254–57 for similar figures).

To illustrate the effects of the terrain on military movements, Chalcuchima's army of 35,000 stationed at Hatun Xauxa at the time of the Spanish arrival may be taken as an example.[17] Single file, about 500 soldiers take up 1 km (cf. Hassig 1988:65–72). If the porters, soldiers' wives, and other camp followers composed a group about the size of Chalcuchima's army, the string would have stretched out to 140 km. If a llama is allowed 3 m in the train, about 333 llamas take up 1 km of road. A llama caravan of, say, 15,000 accompanying the troops would have extended an additional 45 km. The entourage would likely have regrouped, rather than travel single file, of course, and Inka armies were typically deployed in sections, rather than as single bodies. As a unit, however, moving at a rate of 5 km per hour (i.e., 1 league/hour), it would have taken this army and entourage 37 hours to pass through the narrowest point of the road or across a bridge. Traveling constantly from dawn to dusk, the human force would have consumed more than 300,000 kg of food and the llamas 90,000 kg of forage—just to get 5 km outside Hatun Xauxa toward the coast (see Table 5.3 and Figs. 5.5 and 5.6 for calculations).

To evaluate the general capacities of this transport system, reliable estimates are necessary for the subsistence needs of soldiers and support personnel. Although calculation of such values is necessarily an approximation, the estimates provided here should be fairly accurate, because of detailed studies on Andean dietary needs and energy expenditure rates. The consumption rates obtained here are based on data provided for the traditional farming and herding population of the Nuñoa district, Department of Puno (Thomas 1973). Summary data on the caloric values

and rates of consumption of various kinds of staple Andean foods are provided in Tables 5.1 and 5.2. An average soldier on the march would have consumed about 1.5 kg of mixed foods (maize, potatoes, chuño) per day, and a wife accompanying him would consume about 1.2 kg, for a total of 2.7 kg/day for the couple. A male porter shouldering a heavy load would consume about 1.7 kg/day, and a female porter about 1.4 kg/day. Adult drovers for llama caravans would have consumed about 1.5 kg/day, and young male assistants about 1.2 kg.[18] We may assume, for the sake of the argument, that the 2 liters (1 kg) of water needed on a daily basis was readily available.

These figures may be used to estimate the caravan transport capabilities of llamas and humans. Table 5.3 and Figures 5.5. and 5.6 illustrate the ranges of human and llama caravans of varied compositions and carrying differing loads. Taking a situation in which the intent of the transport was to supply an end-depot or besieging army with nothing but food, in which at least half the load was supposed to be delivered, we may see that male porters carrying nothing but fresh potatoes had a limit of about 88 km, females 75 km, and a llama caravan 635 km. If the bearers were to return home, the limit was halved: 44 km for males, 37 km for females, and 317 km for llamas. If we assume a mix of 50 percent shelled maize, 25 percent fresh potatoes, and 25 percent chuño, the ranges approximately double. As the supplies in the vicinity of an army were exhausted, of course, the foodstuffs would have been procured from increasingly far afield, reducing the efficiency of the transport and compounding the supply problem.

An alternative situation, in which the intent is simply to feed an army on the move to another source of food, extends the range as well. An extreme situation may be found in which a drover and an assistant, not intending to return home, herded a remarkably resilient llama train that carried nothing but dried, shelled maize. Under these conditions, they could have traversed about 4,571 km, arriving with 20 llamas, no maize, and no foodstuffs to get home. A more reasonable situation may be described as follows: Five soldiers accompanied a train of 20 llamas that packed 50 percent of the maize-potato-chuño mix and 50 percent other supplies, with the intent of delivering 50 percent of the food at the end to supply the soldiers for a stay of some duration. Under these circumstances, the range of the llama caravan is reduced to only 168 km—barely the distance from the nearest highlands valleys to the coast in many areas. If each soldier had exclusive

Table 5.1. Caloric and Volume Values for Andean Foods

Food source	Form	kcal/kg	Weight/ volume (kg/m^3)	Source
Maize *(Zea mays)*	Various	3,400–3,600		Collazos et al. 1957: main table, items 356–58
		3,600		Leung 1961:13
	Shelled flint		770	D. Fetherston, U.S. Feed Grains Council, pers. com. 1987
Andean grains	Seed	3,420		Thomas 1973:108
Potatoes *(Solanum tuberosum)*	Fresh	790		Leung 1961:37
		990		Thomas 1973:108
			770	G. Porter, Potato Association of America, pers. com. 1987
	Chuño	3,270		Leung 1961:37
		3,960		R. B. Thomas, pers. com. 1989
			385	G. Porter, Potato Association of America, pers. com. 1987
Quinoa *(Chenopodium quinoa)*	Whole grain	3,510		Leung 1961:17
Bean *(Phaseolus vulgaris)*	Fresh	360		Leung 1961:23
Mashwa *(Tropaeolum tuberosum)*	Dried	520		Leung 1961:33
Lupine, or talwi *(Lupinus mutabilis)*	Fresh	1,260		Leung 1961:67
Llama *(Lama glama glama)*	Live animal	957		Sandefur 1988:151
	Edible portion	1,533		Thomas 1973:113
	Entire animal	1,029		Thomas 1973:113
Alpaca *(Lama glama pacos)*	Live animal	1,500		Sandefur 1988:151
	Edible portion	1,521		Thomas 1973:113
	Entire animal	1,019		Thomas 1973:113

Table 5.2. Estimates of Caloric Expenditure

Individual (kcal/day)	Mean daily caloric expenditure (kg)	Weight required in food (kg)						Water required (kg)
		Potatoes	Chuño	Maize	Maize/potatoes (50/50 mix)	Maize/chuño (50/50 mix)	Maize-potato-chuño mix	
Adult male—55 kg (Nuñoa)	2,094 (0.758 FAO)[a]							
Adult female—50 kg (Nuñoa)	1,610 (0.749 FAO)							
Adult male—55 kg (FAO recommendation)	2,764							
Adult female—50 kg (FAO recommendation)	2,149							
Soldier or drover—55 kg	2,500	3.0	0.7	0.8–0.9	0.4/1.5 (1.9)	0.4/0.35 (0.75)	1.5	1.0
Male porter—55 kg	2,856	3.4	0.8	0.9–1.0	0.5/1.7 (2.2)	0.45/0.40 (0.85)	1.7	1.0
Adult female—50 kg	1,750	2.4	0.5	0.6 (0.56–0.63)	0.3/1.0 (1.3)	0.3/0.25 (0.55)	1.2	0.7
Female porter—50 kg	2,040	2.8	0.6	0.6-0.7	0.4/1.4 (1.8)	0.4/0.33 (0.73)	1.4	0.7
Assistant drover (juvenile)	1,750	2.4	0.5	0.6 (0.56–0.63)	0.3/1.0 (1.3)	0.3/0.25 (0.55)	1.2	0.7

[a]FAO = Food and Agricultural Organization of the United Nations (1957).

Table 5.3. Caravan Transport Capabilities

Option	Bearer	Load/individual (kg)	Food mix	Consumers	Consumption rate per day (kg)	Distance per week (km)	50%-delivery range (km)	Round-trip range (km)	One-way range (km)
a	Male porter	30	Maize, potatoes, chuño	1 soldier 1 porter	1.5 1.7	140 140	94	94	188
b	Male porter	30	Chuño	1 soldier 1 porter	0.7 0.8	140 140	200	200	400
c	Male porter	30	Maize	1 soldier 1 porter	0.9 1.0	140 140	158	158	316
d	Male porter	30	Maize, potatoes, chuño	1 porter	1.7	140	176	176	353
e	Male porter	30	Potatoes	1 porter	3.4	140	88	88	176
f	Female porter	21	Maize, potatoes, chuño	1 soldier 1 porter	1.5 1.4	140 140	72	72	145
g	Female porter	21	Chuño	1 soldier 1 porter	0.7 0.6	140 140	162	162	323
h	Female porter	21	Maize	1 soldier 1 porter	0.9 0.7	140 140	131	131	263
i	Female porter	21	Maize, potatoes, chuño	1 porter	1.4	140	150	150	300
j	Female porter	21	Potatoes	1 porter	2.8	140	75	75	150
k	20 llamas	20	Maize, potatoes, chuño	1 drover 1 assistant	1.5 1.2	120 120	1,270	1,270	2,540
l	20 llamas	20	Maize	1 drover 1 assistant	0.9 0.6	120 120	2,286	2,286	4,571
m	20 llamas	20	Potatoes	1 drover 1 assistant	3.0 2.4	120 120	635	635	1,270
n	20 llamas	20	Maize, potatoes, chuño	5 soldiers 1 drover 1 assistant	7.5 1.5 1.2	120 120 120	336	336	672
o	20 llamas	20	Maize, potatoes, chuño (50%); nonfood (50%)	5 soldiers 1 drover 1 assistant	7.5 1.5 1.2	120 120 120	168	168	336
p	20 llamas	20	Maize, potatoes, chuño (50%); nonfood (50%)	1 drover 1 assistant	1.5 1.2	120 120	635	635	1,270

access to only 2 llamas, he would have arrived with no food in hand at all.

Two further points need to be emphasized here. First, many of the goods transported by caravan were not food. Vast quantities of cloth, clothing, and weapons were also carried by llama train. The amount of portage actually given to food cannot be ascertained with present information, but it would probably be an error to suppose that the army trains carried little but food with them. Second, even given that the porters and drovers in transit ate food from state storehouses, their consumption of stored rather than transported foodstuffs had no effect on the ratio of food eaten to that delivered (see Hassig 1985:28). We may take as an

illustration a report by Pedro Pizarro (1986 [1571]: ch. 15, pp. 97–98) that one man from Cajamarca told him he twice carried half an *hanega* of maize (about 21.8 kg) to Cuzco for the Inkas. Along the way, he was fed from goods stored for travelers on state business and was forbidden to touch his load. Given the figures cited above, he would have consumed in the round-trip more than four times the caloric value of the maize that he would have delivered. The transportation of this maize could not have been part of a system supplying subsistence support to the capital.

More generally, we may suppose that the goal was to transport food from any point A (e.g., storehouses) to point D (e.g., battle). The food eaten by the drovers or

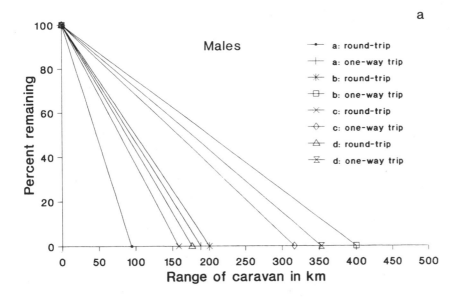

a

Fig. 5.5. Transport capabilities of human males and females under varying conditions. See Table 5.3 for key.

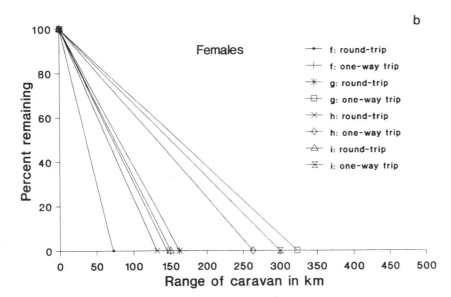

b

porters at any locations B and C along the way could have been more easily and efficiently shipped from those points B and C than from point A. From the perspective of supply, there would have been no point to ship the food from point A. The preferred Inka tactic of having local porters carry supplies from one end of their territory to the other did not make the transport system any more efficient than having a single train walk an entire trek. Its positive effects lay in spreading out the labor burden and reducing the physical breakdown of porters. The key point is that once the amount of food consumed in transport at normal rates exceeds that being shipped, the range of transport cannot be extended without degrading the personnel—an un-

desirable option for military ventures. One expedient, of course, would have been to eat the llamas themselves. This certainly would have extended the transport range of the army, given that the edible portion of a llama weighing 90 kg can satisfy the caloric needs of about 37 adult males for a day (Thomas 1973:112). Eating a supply train is a tactic of military emergency, however, and appears to have been viewed as such by the Inkas (Murra 1980 [1956]: 53).

The implication of this logistical situation is that regular provisioning of armies at a distance of more than a couple of hundred kilometers using llama caravans or human porters was an overwhelming, almost impossible task. Access to local resources was critical

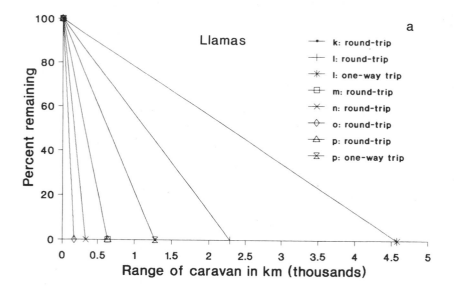

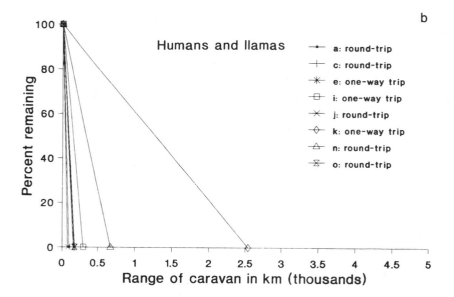

Fig. 5.6. Transport capabilities of llamas and humans under varying conditions. See Table 5.3 for key.

to avoid degrading the physical condition of the troops, porters, or animals. In an empire measuring 4,000 km from end to end, this situation created a pervasive regional demand for supplies. Of the options used by the Inkas in offensive warfare—living off the land, obtaining the cession of provisions before moving into new territory, and setting up a supply system with many local depots—only the last was viable once territory was taken. As early as the reign of Pachacutec, therefore, the importance of the storehouses grew as the options of foraging or living off the enemy's resources became less attractive.

Summary and Discussion

The conquests by the Inka military were a remarkable accomplishment, unparalleled in the Andes and seldom rivaled in the archaic world. In this chapter, elements of Inka military and logistical practice have been outlined to provide a context for explaining the planning of Inka facilities in the central sierra. From the information available, it appears likely that the immediate logistical needs of the military in securing newly won territories played a major role in the original configuration of the system. The location of the major provincial centers at natural points for communication along the length of the Andes and across to the coast or montaña emphasizes the importance of interregional movements of people, goods, and information. Present information suggests that facilitating intraregional administration was less important in the selection of locations for provincial centers (see Chapter 6).

The Inka conquest of the Upper Mantaro region exemplifies several fundamental elements of Inka military strategy. The annexation of much of the region through diplomacy illustrates an economic use of force, key to much of the imperial expansion. This strategy was coupled with reprisal, in the form of deportation for the northern Wanka (Xauxa?) groups who resisted, and evacuation of highland redoubts. This two-pronged approach conserved much of the human and natural resources of both the victors and the vanquished, so the state could make use of the productive capacities of the region with relative ease.

The military use of the Upper Mantaro region is consonant with either a territorial or a defense-in-depth strategy of occupation in the central sierra, given that it was focused on assisting campaigns conducted elsewhere in the empire. The long-term commitment of soldiers to the conquests in Ecuador and to a garrison at Willka Wamán gives some indication of the human costs of imperial military demands, even after the region's submission to Inka rule. Within the valley, the known Inka installations were used more for logistical support of armies on the road than for active defense of borderlands. None of the state settlements appears to have been designed or situated as a fortress, and Hatun Xauxa, the undefended provincial capital, was the most important settlement for Inka military activity. Several times in late prehistory this center hosted Inka armies of tens of thousands. The adjacent storehouses provided a ready supply of food and matériel for the military bivouacked on the valley floor. Because Hatun Xauxa was located at the mouth of the Río Mantaro gorge, it was a focal point for movement of personnel, supplies, and information both along the spine of the Andes and to the coast and montaña.

The Wankas served far afield in imperial armies and contributed leadership, personnel, and logistical support in the civil war, but the presence of Cañare, Chachapoya, and Llaguas mitmaqkuna in the midvalley raises questions as to the degree to which they were pacified. Whether these troops constituted an internal garrison or were part of an interior force intended to back up hard-point defenses along the eastern frontier cannot be resolved with present data. That the first was a realistic possibility, however, underscores the fragility of Inka control even in one of the most intensively integrated provinces of the empire.

In providing a framework for Inka logistics, I have made an effort in this discussion to evaluate realistically the difficulties entailed in supporting the sporadic, always laborious Andean warfare and the solutions attempted by the Inkas. It has been shown that Inka logistical capabilities were restricted, regardless of the labor invested. This limitation was especially notable at the ends of imperial control, where access to subsistence resources was not assured and goods could not be efficiently transported in. The imperial solution was to develop storage facilities distributed throughout the empire, but focused in the central sierra, that could be drawn upon regionally as needed. Given the limitations of Andean transport technology, this was an effective accommodation to the problem, but one that required tremendous inputs of energy and constant maintenance.

The Upper Mantaro region played a significant role in this program. The location of Hatun Xauxa along the main natural route through the Andes and at a cross-point both east and west, coupled with the productivity of the region, made the center a prime locale for bivouacking armies and housing other state personnel on the move. That the Inkas took singular advantage of this situation is apparent in the construction of the valley's extensive storage facilities (see Chapter 8). The volume and range of goods will be assessed subsequently, but a reasonable estimate of the amount of stockpiled foodstuffs suggests that they could have supported a force of 35,000 soldiers for about a year. In their 1558–61 depositions to the Audiencia Real, the Hatunxauxas and Lurinwankas reported having delivered 39 categories of goods to the Spaniards in support of their military and administrative efforts between 1533 and 1554; 32 of them could have conceivably been kept in state storehouses (see Espinoza Soriano 1971; Murra 1975:252, insert). It seems probable that these categories did not exhaust the kinds of materials kept in the facilities.

The range around Hatun Xauxa in which these goods could have been effectively used to support state activities can be assessed from two perspectives (Figs. 5.5–5.7). The first draws on the estimates of transport efficiencies described above, whereas the second relies on the spatial distribution of similar facilities in the

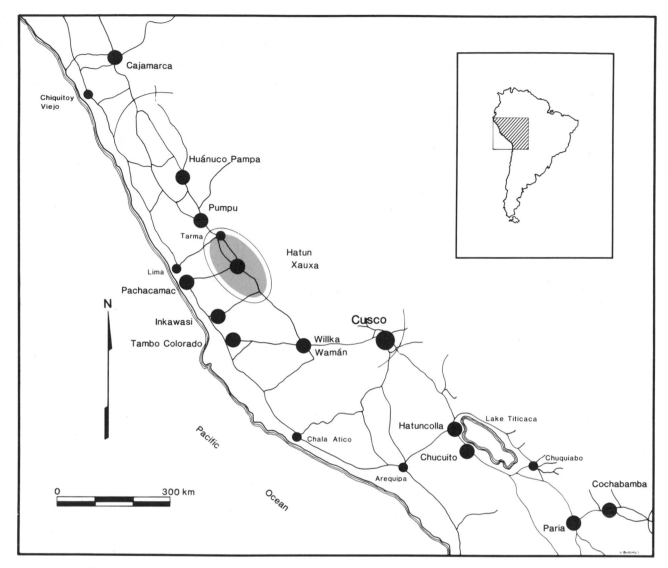

Fig. 5.7. Selected estimated ranges surrounding Hatun Xauxa that could have been supported with foodstuffs transported by humans and animals. Activity within the inner shaded area could have received foodstuffs under conditions *a*, the encircling shaded area under conditions *c*, and the arcs under conditions *m*. (Conditions are described in Table 5.3).

highlands. The estimated rates of consumption for food indicate that porters would have exhausted the food supplies that they could carry in a round-trip by traveling less than 200 km from home, which approximates the distance from Hatun Xauxa to the coast. Pumpu, the next major provincial center to the north, lay about 150 km away, and Huánuco Pampa was situated a similar distance beyond. In contrast, Willka Wamán, the next major center to the south, lay about 300 km away.

Use of llama caravans could have extended the transport range over that of human porters, because a drover and an assistant would have consumed approx-imately 1.6 percent of their 20 llamas' food (maize) load each day. This estimate assumes optimal use of animals and no transport of water, forage, or supplies other than foodstuffs. It is intriguing to observe, how-ever, that the first prestation to Francisco Pizarro in Hatun Xauxa in 1533 included 48,989 loads of grass and 321,354 loads of straw (Espinoza Soriano 1971; Murra 1975:252, insert).[19] Although these loads may not have been entirely used for food, that grass and straw were available in such quantities underscores the state's perceived need to stockpile fodder for pack ani-mals. The conquistadores' horses would have eaten fair quantities of these supplies, but it may also be assumed that the llama caravans placed at Spanish disposal would have consumed much larger amounts, likely carrying much along with them. It was noted above that a 50-50 mix of fodder and human food in a llama caravan would have limited its effective range to about 168 km, assuming a round-trip and 50 percent delivery. Small wonder, then, that the Inkas developed their tampu system such that some storehouses were found every 20 km or so along the road (see Chapter 6). It would have been exceedingly taxing to maintain supply for itinerant state armies with facilities any farther apart.

In sum, the demands of military campaigns and the constraints of logistics were pivotal to Inka imperial strategy. Several factors contributed to the need to develop redundant supply depots throughout the empire and to commit significant resources to transportation. Among them were the shift from offense to defense in military policies (i.e., a move toward territorial control), the empire's longitudinal shape, the severe Andean topography, and the limitations of transport technology. Under the circumstances, the Inkas achieved a remarkable degree of success, but the limits must always be kept in mind when assessing the nature of Inka statecraft.

6

The Imperial Infrastructure in the Central Sierra

During the 70 years of imperial occupation, the Inkas developed an internal network of facilities that formed an umbrella of state dominion over the native populace. In Chapter 5, I argued that the nature and location of military and logistical sites provide key measures of overall imperial strategy. The present chapter shifts attention to the administrative and supporting state facilities in the central Peruvian sierra to assess the nature of imperial rule in this region further. The scale, diversity, and ubiquity of these sites along the imperial highway (*qhapaq ñan*) linking Cuzco and Quito indicate that this region was among the most intensively integrated of the empire (Hyslop 1984:257). Along the length of the main road, the state built a chain of many of its most imposing provincial centers—Willka Wamán, Hatun Xauxa, Pumpu, Huánuco Pampa, Cajamarca, and Tumipampa (Fig. 5.1). Along with a number of sites along the central and southern Peruvian coasts, such as La Centinela and Tambo Colorado (both in the Chincha Valley) and Inkawasi (in the Cañete Valley), the most elaborate imperial administrative construction outside the Cuzco area is found in this sierra region. The imposition of state facilities produced a partially integrated pattern of state and subject settlements in the major valleys, characteristic of a direct or territorial approach to imperial rule. This pattern of imperial settlement is radically distinct from the patterns of the north coast of Peru or the entire empire from central Bolivia south, where large Inka centers are notably lacking.

Because of its location, relatively high populations, agricultural productivity, and potential for military threat, the central sierra was strategically key to maintaining the empire—a situation that the Inkas clearly recognized. By all accounts, the Upper Mantaro region was one of the most favored areas of the Inka domain. The best indication of the region's elevated status may be seen in Thupa Inka Yupanki's and Wascar's reported use of the provincial center of Hatun Xauxa as a prime seat of power, but the Inka presence is readily visible in the extensive archaeological remains distributed throughout the valley. Inka activities in the region were supported by at least 50 storage complexes and a series of strategically placed smaller settlements along the main roads and in subvalleys bordering the main Mantaro Valley (Fig. 6.1).

To set the context for the detailed discussion of the Upper Mantaro region's facilities, this chapter first considers the general character of major imperial facilities in the highlands. The principal sources for this material are the studies carried out by Morris and

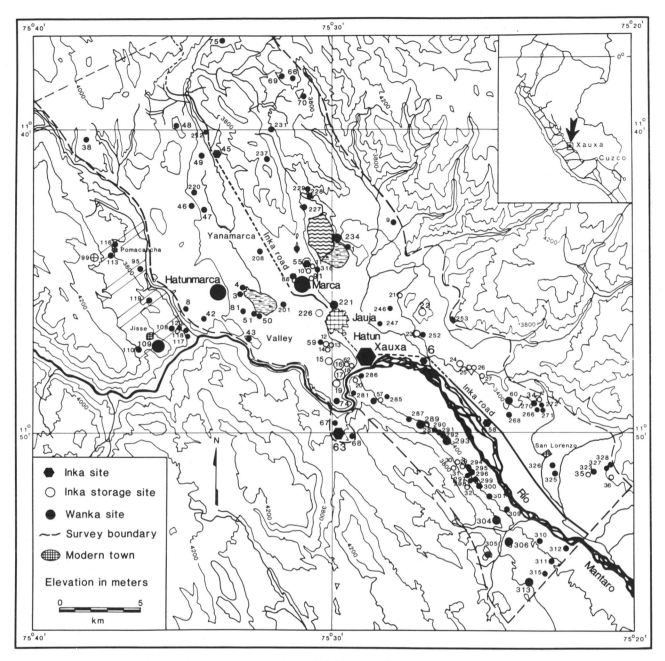

Fig. 6.1. Distribution of sites in the Upper Mantaro region during the Inka occupation.

Thompson in the Huánuco area (e.g., Morris 1967, 1971, 1972b; Morris and Thompson 1985); LeVine's (1985) comparative work in the Huánuco, Pumpu, Tarma, and Hatun Xauxa areas; Lavallée and Julien's (1983) study of Acos; and Parsons and Hastings's work in the Junín and Huasahuasi regions (e.g., Parsons and Hastings 1977; Hastings 1985). The discussion then evaluates the nature of activities at Hatun Xauxa, the layout of the regional road system, and the character of other state settlements in the region.

Economic and Political Considerations in Locating Imperial Installations

The preceding chapter outlined Inka military strategy, describing how shifts over time would have altered the demands placed on support facilities. As the tenor of Inka rule was transformed from conquest to consolidation, administrative and economic access to subject populations and resources potentially began to compete with military needs. The problems of security must have taken precedence sometimes, however, so that a balance had to be struck between provincial administration and imperial security. As was the case with the military facilities, the costs of transportation and, by extension, efficiency of communications underlay the distribution of many Inka administrative sites. Because of the mountainous topography, however, the Inkas could seldom locate centers in a way that would provide efficient movement both within and between regions. The main concentrations of population and productive resources in the central highlands were sometimes situated in warm eastern valleys, such as the Tarma and Huallaga drainages, that were not readily accessible from the easiest routes of transport along the Andes.

Given the strategic importance of the central sierra and the difficulties of bulk transportation, the Inkas appear to have opted for a high-control, high-investment strategy.[1] To make effective use of their labor and resources, the Inkas could consider three basic energetic options in situating these large-scale facilities: (1) minimizing the costs of movement between major nodes of state authority, thus emphasizing the interregional aspects of the support system; (2) minimizing the costs of conducting activities within provinces, thus emphasizing the importance of efficient rule within regions; or (3) optimizing between the two potentially competing alternatives. It should be noted here that the Inkas followed two other policies that helped balance the costs of production and transportation of goods: resettling populations and intensifying production. These two policies will be considered in Chapter 8.

The layout of the road system and settlements suggests that the weight of imperial planning came down heavily on the interregional side of the ledger. The Inka road system played a central role in consolidating imperial control. A marvel of bronze-age engineering, it integrated more than 30,000 km of roads into a single network (see Hyslop 1984).[2] The roads unified the empire physically and conceptually, providing a means for relatively rapid communication, personnel movement, and logistical support. In the northern half of Tawantinsuyu, the road system was structured around two north-south highways, one in the highlands and one on the coast (see Fig. 5.1). Numerous side roads joined the primary routes, and others crossed east into the montaña. Although much of the system followed traditional routes, many new sections were built or upgraded substantially. Under Inka rule, road and

bridge maintenance became a prime labor obligation of many communities. The technical skill reflected in construction was so high that many of the roads remain in use today (Thompson and Murra 1966:634). Several kinds of traffic were permitted to travel along the state's roads and to use its bridges. Military personnel and porters and llama caravans transporting bulk goods for the state were prime users, as were the nobility and various officials on state duty. At intervals of about 6 to 9 km, relay messengers (*chaski*) were stationed to carry information and small loads (Cieza 1967 [1533]: ch. 15, p. 47; see Hyslop 1984:296). Private citizens were also allowed to use the roads, although limitations were placed on their travel and tolls were charged at some bridges.

Several lines of evidence suggest that local logistical costs were secondary in importance to the grand-scale spatial organization of the support system. First, the main road through some highland provinces did not minimize the transport costs between the residences of subject populations and their places of labor at state centers. The highway runs over relatively flat terrain along a high route that bypassed much of the local population from which support was derived. It passes across the puna at the heads of major drainages in the Huánuco, Pumpu, and Tarma regions. Huánuco Pampa and Pumpu themselves lay in the puna, above the valley lands of the subject populations that contributed to their labor pool and supplied much of the foods, raw resources, and finished products on which the state centers depended. Some workers were required to travel several days to discharge duties at the provincial centers. A similar approach was applied in the location of Tarma. This relatively small provincial center, overseeing an eastern, warm-weather valley, was situated just below the edge of the puna at the juncture of the maize and tuber cultivation zones, not among the subject communities, which lay far below. Hatun Xauxa, the Mantaro Valley center, was founded at mouth of the Río Mantaro gorge, at the easiest transport and communications route to Pachacamac, on the coast. This position lies in the sector of the valley that had the lowest population, according to the last Inka census (Vega 1965 [1582]: 167), although the archaeological evidence shows that the neighboring Yanamarca Valley had been a major focus of population in the valley in Wanka II (see Chapter 4).

Second, because much of the population of these provinces was situated in the better agricultural lands, the road layout did not minimize the costs between the points of production and imperial centers. Many of the most productive lands in the central sierra lay in the valleys of the eastern slopes and the montaña. In 1562, peasants in the Huánuco region reported carrying crops or craft goods produced in the Huallaga drainage up to the puna centers of Huánuco Pampa and Pumpu, to Quito and Cuzco, or to wherever else the Inkas required (e.g., Ortiz de Zúñiga 1967 [1562]: 37, 47, 59; Ortiz de Zúñiga 1972 [1562]: 34, 55, 61; see Topic 1985:202). Similar reports can be found for the highlands of Ecuador (Salomon 1986:170), and the Chucuito societies of Lake Titicaca (Diez de San Miguel 1964 [1567]: 81, 92, 116). This apparent willingness to invest peasant labor in transportation implies neither that the Inkas were unaware of transport costs nor that they failed to take them into account in locating their facilities. To the contrary, the Inkas were willing to burden the subject population in an effort to minimize transportation distance and costs between provincial centers—that is, nodes of control in an interregional network (see Chapter 5).

The issue may be phrased in a slightly different way. In the Inka support system, transportation of goods occurred principally between two sets of points. The first was between the loci of production and storage, and the second, between the loci of storage and consumption. The imperial road and system of support facilities were designed to minimize transport costs in the latter instance, when availability of supplies was the prime issue. State concern did not lie primarily with minimizing or optimizing transportation of labor at the time of production (i.e., getting people from their home communities to points of work). Neither did it lie initially in transportation of goods from the fields or workshops to storage depots. Rather, state planners were apparently most interested in minimizing costs—and, not incidentally, maximizing central control—from points of storage to points of consumption. Many of the principal characteristics leading to the location of Inka facilities thus seem to be related to interprovincial planning, not local administration. This strategy makes a great deal of sense in a system designed initially from a military perspective, but less so in a system intended primarily to govern local territories efficiently.[3]

The interregional emphasis in locating principal centers does not imply that state planners showed no concern for efficiency of transport within regions, however. It is argued in Chapters 8 and 9 that the distribution of state farms, storage depots, and local communities in the Upper Mantaro reflects considerable interest in keeping transport costs low, while

maintaining state security. My point here is that decisions concerning the distribution of state facilities followed a hierarchy—interregional concerns first, intraregional interests second.

Planning and Functions of Imperial Centers

The major Inka centers and smaller way stations, or tampu, were built as planned settlements, intended to provide facilities for specific imperial activities.[4] It seems virtually assured that there was a systematic hierarchy to the functions of these imperial installations, given the Inka proclivity for planning. Documentary evidence and the diversity of architecture at the well-studied highland centers in Peru suggest that the functional sizes of the settlements probably corresponded well to their capacity to house a population. This issue deserves a separate study, however, and has yet be addressed in print. To what extent hierarchical levels in the state settlement system were nested spatially in macropatterns also remains to be studied (although see Hyslop 1990). For present purposes, it may be taken that the largest imperial centers between Cuzco and Quito—Willka Wamán, Hatun Xauxa, Pumpu, Huánuco Pampa, Cajamarca, and Tumipampa—probably stood at a roughly comparable level of functional importance in imperial administration. Below them was a series of smaller regional centers, such as Tarmatampu, which served a more restricted population and region and likely exhibited more-limited political, economic, and military functions (Morris 1972b; Hyslop 1985; LeVine 1985). At least a third level of smaller Inka settlements, such as Chacamarca and Tunsucancha, and a fourth level of way stations also dotted the road system. The salient features of the major settlements are described below.

Permanent personnel at the major centers were most directly concerned with administrative tasks, whether governing the local populations, overseeing craft production, or supporting personnel traveling on state duties. Even the major centers supported a surprisingly small permanent population. Although Huánuco Pampa could have housed between 10,000 and 15,000 people, the site's investigators estimate that only a fraction of this maximum was permanently resident (Morris and Thompson 1985:96). The remaining housing was primarily for temporary visitors passing through, discharging labor duties, or participating in grand ceremonies. This circumstance calls attention to a highly distinctive aspect of Inka provincial facilities—the imposed, artificial nature of the urbanism (Morris 1972b). Inka centers did not have many of the features typical of cities that developed in an indigenous context. Although they often employed local architectural techniques and materials, they seem to have lacked independent economic or residential activity. They were not home to a massed local populace, nor did they house independent craft or marketing sectors. Instead, much of the construction belongs to what Gasparini and Margolies (1980:195–305) call the architecture of power—buildings and spaces designed to carry out state business and to reinforce the image of the empire's might.

Morris (1972b) has observed that these centers, typically built in locations previously unoccupied by the local populations, were intrusive into the indigenous ethnic landscape. He notes that they introduced strikingly new architectural forms and settlement plans and employed a stylistically distinct array of material goods (see also Thompson 1967a). The centers shared a set of basic features of planning and architecture, although no two were precisely comparable in layout or details of execution. Site plans were organized around centrally located large plazas, usually trapezoidal in shape. Architectural sectors, often set off from one another by encircling compound walls, surrounded the open areas. These provided housing and work areas for the permanent and temporary residents of the facilities. Even disregarding comparison with the nucleated, labyrinthine communities of the sierra populace, the Inka settlements were models of spaciousness and planning.

The layout of some major centers appears to reflect an intense preoccupation with ceremony and concepts of sacred spatial relationships. The Inkas explicitly conceived of some provincial settlements as "New Cuzcos," built in the image of the sacred imperial capital. Among them were Inkawasi, in the Cañete Valley of Peru; Huánuco Pampa, in the central Peruvian sierra; and Tumipampa, in Ecuador (Hyslop 1984; Morris and Thompson 1985; Salomon 1986). Morris (1990) and Morris and Thompson (1985:72–73) have shown how broad architectural divisions within Huánuco Pampa could be interpreted to parallel the arrangement of sacred places (*wakas*) along *zeque* lines in the vicinity of Cuzco. As analyzed by Zuidema (1964), this complex system, which may have had spatial, social, astronomical, and religious components, seems to have played an important role in organizing state activities in time and space. Following Zuidema's

argument, the layout of Huánuco Pampa can be viewed as based on divisions into two, three, and four sectors.[5] Hyslop (1984) has shown a similar correspondence between the organizational principles used to lay out Inkawasi and the zeque system of sacred lines. Astronomical phenomena, such as the solar zenith and the Pleiades rise azimuth, also appear to have played a role in the orientation of architectural sectors and plazas. Drawing on present knowledge of the layout and activities at Cuzco, however, Morris (1990) suggests that the spatial divisions seem to have been primarily associated with social distinctions. The most important of these divisions were the upper (*hanan*) and lower (*hurin*) social groupings that pervaded Andean kinship and Inka governance.

As it did at Cuzco, the imperial highway took a southeast-to-northwest passage through the central plazas of Huánuco Pampa and Pumpu, and most likely Hatun Xauxa and Willka Wamán. Platform mounds in the shape of a truncated pyramid, called *usnu*, dominated the open spaces. In the central sierra, the usnu varied from the very elegant, dressed-stone masonry of Huánuco Pampa and Willka Wamán (González Carré et al. 1981) to the much simpler, smaller structures built of roughly shaped fieldstone at Pumpu and Hatun Xauxa. The space dedicated to the plazas could be immense. At Pumpu the central plaza was 295 m across the east side, 515 m along the north, 430 m along the south, and 450 m along the open west side (LeVine 1985:180). At Huánuco Pampa it measured 550 m by 350 m (Morris and Thompson 1985:58). LeVine (1985:458) has observed that the vast open areas at these two sites were roughly proportional to the sizes of the populations resident in the province.[6] Given the major role that ceremony played in Inka political relations (see Morris 1990), such vast spaces may have been designed to hold substantial fractions of the regional population at important occasions during the annual ceremonial cycle.

Within the large divisions of the settlements, the principal architectural elements included modular rectangular units and enclosed compounds. The most prevalent unit, called a *kancha,* was a rectangular, walled compound containing a number of one-room structures (Rowe 1944:24; Gasparini and Margolies 1980:181–93; Kendall 1974, 1976, 1985; Hyslop 1985:282–84, 1990:16–18). This form was repeated throughout Inka architecture, whether in the residential sectors of Cuzco-area settlements (e.g., Ollantaytambo and Chinchero) or in the provincial facilities along the road network. At residential communities, most kancha were used to house permanent residents. At provincial centers and tampu, they provided housing and craft quarters for full-time personnel and temporary visitors. Residential sectors of the centers and some tampu were also dedicated to housing the Sapa Inka and his retinue when they were passing through the region.

A second major architectural unit was the *kallanka*, a large rectangular building with an undivided interior space. One of the longer sides invariably opened onto a plaza. Kallanka appeared commonly in Inka centers, particularly the larger ones along the Cuzco-Quito road. Their principal functions were probably to house transient groups, such as the military, and to provide space for ceremonies (Gasparini and Margolies 1980:196–219). Because of their uneven distribution throughout the empire, Hyslop (1984:285) has suggested that they may well have been present primarily along roads with large transient populations, notably the road through the central sierra. Among the other principal architectural forms at major Inka centers were religious structures, such as the temples to the sun, and sequestered sectors devoted to the *aqllakuna*, young, reputedly beautiful virgins dedicated to service of the Inka emperor until given in marriage. Among their duties were brewing chicha (maize beer) and weaving cloth for the state. Their dual religious and craft obligations exemplify the multiple roles played by many state personnel in an administrative system that was only partially differentiated.

Most buildings at the provincial centers and tampu were built and maintained by the *mit'a* labor of local residents, so that the architecture varied substantially in size, number of rooms, quality of masonry, and building materials. In some cases the kancha covered as much as a city block, whereas in others they often were no more than 10 to 20 m on a side (Hyslop 1985:282). Use of the elegant cut-stone masonry for which Cuzco and nearby sites are famous is rare in provincial centers, the royal sector at Huánuco Pampa being the most notable exception in the central sierra. In most cases the architecture was built from locally available materials, especially the fieldstone used in pirka masonry. At coastal sites, such as Tambo Colorado and Inkawasi, the standard material was adobe.

Morris (1972b) has stressed the relative importance of interregional concerns and external ties in these settlements. As he observes, these concerns are exemplified by the concentration of storage facilities, intended principally to support traveling armies and short-term occupants, and by the high proportion of buildings given to temporary housing. The installations lacked important cemeteries and were often rapidly abandoned shortly after the Spanish conquest, further implying that their primary functions were to serve an interregional system. Even though the labor used in their construction and in their productive activities was mostly locally furnished, the centers were clearly organized as part of much larger system. Only where the Spaniards found the locations to be suited to their rather different imperial needs were the major Inka centers occupied well into the Colonial Period. In cases such as Jauja, the first Spanish capital of Peru, the European settlements were shadows of the grand Inka centers, often placed in locations marginal to the imperial facilities.

Distribution of Inka Settlements in the Upper Mantaro Region

Having set the broader context for the development and distribution of the major Inka facilities in the central sierra, the discussion may address the distribution of Inka settlements and the layout of the road system in the Upper Mantaro region. Several sources provide a list of the Inka installations along the royal roads of the central Andes, because the Spanish found it advantageous to use the extant roads, administrative centers, and way stations. The two most complete sources are the *Ordenanzas de Tambos* (Vaca de Castro 1908:442–46), prepared in 1543, and the list of Guaman Poma (1980 [1614]: /1084 [1094]–/1093 [1103], pp. 1000–1007), prepared about 70 years later. Both lists were affected by Spanish patterns of road use, and neither is fully comprehensive. Nonetheless, they allow us to trace the extent and positioning of the imperial facilities within and surrounding the Upper Mantaro region. This section of the discussion has drawn on the work of Hyslop (1984) and LeVine (1985) for information on documentary sources and discussion of the distribution of sites.

Vaca de Castro, in his report, named Hatun Xauxa as a tampu on the highland route from Cuzco to Ciudad de los Reyes (Lima). Between Hatun Xauxa and Willka Wamán—the major Inka installation on the road between the Mantaro Valley and Cuzco—the list of Vaca de Castro's tampu included Chupas, San Juan de la Victoria, Yangar, Marses, Parcos, Picoy, Aco, Llacaja Paraleanga, and Patan. Although Acostambo was the principal Inka settlement in Asto territory, neighboring the Wanka domain on the south, the remaining installations were smaller way stations. Hyslop (1984:277), in his study of the imperial road system, estimates that at least 1,000 and perhaps 2,000 similar tampu were established along the imperial roads. Spaced about a day's walk apart, they were intended primarily to lodge and provision itinerant state personnel. Auxiliary functions identified at various tampu included some ceramic manufacture, road control, mining, military support, coca exploitation, ceremonial activities, chaski duty, spinning, and even residence for local populations (Hyslop 1984:279–80).

The tampu Llacaja Paraleanga probably lay in the southernmost sector of Wanka Wamaní, about 8 km south of modern Huancayo, at modern Sapallanga (LeVine 1985:445). The early historical literature makes several references to this settlement, but no details are provided beyond its general location (see Regal 1936:54). Cieza (1984 [1551]: ch. 84, p. 242) used the term *Laxapalanga* to refer to the entire southern saya (here called Ananwanka) of the province. This term probably reflects the habit of early commentators to interchange district names, place names, and names of local lords.[7] The tampu was maintained in part by mitmaqkuna brought in from the Chucuito Urinsaya, whose lords recalled that they "had given Indians [to the Inka] to place as mitmaqkuna in Xauxa and in Llajapallanga" (Diez de San Miguel 1964 [1567]: 81).[8] By 1543 the *indios* in charge of maintaining the tampu had been assigned to doña Inés Muñoz, the wife of Francisco Martín de Alcantara (Vaca de Castro 1908 [1543]: 446). An additional location for a possible tampu lies in northern Huancayo's suburb of El Tambo (Browman 1970:242). Espinoza Soriano (1971: inset map) records a tampu just north of Huancayo that may correspond to this facility. At a distance of about 10 km north of Sapallanga, this site would have been appropriate for a small state installation, perhaps no more than a chaski post or a minimal tampu. Patan does not have a modern counterpart on modern maps of the region but was likely located at Maravilca, about halfway between modern Huancayo and Jauja (LeVine 1985). Guaman Poma's citation (see below) of Maray Bilca as a tampu in this location suggests that the name *Patan* was lost very early in the Colonial Period, but that the role of road station continued at a midvalley settlement (see also Cieza 1984 [1551]: ch. 84, p. 242).

The Spanish route from Cuzco to Lima turned west to the coast at Hatun Xauxa, over the Cordillera Occidental. Vaca de Castro's list of tampu on this section of the road included Chupayco, Pariacaca, Huarochirí,

Chondal, Natin, and ultimately Ciudad de los Reyes. Cieza (1967 [1553]: ch. 59, p. 196) described this pass effusively: "[T]hey say that Thupa Inka Yupanki conducted grand sacrifices and festivals in Pachacamac [and that], once they were done, he returned to Cuzco by a road that was built for him, that comes out at the Valley of Xauxa, that crosses through the snowy mountains of Pariacaca, that it is no small thing to see and to note its grandness and how many grand stairways it has."[9]

The tampu list of Guaman Poma (1980 [1614]: /1084 [1094]–/1093 [1103], pp. 1000–1007) differed somewhat from that of Vaca de Castro. Between Lima and Hatun Xauxa, Guaman Poma noted the following tampu: Cicaya, Chorrillo, Huarochiri, Pariacaca, and Xulca.[10] From Hatun Xauxa south to Willka Wamán, he listed an additional 11 tampu, the first 3 of which were Maray Bilca, Huancayo, and Aco. Xulcatambo, mentioned in Guaman Poma's list as the first tampu to the west of Hatun Xauxa, was not included by Vaca de Castro. Located along a lateral road to the coast, it has been identified and described archaeologically by UMARP personnel (cf. LeVine 1985:353–57).[11] Modern maps record at least three other small settlements named *tambo* (way station) to the west of Hatun Xauxa. Tambo (4,200 m) and Tambojasa (3,900 m) lie about 15 and 25 km west of the provincial center, respectively, and about 10 km south and hundreds of meters above the course of the Río Mantaro. They are in the general vicinity of the main route to the coast, but the precise relationship of the hamlets to the highway has yet to be verified. Almost 50 km upriver from Hatun Xauxa, at the confluence of the Río Huayhuay, lies the settlement named Tambopuquio. Its nature has not been examined archaeologically.

To the north of Hatun Xauxa, the imperial road to Pumpu and Huánuco Pampa was dotted with an additional series of tampu. In Vaca de Castro's report (1908 [1543]: 446), a marginal comment simply noted that the road to Huánuco and the City of the Frontier of the Chachapoyas parted from Xauxa. Guaman Poma (1980 [1614]: /1087 [1097], pp. 1003–4) provided more-specific information, listing eight tampu between Huánuco and Tarma, including the major installation at Pumpu. Although Tarma was the imperial center for the province of Tarma, which bordered Wanka Wamaní to the north, it was a modest center by Inka standards, covering only about 20 ha. Located in the upper Tarma drainage about 50 km north of Hatun Xauxa, the settlement was established at 3,600 m, far above the warm valley to the east (Parsons and Hastings 1977; Hastings 1985:157–62; LeVine 1985:330–50). This positioning underscores the Inka concern with interprovincial ties in locating their provincial centers. The sierra highway passed a few kilometers to the west of the tampu, a substantial hike up from the lush valley lands below, through the extensive hillside terraces that were almost surely of Inka construction.

Neither Vaca de Castro nor Guaman Poma listed any tampu between Tarma and Hatun Xauxa, but current maps record two small settlements, named Tambo and Tambopaccha, between the provincial centers and near vestiges of the Inka highway (LeVine 1985:444). Both hamlets lie just north of the little gorge that gives out onto the north end of the Yanamarca Valley, about 15 km north of Hatun Xauxa. An additional settlement, called Hacienda Tambo, lies 5 km south at the other end of the gorge. The archaeologically recorded site J45 is found at this spot; no more than a sherd scatter across half a hectare of farmland, it was likely a small roadside station (see "Road Stations," in the section "Auxiliary State Settlements," below).

The distribution of named Inka facilities east of Hatun Xauxa is less well defined than in the other three directions. One Inka road traversed the first range of the Cordillera Oriental and descended to Comas. Paved sections of the Inka highway are exposed in the modern roadbed on the way down to this montaña settlement, a coca-cultivating community occupied by the Wankas under Inka rule. Such place names as Tambo Muyoc and Tambillo occur on modern maps along the trails that connect the montaña to the Mantaro Valley (LeVine 1985:446).

Care should be taken not to accept all modern locations called tambo as formal state way stations, because hundreds of settlements in the region show evidence of Inka presence in the form of imperial pottery. The vagaries in the ways that distances were recognized by the Inkas and recorded by the early Spanish travelers make it difficult to use modern measures as a sufficient criterion for identifying which of the locations called tambo were actually Inka tampu. Ostensibly, tampu lay about a single day's walk apart (e.g., Zárate 1879 [1555]: 471), and major installations were separated by about a five- to six-day walk. In a review of distance measurements over the Inka road system, Hyslop (1984:294–303) describes the tremendous variation in the distances that could be traveled in a single day's walk. The chief Inka measurement, the *tupu*, was reported to be equivalent to varied distances recognized by the Spaniards. In general, the

tupu works out to about 1.5 leagues—that is, anywhere from 6.2 to 9.5 km (Hyslop 1984:297). The traditional Andean concept of a league, however, appears to have been more closely related to the distance that could be covered in an hour's walk than to a linear distance between locations.

Despite these problems, the spacing of state facilities along the Inka road in all directions from Hatun Xauxa seems to fit the historical descriptions of tampu locations fairly well. Between Hatun Xauxa and Acostambo, the provincial center to the south, lay the named tampu of Patan and Llacaja Paraleanga, with another possible tampu located at El Tambo. The first two small installations were situated 25 to 30 km apart, a distance that could have been easily covered in a day over the flat Mantaro Valley terrain, as LeVine (1985:445) observes. From Hatun Xauxa to Tarma is about 50 km, a distance that could be traversed in a day but would be more comfortably covered in two. The presence of one or two small Inka installations along this section of road therefore seems appropriate. To the west, Xulcatambo was the first tampu on the route to Pachacamac to be named in the available documentary sources. This site lies in the valley of the Río Cochas, about 50 km (9 leagues) from Hatun Xauxa. LeVine (1985:439) cites an unpublished report from 1638 in which chaski stationed at Xulca petitioned the Spanish authorities for back payment for mail service along the route to Hatun Xauxa. Given the relatively long distance between these two installations, it would not be surprising if another station was located along the way, such as those mentioned above.

Hatun Xauxa

Historical Descriptions

The ruins of Hatun Xauxa lie on the north bank of the Río Mantaro, where the river emerges from a narrow gorge onto a broad floodplain (Figs. 6.2 and 6.3). A few scattered building fragments and a reconstructed platform mound make up most of the architectural remnants, but immense piles of rubble throughout the site attest to the past existence of many more buildings. Even though its current state belies its imperial status, Hatun Xauxa must have been an impressive sight in the sixteenth century. The settlement figures prominently on virtually every early historical list of important Inka centers. The master Inka chronicler Cobo (1956 [1653]: vol. 2, bk. 2, ch. 32, p. 129) classed the center as one of the major Inka establishments in the sierra, as did Vaca de Castro (1908 [1543]: 442–46) and Guaman Poma (1980 [1614]: /1087 [1097], pp. 1003–4), among others.

Some accounts accorded Hatun Xauxa an importance far exceeding a dominant role in managing the region's affairs. Although Tumipampa is generally considered the most important state installation north of Cuzco, the Mantaro center was a prime node of imperial control in the sierra. Sarmiento (1960 [1572]: ch. 52, p. 257), among the most sober of the Inka historians, reported that a governor ruled the northern half of the empire from this center, during the reign of Thupa Yupanki: "This Inka had two general governors in all the land, called *suyuyoc apo;* one resided in Xauxa and the other in Tiwanaku, town of Kollasuyu."[12] Wascar, Thupa Yupanki's ill-fated grandson, similarly used the valley as a base of power in the last years before the Spanish invasion, according to Guaman Poma (1980 [1614]: /116 [116], p. 94): "From the Valley of Xauxa, [territory of the] Wanka Indians, said Inka [Wascar] governed and reigned."[13] From Guaman Poma's brief reference, it is not clear if Wascar's use of Hatun Xauxa resulted from his loss of control of the northern lands to Atawalpa, if it was simply a preferred site of power, or if its logistical position made it the most desirable location from which to base military operations during the civil war. Regardless of the motivations for the use of the installation, these accounts place the settlement in the uppermost echelons of provincial centers for at least the last 40 years of Inka rule.

To judge from the earliest Spanish descriptions, which universally acclaimed it as a vibrant urban center, Hatun Xauxa was built in a fashion appropriate to an elevated status. At the moment of Hernando Pizarro's foray into the valley on Sunday, March 16, 1533, the center was unwilling host to the newly victorious Ecuadorian army under Chalcuchima. Miguel de Estete (1917 [1532–33]: 96–97), who was on this reconnaissance mission to assess the lands and Inka strength, left the best initial account in his official diary:

The town of Xauxa is large and is in a very attractive valley, and the land is temperate: a strong river passes by one part of the town. It is abundant in supplies and herds; it is constructed in the manner of a town of Spain, very nucleated and with its streets well laid-out. In its view are many other towns subject to it, and the people were so numerous that it appeared to be that, of the town itself and the surrounding area, nothing similar has been seen in one town in the Indies,

because it seems to many Spaniards [who] saw it [that] more than one hundred thousand souls assembled daily in the principal plaza, and the markets and other plazas and streets of the same town were so full of people that its great multitude seemed a thing of wonder. There were men who had the duty of counting people there daily, to know those who came to serve the soldiers: others had the duty of watching everything that entered the town.[14]

In his letter to the Spanish authorities in Panama, Hernando Pizarro reported that the khipu kamayoq had counted off 35,000 soldiers among Chalcuchima's forces (Pizarro 1959 [1533]: 89). He also echoed Estete's description of the center's size and number of people present: "The plaza is large and one-quarter league long. . . . [I]t is true that there were over one hundred thousand souls. . . . This town of Xauxa is very fine and beautiful and [has] many flat exits [streets]" (p. 90).[15]

These descriptions should be taken with a grain of salt. A number of authors have pointed out that the Spanish perceptions of the size of the settlement may have been amplified by the presence of the bivouacked Inka army and the attendant festivities (e.g., La Lone 1982:303–4). The Europeans in fact complained that they could get nothing done for five days because of the debauchery of the local populace. The early commentators were also prone to express large numbers in an exaggerated form; "one hundred thousand" is undoubtedly a shorthand expression for several tens of thousands. Although the army and its entourage may have given the Spaniards a distorted view of the center's activity and size, Hatun Xauxa must still have been a substantial settlement.

A more detailed description of the architecture and activities can be found in Pedro de Cieza de León's travelogues. A soldier who passed through in 1547, Cieza (1984 [1551]: ch. 84, pp. 242–43) described the former capital expansively:

In all these parts there were great lodgings of the Inkas: although the principal ones were at the beginning of the valley in the part they call Xauxa: because there was a large enclosure, where there were strong and very excellent stone lodgings: and a house of women of the sun: and a very rich temple: and many storage structures full of all the things that could be had. Besides that, there was a large number of smiths, who worked large and small vessels of silver and gold for the service of the Inkas and [for] temple ornaments. There were more than eight thousand Indians for service of the temple, and of the palaces of the lords. All buildings were

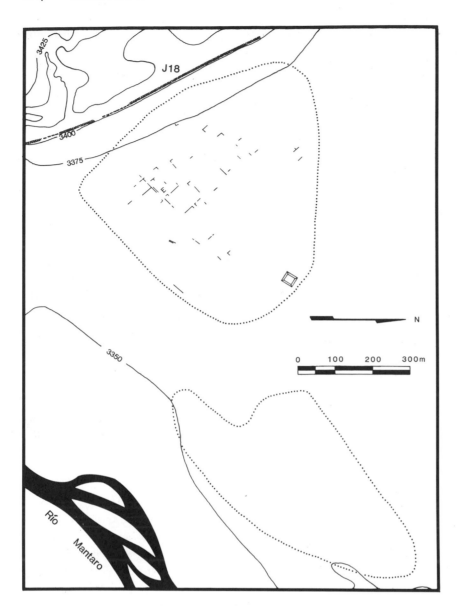

Fig. 6.2. Inka provincial center of Hatun Xauxa, at the mouth of the Río Mantaro. Modern Sausa overlies the archaeological site, which is delimited by dotted lines.

of stone. The tops of the houses and lodgings were immense beams, and for roofing they had long straw.[16]

Because Cieza saw the abandoned capital 15 years after the Inka collapse, his information on state activities must have been secondhand, probably drawn from local residents. Moreover, Hatun Xauxa had been extensively burned in 1533 and had long since ceased to function as a state center (see Sancho 1917 [1532–33]: 141), so one wonders how much of the grandeur of the capital was still preserved in the ruins.

Site Layout, Population, and Architecture
The documentary information makes it amply clear that Hatun Xauxa was a major Inka establishment and

informs us about some of the activities conducted there. In contrast, we know little about the center from archaeological research. The best, early modern reference to the ruins was written by Charles Wiener (1880:242–43), a traveler who described the layout briefly and illustrated a platform that is still present (Fig. 6.4):

The ruins of the plain, in the middle of which the huts of the hamlet of Tambo [Sausa] are erected today, are of constructions probably even grander than those of Tarmatambo ever were. By their general disposition, they appeared to have been of the same architectural order. One may note not only the remains of a royal residence, of palaces with grand galleries and vast courts, but also monuments constituting an

Fig. 6.3. View looking west at Hatun Xauxa. Rubble remains from destroyed Inka buildings, and storage structures line the hillslopes above the center. (Photo courtesy of Servicio Aerofotográfico Nacional, Lima, Peru [#0-1309])

important sanctuary. The center is formed by a platform similar to the one we have seen at Huamachuco, and on which, as one might have expected, the Spaniards have erected a chapel even more dilapidated than the ruins of the shrine over which it was built.[17]

Wiener, among others, erroneously identified the storage complexes above the center as habitation zones, an error that Morris (1967:147–52) corrected (see also Horkheimer 1951:11; Parsons and Hastings n.d. [1975–76]). The presence of massed storehouses on the hills to the west has led some researchers to the mistaken attribution of the upper (storage) and lower (main center) architectural zones to the hanan and hurin sociopolitical divisions. It has also been erroneously suggested that the upper sector may have been a

pre-Inka village (García 1942:97; Guzmán Ladrón 1959:248). The site has been described briefly by a number of professional scholars in the twentieth century, but virtually no investigations into its internal organization were ever undertaken (see García 1942: 97; Porras Barrenechea 1950; Guzmán Ladrón 1959: 248; Morris 1967:167; Browman 1970:265; Parsons and Hastings 1977:49–51; Matos Mendieta and Parsons 1979:168–70). Even the Junín survey project of 1975–76 recorded only the location, general size, and condition of surface remains (Parsons and Hastings 1977:49–51), because the extensiveness of the project precluded more-detailed study.

The present research into the plan and activities at Hatun Xauxa was severely hampered by the presence of modern Sausa over the ruins and by the badly deteri-

Fig. 6.4. Sketch of the platform mound (usnu) at Hatun Xauxa, by Charles Wiener (1880:243).

orated condition of the visible site. A detailed study comparable to studies conducted at other Inka centers was therefore not feasible.[18] The present research focused on determining the nature and organization of the basic activities in the areas accessible to research. A two-stage research program was adopted to address the problem. The intent was first to map the site and to study the standing architecture. The site was then surface-collected, based on a site stratification derived from distribution of visible architectural remains. Excavation was ruled out at this stage because adequate time and personnel were lacking and because the cuts for new houses in modern Sausa indicate that the depth of the deposit may not exceed 30 to 40 cm in many places. The soil has been turned over many times for agriculture, so a surface collection in these areas should have yielded essentially the same material as a shallow excavation.

Mapping of Hatun Xauxa was unfortunately expedited by the paucity of visible structural remains. The destruction of the capital has been a long-term affair, beginning in 1533. Anticipating a withdrawal from Hatun Xauxa, Quisquis's retreating army sought to render it useless to the invading Spaniards by burning the main facilities and storehouses. Pedro Sancho de la Hoz (1917 [1532–33]: 141), a witness to the event, described the action: "[The Inka military leaders] had sent those six hundred men to finish burning the city of [Hatun] Xauxa, having already burned the other half seven or eight days earlier, and then they burned a large building that was on the plaza and other things in the view of the people of the city along with a great deal of cloth and maize, so that the Spaniards did not benefit."[19] The destruction prompted the Spaniards to move their first capital about 5 km north to the location of modern Jauja, rather than use the Inka center (see also Pizarro 1986 [1571]: ch. 17, pp. 113–14). Recent construction of the village of Sausa over the archaeological site is rapidly advancing the job begun in 1533.

The ruins of the site are divided into two sectors (Fig. 6.2), only the western of which contains any standing architecture (Fig. 6.5). The remainder of the surface materials consists of massive piles of rubble interspersed among agricultural fields and among the buildings of modern Sausa. The ceramic deposit used to define the limits of Hatun Xauxa covers 48.4 ha— 31.1 ha in the north sector and 17.3 ha in the south. With the early destruction and the modern rebuilding, only 14 clearly definable building fragments and the usnu are now preserved above ground surface. The buildings are concentrated in a small zone in the center of the northern sector, about 300 m west of the platform. Not one building is complete, and most are represented only by fragmentary wall sections. A few old terrace support walls are also scattered throughout the site, although their association with the Inka occupation is problematic.

The relatively small size of Hatun Xauxa belies its apparent importance as the capital of a populous prov-

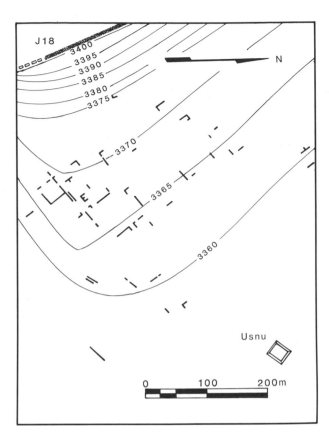

Fig. 6.5. Distribution of wall remnants at Hatun Xauxa.

persal of regional authority. It seems likely that a high proportion of the populace was core state personnel, not temporary laborers. By having access to a large population in the immediate vicinity, the Inkas need not have housed corvée workers but could have conscripted them from their home communities on a daily basis. Because this tactic would have significantly reduced the need for a capacious center, the number of state personnel at Hatun Xauxa may have been comparable to that at Pumpu and perhaps even at Huánuco Pampa. The high number of subject sites with state ceramics and state-inspired architecture also suggests that the Inkas may have been delegating authority extensively in the area. Historical evidence on the Late Horizon political organization corroborates this interpretation to a large degree (see Chapter 7).

The surface remains at Hatun Xauxa are insufficient for reconstructing even the best-preserved area in detail, so the precise organization of the architectural plan cannot be determined. All preserved structures were rectilinear and were laid out in the same orientation, roughly 54° to 144° from magnetic north. Although the preserved walls lie in rough conformity with the plan of Sausa, it is unclear whether the site was originally laid out in this form. Possibly only the walls that fit the preferred Colonial rectilinear layout were left standing. As was noted earlier, planned Inka settlements differed in layout throughout the empire, according to a variety of considerations, such as topography. The preferred plans of other major provincial centers often were not rectilinear but frequently exhibited trapezoidal central spaces, especially where topography did not constrain layout. At present, even this basic element of organization cannot be determined for Hatun Xauxa.

Neither can the size of the central plaza be estimated accurately with present information. Hernando Pizarro's informal description of the plaza as one-quarter of a league long yields an estimate of about 1.0 to 1.5 km on at least one side—that is, two to three times the length of the maximal dimensions of the plazas at Huánuco Pampa and Pumpu. Although this measure would make the plaza the largest in the central sierra, LeVine (1985:315–16) suggests that the estimate may not be excessive. If the space were meant to be proportional to the size of the native population, as she suggests, a plaza almost four times the size of that at Huánuco Pampa (19 ha) would have been appropriate. LeVine estimates that the open area covered 50 ha but terms this figure an educated guess, because the eastern and northern limits cannot be defined on the

ince and its critical logistical position. Architectural deterioration has made it extremely difficult to estimate the size of the resident population accurately. Morris and Thompson (1985:96) have estimated that the architectural zones of Huánuco Pampa, which covered about 90 ha, could have easily housed 10,000 to 15,000 people. As they point out, however, much of that population was probably transient personnel serving rotating corvée duties. If the residential density of Hatun Xauxa can be assumed to be roughly equivalent to that of Huánuco Pampa, it may be reasonable to estimate that 5,300 to 8,000 people were housed permanently at Hatun Xauxa. An alternative approach, in which the population density is assumed to be comparable to that of the region's Wanka III settlements (150 people/ha), puts the site's potential population in the same range—6,990. For purposes of the present analysis, these figures have been rounded to 7,000.

The apparent small size of the center, relative to the size of Huánuco Pampa, may be attributed to two factors: housing of support personnel elsewhere and dis-

Fig. 6.6. Usnu in the main plaza at Hatun Xauxa, looking west. A small modern chapel sits atop the structure.

Fig. 6.7. Section of southeastern face of the usnu at Hatun Xauxa, showing original (right-hand three-quarters) and reconstructed (left-hand quarter) areas.

basis of the present surface architectural or artifactual remains.

The platform mound within the plaza almost certainly dates to the Inka occupation, even though its surface has been badly disturbed (Fig. 6.6). This structure, which measures about 28 by 32 m on a side and stands to a maximum height of 2.7 m, retains only small segments of pirka wall from the original (Fig. 6.7). García (1942:97) has reported that the "usnu [was] supported by thick walls of polygonal stones and granite corners."[20] Either the platform has been rebuilt since his visit or García exercised some literary license, because the present structure exhibits neither of those features. Much of the platform has been re-

Fig. 6.8. Section of pirka (fieldstone) wall at Hatun Xauxa, with series of trapezoidal niches in the imperial style.

built, and a small chapel stands atop it; neither the corners nor the stairway of the platform is original. Although no excavations were conducted in the structure, it appears to have a rock-and-earth core, with a pirka facing around the exterior. The tops of some pirka sections are smoothly finished, suggesting that the modern height conforms fairly closely to that of the original platform. The facing measures about 0.70 m in cross section, and there is no surface evidence of a rock floor on top of the platform.

Similar usnu dominate the central plazas of Huánuco Pampa and Pumpu. The first of these was an elegant, two-tiered structure built of finely dressed stone in the center of a vast open space; at the base it measured 32 by 48 m (Morris and Thompson 1985:59). At Pumpu the usnu was far smaller—28 m north-south by 18 m east-west at the base—and was built of pirka (Thompson 1968b; LeVine 1985:182).[21] At both highland centers the platform lies in a plaza, separated from elite architecture by an open space. The usnu was apparently a focus of public ceremony, and the nearby buildings may have been for elite residence (Thompson 1968c:68; Morris and Thompson 1985). The layout at Hatun Xauxa is comparable to that of

Pumpu, in that most of the preserved architecture is concentrated in a small area slightly removed to the west. The preservation of walls implies that the architecture in this sector was superior to that found elsewhere in the center, as one would expect in an elite structure. Concentration of high-quality ceramics in the area tends to corroborate this inference (see "Spatial Segregation of Activities," in the section "Analyses of Surface Materials," below).

Assessing the planning and functions of the remaining structures is difficult, although some clues can be gleaned from the architectural remains. All preserved structures at Hatun Xauxa were built of local yellowish limestone and variously colored river cobbles, set in a mud-and-rock mortar (Fig. 6.8). The walls presented rough faces to the interior and the exterior, separated by a core of small rocks and mud mortar (Fig. 6.9). Neither the interior nor the exterior face on any preserved building was smoothly finished. Although rocks were often trimmed roughly, particularly for corners, no effort was made to dress them carefully, perhaps because of the use of plaster over the surface. The rocks were not laid in neat rows in any preserved wall section but were laid with their longest dimen-

Fig. 6.9. Cross section of wall at Hatun Xauxa.

tor, 25.6 m long, contains seven well-preserved niches (Fig. 6.10), each lined with shale and capped with a single, carefully shaped lintel stone. A row of five niches in a wall fragment 22.4 m long on the southeast part of the northern sector displays similar dimensions and masonry. No other niches are fully preserved.

This style of construction, using fieldstone and mud mortar, is common in local and Inka architecture in the highlands. None of the standing walls evinces the close-fitting, polygonal, cut-stone masonry found in some other imperial Inka architecture—a somewhat surprising finding, given that cut-stone work is found at Huánuco Pampa (Morris and Thompson 1985) and perhaps near Huancayo (Horkheimer 1951:15; Browman 1970:23). It must be emphasized, however, that the more elegant style is characteristic of only a small portion of Inka public and elite architecture and is not found in lower-status domestic or storage buildings, where pirka and sod dominate (see Rowe 1946:222–

Fig. 6.10. Niche in Inka wall in central preserved architecture sector at Hatun Xauxa (detail of wall in Fig. 6.8).

sions horizontal, giving the walls a coursed appearance. The maximum dimensions of the rocks range from about 30 to 80 cm, with a mode toward the lower end of the continuum. This estimate should be taken as a rough one, because no systematic measurements were taken.

Wall thicknesses of 0.55 to 1.10 m ($\bar{X}$ = 0.79 m; SD = 0.14 m; N = 15) lend the buildings a massiveness not found at any other site in the region. The maximum height of preserved wall is slightly less than 3.0 m, and no wall remains standing to a level at which the roof would have been attached. Although no ledges for beams remain in place nor are any tenons preserved, Cieza's comments (see the section "Historical Descriptions," above) imply that the roofs were thatched. Trapezoidal niches, found in imperial architecture throughout the empire, are preserved in three walls only; it is not clear if these were building or compound walls. One wall section in the central sec-

23; Gasparini and Margolies 1980). It is possible that excavations at Hatun Xauxa would uncover remains of cut-stone masonry, but at present there is no evidence to this effect at the site.

Despite the apparent inelegance of the standing architecture at Hatun Xauxa, it contrasted markedly with the indigenous structures. Wanka buildings were typically circular in plan, grouped into irregular compounds, and much less substantial (see Chapters 4 and 9). Although efforts were made to present flat rock surfaces on both wall faces to give a smooth finish, especially in elite compounds, the effect was never elegant. Even the pirka Inka architecture thus differed from the local in structure and compound plan, size of buildings, and massiveness of construction.

Analyses of Surface Materials

In an effort to assess the nature of the Inka occupation of Hatun Xauxa more thoroughly, four issues were addressed through analysis of surface collections:[22] (1) determination of the Inka settlement as new or imposed on a prior occupation, (2) spatial segregation of activities at the center, (3) the presence of craft specialists, and (4) the presence of a newly founded, associated Wanka residential area.

HATUN XAUXA AS A NEW SETTLEMENT The selection of a previously extant town as the base of state power or the choice of a new site had a direct bearing on the state policy of separation of state and local powers in the region. Evaluating the possibility that Hatun Xauxa was a new settlement required determining if Wanka ceramics and architecture were distributed throughout the site. It was expected that a newly founded Inka settlement would show no evidence of local occupation. Conversely, construction of the center in a previously occupied zone should result in mixture of Inka and subject pottery in the same surface collections, because it would not be expected that the relatively brief Inka occupation could have eliminated all surface traces of an earlier settlement.

The surface collections and shallow cultural deposit (30 to 40 cm) showed that the Inka center was founded in a location that had not been occupied during the Wanka II phase. Virtually no ceramics attributable to the Wankas were among the sherds recovered.[23] Those recovered were found in 14 of 16 collections and may have resulted from a light post-1533 occupation. A small Early Intermediate Period–Middle Horizon component, covering about 5 ha, was recovered from the north end of the northern sector. This component

agrees with LeBlanc's (1981) finding that sites that were occupied during the Early Intermediate Period–Middle Horizon and Wanka I were abandoned systematically during the Wanka II phase and then reoccupied selectively. Typically, such sites were found along the lower flanks of the hills lining the valley floor. They were adjacent to prime lands for agriculture and were readily accessible to foot traffic.

SPATIAL SEGREGATION OF ACTIVITIES It was expected that an elite residential zone would be present, characterized by high-quality masonry, a central location, and a dense ceramic assemblage with relatively high proportions of fine-quality domestic pottery. Similarly, a religious enclave should also have been centrally located. The ceramic assemblage associated with these areas should contain a relatively high proportion of fine-quality small vessels, including domestic and ceremonial types, such as plates for offerings (Morris 1966, 1971). Such a zone might also be characterized by evidence of spinning and weaving, such as concentrations of spindle whorls, because the aqllakuna, whom Cieza mentioned as being present, reportedly wove for the state (Morris 1974:57). Distinguishing a religious sector from an administrative elite area was considered difficult, however, because of the ceremonial roles of governmental officials. It was considered likely that the principal distinguishing characteristic would be disproportionate evidence for craft activity in the religious sector. It was also considered possible that a housing area for transient military or corvée personnel might be present, characterized by large buildings peripheral to the center of the site. The ceramic assemblage, if present, should have been dominated by utilitarian vessels used for food preparation, serving, and storage; they should have been almost exclusively Incaic in style, particularly the storage vessels. It was anticipated that few fine-quality plates or bowls would be recovered.

The variable density of ceramics recovered in the surface collections showed differential use of the areas within the site. Densities within strata varied from 0.38 to 7.94 sherds/m². As is shown in Figure 6.11, the greatest concentrations occurred where they might have been expected, in the strata containing the preserved architecture, especially stratum 1B and immediately adjacent collections in strata 1A, 1C, and 2A. It should be observed that the samples from strata 4 and 5 (collections J5=13 and J5=17) may be misleading, because the fields randomly selected for collection seemed to contain an unusually high concentration of

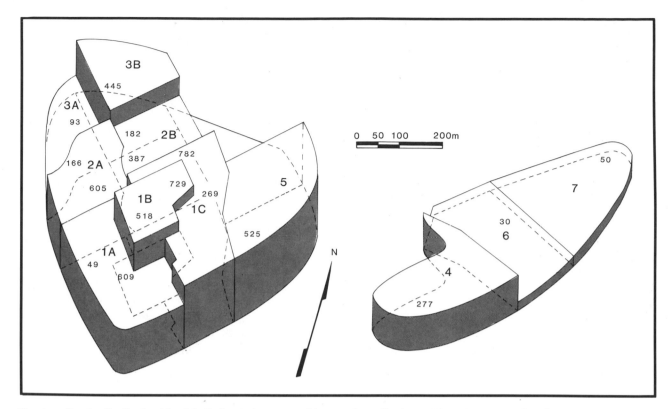

Fig. 6.11. Density distribution (sherds/m²) of ceramics recovered from surface collections at Hatun Xauxa. Heights of strata are proportional to mean densities of ceramics recovered in surface collections. Small numerals indicate locations and numbers of diagnostic sherds recovered from collection circles of 10 m in diameter.

pottery for their respective strata. Nonetheless, the occurrence of relatively dense ceramic scatters in these areas did reflect some concentrated activity.

The variable density of surface ceramics can probably be attributed to either of two causes. First, the Inkas designed their centers around plazas. The concentration of pottery in areas of preserved architecture may partially reflect use of ceramics in or adjacent to buildings, rather than in plazas. Second, the standing architecture may be a zone of permanent elite residence, which may be expected to have contained heavier depositions of pottery than the areas used by military, corvée laborers, or itinerant state personnel, who were present on a seasonal or intermittent schedule.[24]

The distributions of functional categories within the total Inka assemblage also reflected differential use of space within the center. It was assumed that a difference of proportions of certain shapes of vessels would reflect differing activities. Ceramics were therefore grouped into categories of flared-rim jars (constricted and open-mouth) and small domestic vessels (cooking and serving pots, bowls, and plates; see Figs. A.1–

A.13, in the Appendix). As is shown in Table 6.1, there was a significant variation in the distribution of these gross categories. The ratio ranged from 1.64 : 1 (stratum 6) to 10.25 : 1 (stratum 1C). A chi-square test for the randomness of the distribution of these two categories across the site was significant at $p = .05$ ($p < .001$). The heaviest concentrations of flared-rim jars occurred in the central portion of the western sector, particularly in the area of preserved architecture.

The distribution of the flared-rim jars alone evinced a similar pattern. Each stratum's jars were divided into two classes: those with rim diameters greater than the mean (26 cm or greater) and those with smaller than mean diameters (25 cm or less).[25] The null hypothesis that the two ranges of jar sizes were proportionally distributed among strata was rejected at the $p = .05$ level of significance (.01 $< p <$ .02). Inspection of Table 6.2 shows that the differences in distribution are attributable to an east-west dichotomy. This conclusion is reinforced by the high proportions of smaller jars in the collections from the eastern strata (4, 6, and 7) with quantities too low to be included in the test.

Table 6.1. Chi-square Test for Distribution of Flared-Rim Jars and Small Domestic Vessels at Hatun Xauxa (J5), by Surface Collection

Collection stratum	Flared-rim jars	Pots, bowls, plates	Total
1A (J5=5, 6)	523 (518.2)	66 (70.8)	589
1B (J5=2, 3)	1,042 (1,040.8)	141 (142.2)	1,183
1C (J5=1, 4)	861 (831.4)	84 (113.6)	945
2A (J5=8, 9)	60 (615.0)	90 (84.0)	699
2B (J5=7, 10)	426 (423.2)	55 (57.8)	481
3A (J5=11)	70 (76.5)	17 (10.5)	87
3B (J5=12)	382 (363.4)	31 (49.6)	413
4 (J5=13)	205 (207.6)	31 (28.4)	236
5 (J5=17)	381 (407.4)	82 (55.6)	463
6 (J5=14)	18 (25.5)	11 (3.5)	29
7 (J5=15)	22 (29.9)	12 (4.1)	34
Total	4,539	620	5,159

H_0: The two categories of vessels were randomly distributed across the sampling strata.

$$\chi^2 = \sum \frac{f_o^2}{f_e} - N = 5{,}231.40 - 5{,}159 = 72.40;\ df = 10;\ p < .001.$$

Note: Expected values are given in parentheses.

In neither data set, however, was there a strong degree of association between the collection stratum and the kinds of vessels recovered. A τ_a coefficient of .01 may be calculated for Table 6.1 (see Thomas 1986: 423–26), when the collection stratum is treated as the independent variable and the two vessel categories as the dependent variable. Applied to Table 6.2 data, the same statistic yields a stronger but still very weak association ($\tau_a = .09$) between collection stratum (independent) and size categories of flared-rim jars (dependent). To put these statistics in more-concrete terms, knowing the location of the collection provided little information about composition of its ceramic assemblage.

With the caveat of the low measures of association

being kept in mind, the pattern elicited from these distributions was as follows: (1) The western sector had a higher density of sherds overall than the eastern sector. (2) The central area in the west, with standing architecture, had the densest concentration of any part of the site. (3) The central area in the west sector (strata 1B, 1C, 2A, 2B) had a higher proportion of jars, particularly large storage jars, than the eastern sector (strata 4, 6, 7) and the peripheral strata in the western sector (strata 1A, 3A, 3B, 5). (4) The distribution of two infrequent vessel forms—an incurved bowl and high-necked jars—underscored these distinctions; both forms, found only in the central strata of the western sector, were characteristically small and finely made and were likely reserved for elite consumption.

To judge from these data, it may be tentatively proposed that stratum 1C, with the preserved architecture, was a zone of elite residence. The high-quality masonry and dense pottery deposit, including elite

Table 6.2. Chi-square Test for Distribution of Size Categories of Flared-Rim Jars at Hatun Xauxa (J5), by Surface Collection

Collection stratum[a]	Smaller than mean diameter (≤ 25 cm)	Greater than mean diameter (≥ 26 cm)	Total
1A (J5=5, 6)	10 (8.1)	5 (6.9)	15
1B (J5=2, 3)	23 (23.3)	20 (19.7)	43
1C (J5=1, 4)	20 (22.7)	22 (19.3)	42
2A (J5=8, 9)	14 (14.6)	13 (12.4)	27
2B (J5=7, 10)	3 (8.7)	13 (7.3)	16
3B (J5=12)	6 (5.4)	4 (4.6)	10
5 (J5=17)	23 (16.2)	7 (13.8)	30
Total	99	84	183

H_0: The two size categories of flared-rim jars were randomly distributed across the sampling strata.

$$\chi^2 = \sum \frac{f_o^2}{f_e} - N = 199.26 - 183 = 16.26;\ df = 6;\ .01 < p < .02.$$

Note: Expected values are given in parentheses.
[a]Strata 3A, 4, 6, and 7 were not included in the test, because of the small size of the collections of flared-rim jars. Stratum 3A (J5=11): 1 jar smaller than mean diameter, 0 greater than mean diameter. Stratum 4 (J5=13): 10 smaller, 2 greater. Stratum 6 (J5=14): 1 smaller, 0 greater. Stratum 7 (J5=15): 4 smaller, 0 greater.

forms (e.g., finely painted modeled plates), likely indicate habitation of permanent state personnel. The concentrations of large storage jars in adjacent strata 1B and 2B suggest that these areas may have housed goods used by the centrally located elites. The proximity of this area to the usnu may also indicate elite or religious residence.

Because of the poor condition of the architecture, isolating areas of temporary housing for military or corvée personnel has proved difficult. Three lines of evidence suggest that the eastern sector might have been reserved for this function, however. First, the dislocation of the area from the core of the center seemed to be analogous to the segregation of elite and non-elite sectors at Huánuco Pampa. Second, the low pottery frequency suggested lighter use of the eastern sector than the western. If personnel were stationed only intermittently on state business, the lighter use should have produced less broken pottery than permanent residence. Third, the extremely low density of large jars and the high proportion of small vessels suggested that food was consumed there, not stored. The second and third features also appeared to fit the pattern at Huánuco Pampa, where excavations in a kallanka yielded virtually no artifacts. The differential preservation of architecture and distribution of pottery thus suggested that activities were spatially restricted at the Inka center and that the area to the west of the usnu was the focus of most concentrated elite activity. Whether this usage plan corresponds to that of the elite compound described by Cieza is still open to question.

These conclusions, however reasonable, must be drawn with care. Jones et al. (1983) have pointed out that a strong relationship often exists in archaeological assemblages between the diversity of categories and the frequency of artifacts in those categories (see also Thomas 1983:425–31). In analysis of assemblages from surface collections and excavations, these researchers have shown that much of the assemblage variation that is typically attributed to the breadth of activities at particular sites is statistically attributable to the size of the collection. This problem is apparent in the Inka rim assemblages from Hatun Xauxa. Regression of the logarithm of category frequency (count of rim types; see D'Altroy 1981:373–77) against the log of the artifact frequency (rim counts) yields $r = .8898$ (range of $N = 2$–75; $S_{\hat{y}} = 0.1206$). That is, about 79 percent of the variability in diversity is explicable by sample size alone.[26] This relationship, graphed in Figure 6.12, is clearly log-linear. Much of the residual variance lies in the lower end of the graph,

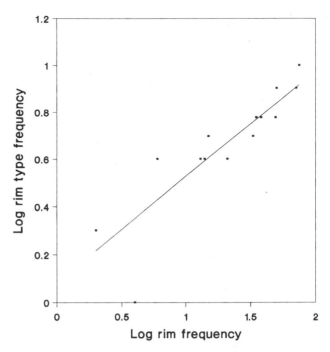

Fig. 6.12. Scatterplot of log of rim frequency against log of rim type frequency at Hatun Xauxa. $R^2 = .7917$; y-intercept $= 0.0825$.

although only one collection, with all four rims being from flared-rim jars, was a real outlier ($J_5 = 15$) from the east end of the site. It is intriguing to note that if the two smallest collections are removed from the plot, the remaining points display a curvilinear relationship. That is, diversity of activity increases at a faster rate than expected as the collections get larger.

These results imply that the diversity of activity at any location at Hatun Xauxa was not solely a direct function of intensity of activity. Assuming that the Inkas considered all areas to have been part of the site for essentially the same length of time, diversity of activity cannot be accounted for just by relative permanence of occupation. This statement may be taken in either of two ways. First, we may conclude that the area of standing architecture was both the most intensively occupied area and the location of the most diverse kinds of activities, but we must recognize that these are largely measures of essentially the same thing. Second, the less intensively occupied an area, the more likely it was to be specialized, as far as use of Inka ceramics was concerned.[27]

CRAFT SPECIALIZATION   It was considered likely that full- or part-time craft specialists manufactured a range of products in restricted areas. As discussed in

Chapter 8, the state production system was based in part on use of attached craft specialists resident at provincial centers. Both Cieza and Estete (1917 [1532–33]: 97) recorded that metalsmiths and carpenters produced goods at Hatun Xauxa, but there were no reports of the major industries of textile weaving or ceramic production. Textile manufacturing could potentially be identified through concentrations of spindle whorls or bone implements (Morris 1974), and metal slag or crucibles could be used to identify areas of metallurgy. Similarly, quantities of vitrified ceramics or dumps of potsherds could be interpreted as reflecting pottery manufacture. Ceramics were often made for the state at specialized manufacturing centers, where they could be closely controlled for quality, style, and morphology (Chapter 8). Isolation of weaving, metalworking, or potmaking areas at Hatun Xauxa would provide direct evidence of state economic organization in the province.

Surprisingly, no evidence was recovered in any of the surface collections to indicate that craft-specialized activity was pursued at Hatun Xauxa. The measurement of rim sherd frequency against rim type frequency has already provided one line of evidence in this regard. Similarly, only two ceramic spindle whorls, no metalworking tools or products, and no vitrified sherds were found. Because of the isolation of an apparent weaving compound at Huánuco Pampa (Morris 1974:53) and Cieza's reference to aqllakuna, the entire surface of Hatun Xauxa was intensively surveyed for spindle whorls. The hope was that any substantial concentration would be found, but this tactic proved unsuccessful. The lack of evidence for spinning may be attributable to (1) lack of the activity in the preserved sectors of the center, (2) use of perishable materials, such as wood, for spindle whorls, or (3) inadequacy of the recovery technique. Because similar collecting techniques regularly recovered spindle whorls at other sites in the study area (Earle et al. 1980), it seems likely that the lack of evidence reflects a true lack of spinning in the areas accessible for research. It is possible, of course, that a weavers' compound lies under modern Sausa.

The problem of state ceramic production in the region is intriguing. Materials analysis of imperial Inka and Wanka pottery has shown that the state exerted close control over manufacture of the vessels in the state style (D'Altroy and Bishop 1990). However, no site of state ceramic production has been located in the region. Neither pottery dumps nor scattered wasters were observed in the mapping and surface collecting at

Hatun Xauxa. In contrast, fieldwork at the nearby town of Marca (J54) shows that the settlement was a ceramic production center during Wanka III (Costin 1986). However, only two wasters from state polychrome jars were recovered in UMARP fieldwork, both from Marca; both were collected in surface work, not excavations. Because wasters were also recovered from surface collections and excavations at several other settlements preceding and under Inka rule, the scarcity of by-products at Hatun Xauxa may reasonably be attributed to the organization of craft production rather than to the recovery technique. Possible causes include lack of a ceramic industry and covering of the production areas by modern Sausa. Although the latter cannot be discounted, we cannot assign all activities for which we have no evidence to a deposit under the modern town. It must be considered likely that ceramic production did not occur at Hatun Xauxa.

Even though no archaeological evidence was found for craft activity, it seems almost assured that attached specialists worked at the center. Cieza's secondhand statement that silversmiths and goldsmiths were resident and Estete's (1917 [1532–33]: 96) firsthand reference to woodworkers both indicate that specialists were present. Study of Inka practices from other provinces leads to the same conclusion (e.g., Espinoza Soriano 1970, 1973a, 1983, 1987; Williams 1983; Morris and Thompson 1985).

The development of a separate class of state-dependent economic specialists, among them craftworkers, was key to the independence of the Inka economy (Chapter 8; see also Murra 1980 [1956]). By supporting specialists, whose purpose was to manufacture prestige and state utilitarian goods, the Inkas were able to regulate the distribution of the status-marking goods critical to ceremonial and political activity. This practice also permitted the state to reduce its dependence on local artisans for its material support. The extent to which this transition to economic independence was achieved in the region is not clear from the present data. From information on the organization of state storage, it appears that the state was making an extensive effort to integrate its subjects into the state support system at the local villages. The proportion of craft specialists housed permanently at Hatun Xauxa may therefore have been smaller than at other, more autonomous state centers.

WANKA RESIDENTIAL AREAS   Evidence supporting the proposition that residential areas inhabited by

Wankas were constructed within or adjacent to Hatun Xauxa would include concentrations of circular structural foundations or Wanka ceramics in areas peripheral to the site's center. Wanka III occupations could be distinguished from pre-Inka occupations by their ceramic assemblages and spatial limitation, because the state characteristically kept its elite areas segregated from local groups. The possibility of a Wanka presence at Hatun Xauxa was raised by the anomalous number of subject communities with state wares in the main valley and by the close political ties between the state and native elites (Chapter 9). This situation contrasted markedly with the restricted circulation of Inka pottery at local sites in the Huánuco area (Thompson 1967b, 1972b; Morris 1972a) and in the Junín, Tarma, and Huaricolca areas (Parsons and Hastings 1977; Hastings 1985:608). The apparent difference in state-local interaction suggested that subject access to the provincial capital may have been less restricted than among other groups elsewhere.

Only 78 sherds of Wanka style were recovered from the surface collections. The low number is comparable to that of the core of Huánuco Pampa, at which fewer than 5 sherds of a collection approaching 100,000 could be attributed to subject styles (Morris and Thompson 1970:359). This finding suggests strongly that the Inkas strictly regulated activity within their center and supplied any workers with state ceramics while at the center. In contrast to Huánuco Pampa and Pumpu (Thompson 1968b), no area of apparent local residence exists on the periphery of Hatun Xauxa. It may therefore be inferred that subject activities were limited to discharge of obligations owed to and defined by the state.

Summary of Archaeological Research

Despite its present deteriorated condition, Hatun Xauxa was clearly the central Inka establishment in the region. The settlement exhibited many of the basic features of highland administrative centers. It was a planned settlement, placed in a previously unoccupied spot and probably laid out in a regular design, with a focus on a central plaza and a platform mound. The architecture was typically Inka, and the artifact assemblage was dominated by goods of imperial manufacture. The main highway passed either directly through it or by it, and massive storage facilities were constructed just outside the residential areas on elevated ground. A range of spatially restricted activities was pursued, including administration, military garrisoning, craft production, and religious ceremony. The craft activity and military presence were best verified by historical data, because the archaeological fieldwork yielded little evidence on these aspects of the occupation. Nonetheless, the surface work did confirm the Inka character of the center, both from distinctly Incaic architecture and from the overwhelming dominance of state-manufactured ceramics.

The Road System

The Inka sierra highway passed directly through the Mantaro Valley, joining Hatun Xauxa to the other state centers in the central highlands. The main road in the Mantaro Valley lay along the eastern side of the Río Mantaro, crossing a tributary drainage at site J6, about 5 km east of Hatun Xauxa (Figs. 5.1 and 6.13). Once beyond Hatun Xauxa, the road passed directly through the Yanamarca Valley and rose over the Huaricolca puna on the way to Tarma, the next Inka center to the north.

The best-preserved segments of the major road lie at the north end of the Yanamarca Valley and in the main Mantaro Valley, south of Ataura (von Hagen 1955: 168–76; Parsons and Hastings n.d. [1975–76]). The southern section consisted of a generally straight road, with a few minor changes in angle to accommodate bends in the river course. About 8 m wide, it was lined on either side with a row of stones. None of the road there retains stone paving, nor is there any evidence of water control improvements, although the bed may have been smoothed. From J6 to Hatun Xauxa, the road has been obliterated by agricultural activity and construction, so that its relationship to the center cannot be firmly established. It seems likely that the highway passed through the center in a southeast-northwest direction, traversing the main plaza in the process. This orientation was consistently the case in neighboring highland centers, such as Huánuco Pampa (Morris and Thompson 1970:346) and Pumpu (LeVine 1985:178). It is probably no coincidence that the main road through Cuzco—to Chinchasuyu and Kollasuyu—followed a similar path (see Gasparini and Margolies 1980:46).

About 5 km north of Hatun Xauxa, two short segments of old road are preserved on either side of the pass between the Mantaro and Yanamarca Valleys. The beds of these sections, which are no more than a couple of hundred meters long and about 5 m wide, have been slightly flattened and lined with rocks along the edges. Within the Yanamarca Valley itself, the trace

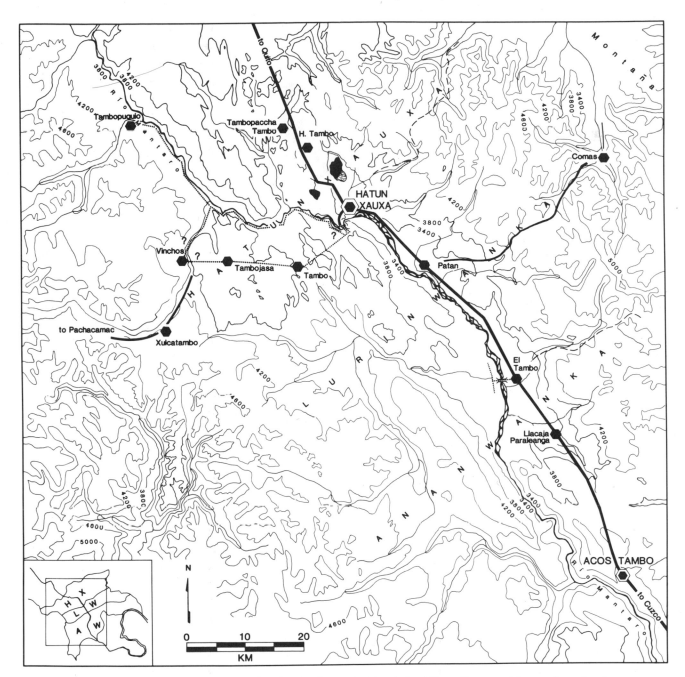

Fig. 6.13. Inka road system through the Mantaro Valley, showing the provincial capitals of Hatun Xauxa and Acostambo and various smaller tampu along the highway. Trunk routes to the coast and the jungle are also shown. *HX* = Hatunxauxa; *LW* = Lurinwanka; *AW* = Ananwanka.

of the road is lost until it exits the north end, but its location at the base of the flanks of the eastern hills may be inferred. Von Hagen (1955:168) reported that the road was still visible through the valley in the early 1950s, although he did not specify the location of the preserved section.

The highway exited the Yanamarca Valley through the Quebrada Huaripchacún, rising 75 m above the east side of the Río Grande (Fig. 6.14). About 5 km north, at the end of the bottleneck, the road descended to the stream and traversed it via a stepping-stone bridge. Whether the bridge was covered with a wood structure in Inka times is unclear, although the narrowness and shallowness of the channel would not really

Fig. 6.14. Inka road through the Quebrada Huaripchacún, about 20 km north of Hatun Xauxa, looking north.

have required it. In the section of road elevated above the stream, the exterior side was buttressed by a dry-laid stone wall, which occasionally exceeded 2.0 m in height. Because of variations in topography, the road ranged from about 8 m in width in a broad flat section at the south end of the gorge to little more than 1 m in short sections that hug a cliff face halfway through. At particularly steep points, the roadbed was built up with rocks. Occasionally, wide stone steps about 25 cm high were built, although they do not appear to have been structurally necessary and do not really facilitate walking. In the sections with the steps, some short stretches, perhaps 50 m in length, were paved with flat stones, perhaps to minimize erosion (Fig. 6.15). Some concern for water control can be seen in the construction of narrow, stone-lined channels where small drainages intersect the road. Overall, the improvements to the road give an impression more of solidity and serviceability than of grandeur.

The Hatun Xauxa–Pachacamac road was not lo-cated precisely within the archaeological survey area, and it may be that it has been destroyed in this part of the valley. A short road that joined the main storage facilities above Hatun Xauxa was likely the start of the highway to the coast, because the bridge over the Río Mantaro lay in a direct line beyond the qollqa (store-houses). This road shared the characteristics of other prehispanic routes in the area: some bed preparation, a border of a single row of stones on either side, and a maximum width of about 10 m. Far to the west, sec-tions of the road that rose rapidly over the mountains are still in good condition (J. Rick, pers. com. 1983). A trunk road, running off this western route, led up to a small administrative post (J63) and beyond to the south. The road here wound up the valley above mod-ern Miraflores, about a kilometer west of the main bridge across the Río Mantaro. About 5 to 7 m wide where preserved, it was also bordered by a single line of stones on either side; no steps or paving are visible in the section preserved.

Fig. 6.15. Paved bed of Inka road about 20 km north of Hatun Xauxa, looking north.

Paths also run north onto the puna from Laguna Paca, east into the montaña from the area of modern Yauli, and north from Concho and Yanamarca in the Yanamarca Valley. It seems probable that these routes were used during the Late Horizon, particularly because Inka sites lie along their probable paths. The last of these paths bears the marks of Inka construction (Hastorf, pers. com. 1986) but was not investigated during the present fieldwork.

Farther out from the archaeological survey area, the Inka roads become more readily visible. To the north,

well-preserved sections of the main road have been recorded across the Huaricolca puna, on the way to Tarma (Parsons and Hastings 1977, n.d. [1975–76]; see also LeVine 1985:434–36). To the east, the modern road from Matahuasi (3,400 m) over the puna (4,500 m) and to Comas (3,300 m) runs along the Inka roadbed for lengthy stretches. Segments of the old road are still well preserved in the high puna and on the descent to the east. Above Comas, the road was paved with stones for several kilometers and was carefully buttressed by stone walls lining the downhill side of the route. LeVine (1985:441–44) suggests that travelers on the way to the montaña and selva villages may well have used a series of other passages that are simply noted as "important trails" on modern maps. Pedestrians could have readily passed east through the Quero Valley, for instance. The easiest routes to the lowlands, however, were through Tarma and Comas, which is where the preserved sections of Inka road have been recorded. Whether any of the more minor paths were established or improved under Inka rule is not clear at present.

At several points, bridges or fords were required to cross the various drainages in the region. The principal bridges crossed the Río Mantaro near Hatun Xauxa and near modern Huancayo, at the south end of the valley. The bridge near Hatun Xauxa lay a short distance upstream on the sierra-coast road. The location of this bridge played a role in the tactics of the initial encounters between the Spaniards and the Inka army at Hatun Xauxa. In mid-March of 1533 a contingent of conquistadores arrived at Hatun Xauxa, under the leadership of Hernando Pizarro. The Inka general Chalcuchima had previously withdrawn from the center, setting up a bivouac across the river as a protective maneuver (Hemming 1970:66). Hernando Pizarro (1959 [1533]: 90) reported, "[Chalcuchima] had gone with his soldiers, and had crossed a river that was just next to the town, by a network bridge [woven or braided suspension bridge]."[28] The following day, Chalcuchima crossed back to Hatun Xauxa to parley with the Spaniards, ultimately accompanying them to Cajamarca and delivering himself to his death.

In October of the same year, the main Inka force stayed on the far side of the river from Hatun Xauxa, while 600 men were detached to torch the tampu and its storehouses (Sancho 1917 [1532–33]: 141). The Spaniards charged this contingent, and both forces forded the river to Huaripampa. Following a pitched battle, the Inka army was routed down the valley. No mention of the bridge was made in the accounts of this event, most likely because the bridge was too distant for ready crossing of the river. Neither has any evidence of a foundation been found adjacent to the tampu during fieldwork. The modern highway crosses the river at the most likely point for a prehispanic bridge immediately adjacent to Hatun Xauxa, and any foundation that may have been there at one time has been destroyed.

It seems almost certain that the principal suspension bridge lay about 3 km upstream from the provincial center, on the main road to the coast (Figs. 6.16 and 6.17). The stone foundation of a well-made Inka bridge stands next to the ruins of an arched Colonial bridge, at the narrowest constriction of the Río Mantaro for many kilometers in either direction. Access to the location from Hatun Xauxa can easily be gained by crossing over the rolling hills at the south end of the Yanamarca Valley and descending about 50 m along a road cut into the cliff face. Because this point is somewhat inconvenient for southbound travelers crossing from Hatun Xauxa to the right bank of the Río Mantaro, it seems possible that there was a minor means of crossing the river at Hatun Xauxa, perhaps a balsa raft ferry.

The base of the Inka bridge is well preserved, having withstood the pounding of the rapidly flowing river for centuries. A core of earth and small rocks was covered with a thick skin of dressed blocks of rock (up to 80 cm maximum dimension) set without mortar. The corners were columnar, and the sidewalls were canted slightly inward, perhaps for stability. To judge from the shape of the stone base and from the following tortured description by Guaman Poma (1980 [1614]: /357 [359], p. 329), a woven suspension structure spanned the river here: "Bridges of great woven ropes that there were in the time of the Inka, as are those of Pumpu, Xauxa . . . and other bridges of poles and balsas [rafts] that the Indian boatmen ply, as in the plains and in Collao and Cangallo and Huancayo. . . . And afterward the lord Viceroy Marquis of Cañete, the elder, ordered that the bridge of Lima and the bridge of Xauxa and the bridge of Ango Yaco be made of mortar and stone."[29] Illustrations by Regal (1972:27, 109) and Hyslop (1985:326; Fig. 6.18 here) give an idea of what this bridge probably looked like (see also Thompson and Murra 1966).

As Guaman Poma recounted, a Colonial stone-and-mortar structure spanned the river at the same location as the Inka bridge. Also built with an earth-and-rubble core, it was distinguished from the Inka bridge by having a gently curving arch and turquoise-colored tiles facing the sides. From the repeated use of this location, it is apparent that the peculiarities of topography made this an ideal location for foot traffic to gain the other bank. When motorized vehicles came into use, a point with broader banks at the mouth of the river gorge became a more desirable location for a bridge.

Sancho (1917 [1532–33]: 147) reported that the Spaniards traveled south for three days from Hatun Xauxa before reaching a network bridge across the Río Mantaro: "The governor traveled for two days through a very low valley, on the border of the Río

Fig. 6.16. Inka and Colonial bridges over the Río Mantaro, about 3 km west of Hatun Xauxa.

Fig. 6.17. Close-up of Inka and Colonial bridges over the Río Mantaro. The Colonial bridge is distinguished by its true arch and tiles.

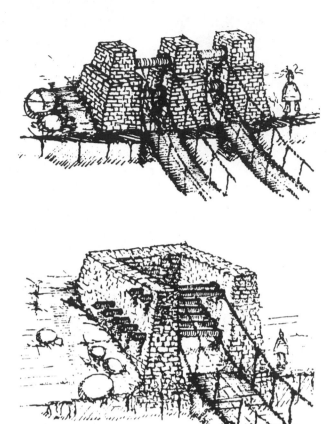

Fig. 6.18. Inka suspension bridges, probably similar to the one over the Río Mantaro above Hatun Xauxa. (After Hyslop 1984:326)

Mantaro, which is very delightful and populated in many places, and on the third day he arrived at a network bridge that is over the river, which had been burnt by the [Inka] Indian soldiers after they had crossed over."[30] This bridge may have been the one recorded by Guaman Poma at Huancayo. Today a vehicle bridge crosses the river at the most logical point for the Inka and Colonial structure, a constriction in the river between Huancayo and Pilcomayo. The proximity of a state facility at El Tambo suggests that the site of the station was chosen both to serve travelers along the main north-south highway and to watch traffic crossing the river.

Three other locations for bridges or fords have been identified in the archaeological study area. One of them lies just north of modern Ataura, where the Inka highway crosses the Río Yauli. Unfortunately, the modern highway has obliterated any traces of a possible structure. An archaeological site (J6) adjacent to this point may have served as a state installation. A stepping-stone bridge, described above, is found

where the main road crosses the Río Acolla, north of the Yanamarca Valley.

An architecturally intriguing bridge lay across the Laguna Tragadero drainage stream, next to the site of Tragadero (J4). It consisted of a series of large dressed stones, about 1 m across, separated by gaps of 1 to 2 m. For this bridge to have been serviceable, a superstructure of wood or other material must have spanned the apertures, resulting in a structure much like that illustrated by Hyslop (1985:320) at Lake Lauricocha. That a bridge was thought necessary or desirable here is an interesting point, because a modern road easily passes behind the adjacent sinkhole into which the lake drains. Across the road from the drainage hole sits a small chapel, which overlies an Inka shrine, according to local oral tradition. Some credibility can be given this account, because the Inka site of Tragadero lies next to this location. If passage by the sinkhole were constrained, constructing a bridge at this point would have been the only way to avoid walking around the lake.

Given the information available at present, it is not possible to determine if these last two or three bridges were built initially by the Inkas or if the state simply took advantage of existing facilities. Once the crossings were adopted into the state highway system, however, their use would probably have been restricted and the local populace may have found its travel capabilities curtailed rather than expanded (see Xérez 1917 [1534]: 32; Rowe 1946:232).

Auxiliary State Settlements

The principal state facilities in the Upper Mantaro region complementary to Hatun Xauxa and the road network consisted of a series of small settlements along the roads and in side valleys, and the storage complexes. As Cieza (1984 [1551]: ch. 84, p. 242) put it, in describing the Mantaro Valley: "In all these parts there were great lodgings of the Inkas, although the principal ones were at the beginning of the valley, in the part they call Xauxa."[31]

Archaeological evidence suggests that a series of six small settlements may have functioned as state administrative posts (J63), traffic control stations (J6, J45, J58), and religious centers (J55, J4). Each settlement bears the stamp of state construction or staffing, to judge from ceramic and architectural evidence, topographic location, or proximity to the highways. Of these sites, four appear to have been almost exclusively state-maintained: J6, J45, J55, and J63. J4 retains components of both state and Wanka ceramics in the surface assemblage, along with Inka and local architectural features. It is included here because important state functions may have been conducted there, along with its having resident subject villagers.

Cutocuto

Cutocuto (J63) has been tentatively identified as a small administrative facility, based on its location, Inka architecture, and Inka-dominated ceramic assemblage. Situated high on the slopes of a small valley, Cutocuto commands a view of the Río Mantaro gorge, along which passed the road to Pachacamac (Fig. 6.19). The site seems to have been loosely organized around open spaces, with small groups of buildings aligned internally, in a plan reminiscent of that of Chilecito, Argentina (González 1983:348). Of the 58 buildings still visible on the ground surface, 5 large rectangular buildings dominate. The best-preserved of these (structure 18) stands 5.0 m high at the peak of the gable and measures 14 by 7 m on the exterior (Fig. 6.20). It contained an interior ledge apparently designed to support beams for a second story or attic; the ledge sits approximately 2.5 m above the present

ground surface. Four wall niches line the interior of each of the two long walls, and a single doorway faces downhill to the northwest. Each niche is capped with a single lintel stone and is neatly built, although not as smoothly finished as the comparable niches at Hatun Xauxa. The doorway has been largely destroyed, so that details of construction were not preserved. The foundations of three other rectangular structures of a similar size lie nearby, but none is preserved above ground level.

The largest structure on the site is an enclosure about 29 by 28 m, with a maximal height of 2.3 m. It seems likely that it did not have a roof, because of its size; the smooth finish applied to the wall tops tends to support this interpretation. The structure has the appearance of a large corral and is currently used as a cemetery, but its masonry is the finest of any building preserved in the study area, including those at Hatun Xauxa. The stones were either selected for shape or were partially dressed, but the masonry is not as fine as Inka polished polygonal stonework (Figs. 6.21 and 6.22). The walls comprised courses of large, roughly rectangular stones (up to 80 cm maximum dimension) alternating with courses of stones angled at 45° or laid flat. Corners were well joined, rather than columnar,

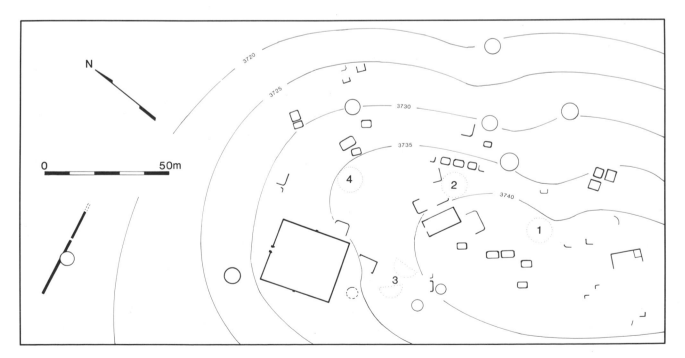

Fig. 6.19. Site plan of Cutocuto (J63), an Inka installation about 10 km west of Hatun Xauxa. Dotted circles and semicircles are collection areas.

Fig. 6.20. Main architecture preserved at the Inka installation of Cutocuto.

Fig. 6.21. Patterned stonework of large enclosure at Cutocuto.

as was characteristic of most other rectangular buildings in the area, both Inka and Wanka. Stone columns flanked the entrance and abutted the exterior of the side walls.

Most of the remainder of the site's architecture consists of small rectangular structures, up to 4.0 m long on a side (Fig. 6.23). Several of these buildings retain portions of corbeled-arch roofs, all of which are plastered in the interior. In most structures the quality of the architecture is exceptionally high. Occasional at

tempts at decorative masonry are visible on the exterior, and several buildings retain step tenons in exterior walls. The remains of some 15 circular buildings are still preserved. This architecture seems to reflect a combination of Inka and Wanka styles. Apart from four or five sherds attributable to the Early Intermediate Period–Middle Horizon, the ceramics at J63 were all Late Horizon. Inka ceramics dominated the assemblage (65.0 percent), although local types, composite Wanka-Inka, and an imported kaolin sherd were present as well. A full range of small Inka jars, cooking and serving pots, bowls, and plates was distributed throughout the site.

Present interpretation of Cutocuto is that it was a relatively small state establishment charged with administering its valley. At least two other Late Horizon habitation sites lie within 1 km of it, each of which is also dominated by the small rectangular buildings apparently favored by the Inkas. Cutocuto may also have controlled traffic on the trunk road to Pachacamac passing somewhere nearby. The presence of high-quality Wanka pottery belies strict state supervision of quotidian activity. Rather, it may be suggested that both state-supported and locally supported personnel occupied the settlement or at least supplied it. Conversely, the same personnel living at the settlement may have been only partially supported by the state, depending on the activities pursued at any given time.

Road Stations

The Junín survey recorded three Late Horizon sites—J6, J45, and J58—at points that could have served as traffic control stations. I have tentatively assigned these sites that function, based on their ceramic assemblages and locations. Site J6 (0.6 ha) consisted solely of a ceramic scatter (92.4 percent Inka) in a flat plowed field on a river terrace, with no surface evidence of structures visible. It lay on the north side of the Río Yauli, a tributary of the Río Mantaro, about 4 km east of Hatun Xauxa, near Patan. Because this is the only

Fig. 6.22. Exterior column on large enclosure at Cutocuto.

Fig. 6.23. Small rectangular buildings with corbeled-arch roofs at Cutocuto. Note the step-tenons on the exterior.

Provincial Power in the Inka Empire

easily passable point over this stream, it is likely that a small bridge or ford was located there. The location on the flat river terrace is atypical of local residential sites, and the ceramic scatter confirms the state presence. The state wares are dominated by large storage jars; no bowl or plate fragments were recovered.

Site J45 was situated at the north end of the Yanamarca Valley, where the Inka highway entered a narrow gorge before rising over the Huaricolca puna. The Inka sector of J45 (1.0 ha) contains no standing architecture. All Late Horizon ceramics recovered were either Inka or Inka-related (e.g., composite Wanka-Inka style). An intriguing element of the ceramic collection there is that the six sherds that were chemically characterized corresponded to the Hatun Xauxa source group (Chapter 8). Because none came from the Hatunmarca source group, a close state affiliation in supply of the goods consumed here is indicated. The state pottery was again dominated by large jars (64 of 74 sherds, or 86.5 percent), but several high-quality plates were found, in contrast to the assemblage from site J6. The plates included an example with a bird-head effigy, the finest modeled piece recovered from any state site in the study area. This ceramic evidence strongly suggests that state personnel were sustained, and perhaps resident, here.

J6 and J45 lie at points where natural travel routes were constricted. Neither site was sufficiently distant from Hatun Xauxa to have been an overnight way station for personnel traveling on state business. Rather, it seems more likely that they housed functionaries who monitored and perhaps controlled traffic approaching and leaving Hatun Xauxa. It is also possible that they served as shelter stations for state messengers, but I saw no ready means for testing for this last function.

J58 (2 ha) lies on the edge of the main river terrace, about 200 m west of the main Inka highway. The partial foundations of four rectangular buildings are still preserved, and several other buildings probably existed, to judge from the piles of rubble. The surface ceramics indicate that the Inka occupation was the most extensive, although J58 was originally occupied in the Early Intermediate Period–Middle Horizon and continued to be used into the Colonial Period. All Inka sherds come from flared-rim jars or from small cooking or serving pots; no bowl or plate fragments were recovered. None of the remaining diagnostic pottery is attributable to the dominant late Wanka styles. This assemblage appears to correspond to that of a small way station on the main highway, perhaps responsible

for putting up state travelers. The site's location just off the highway and the small number of rectangular buildings would seem to support this interpretation. An administrative function seems less likely, because the valley is quite wide and flat here, and the site lies at an ineffective position for controlling activities on its side of the river.

Possible Religious Facilities

Three sites have distinctive characteristics that may reflect a religious function. One of these, J22, consists of an elliptical set of 74 probable storage structures on the highest hill on the east side of the main Mantaro Valley (Fig. 6.1). Within this formation lie an earth-and-rubble mound and a rectangular rock feature that indicate a potential ceremonial element to use of the site.

A second potential religious establishment, J55, lies atop a relatively high peak between the Yanamarca Valley and main Mantaro Valley, about 450 m above Laguna Paca. It commands a view of the entire Yanamarca Valley as well as the main Mantaro Valley and the puna to the north. Using surface collections, LeBlanc (1981) determined that the site had been occupied during Wanka I, was abandoned during Wanka II, and was reestablished during the Inka occupation. The dominant Late Horizon ceramic type was Inka (19.4 percent of diagnostics). The architecture of J55 distinguishes the site from the normal residential sites in the region. Only six J55 structures are still partially preserved, widely spread over an area of about 1.1 ha. Two structures are identifiable as circular in floor plan, and at least two others are rectangular or circular. The largest structure comprises three concentric stone circles, joined at variable intervals by short cross-walls.

The layout is reminiscent of a feature at Saqsawaman (just outside Cuzco), purported to be a fortified tower (Valcárcel 1946:178) or a focus of religious ceremony (Lumbreras 1974:221). Whether either interpretation is accurate for the structure at J55 is uncertain, but the layout is undeniably unusual. The remaining architecture is not appropriate for normal habitation sites, and the ceramic assemblage is clearly Inka. These characteristics, coupled with the commanding location, suggest that some state-related activity other than storage, residence, or administration was conducted here. The two most likely possibilities are religious ceremony and military surveillance, but establishing precedence of either interpretation is not possible with the present data.

A concentration of high-quality state pottery at the

lakeshore site of Tragadero (J4) suggests that it may have held unusual importance for the Inkas. The site consists of a ceramic scatter (4.8 ha), dominated by the Inka component, at the point where Laguna Tragadero drains into a stream, sinking underground several hundred meters to the northwest. Springs and stone were the most commonly revered natural objects in the Cuzco area (Rowe 1946:298), and the Wanka-origin shrine of Wari Willka near Huancayo is also the location of a spring (Cieza 1984 [1551]: ch. 84, p. 243; see Flores 1959). It seems reasonable to assume that a feature as unusual as an underground drainage should have had some religious significance for the Inkas as well. The presence of the central state ceramics component confirms the importance of the site, and at present a religious function seems to be the most likely explanation.

Summary of Imperial Settlements

This chapter has discussed the archaeological sites interpreted to be state establishments in the Upper Mantaro, in the context of general state settlement patterns in the central sierra. The diversity and extensiveness of imperial construction in the region provide some of our best evidence for the intensity of state rule. State sites include the provincial capital of Hatun Xauxa and several smaller sites taken to be administrative posts, traffic control stations, possible religious centers, or military posts, accompanied by more than 50 storage complexes (see Chapter 8). Most lie directly along the main routes of transit, and at least 2 appear to have been intended to regulate highway traffic. Except for J63 and some of the storage sites, these state sites have deteriorated severely, leaving few architectural remains. Nonetheless, the concentration of high-

quality state pottery and the occasional architectural fragments mark them as state sites.

The location of Hatun Xauxa is explicable primarily from two factors: interregional logistics and provincial administration. The center was well suited for administration, lying within a densely populated zone, at the juncture of the main highland road and an important trunk route to the coast. The immediate vicinity was also a source of a wide range of agricultural and industrial resources. The field data show that Hatun Xauxa was built in a spot occupied in the Early Intermediate Period–Middle Horizon but not during the Late Intermediate Period. Architectural preservation and differential distribution of ceramics suggest that the central portion of the site was used for elite residence and that the peripheral sectors were possibly used for more-temporary personnel. The centrally located platform mound appears to confirm the presence of a religious enclave, alluded to in the documentary sources. No archaeological evidence was found to confirm the presence of craft specialists, but historical accounts attest to the presence of metalsmiths and woodworkers. Finally, no evidence was found for a Wanka sector at the center, which appears to reflect the strong state-local dichotomy found at provincial centers elsewhere in the central part of the empire.

In sum, the archaeological and documentary evidence for the Inka occupation of the central sierra indicates a high-control, high-investment strategy of rule, focused around major provincial centers. The state facilities in Upper Mantaro region, though tailored to the local situation, clearly illustrate this pattern. Chapter 7, which examines provincial politics, shows that the state's investment in facilities was coupled with extensive use of subject elites in its administration to attain effective control over the region.

7

Political Organization

The imposition of the Inka administrative system and the adaptations made by subject societies resulted in dramatic changes in the political landscape of the Andes. This chapter begins by outlining the administrative options available to the Inkas, given the conditions present at the outset of imperial dominion. It pays particular attention to political structure and to Inka administrative accommodation to the varied political systems of subject groups. I suggest that four basic kinds of political strategies were available within the hegemonic-territorial continuum: destructuration, patron-client relations, alliance, and intensive bureaucratic incorporation. The last of these strategies was implemented in the Upper Mantaro region, because of the area's strategic location, large population, and agricultural productivity. The coordination of imperial and local politics was facilitated by the similarities that existed between the pre-imperial Inka and Wanka sociopolitical organizations. The success of the Inkas in centralizing rule in the region, using native elites, was such that the Wanka paramounts readily mobilized personnel and matériel in coordinated support of the Spanish invasion in 1533 and for decades thereafter.

Imperial Administration

Although commentators have debated the nature of imperial rule and its effects on subject political life for decades, agreement in the near future does not seem likely. Early analyses of the Inkas by the Spanish chroniclers (e.g., Cobo 1956 [1653]; Garcilaso 1960 [1609]) and more-recent treatments by scholars who have depended on the general accounts (e.g., Métraux 1969; Katz 1972) have portrayed the empire as a well-integrated polity. These expositions often treated the structure of government and the policies of rule as though they had been consistent across the length of the empire and throughout the century of its existence. Among the modern views are those that see the empire as a socialist utopia (Bauden 1928), a benevolent or feudal monarchy (Schaedel 1978), or an Asiatic state (Godelier 1974; Espinoza Soriano 1978; cf. Patterson 1985, 1986).[1]

In part, early monolithic views derived from a lack of information on the diversity of the societies that the Inkas conquered and drew into the empire. More-recent research into the ethnic groups that composed the subject population is reforming current perspectives (e.g., Diez de San Miguel 1964 [1567]; Ortiz de Zúñiga 1967 [1562], 1972 [1562]; Murra 1975, 1980

[1956]; Pease 1977; Rostworowski 1977b, 1978). It is now apparent that varied political and economic relationships among these societies and with the Inkas contributed to a volatile political climate in the late fifteenth and early sixteenth centuries. The dynamic nature of the state itself intensified the instability of political relations. Even taking into account the mythologized nature of the Inka history, the early sources imply strongly that lethal factional infighting characterized each succession to Inka paramount leadership. The conflict over Wayna Qhapaq's throne that led to the civil war between Atawalpa and Wascar in the 1520s may have been just the last link in a chain of fraternal clashes.

Until recently, archaeological work appeared to support the chroniclers' view of a fractious political landscape in the southern highlands just before the imperial expansion (Rowe 1944; Dwyer 1971; see Bauer 1990:98–102).[2] Despite the presence of pre-imperial Killke-phase fortifications outside the Cuzco Valley, a survey by Dwyer (1971:146) indicated that the area may have been an "oasis of tranquility" in the war-torn sierra. Bauer (1990) suggests, however, that the Inkas may have begun to develop an unusual breadth of regional control in the 200 years before their fifteenth-century conquests. Survey data from the Paruro area, up to 60 km from Cuzco, show continuity in the settlement pattern from the Killke phase into the imperial phase, coupled with a lack of late-prehistoric fortified sites. Noting that the Paruro populace shared the Killke ceramic style with the inhabitants of Cuzco, Bauer argues that the pre-imperial Inkas had integrated an extensive area into a single realm. Whether this integration implies the presence of a state-level polity remains to be ascertained, but the argument provides greater time for Inka state development than prior work had suggested.

To understand imperial rule, nonetheless, it is essential to recognize that the Inkas developed much of their administrative apparatus as a consequence of a need to rule newly acquired imperial territories. Variations in Inka rule stemmed initially from the nature of Inka society at the time of the first conquests. Societies with organizational capacities most similar to those of the Inkas were most readily assimilated, whereas those that were markedly more or less complex presented administrative problems. Political interaction between the Inkas and their subjects thus ranged from patron-client relations with the elites of small-scale and peripheral societies (e.g., the Pasto of northern Ecuador) to treaty or favored-status relations with some internal polities (e.g., the Chincha and the Lupaqa) and intensive assimilation with a well-developed bureaucracy (e.g., the core region around Cuzco and, to a lesser degree, the Upper Mantaro region). In contrast, the Chimu state of the north coast of Peru was decentralized into valley-wide polities because of the threat that the larger polity posed to imperial stability (see Netherly 1978 and Ramirez 1990; cf. Pease 1978).

Overall, the administrative system in the provinces was designed to supervise regional projects associated with state expansion, military support, political consolidation, security, and maintenance of permanent and temporary state personnel.[3] It provided an overarching superstructure and often invaded the local system by creating offices within communities, below the maximal units of existing native authority (see, e.g., Toledo 1940a [1570]; Cock 1977). Because the state depended heavily on local elites, the apparatus of government was tailored to use the authority of ethnic leaders among their own people. Conversely, the local political structures were modified to facilitate state rule.

The evidence for provincial variations necessitates caution in applying specific administrative models to any given province. This problem is particularly acute where information on either the state or subject structures per se is highly fragmentary, as in the present study area. Moreover, governmental approaches that relied heavily on native authority—effective shortly after conquest—were transformed as subject polities became more fully integrated into the empire. Despite the variation, however, Inka governance was not an ad hoc affair, assembled piecemeal as the conquests rolled on. Rather, the Inkas seem to have developed systematic policies, adapted to accommodate existing social, political, and economic institutions.

State policies suggest that the Inkas were attempting to balance two potentially conflicting political goals: (1) coordinating local political organizations and (2) minimizing the possibility of allied resistance. Initially, they needed to set up an administration that could conduct state affairs in the absence of adequate loyal personnel. Conversely, increasing the organizational abilities of subject groups and the power of subject elites magnified the potential internal threats to the empire.[4] Schaedel (1978:308) has suggested that a central Inka principle was thus to develop central state control over individual provinces while discouraging horizontal bonds between provinces. Governance was vertically oriented, for political control was vested hierarchically in offices filled by ethnic and honorary

Inkas and elites from subject groups. A number of policies imply that limiting interethnic relations may have been an initial key to Inka rule, because it discouraged alliances against the state. Forced internal resettlement, through the mitmaqkuna program, was among the foremost of these stratagems. The Inkas also encouraged the use of localized resources by multiple ethnic groups, which minimized subject dependence on specialization and on exchange between groups. To govern the empire effectively, however, the Inkas frequently found it necessary to empower subordinate elites to carry out state business—a policy followed in the Upper Mantaro region.

The structure of the overarching government incorporated notions of Inka kinship, but the extent to which these concepts were applied to administration within subject provinces is not yet clear.[5] The emperor stood at the apex of the political (and religious) pyramid, surrounded by his lineage and the 10 royal ayllu. The highest level of political division consisted of four administrative quarters (*suyu*) centered at Cuzco (Rowe 1946:262; Schaedel 1978:292). One administrator supervised each quarter, among which were scores of provinces.[6] Many of the provinces corresponded to territories of pre-Inka polities, in keeping with the Inka policy of using extant political systems to govern. Each province was headed by an Inka-appointed governor (*tokrikoq*), usually an Inka noble, who directed an array of imperial and local elites and functionaries. The vertical orientation permeated the provincial structure, because the tokrikoq administered the local elites directly below him in the pyramid, rather than the people themselves (Cobo 1956 [1653]: vol. 2., bk. 2, ch. 25, pp. 114–15). The officials from the provincial governor up were recruited from the core Inka nobility, although the offices were not strictly hereditary and ability was considered in making appointments (Rowe 1946:262; Wachtel 1977:75–79; Schaedel 1978:300–306).

Each province was further subdivided into two or three political units, apparently with a bounded territory, often called saya (Quechua) or *repartimiento* (Spanish) in the documents.[7] Each division subsumed a variable number of ayllu, the corporate group that appears to have formed the basic social unit from Bolivia to northern Peru. Present evidence suggests, however, that the ayllu did not extend into northwest Argentina or highland Ecuador as the basic social unit (Salomon 1986; Lorandi and Boixadós 1987–88). The tie between the ayllu and its land and other resources meant that Andean communities were bound

together socially, politically, and economically (Moore 1958:22), making them convenient units for resettlement or mobilization for state activities. Under Inka rule, the saya and ayllu were often hierarchically ordered internally; their political structure in the Mantaro region is discussed later in this chapter. Because the imperial bureaucracy penetrated local political systems, many of the native elites who held positions of authority in their ayllu were precisely the individuals who were recruited by the Inkas to hold low-level administrative roles in the imperial government.

The Inkas and many provincial groups were also partitioned sociopolitically on a numerical basis (see Rowe 1946:262–64; Zuidema 1964; Wedin 1965; Netherly 1978). The difficult analysis of the kinship-political structure of Cuzco made by Zuidema (1964, 1977, 1983; see also Zuidema and Poole 1982) presents the most detailed argument for rule through a numerical hierarchy.[8] Zuidema argues that Cuzco, its populace, and, by extension, the empire were quadripartitioned; pairs of quarters formed opposing, hierarchical halves. The halves have often been termed moieties, despite their apparent divergence from classic kinship moieties at the more comprehensive levels (see Keesing 1975:150). Various levels in the structure were divided into upper (hanan) and lower (hurin) halves, including the entire empire, the province, the residential community, and the ayllu.

The repeated descriptions of dual divisions in documents on local societies in the early Colonial Period have contributed to a conflict of interpretations on the fundamental character of Inka rule.[9] Zuidema has contended that true dual rule may have existed at both state and local levels; he attributes the lack of fuller documentation to the Spaniards' failure to recognize the structure. Thus, Inka king lists may have recorded parallel, not directly successive, rulers (see Conrad and Demarest 1984). Rowe (1946:254, 257, 260), conversely, has pointed out that early documentation overwhelmingly favors the view that rule lay in a single patrilateral line in the numerical orderings. Rostworowski (e.g., 1961, 1977a) has partially resolved the conflict by showing that local and imperial successions were not simple patrilineal processes but varied among societies of the coast and highlands. Even if only males belonging to particular kin groups could inherit power, rights to office in many subject societies often shifted between brothers before passing to the succeeding generation.

Zuidema has also argued that divisions by units of three were basic to Inka ethnic and imperial organization. Hierarchical tripartite divisions—*qollana, payan,* and *kayao*—were applied to a variety of sociopolitical and religious relationships (see Wachtel 1977: 77–79). Although these divisions were theoretically based on kin divisions, the Inkas ostensibly applied them to territorial and political structures. A partial explanation of the uneven presence of elements of Zuidema's model lies in the possibility that it may have been most fully elaborated in the social organization of Cuzco and not widely applied to provincial populations.

In central areas of the empire, a decimal hierarchy paralleled and intersected these structures and other forms of native authority. It was particularly well developed in the sierra from the Bolivian altiplano to the northern Peruvian highlands. Officials in this system exercised jurisdiction over units ranging up to 10,000 heads of household. Their titles were as follows: *hunu kuraka* (lord of 10,000 heads of household), *pichqawaranqa kuraka* (lord of 5,000), *waranqa kuraka* (lord of 1,000), *pichqapachaca kuraka* (lord of 500), *pachaca kuraka* (lord of 100), *pichqachunka kamayoq* (lord of 50), and *chunka kamayoq* (lord of 10). Officials down to and including the pachaca kuraka were recruited from local elites and loyal foreigners, with heredity and ability taken into account in succession (Rowe 1946:262; Schaedel 1978:300–306; Niles 1987:53).

The decimal structure was an ideal system, unevenly applied throughout the empire (Murra 1958). The most thorough implementation of this hierarchy and other elements of imperial government apparently occurred in societies closest to the homeland of the Inkas—that is, in highland Bolivia and along the central spine of the Peruvian sierra (e.g., Pease 1977; Julien 1982, 1988). A likely reason for this more formal jurisdiction lay in the imperial need for tight control over the heartland. The process of installing a centralized authority system, based on principles of duality integrated with decimal hierarchies, was facilitated by the similarities of the sociopolitical systems of the Inka and surrounding societies. In the highlands of Ecuador, the system was present most clearly in imported mitmaqkuna settlements (Salomon 1986:191) but not among the native populace. It was not well developed in northwest Argentina (Raffino 1983; Lorandi and Boixadós 1987–88) and seems to have played a minimal role in the political hierarchies of the north coast of Peru (Netherly 1978; Ramirez 1990). The irregular application may have stemmed from incomplete consolidation of the provinces and from the

difficulties of standardizing rule among diverse societies.[10] Alternatively, the lack of implementation in peripheral areas may be attributable to the brief length of time that the territory was under imperial control. The degree to which the key to pacification of a region lay in decentralizing native authority was also likely significant—for instance, in the Chimu state, the single greatest regional threat to Inka imperial expansion.

It is intriguing that the span of control of decimal officials was 5 subordinates, not 10. If each official concurrently held a position in each succeeding level below, his span was even less—perhaps 4. This calculation conforms generally to Johnson's (1982, 1983) finding that the mean span of control in decision-making hierarchies tends to be about 6; individuals with broader spans tend to get overwhelmed with information, and decision-making becomes less efficient. Skinner (1977:321) argues that a narrow span of control (i.e., few officials below any given official) was desirable in centers that were vulnerable to military or other violent disruptions, because it entailed "close supervision and minimal competition for channels of communication." Combined considerations of economic strategy and defense would lead us to expect narrower spans in fractious regions, in lower levels of the administrative hierarchy, and toward the perimeters of imperial control (Skinner 1977:309–14, 321).

Given current information, it is difficult to assess variations that may have occurred in the breadth of Inka officials' spans of control. This difficulty is especially apparent when considering the crosscutting sociopolitical structures arrayed within Andean society, especially the pervasive duality. However, the scant evidence for mobile officials, such as inspectors and judges, whose apparent function was to ensure the honesty and loyalty of the provincial administration, suggests that they tended to be specialized (see Moore 1958:101–21; Schaedel 1978). Broadly speaking, this suggestion conforms to the general administrative principles for which Skinner and Johnson argue.

The functions of the base-10 system have elicited disagreement among Inka scholars. Rowe (1946:264) considered the decimal count to have been used rigorously in census taking, taxation, and military recruitment. In contrast, Murra (1958:33–34) has argued that this bureaucratic approach is more readily understandable as a census taker's vocabulary than as demographic reality. Wedin (1965) completely dismissed the civil applications of the system, arguing that it was applied only to military personnel and that the apparent civil uses were an invention of late-sixteenth-century chroniclers. This last position is no longer tenable, given the detailed documentary evidence for mobilization of corvée personnel through the decimal system in the Chucuito and Huánuco regions (Diez de San Miguel 1964; Ortiz de Zúñiga 1967 [1562]; see Julien 1982 and LeVine 1987).[11]

Whatever the structure, political control was not applied evenly across all societies. Although the Inkas exerted their tightest control near the core of the empire, regions at varying distances from the capital were integrated more fully than were other closer regions, and their human and natural resources more fully exploited. The regions' productive capacities contributed to the groups' importance as targets of intensive imperial assimilation. The breadbaskets of Cochabamba, Abancay, Yucay, and the Upper Mantaro Valley were prime examples of localized state control and economic intensification. Smaller, less productive valleys, such as those in the Acos, Tarma, and Carahuarazo areas, show significantly less evidence of imperial development (Lavallée and Julien 1983; Hastings 1985:740–41; Schreiber 1987).

A relatively indirect form of political relations between state and subject can be found in the initial integration of some peripheral societies, of which the simple chiefdoms of northern Ecuador are the best-documented (Salomon 1986:172–86; Salomon 1987). Often formidable military foes who occupied difficult terrain, these societies presented administrative problems for the state. They were economically interdependent and maintained contacts with societies outside imperial territory that produced sumptuary goods that the Inkas desired. However, they were politically decentralized, making it difficult for the Inkas to conduct state business. Even in more southern Ecuador, the local societies were not readily drawn into the hierarchical state government.

Salomon (1986) has shown that, at least initially, the Inkas found it most effective to deal with the Ecuadorian populations through a single point of native authority—a paramount chief, sometimes elevated to represent a pooled set of smaller chiefdoms. As the rulers of the empire attempted to forge stronger control over the region, they gradually transformed the military occupation into social and political integration. They resettled elites from native societies in the sacred city of Quito, where they could be watched. At the same time, the elites were granted economic perquisites, giving them a vested interest in maintenance of the state economy. In a parallel tactic, the Inkas promoted small replicas of the hierarchical state trib-

ute apparatus and political relationships within the chiefdoms (Salomon 1986:185). Both Salomon and Idrovo (1988) suggest that there is more tangible evidence of these efforts in the southern Ecuadorian highlands than among the Pasto in the north. They attribute this difference to both the greater duration of imperial dominion in the south and the greater distance that the northern lands lay from the limits of imperial territory.

As was noted earlier, the Inkas adopted an opposing strategy in the Chimu area: decentralized political control to defuse a threat to state security. The Chimu king Minchançaman was held as an honored hostage in Cuzco, while political control among his lands was dispersed among local lords, who each headed up a territory roughly corresponding to a valley (Rowe 1948; Netherly 1978, 1988; Ramirez 1990). Physical evidence of the imperial presence in the area is scant (cf. Conrad 1977; Hyslop 1990), with no major state installations such as those found in the highlands or farther south on the Peruvian coast. It appears that a principal imperial goal in this region was to reduce the opportunity for orchestrated actions by subject elites. Whether by design or because of insufficient opportunity to install a centralized bureaucracy, the political system depended upon a local structure, based on a dual and perhaps quadripartite organization, instead of the decimal hierarchy.[12]

Regardless of the precise form of the political tie between the state and its subjects, ceremonial activities appear to have been focal to the actual interaction between state and subordinate personnel. The Inkas invested considerable effort to construct such cities as Quito, Inkawasi (Cañete), and Huánuco Pampa in imitation of the sacred geography of Cuzco. Other energy that was put into ideological endeavors, especially ritual hospitality underwritten by state supplies, underscores the importance of ceremonial activities in political relations between state and subjects. Morris (1982:155) has suggested that, at its provincial centers, the state emphasized ritual and ceremonial activity over coercion or secular administration in its political relations with subjects.

This emphasis draws attention to three central elements of Inka rule. First, the Inkas still had to court the compliance of subject populations. Even in the sixteenth century, the state relied on subject collaboration to mobilize labor and goods and to transform the institutions of Andean societies. Second, local and imperial ideologies were a very active part of sociopolitical relations. Administrative functions were often couched in terms of traditional reciprocities, so that administration was not well differentiated from other aspects of relations between the state and its subjects (Wachtel 1977:75–81; Murra 1980 [1956]). Third, the assimilation of subject societies into the empire was not simply political or economic exploitation. The Inkas were quite deliberately trying to reshape at least some of the peoples of the Andes into coordinated elements of a grandly conceived, unified culture (see Rowe 1982).

The questions remain as to how decision-making worked and what levels of the political structure were responsible for what kinds of decisions.[13] Although evidence on these issues is scant, it seems to point to a great deal of authority in the hands of the subject elites (Morris 1982:165). The detailed visitas of the Huánuco (Ortiz de Zúñiga 1967 [1562], 1972 [1562]) and Chucuito (Diez de San Miguel 1964 [1567]) areas provide examples of the manner in which the state assessed labor obligations and the native elites applied them to their subjects. Julien (1988) has argued that decision-making about labor assessments in the Chucuito area occurred in two stages: (1) before the execution of the assessment, when the population was organized into accounting units, and (2) when the quotas were levied. The decimal groupings were based on periodic censuses conducted by state officials (*runakhipu*), who adjusted the structure as the population changed in composition and size. Local variations in population distribution seem to have led to greater divergence from the ideal units at the lowest levels of the structure than at the highest. Elites acting on behalf of the state ultimately applied labor obligations in fairly strict proportion to the number of households present, not to an idealized decimal unit (Julien 1988). LeVine (1987) has shown that decisions concerning allocation of labor in the Huánuco region were made at different levels of the hierarchy, depending on whether services or goods were the intended output. This information suggests that different levels in the hierarchy were responsible for mobilizing different kinds of resources for the state's use.

The degree of independence accorded native elites in these decisions is a central issue in understanding the variations within imperial rule. It was argued earlier that a principal measure of imperial integration is the extent to which the state intrudes into the local society with respect to decision-making. Moore (1958:99–125) has pointed out that the Inkas appear to have appropriated the right to make certain kinds of decisions, such as adjudicating land disputes between ethnic groups and major corporate or political units

and administering punishment for murder and other crimes (see Cobo 1956 [1653]: vol. 2, bk. 2, ch. 26, pp. 116–18). Although it is not clear whether specific rules were applied universally throughout the empire, the state seems to have progressively removed the right to resolve major disputes over property and life from the hands of the native elites. To the extent that these rules were actually enforced and were not simply codified guidelines, the Inkas were transforming the subject societies into fully assimilated provinces of a territorial empire. In contrast, to the extent that adjudication of many of these issues remained in the hands of the subject elites or the parties involved, the Inkas were still ruling through a hegemonic strategy that emphasized indirect exploitation over direct integration.

In sum, the Inka political system was initially built on the authority systems of a widely diverging set of subject societies. The evidence suggests that the Inkas were attempting to apply systematic policies to subject groups within the empire. Regional variations in demography, political complexity, native social and economic forms, and security threats—coupled with limited imperial resources, transport, and communications capacities—contributed to variable imperial policies. With this review as context, we may now sketch out the major political changes effected in the Upper Mantaro region under Inka rule.

Provincial Imperial Authority in the Upper Mantaro Region

Following their conquest of the region, the Inkas called the Upper Mantaro Valley and adjacent lands Wanka Wamaní—Valley or Province of the Wankas (Vega 1965 [1582]: 166). From that point until the Spanish invasion, state and local political systems exercised intersecting control over the populace. The effectiveness of this approach is attributable to increased centralization of local authority, although the partially discrete jurisdictions and the roles played by Wanka and Xauxa elites in each system also contributed to the efficacy of Inka rule. Because some local elites occupied positions whose legitimacy derived from both state and local sanction, the two systems were not totally discrete structurally. Some of the difficulty in distinguishing between local and imperial rule may be credited to Inka efforts to create an integrated administration. It appears that the two interest groups were still molding a working relationship at the time of the

Inka demise, however, and a static political system was never achieved.

Apart from repeated allusions to the decimal system in the 1570 visita of Toledo (1940a), documentary evidence for state offices in the province is scant, but it suggests an elevated role for the administrators resident in the Mantaro Valley. The inconsistently detailed data may be largely attributed to the nature of the available documents[14] and probably not to a lack of state bureaucrats. Much of the available evidence in the Toledo visita, for instance, concerns the organization of the Wankas before and under Inka rule, whereas the Inka system per se is seldom addressed. The state administration is alluded to largely in the context of the role played by the Wankas and of the succession and conquests of Inka emperors. It should therefore be kept in mind that the organization described here was recounted by the Wankas and that the previous discussion of the state should be retained as a balance to the Wanka testimony.

The political importance of the region within the empire is touched on only in tantalizingly brief references. As was described in Chapter 6, Thupa Yupanki installed a governor at Hatun Xauxa to oversee the northern half of the empire on his behalf (Sarmiento 1960 [1572]: ch. 52, p. 257). Wascar also used the valley as a center of imperial authority during his brief, contested reign (Guaman Poma 1980 [1614]: /116 [116], p. 94). These comments do not provide sufficient detail for us to know precisely what duties the governor had, nor is it apparent for what purposes Wascar used the center. But it does seem clear that, in terms of political rank, Hatun Xauxa was among the most elite provincial centers in the empire.

Organization of the Saya

The three saya—Hatunxauxa, Lurinwanka, and Ananwanka—formed the largest political units within the Inka province that were headed by native elites. The evidence suggests that these divisions antedated the Inka conquest (see Chapter 4). To recapitulate, the salient characteristics of the regional divisions were as follows. According to the 1582 inspection by Vega (1965:167), there were about 27,000 "war Indians" in the province at the time of the Spanish conquest. Six thousand of them were counted in Hatunxauxa, 9,000 in Ananwanka, and 12,000 in Lurinwanka. Because this unequal division of population was present among the saya even after the last Inka census in the mid-1520s, it seems likely that the distribution followed borders that had been at least generally established

before the conquest, especially considering that the last major territorial dispute of which we are aware was settled by Wayna Qhapaq (Cieza 1967 [1553]: ch. 64, p. 215). The demographic imbalance retained by this late settlement suggests that the Inkas largely respected pre-conquest ethnic divisions. The need for Inka intervention to resolve the dispute (which may have been initially caused by Inka apportionment) raises the point that the incorporation of small polities into the state did not eliminate intergroup hostilities. It simply channeled conflict resolution from warfare into litigation (Murra 1980 [1956]: 32).

The other principal lines of evidence suggesting that the Inkas ordered the saya along indigenous ethnic lines include the linguistic and dress differences among groups that almost certainly antedated the Inka conquest. The names of the divisions themselves suggest a distinction between the northern group (Hatunxauxa) and the central and southern Wankas (Lurinwanka and Ananwanka).

The territories of each saya encompassed each of the major ecozones in or near the Mantaro Valley: valley floor, hillslopes, upland valleys, puna, and montaña (Espinoza Soriano 1971: inset map; LeVine 1979). The 1582 visita of Vega (1965) illustrates the continuing sierra-montaña relationship. By 1582 the number of communities had diminished considerably from the prehispanic situation, as a result of war, disease, and the 1571 Toledan reduction. In Table 7.1 (modi-

Table 7.1. Distribution of Settlements in Xauxa Province in 1582

Repartimiento	Mantaro Valley settlements	Montaña settlements
Xauxa	Hatunxauxa (Jauja) Guaripampa Yauyos	Monobamba Uchubamba (under Lurinwanka)
Hurin Guanca	Apata Mataguaci La Concepción Cincos Mito Urcotuna	Uchubamba Comas Andamayo
Hanan Guanca	Chupaca Guancayo Cicaya Chongos	Uchubamba (under Lurinwanka) Paucarbamba Uítoc (Tarma's jurisdiction)

Source: Modified from LeVine 1979:26.
Note: Spellings are according to Vega 1965 [1582].

fied from LeVine 1979:26), the communities that the census recorded are provided (Vega 1965 [1582]: 172–74).

The montaña settlements among these communities were listed as "*sujeto*" to the main valley, an ambiguous relationship that may have implied only political dominance (LeVine 1979:26). The montaña communities could have been conquered, populated voluntarily by Xauxa and Wanka colonists, or even assigned by the Inkas as part of their territorial reorganization. Regardless of the process of settlement, it appears from the manner in which the montaña communities are cited in the inspection that their inhabitants were a politically integral part of each saya. For example, Uchubamba lay within Lurinwanka territory, but individuals from the other two saya living there were counted as belonging to their own groups: "This division [saya] of Lurinwanka has toward the montaña, which they call the Andes, a community named San Juan Bautista de Uchubamba. . . . [A] few Indians from the saya of Hatunxauxa and from the saya of Ananwanka are resettled in it" (Vega 1965 [1582]: 173).[15] Spatial sovereignty of saya is also reflected in the identification of Ananwanka settlers in Vítoc, a community under the jurisdiction of Tarma (Vega 1965 [1582]: 174). Testimony in a 1560 Wanka petition to the Audiencia Real in Lima noted that the paramount of Lurinwanka had subjects tending his aji fields in the montaña settlement of Andamarca during the first few postcontact years, while the Inkas were still actively resisting Spanish rule in the central highlands: "Manco Inka . . . came with many soldiers that he brought from the montaña to some towns subject to the Valley of Xauxa, especially Andamarca, which is where don Jerónimo has his aji fields[.] Manco Inka robbed his land and burned his towns and killed many of his Indians, the most valiant of the valley" (Guacrapáucar 1971c [1560]: 223).[16] These settlements in the montaña almost certainly antedated the Spanish incursion into the valley in 1533, given that the villages would not likely have been established during the widespread warfare of the 1530s.

Murra (1975:58–116) has suggested that such multizonal occupation by single communities preceded the Inka conquest. Archaeological remains from montaña products suggest that exchange relationships between the highlands and the montaña antedated the Late Horizon, so the key here lies in the nature of the ties (Earle et al. 1987). Among the various economic relationships (examined in Chapter 8), the most likely possibilities for sierra-montaña ties are dyadic rela-

tionships between communities, exploitation through estates of landed elites, and pooling within communities distributed in extended settlement patterns. The residents of the montaña communities were considered political subjects of specific saya, regardless of the economic relationships and regardless of the presence of individuals from other political units.

The Decimal Hierarchy

Because of the extent and rapid growth of the empire, the Inkas were beset with a major administrative problem: staffing a workable system with limited true state personnel. The decimal hierarchy provided a partial solution in the Xauxa region, because native elites were employed as administrators. The structure seems to have been introduced fairly early in the Inka occupation, for witnesses testifying in 1570 to Toledo (1940a:36) unanimously credited the system to Thupa Inka Yupanki, who was also cited as the valley's conqueror: "[Thupa Inka Yupanki] established the lords who are called hunu for ten thousand Indians, and pichqawaranqa who are of five thousand Indians, and waranqa who are of one thousand Indians, and pichqapachaca who are of five hundred Indians, and pachaca who are of one hundred Indians, so that they would be governed"[17] (see also Toledo 1940a [1570]: 21, 26, 29). It should be kept in mind, however, that this testimony may be an apocryphal compression of Inka history, because the Wanka informants tended to attribute most acts of state reorganization to Thupa Yupanki (see Rowe 1946:201–9).

The highest-order decimal office established in both the Lurinwanka and the Ananwanka saya was almost assuredly an hunu kuraka (lord of 10,000). Only Lurinwanka had sufficient population (12,000 soldiers) to have merited this official strictly on the basis of population. A petition dated 1563 and filed with Toledan subordinates in Cuzco in 1571 states that the head of the Ananwanka saya (9,000 soldiers) was also accorded the status of hunu kuraka under the Inkas: "[Don Carlos Alaya] petitioned that, in continuation of the custom that the Inka had, the favor be granted of giving him the seat and clothing that said Inka was accustomed to give for the insignia of lordship to similar lords of ten thousand Indians as he was and ought to be" (Toledo 1940b [1571]: 96).[18] The thrust of the petition was that don Carlos Alaya be recognized legally as the successor to his deceased father, don Cristóbal, and that the latter's brother, don Hernando, be accorded the status of regent because don Carlos was underage. None of the available documents provides data on the decimal title of the paramount of the Hatunxauxa saya, but it seems reasonable to assume that the highest position in each saya was functionally equivalent vis-à-vis the state.

The pachaca (100 households) is the only other decimal office specifically alluded to in a context other than simple enumeration of state offices. Don Felipe Pomacao, a Toledan informant, identified himself as a leader of a pachaca in Lurinwanka: "don Felipe Pomacao, lord of the pachaca of the pueblo of Santana, which is in this saya of the Lurinwankas" (Toledo 1940a [1570]: 26).[19] Other social units conceptualized as having 100 households apparently survived the Toledan resettlements or were reconstituted by the Spaniards for taxation. In testimony for a lawsuit in 1598, litigants argued that a particular individual was not entitled to be lord of an entire ayllu, because his ancestors had been lords over only 100 households, not the entire ayllu: "[T]hese witnesses said that don Cristóbal Cargua Alaya was never lord of said ayllu, over which the suit is brought, but that his ancestors were lords of one hundred Indians of the ayllu" (Espinoza Soriano 1969 [1598]: doc. 4, p. 68).[20]

Although it is not explicitly stated anywhere in the 1570 and 1598 documents, the testimony indicates that units of 100 households were an active component in the provincial Inka administration. The intrusion of the pachaca into ayllu organization has been recorded in the Guancayo, Huallaga, Collaguas, and Chucuito regions, among others, even though it resulted in odd numbers of pachaca within the local sociopolitical units (Espinoza Soriano 1963; Martínez Rengifo 1963 [1571]: 59–60; Zuidema 1964:221; Murra 1975: 171–92; Wachtel 1977:79; Julien 1983:59). The policy of creating odd numbers of pachaca in local sociopolitical groups may have been a principal means by which the Inkas structurally justified conflicting numerical orderings among the populations of the Upper Mantaro.

Powers and Responsibilities of Officials

The available documents from the Xauxa area provide little information on the precise duties and perquisites of decimal office. It is therefore necessary to rely partially on information from other parts of the empire to evaluate the roles of the decimal elites. Chroniclers and commentators generally agree that census taking and supervision of state corvée service were among the principal duties (Rowe 1946:264, 267–68; Moore 1958:116; Murra 1975:23–44). It was undoubtedly an Inka provincial census that allowed the Wankas to

estimate their population of soldiers at 27,000. Although the officials who took the census did not have discretion over the amount of tax to be levied, they did have the authority to delegate tasks within their domain (Moore 1958:70). The right to allocate preferred or odious labor must have given the decimal elites great leverage over subordinates.

Decimal officials were also generally responsible for maintenance of state facilities, particularly lodgings, storehouses, and lands (see Cobo 1956 [1553]: vol. 2, bk. 2, ch. 26, pp. 116–18). In the Xauxa area the construction and maintenance of the administrative center must have required a substantial expenditure of managerial energies, especially if the estimate by Cieza (1984 [1551]: ch. 84, p. 242) of 8,000 possibly rotating attendants is accurate. The road system and wayside traffic control stations also required active supervision, as did management of the extraordinary state storage system.

The present analysis is not sufficiently detailed to determine precisely how the range of activities supervised by a given official varied up and down the hierarchy, although there are some clues. The provincial governor's administrative entourage, for instance, clearly included a number of officials intended to oversee subordinates in the decimal hierarchy. That labor to produce goods or provide services was implemented at differing levels also suggests some systematic variation in decision-making. The removal of the right of local elites to adjudicate certain kinds of disputes further indicates that the scope of decision-making by officials was consistently reduced, going down the ladder of administration. The details of this picture, however, remain to be sketched out.

In return for his labors, the decimal official received extensive rights and privileges, proportional to the individual's position in the hierarchy. According to the petition cited above in which the Ananwanka paramount's son requested recognition of his right to succeed to office, an hunu kuraka was entitled to particular gifts as a mark of office: ". . . the seat and clothing that said Inka was accustomed to give for the insignia of lordship to similar lords of ten thousand Indians as he was and ought to be . . . and Your Excellency gave to said don Carlos and don Hernando, from your hand, two pairs of clothing from that which the Indians are accustomed to wear so that they would have them as insignia of office [of hunu kuraka] and investiture" (Toledo 1940b [1571]: 96–98).[21] The Inkas often presented gifts, such as *qompi* cloth, to elites in ritual ratification of the services provided and of the hierarchical relationship between statuses (Murra 1975:165–66). An instance of this practice occurred when the allegiance of a Lurinwanka leader was wooed through gifts from the conquering Inka army: "[S]aid Thupa Inka . . . had given [the witness's] great-grandfather several elegant shirts and blankets and several cups from which to drink" (Toledo 1940a [1570]: 20).[22]

Ethnic elites could also be termed "Inkas by privilege," a title occasionally given to entire ethnic groups (Rowe 1946:261), but it is not clear what privileges accrued to a person so honored. The favor was apparently granted to the paramount of the Hatunxauxa saya, who was referred to as the "*inga Surichaca*" (Cusichaca et al. 1971 [1561]: 264).[23] In several regions of the empire, some decimal elites were also relieved of corvée duties; favorites were also reportedly awarded private lands (Murúa 1962 [1590–1600]: vol. 1, ch. 26, p. 64; see Murra 1980 [1956]: 36 and Moore 1958:91–92). Each administrator from the pachaca kuraka upward was entitled to support from his community in the form of working his fields, building his house, and guarding his flocks and fields. Similar privileges were requested in 1571 by the petitioner for paramountcy of the Ananwanka saya:

. . . and that [Your Excellency] ordered the Indians who were present and the other Indians of said province of Ananwanka to obey and take said don Carlos as paramount lord and they protect and ensure the protection of all the honors, preeminences, liberties, and exaltations and other things that by reason of said office he ought to have and enjoy and they ought to protect for him and that they should not place any impediment on his rights because Your Excellency has received from that time the use and exercise of said office and ordered [don Carlos] to treat said natives well and not to extract more tribute than that which they were obliged to give.[24] (Toledo 1940b [1571]: 97)

Personal service was also supposed to be a perquisite of office, with officials theoretically having the right to 1 servant per 100 households administered (see Moore 1958:51, 63). Some personal servants attended the Xauxa and Wanka paramounts in the early Colonial Period, but it is not clear how many of them were residual from Inka grants or from previously extant Wanka rights. Shifting the source of legitimacy from the local group to the state may have symbolically accentuated the loss of autonomy suffered by the subject elites. As will be shown later, however, the support of elites occupying positions established by the Inkas was accepted to the extent that it continued well into the Colonial Period.

Recruitment and Succession to State Office

As the following quotation from Toledo (1940a [1570]: 25–26) suggests, the principal criteria for appointment to decimal office apparently were political submission, reliability, and capabilities: "[W]hen some cinchecona came with the Indians who respected them to show obedience to Thupa Inka Yupanki, he made leaders and lords of the Indians, and those who did not come in peace were conquered and he assigned lords himself, those whom he wanted, and of the captains who served him best and from among other Indians he placed leaders and lords as he chose from the captains who served him and from other allies, in this manner without any other consideration"[25] (see also Toledo 1940a [1570]: 29, 32, 36; Vega 1965 [1582]: 167). In the oral history of the Lurinwanka, a native cinche was appointed to a position of status by Thupa Inka Yupanki after having capitulated without a fight (Toledo 1940a [1570]: 19–20). The guiding principle here, as elsewhere in the empire, was to permit loyal local elites to remain in power and to appoint officials from outside to oversee less reliable groups (Moore 1958:92).

Rules governing succession to decimal office are difficult to discern because of bias in the documentary sources and because one individual could hold both state and local office. Toledan informants often contradicted themselves when discussing succession (Moore 1958:90). They would argue, first, that positions were inherited, subject to the successor's having the requisite abilities, and, second, that the Inkas appointed whomever they chose. The latter statements allowed the Spaniards to justify supplanting Inka authority by using the argument that the Inkas ruled arbitrarily and despotically: "[N]either sons nor other relatives succeeded to these offices except at those times when an official died [and] the Inkas saw that a son had ability, they named him to his father's office" (Toledo 1940a [1570]: 29).[26] Similar denials of inheritability of office are refuted by further testimony on succession by sons (Toledo 1940a [1570]: 22, 26, 33, 36).

In addition, the Toledan testimony indicates that offices appointed and recognized by the Inkas were inherited lineally among the Wankas during the sixteenth century. Five informants professed descent from lineages of caciques (Toledo 1940a [1570]: 17, 22, 27,

30, 33); two even contended that their lines dated to appointments made by Thupa Inka Yupanki:

[T]o the second question this witness said that he did not recollect that which occurred before the Inka governed because he did not see it but heard his father, Guamachiguala, and his grandfather Xaxaguaman say who were [the] lords named by the Inka who conquered this land.[27] (Pp. 17–18)

To the first question, he said that he is ninety-three or ninety-four years old and that he descends from a lineage of lords appointed by Thupa Inka Yupanki.[28] (P. 30)

Claims of Inka appointment may have been self-serving efforts to establish legitimacy and thereby obtain benefits under Spanish rule. However, lineally related Wanka and Xauxa elites showed a remarkable capacity for maintaining status as native leaders for the entirety of the sixteenth century. Continuity in office is shown by the lineal retention of the three offices of saya paramount from the time of the Inka emperor Wayna Qhapaq (ca. 1493–1527) at least until 1582 (Vega 1965 [1582]: 166). The details of this succession and its impact on political life are treated below.

From the phrasing in the Toledan documents, it seems almost certain that the officials named were ethnic Wankas. The sole exception was the mitmaqkuna leader don Diego Lucana, who identified himself as a leader of a foreign group, not as a decimal official. This, more than anything else, emphasizes the use of the members of the conquered groups as state officials. The citations also show that several officials attributed their positions directly to appointment by the Inkas and may not have been elites before the Inka conquest. If these stories are correct, they exemplify one of the two principal means by which subjects could reach an elevated status in the empire: worthy administrative service and military valor.

This information raises basic questions in evaluating accession and succession to state office. Given that the Inka and subject rules for succession may have differed somewhat, according to whose rules did local elites normally succeed to state office, and did the rules shift situationally? These questions are critical, because they address whether the state simply used local structures to enact state programs or established its own system of government within the province. The former solution was apparently used in Ecuador, where decimal hierarchies were not installed (Salomon 1986). An alternative system was to modify the decimal hierarchy such that the local and state units were congruent where possible and then let succession continue among the local units, subject to state review. This policy seems to have been followed in several parts of the southern highlands (Zuidema 1964:221; Cock 1977; Julien 1983:57–64) and on the central Peruvian coast (Martínez Rengifo 1963 [1571]).

The data just reviewed for the Upper Mantaro area suggest that the second solution was applied to the Xauxas and Wankas. Rules for direct succession to state offices were probably those of the local societies, because state and local offices were often identical. This conclusion makes sense, given that the sociopolitical groups that formed the basis of state economic support were left essentially intact, even if moved around.

Native Authority at the Saya Level

Political Structure of the Saya

At present, the organization of the indigenous saya hierarchy is only partially explicable, because the Spaniards applied terms of leadership to various offices with little discrimination and because individuals could occupy more than one office simultaneously. Nonetheless, it is clear that native authority above the ayllu and residential community was vested in a limited number of offices dominated by elite kin groups. The key positions are identified in the documents as the *cacique principal* (paramount lord), *segunda persona* (second lord), and *principal* (lesser elite). In brief, the cacique principal was recognized as the paramount of each saya under the Inkas and during Spanish rule. He was assisted by the segunda persona, an immediate subordinate. Below these two highest elites was a series of principales, whose jurisdictions ranged from subsections of the saya to subsections of ayllu.

The relationship between the cacique principal and the segunda persona very likely reflects a dual social division carried into the political sphere (see Cock 1977; Rostworowski 1977a; Julien 1978; Netherly 1978; Salomon 1986). The cacique principal headed the higher of two paired divisions, and the segunda persona headed the lower. The dual structure was widespread in the Andes at the saya level (Rowe 1946: 262) and seems likely to have played a role in saya organization among the societies of the Upper Mantaro. Allusions to principales and caciques principales are common throughout the sources used in this study, but only the Vega visita (1965 [1582]: 166) explicitly mentions segundas personas. At the audience in Santa

Ana de Cincos, in Lurinwanka, four segundas personas accompanied the three caciques principales and other witnesses to give testimony.

One major exception to the dual organization of the saya hierarchy may be found in the available documents. The Hatunxauxa *Memoria* of 1561 (Cusichaca et al. 1971:278) lists a cacique principal and two immediate subordinates. If the premise of duality is to carry through, only one cacique principal and one segunda persona should have existed coevally. One possible explanation is that the saya was divided into three units, rather than two. The principle of division into three parts has also been seen in the existence of three saya and is visible in the organization of some ayllu of Hatunxauxa.[29] Zuidema (1964) argues that the triad division was a fundamental feature of Inka sociopolitical organization. If that was the case, the three units were probably comparable to the dual divisions, in being discrete segments of a larger political unit, perhaps related through kin ties. An alternate explanation is that the two subordinates to Cusichaca corresponded to pichqawaranqa kuraka (lord of 5,000) under the Inkas and that Cusichaca himself was hunu kuraka (lord of 10,000). This fits the Inka structure nicely but is unfortunately not supported by any direct documentary evidence.

Below the segunda persona, the organization is singularly unclear. Constant reference is made to *parcialidades,* which Netherly (1978:118) suggests were "bounded social groups of varying sizes subject to lords of differing ranks." The term *parcialidad* was also regularly applied to each of the two halves of moiety groups in the southern highlands (Pease 1977). The lack of discrimination in the sources suggests that the term was used generically for several distinct groupings, which simply shared the characteristic of being sections of larger units.

The title *principal,* a Spanish catchall for lower elites, was applied to leaders of parcialidades. The title was also accorded to heads of three other distinct political or territorial units: the *pachaca,* which consisted of 100 households (Toledo 1940a [1570]: 26); the *pueblo,* usually a residential community (Toledo 1940a [1570]: 17); and the ayllu (Espinoza Soriano 1969: 36). It is not yet clear whether the Spaniards applied the term *parcialidad* equally to each of these units.

Kinship Basis of the Saya Hierarchy

The title and privileges of the upper echelons of each saya appear to have been vested in a restricted kin group. At the time of the Hatunxauxa and Lurinwanka petitions to the Audiencia Real in Lima in 1558–61, direct descendants of the regional paramounts at the time of Wayna Qhapaq's land reapportionment were still in control (see Cieza 1967 [1553]: ch. 64, p. 215). As was the case at the ayllu level, either brothers or sons could succeed to office.

In the Hatunxauxa saya, don Francisco Cusichaca assumed control of Hatunxauxa sometime after the death of his father, Sulichaque (Cusichaca et al. 1971 [1561]: 278). Between their tenures, an individual referred to only as don Alvaro may have been paramount (Guacrapáucar 1971a [1558]: 201, 202); his relationship to either man is unspecified. Don Francisco Cusichaca was succeeded by Juan Ticsi Cusichac, who held office at least until the end of the sixteenth century (Espinoza Soriano 1969 [1598]: doc. 11, p. 93).

In the Lurinwanka saya, don Felipe Guacrapáucar inherited the title of paramount from his father, don Jerónimo, but lost it to his brother, Carlos Lima Illa (Vega 1965 [1582]: 166; Guacrapáucar 1971c [1560]: 216). Don Felipe Guacrapáucar may have forfeited his title as a result of legal troubles with the Spanish authorities, which plagued him for decades. Dunbar Temple (1942:152) has suggested that Carlos Lima Illa simply held the position on an interim basis, but the evidence on this point is not clear.

The data on sixteenth-century succession in Ananwanka are more complicated (Dunbar Temple 1942: 147–52).[30] Until about 1525 the brothers Sinchi Roca and Sinchi Canga Alaya Sor. had been hunu kuraka of the saya. The latter's son, Macho Alaya, who was serving with Wayna Qhapaq at the time, succeeded to the position. Upon the emperor's death, Macho Alaya accompanied the corpse to Cuzco, apparently an act for which he was awarded two wives. One of these was an aqlla from Hatun Xauxa, and the other reportedly an Inka from Cuzco. He was succeeded in 1546 by his son, don Cristóbal Alaya, who was paramount until some point between 1558 and 1563 (Guacrapáucar 1971a [1558]: 201). A petition dated 1563 was filed with Viceroy Toledo's subordinates in Cuzco in 1571, requesting official sanction of the transfer of power to Carlos Guaina Alaya, son of Cristóbal (Toledo 1940b [1571]: 96–98). Carlos was still underage in 1563, and the petition therefore requested that Cristóbal's brother, Hernando Viza Alaya, be named to rule as regent in Carlos's stead. In 1582, Hernando Viza Alaya was still in office but was called *gobernador,* not cacique principal (Vega 1965 [1582]: 166). This title suggests that Hernando's continued tenure in office was legally respected by the Spaniards even though Carlos had already succeeded to office.

Kin ties between members of the upper echelons of native authority can be shown for the same period. Don Cristóbal Canchaya and don Diego Ñaupari were immediate subordinates to the saya paramount don Francisco Cusichaca. The following somewhat ambiguous statement asserts that the first two men were related either to don Baltazar Canchaya, a principal in the saya, or, less likely, to the saya paramount. Don Baltazar testified "that don Francisco [Cusichaca] is paramount at this time and that don Cristóbal is his relative and don Diego Ñaupari is as well" (Cusichaca et al. 1971 [1561]: 345).[31] Yet another principal of Hatunxauxa—don Alonso Malqui-Cusichac—shared the surname of the paramount, perhaps indicating a real or fictive kin relationship. Similarly, the lord of the Wanka mitmaqkuna at El Quinche, Ecuador, was named don Diego Guaman Ñaupa (Salomon 1986:162). It may therefore be possible that the three top officials and a number of lesser elites were all part of the same close kinship network.[32]

The kin relationships between the paramount lords and immediate subordinates indicate that by the time of the Spanish conquest a separate level of elite native rulers had assumed control of the major provincial offices. In many other ethnographically recorded complex societies, separate elite classes arose, from which leaders were derived, regardless of their relationship to the groups over which they ruled (e.g., Hawaii—see Earle 1978). The Inkas used this system in the upper echelons of government, and they may have promoted a similar system among the Xauxas and the Wankas. The local elites are likely to have been amenable to this arrangement, because the sanctioning of their position by the state would have solidified their position among their own people (see "Coordination of Imperial and Native Authority Systems," below).

Powers and Responsibilities of the Paramounts
As paramount among his own people, the cacique principal represented the saya in relations with outside agents. For instance, when the Inka emperor Wayna Qhapaq settled a boundary dispute in the province, he assembled the three caciques principales (Cieza 1967 [1553]: ch. 64, p. 215). As part of his powers in external affairs, the paramount could delegate business to other saya elites. The Hatunxauxa paramount Sulichaque sent an immediate subordinate to Cajamarca

with gifts for Pizarro in 1533, while the Inka armies still occupied the provincial capital, Hatun Xauxa: "And this witness saw that Sulichaque, the cacique principal who at that time was from said saya [Hatunxauxa], sent all the aforementioned [goods] to Cajamarca with don Diego Ñaupari with three hundred Indians, more or less, to give to said marquis [Francisco Pizarro]" (Cusichaca et al. 1971 [1561]: 345).[33] Sulichaque's ability to dispatch the second-ranking individual in his saya on a mission directly contravening Inka authority verified that he wielded real power among his own people and was not merely a titular head installed by the Inkas.

In 1558–61 the Xauxa and Wanka paramounts filed petitions with the Audiencia Real in Lima to gain restitutions for material goods, food, camelids, and human workers provided the Spaniards from 1533 to 1554 in support of the conquest and later wars. The native lords filed for royal concessions, consisting primarily of rights to land and labor for the paramounts. These petitions show that the leaders continued to represent their people in external affairs in the Colonial Period and that they held the power to mobilize large quantities of goods for political purposes. They also show a willingness on the part of the lords to profit on the behalf of their people.

In the first Memoria of 1558, representatives of each paramount appealed for repayment in the name of the elites and members of the saya: "To Your Highness, we ask and petition in said names [of the paramounts and their representatives] and the other lords and Indians of said valley that you order it seen and accounted that we be paid for that for which we ask equity and costs" (Guacrapáucar 1971a [1558]: 201).[34] The native lords recorded the goods given the Spaniards in detail on khipu, permitting precise itemization of goods provided on specific occasions. The contents of the khipu have been discussed elsewhere (e.g., Espinoza Soriano 1971; Murra 1975:243–54; LeVine 1979; Earle et al. 1980; D'Altroy 1981), and their implications for the state economy are raised in Chapter 8. The lists draw attention to two critical features of the subject political organization, however, in addition to their more obvious economic implications.

First, the paramounts' abilities to repeatedly mobilize large quantities of goods confirm the real power that they exercised. The lords also mobilized more than 7,000 men and women as soldiers and porters for the Spaniards during this period, although these forces were not mobilized according to the proportions used for material goods, as described below (see Murra 1975:246). The centralized political structure within saya, instituted by the Inkas, had apparently become well established among the subjects themselves.

Second, the paramounts coordinated their activities when providing the conquistadores with matériel, underscoring the role of the paramounts in representing their saya in relations with outside agencies. From 1533 until 1537 they often mobilized certain classes of goods in direct proportion to the census enumerations of Hatunxauxa (6,000 soldiers) and Lurinwanka (12,000). Many of these goods were taken from the region's Inka storehouses, maintained by the native lords as a means of protecting their communities from Spanish depredations. When visiting the Mantaro Valley, Cieza (1967 [1553]: ch. 12, pp. 36–37) was highly impressed by the accounting of these mobilizations, maintained by the Lurinwanka paramount Guacrapáucar and his khipu kamayoq.[35] He wrote that, after provisioning the Spaniards with all manner of goods, the lords gathered to even out the amounts in their records: "[A]fter [the Spaniards] had departed, the assembled lords went over their accounts with their khipu and through their use [balanced the accounts], [so that] if one had expended more than another, those who had provided the lesser amount paid him, so that they all were equal" (Cieza 1967 [1553]: ch. 12, p. 37).[36]

The first years of this provisioning, before the first European goods (e.g., chickens) were introduced into the lists in 1537, are particularly significant because Spanish reorganization had yet to take major effect. The 1 : 2 ratio for Hatunxauxa and Lurinwanka can be seen principally in goods with prestige value and in food, including precious metals, mature camelids, qompi cloth, blankets, maize, quinoa, and potatoes (see Earle et al. 1980:36–37 and D'Altroy 1981: Table 7.2; cf. Murra 1975:252, insert, and LeVine 1979). The first gift to Pizarro in Cajamarca in 1533 effectively demonstrates the coordination between saya. These goods, almost certainly given by volition rather than in response to a request from the Spaniards, reflect the 1 : 2 ratio in all classes of goods provided, with the exception of 20 hanegas of potatoes given by Hatunxauxa. Later prestations, particularly those involving a large quantity of goods, such as maize, quinoa, and potatoes, show that the Hatunxauxa saya provided slightly more than 33.3 percent of the goods. It may be that the population of Hatunxauxa exceeded one-half that of Lurinwanka by a small margin. When large quantities of goods were involved, such varia-

tions in population levels may have become important in mobilization. The khipu lists thus show that the Xauxas and Wankas were politically centralized, independent of Inka sanction, and that they coordinated some activity among saya. The lists also demonstrate that the system of mobilizing labor by population under the Inkas also could be extended directly to mobilizing goods. This point is elaborated in Chapter 8.

Most of the perquisites of office of the native lords have been described above in the discussion of the decimal elites. Among the benefits was the grant of noble wives to the favored Macho Alaya. Some of the perquisites of office of paramount lords can also be seen in grants confirmed by Spanish authorities in the first decades of the Colonial Period. The 1563 petition (Toledo 1940b [1571]: 96) on behalf of don Cristóbal Alaya for rights to the clothing, throne, and other insignia of office has already been noted. Other, earlier grants were awarded, notably the confirmation in 1558 in Sicaya, by Garci Diez de San Miguel, of the rights of office for all saya paramounts (Dunbar Temple 1942:151). At that time don Cristóbal Alaya was awarded 200 servants by the Lic. Gasca. Although the Spaniards undoubtedly tailored colonial grants to meet their interests, the grants awarded conform well to those noted for other regions of Tawantinsuyu before the Inka collapse.

Native Authority at the Ayllu Level

The ayllu was the basic corporate, socioeconomic unit for Peruvian highland societies.[37] Each ayllu was a sociopolitical unit with a formally recognized paramount, variously called the cacique principal, the cacique, the kuraka, or the principal in the sources (Espinoza Soriano 1969:30; doc. 1, p. 53; doc. 3, pp. 63, 65; doc. 4, p. 68). It seems highly likely that the ayllu was formally divided into subunits, each of which had a recognized office of leader, although the number and organization of these subunits are unclear. Most studies of ethnic groups under the Inkas emphasize the pervasive dual character of sociopolitical organization. Units at several levels of organization, including the ayllu, were divided unto upper (hanan) and lower (hurin) divisions. The guiding principle is that the overall paramount headed the hanan division and spoke for the group as a whole in external relations, and a lower elite headed the hurin division.

To a certain extent, the principal of duality can be documented as a part of the Upper Mantaro societies.

For instance, the ayllu Lurinhuaila had an Ananhuaila counterpart (Espinoza Soriano 1969 [1598]: doc. 4, p. 66). The ayllu Llampa y Pallpa also had a dual name. Additionally, the name of the ayllu Ichoca means "left" in Quechua, the implication being that there existed a right ayllu (Allauca) and perhaps even a center ayllu (Chaupi) (Espinoza Soriano 1969 [1571]: doc. 1, p. 54). Whether these matched ayllu were corporate entities themselves or were sectors of larger units is not clear.

An alternative division can be seen in a quotation cited in the next section ("Ayllu Population"), which states that the ayllu Lurinhuaila contained at least one subunit of 100 Indians, with a formal leader. Espinoza Soriano (1969:15) suggests that Lurinhuaila and another ayllu called Llampray, Cacras, y Purac were each divided into three pachaca. He offers no evidence to substantiate this number of divisions for Lurinhuaila, and the evidence for the other ayllu seems to be based solely on the tripartite name. In favor of this interpretation, it should be noted that the ayllu Jauja-Collana may correspond to one part of the qollana-payan-kayao structure that Zuidema (1964) contends formed the basis of the Inka organization in Cuzco and throughout the empire. This structure has been documented for the Collaguas and Chucuito areas, among other regions, and it may apply to the Xauxas and Wankas as well (Zuidema 1964:221; Cock 1977:108; Wachtel 1977:79).

With the present data, the conflict between the dual and triad principles cannot be structurally resolved (cf. Netherly 1978:330). The importance inferences can be taken, however, that the ayllu contained a formal internal structure and that Inka decimal units may have been equated with some of the subunits.

Ayllu Population

As might be expected from groups founded on kinship, the population of ayllu could vary substantially, with the size potentially ranging into the thousands. According to the census data reported in the 1582 visita of Vega (1965:167), the saya of Hatunxauxa contained about 6,000 soldiers. The partial list of ayllu in the saya compiled from legal documents published by Espinoza Soriano (1969: docs. 1–4, pp. 51–72) contains 12 indigenous and 1 mitmaq ayllu: Jauja-Collana; Marco; Paca; Ichoca; Guamachuco (mitmaq); Llampray, Cacras, y Purac (or Sacras); Llocllapampa; Guacras; Lurinhuaila; Ananhuaila; Llampa y Pallpa; Huarancayo; and Guaillas.[38] Judging from the number of ayllu and from regional population estimates, each

ayllu may have contained no more than about 500 soldiers or heads of household. On average, that figure would indicate a population of 3,000.

Specific demographic information is available for only one ayllu: Lurinhuaila in the village of Huacjrasmarca. The ayllu was divided into units considered to encompass 100 households each (pachaca). One deposition in the litigation over succession to the *cacicazgo* of Lurinhuaila reads: "[T]hese witnesses said that don Cristóbal Cargua Alaya was never lord of said ayllu, over which the suit is brought, but that his ancestors were lords of one hundred Indians of the ayllu. And that the part [lineage?] of don Juan were those that were paramount lords of the ayllu" (Espinoza Soriano 1969 [1598]: doc. 4, p. 68).[39] The 100 Indians referred to were probably heads of household, that being the normal manner of counting population. The kurakas of 100 Indians may therefore have been lords of about 600 individuals, on average, assuming that the pachaca really contained that many households. Because the lord of 100 Indians was, by implication, not the paramount of the ayllu, there must have been more than one pachaca. This ayllu could thus have encompassed 1,200 or more people (2 pachaca of 600 people each). The apparent discrepancy between the mean ayllu population and that of Lurinhuaila may be attributable to imprecise correspondence between real pachaca, whose population undoubtedly varied, and pachaca legally considered to have 100 householders. The number of pachaca within ayllu may also have varied, and the list above is most likely incomplete for the saya.

Succession of Ayllu Leadership

The available evidence is overwhelming for patrilateral inheritance of office in the ayllu and at the saya level. According to the litigation for rights to the office of ayllu paramount, only males held office and only sons or brothers (and maybe parallel cousins) of officeholders succeeded them. The reader is referred to Espinoza Soriano (1969) for a detailed examination of this case (see also LeVine 1979; D'Altroy n.d.), but two aspects of succession should be emphasized. First, the leadership of the contested Lurinhuaila ayllu was ostensibly maintained within a single kin group from the time of Thupa Inka Yupanki's rule (ca. 1471–93) until 1571 (Espinoza Soriano 1969 [1571–1602]: docs. 1 and 4, pp. 53, 66, 71). The litigation arose only when the Spaniards installed a lower elite in office, apparently with the collusion of the saya paramount. Second, succession was not directly lineal. In the succession traced by Espinoza Soriano (1969:48, insert), each male in a generation apparently succeeded to office before the position passed to the descending generation. This policy is one of three general options for succession followed in the Andes (Rostworowski 1961, 1988:140–42). The other two were direct primogeniture and succession through the son of the paramount elite's sister (SiSo). Because the local rules for succession were familiar to the Inkas, incorporation of native elites into the Inka authority system, from top to bottom, would have been greatly facilitated.

Multi-ayllu Authority

The ayllu may not have been the maximal residential unit, because one loosely defined community could subsume several ayllu. In the case of the unreduced village of Huacjrasmarca (also called Guacras or Huajlasmarca), on the southwest side of the Río Mantaro gorge, at least two and perhaps three of the ayllu listed above may have resided in the village before 1571: Guacras, Lurinhuaila, and Ananhuaila. Mango Misari, paramount of Lurinhuaila, lived in Huacjrasmarca with his ayllu in about 1533. The following citation, a question asked by a Spanish legal authority in the litigation, implies that the lord of Lurinhuaila was also lord of the pueblo itself: "After the death of said Mango Misari, who was the lord of said town of Guacras and came to govern its Indians?" (Espinoza Soriano 1969 [1571]: doc. 1, p. 56).[40] Mango Misari's son, Juan Mango Misari, was ayllu paramount circa 1571–86 and also lived in Huacjrasmarca, as is apparent in this reference to him: "Juan Mango Misari, lord who at present is from the town of Guacras" (Espinoza Soriano 1969 [1571]: doc. 1, p. 53).[41]

A further reference establishes that the ayllu Guacras and Lurinhuaila were discrete entities, although closely affiliated: "Hernando Guaman Alaya, who is from the ayllu of Sacras and not from that of Guacras, which is conjunct with [united with? adjacent to?] the ayllu of Lurinhuaila" (Espinoza Soriano 1969 [1599]: doc. 3, p. 106).[42] This distinction was important to the litigation discussed above, because Alaya claimed a tie to Lurinhuaila by being a member of the ayllu Guacras Lurinhuaila (Espinoza Soriano 1969 [1597]: doc. 4, p. 64; see also Espinoza Soriano 1969 [1571]: doc. 1, p. 54, for another reference to the ayllu Guacras). Conversely, the other side in the suit argued that Alaya and his father were members of other ayllu—either Llampa y Pallpa or Sacras—and therefore had no rights to land, power, or services in Huacjrasmarca (Espinoza

Soriano 1969 [1597, 1599]: doc. 4, p. 65; doc. 13, p. 106). This information suggests that the other ayllu were resident in other communities, at least at the time of the litigation. It also confirms the ayllu as the fundamental source of rights and identification among the local populations.

One deposition also refers to the ayllu of Ananhuaila, resettled in the town of Huaripampa in the Spanish reduction of 1571, along with Lurinhuaila and several other ayllu (Espinoza Soriano 1969 [1598]: doc. 4, p. 66). It seems probable that Ananhuaila and Lurinhuaila formed paired ayllu, composing a greater unit. Whether Ananhuaila also resided in the town of Guacras is not specified in the documents.

Another apparent instance of residential pairing—between the ayllu Llocllapampa and Llampray, Cacras, y Purac—is evidenced in the following references: "Don Martín Carbanampa, of the ayllu of Llocllapampa, who seemed to be more than fifty" (Espinoza Soriano 1969 [1571]: doc. 1, p. 54),[43] and "Indians of the ayllu and parcialidad of Llampray, Cacras, y Purac, of which Hernando Carua Arannia is lord, who are settled in the town of Llocllapampa [and are] subjects of the cacique don Hernando Pascual Riquira" (Espinoza Soriano 1969 [1599]: 30).[44] The members of these groups most likely resided in the village that is now known as the archaeological site of Llocllapampa, above modern Parco.

The likely presence of multiple ayllu in one village raises two questions pertinent to the political organization of the time. First, did a central authority coordinate all ayllu in a given settlement? Political relationships assuredly existed and problems arose among ayllu or concerning all members of the community. In the case of paired ayllu or subayllu, such as Lurinhuaila (lower) and Ananhuaila (upper), evidence from elsewhere in the Andes is overwhelming that Ananhuaila would have been dominant (e.g., Rowe 1946:262; Zuidema 1964; Netherly 1978). In the case in which unmatched ayllu lived adjacent to one another, two solutions seem possible. One is that they kept segregated enough spatially and territorially that they considered themselves to be independent of one another. The quotations cited above, however, suggest that the lord of the ayllu Lurinhuaila was also the lord of the town Guacras and that the ayllu Guacras and Lurinhuaila were joined in some fashion. The existence of the lord don Hernando Pascual Riquira as superior to the ayllu lord(s) of the town of Llocllapampa further implies some form of coordinated authority among ayllu. It therefore seems likely that a hierarchy of authority existed between co-resident ayllu, even if they were not paired by name.

One comment by Cieza (1984 [1551]: ch. 84, p. 243) helps clarify the situation. In describing the pre-Inka settlements, fortified and set on hilltops, he notes that they were divided into *barrios*. Architectural remains of some Wanka II and III settlements—especially Llamap Shillón and Tunanmarca—are divided into residential sectors internally divided by stone walls. Tunanmarca is also notable for its complex of central plazas and public architecture, likely shared by all residents of the community. Although UMARP has not addressed the problem of segregated neighborhoods through archaeological research,[45] the split residential zones strongly suggest that socially discrete groups lived in the settlement. Whether these groups conform to ayllu or to some other social unit remains open to question.

A second question concerns why multiple, discrete corporate groups lived in the same settlement before the Spanish reduction of 1571. One possibility is that the warfare of the Wanka II period forced consolidation of independent groups into defensible villages for security. These associations may have been maintained under Inka rule in communities that did not resettle in new locations. Alternatively, demographic reshuffling under the Inkas may have combined previously separate social units. If so, the coordinated political relationships among ayllu may have been a response to state requirements or census practices. Present data are unfortunately inadequate to resolve these questions satisfactorily, despite their importance to reconstructing the local authority system under Inka rule.

Coordination of Imperial and Native Authority Systems

In the Upper Mantaro Valley, state political organization did not appear as an indigenous, evolutionary development. Rather, it was an imposed solution to managerial problems, the result of a need to satisfy economic and political goals associated with imperial expansion. At the time of the Inka conquest, the political fragmentation of the Xauxas and Wankas had posed immediate administrative problems for the new sovereigns. No unified authority system existed through which the state could govern the province as a unit. Yet the Xauxas and Wankas were sophisticated enough to pose a substantial military threat. Moreover, the Inkas could not effectively pursue the imperial goals of economic and political exploitation without some kind of integration of the state and local authority systems.

In the province of Wanka Wamaní, the Inkas created a state political system using principles of authority differentiation already present among the native populace. If we accept Wright's (1977) model of a state's constituting a polity with a three-tiered administrative hierarchy, the addition of a supralocal authority system would have brought the Wankas into the state sphere. At least four administrative levels were present: the paramount authority at Cuzco, the provincial governor and staff, the saya paramounts, and the lesser saya and ayllu elites. It seems likely that before the Inka conquest the local hierarchies had not developed a system more complex than a complex chiefdom; that is, they did not have personnel whose role consisted of policymaking. The decision-making hierarchy at and above the level of saya paramount was thus clearly an Inka introduction.

A decision-making structure alone does not describe a state adequately, however. States normally entail a ruling class, a centralized monopoly of force, arrogation of juridical rights to the central authority, and often an administered sector to the economy (Flannery 1972:403–4). The integration of these features into a more or less coherent whole characterizes a territorial state and separates it from a polity with tributary relationships outside the zone of political control. This transition from indirect, hegemonic control to territorial rule is precisely what the Inkas undertook in Wanka Wamaní. The persistence of some Incaic political features—notably the consolidation of entire saya under local paramounts—into the Colonial Period shows the effectiveness of the Inkas in increasing subject political authority.

In altering the character of regional authority, the Inkas applied several complementary policies. They introduced a state bureaucracy while increasing the complexity of the native authority systems, a move that benefited both local elites and the state. The role of the native elites altered to incorporate the demands of the state as well as the continuing needs of the commoners. This change reduced the elites' power to make independent decisions over subordinate populations but provided them greater leverage in maintaining their positions. Features of the native system that had been in flux, such as the territory of political units, were frozen in the process. In effect, the Inkas used a complex nonstate system as the foundation of a state organization, whose goal was to expedite exploitation of the regional resources.

The coordination of the two systems created structural problems for the Inkas. The central issue was justifying a decimal system with a local system built on dual or triad principles of organization. Although the precise solution is still sketchy, some aspects can be inferred. As was argued earlier, the tripartite provincial division into saya seems to have reflected an antecedent Wanka II form (Late Intermediate Period). The pre-Inka organization was fluid, however, and the creation of the three saya thus imposed greater regional unification than had existed previously.

Each saya had a paramount lord, an office established by the Inkas but filled by local elites. The paramounts in this system held decimal offices at the same time that they filled native elite positions. The decimal hierarchy also invaded the ayllu, as shown by the presence of multiple pachaca within kin-based corporate units. It is highly likely that the native elites between the saya paramounts and the pachaca leaders filled the other positions in the decimal hierarchy. Ayllu paramounts may have filled lower intermediate positions, or several ayllu may have been drawn together for state administrative purposes. The apparent modification of the decimal system to accommodate local organization and demography confirms Murra's (1958) contention that the decimal hierarchy was only an ideal structure that did not really reflect population distributions. The policy of minimizing the discontinuity between the two political systems may have been adopted because the economic system supporting the state in its early years was founded in the local units. By interfering with the operation of the local groups, the Inkas would have reduced the productivity of the system supporting the state.

The dual role played by the local elites was key to the effective administration of the province. With respect to the local group, the lord was both an aristocrat and a leader, and the group was a source of economic support and a constituent body. Under the Inkas, the native lord who took on the role of state administrator was saddled with the additional responsibility of passing on state requirements for labor and goods. From the perspective of the state, the local elites were state functionaries responsible for low-level management of state projects. It was to the state's benefit, therefore, to cultivate the lords with prestigious gifts and economic support. By retaining right of approval over all official positions, however, the Inkas ensured that the personnel were amenable to state supervision.

In sum, the political organization of Wanka Wamaní in the Late Horizon was more complex and integrated than it had been in the Late Intermediate Period. This development was a direct consequence of imperial managerial problems, but the Wanka elites adopted the centralization into a continuing system because of the increase in power it afforded them.

8

The Imperial Economy

The Inka conquests created a need for an economic support system that could sustain imperial personnel and underwrite political relations between the state and its subordinate elites. This need was met through two interlocking components of the imperial political economy: a staple finance economy and an associated system that produced prestige or wealth support (cf. Polanyi 1957; Murra 1975, 1980 [1956]; D'Altroy and Earle 1985). In the staple finance sector, goods were mobilized either indirectly as products of corvée or more directly through attached specialists, satisfying requirements for subsistence and utilitarian goods and for basic services. The complementary sumptuary system produced the goods that were used to legitimate hierarchical linkages and to fund ceremonial activities and political relations. Both economic components entailed production, consumption, and exchange of the resources used to maintain the state institutions that integrated and controlled the subject polities.

The imperial political economy was initially developed as an extension of the subsistence and political economies present among the highland societies that were first drawn under Inka control. Dependent at the beginning on the corvée of subject communities, the economy progressively underwent a shift toward independent production (see Murra 1980 [1956]: 183–86). The principal steps in this shift included creation of specialized labor statuses and establishment of state centers of production, coupled with intensification of productive resources. By the time of the Spanish conquest, the state supported a wide range of agricultural and craft production settlements that provided an increasing proportion of the goods that underwrote state activities. The periodic labor of the peasantry remained the bulwark of state production even at the end, but a trend toward attached, specialized production was unmistakable.

Because the political economy served the purpose of supporting the state and its personnel, it extracted and exploited the labor and resources previously at the disposal of subject populations. Some subjects benefited economically in some ways from imperial rule, such as in more-diversified diets, in increased elite access to some long-distance goods, and in increased access to lands previously off-limits because of chronic conflict. The essence of the political economy, however, was intensification of production, through increased specialization of labor and development of state resources, and distribution of goods and services for state disposal.

This chapter explores the institutional forms that state demands took and the energetics involved in implementing some of those strategies. Of particular interest here are the production of food and the distribution of ceramics and other goods of state manufacture. The chapter begins with a sketch of the foundations of the Inka political economy in the sierra societies upon which it was initially based. That discussion is followed by a more theoretical consideration of the overall structure of the political economy. Together they provide the context within which to consider the nature of the Inka economy in the Upper Mantaro region.

Foundations of the Inka Political Economy

The sierra societies upon which the state depended for its early model tended to be generalized in subsistence production. As was described previously, the ayllu formed the basic resource-holding unit in the central Andes.[1] Ranging up to several thousand members, the ayllu held lands communally, allocating them through usufruct. The basic principle underlying access to resources was that one held rights to agricultural land, pastoral grasslands, water, and other critical resources through membership in the kin group. The elite members of the community had rights to have their lands worked, herds tended, and some craft products manufactured, theoretically in return for their role as leaders of the community (Murra 1980 [1956]). Although it is not clear how widespread the practice was, some elite males were also apparently entitled to multiple wives, who provided, among other amenities, an increase in politically useful household labor. In return for these privileges, the kurakas were responsible for adjudicating disputes, providing military and ceremonial leadership, and providing ceremonial hospitality. The ideology propounded throughout the Andes was that this relationship was one of reciprocal obligations (see Wachtel 1977:70–73).

The ideal ayllu territory recorded in the early documents encompassed all basic ecological zones in the region within lands held by the corporate group. According to Murra (1972), sierra community members resided in settlements distributed throughout their territory, pooling and exchanging resources internally. The principal community would normally be located near the ecotone between the maize- and tuber-growing zones, and satellite villages would be located

from the high puna, where camelid herds were most effectively raised, down to the upper edge of the jungle, the source of coca, pepper, and tropical fruits. Murra has suggested that communities could also establish small settlements at points of specialized productivity, such as in zones favorable to coca cultivation or salt collection. Although solid evidence exists for the establishment of such vertical archipelagoes under Inka rule, especially along the eastern slopes, widespread hostilities throughout the Andes immediately preceding the imperial expansion would have made such an arrangement of multiethnic resource sharing highly unlikely.

Upon conquering a region, the state appropriated rights to all resources within the subject territory. The resources were then divided up among the state, the state religion, and the subject communities. The available evidence suggests that the administrative side of the state superstructure had substantially more resources at its disposal than did the religion. In exchange for corvée (mit'a), the state allocated access to productive agricultural and pastoral lands back to the communities, but it retained a monopoly on many wild and mineral resources, notably metals. In practice, communities retained a high proportion of their original resources, but they yielded prime land to the state in many areas.

Members of the local communities were required to perform myriad duties for the state. In 1549 and 1562, for instance, members of the Chupachu ethnic group of the Huánuco region reported having fulfilled 31 separate classes of productive and service duties for the Inkas, including generalized agricultural production; construction near the home communities, at provincial centers, or at Cuzco; mining gold and silver; performing guard duty in locations ranging from Quito to Cuzco; growing coca and peppers; collecting feathers and honey from the lowlands; tending state herds; and manufacturing sandals, pottery, and wooden objects (Helmer 1955–56 [1549]; Ortiz de Zúñiga 1967 [1562], 1972 [1562]; see Julien 1982, 1988, and LeVine 1987). Each of these and other assignments was allocated according to the population of the region. In return for their efforts, the laborers were entitled to be supported with food and chicha while they were carrying out state directives. Other rights included the annual distribution of sandals and a new set of clothing to soldiers.

The goods that were produced or gathered were stored in massive storage facilities at Cuzco, provincial centers, and tampu. The storehouses played a pivotal role in the state political economy, for goods were made available to permanent and temporary personnel housed at the imperial installations and to itinerant state travelers. The principal purpose of the stockpiles, however, was to support state laborers and the imperial armies.

The Inkas and their subjects insisted to the Spanish inspectors throughout the empire that the peasants owed only their labor and no material products (e.g., Polo 1917 [1567]; see Murra 1986). For instance, cloth woven for the state by the women of the peasant communities came from wool sheared from state herds, and seed sowed on state lands came from imperial supplies. Moore (1958:49) has observed, however, that the Inkas received both labor and services as products of subject efforts. Moreover, the Inkas reportedly determined the amount of seed to be sown and the amount of cloth to be woven on an annual basis, according to state needs. Thus, the labor input of the subjects varied according to state requirements and was not an immutable, fixed obligation. At present, it is unclear precisely how state personnel estimated the state's needs, but it may be inferred that the labor tax was the dependent variable in the state economy and that projected needs for services and matériel conditioned state demands (see D'Altroy and Earle 1985).

The Inka Political Economy as a Dendritic System

Most recent authors who have addressed the nature of the Inka political economy have followed either a substantive or a Marxist economic perspective. The former perspective, derived initially from the writings of Karl Polanyi (esp. 1957) and elaborated through the influential work of John Murra (e.g., 1975, 1980 [1956]), subscribes to the premise that economic relations were embedded in the sociopolitical matrix. This premise assumes that the nature and development of economic relations are specific to the society within which they occur. Many studies of the Inka economy thus concern how economic processes, such as production and exchange, were undertaken in contexts peculiar to a given historical circumstance. The values, motives, and policies of Andean societies are taken to have determined economically rational behavior. From this view, the processes that contributed to economic developments are comparable across societies only to the extent that the social and political contexts, the motivations, and the values are comparable.

Two substantivist economic notions receiving great attention in the Andean literature derive from Polanyi's (1957:128) classification of exchange into reciprocity, redistribution, and (market) exchange. In Andean studies, *reciprocity* is generally taken to imply an obligatory relationship of exchange defined by social or political relationships. The term has been applied to varied contexts, among them simple dyadic exchanges between members of social groups occupying zones that produced specialized cultivated or gathered subsistence crops. Examples of this kind of reciprocity are found in the exchange of salt and maize among the Tarama and Upper Mantaro societies early in the Colonial Period (e.g., Vega 1965 [1582]: 171) and of coca and *ch'arki* (dried meat) between montaña and puna societies. *Asymmetrical reciprocity* is taken to be the fundamental form of political exchange that characterized relationships between native elites and commoner populations throughout the Andes in late prehistory (e.g., Wachtel 1977:62–75). This relationship, often described in structural terms, consisted of mutual obligations between the elite stratum of society and the subject groups that supported it. In this relationship the elites received labor and material support, in return for which they provided political, economic, and religious leadership, as well as food, chicha, and various other material goods. Although these exchanges were consistently couched in terms of mutual responsibilities, it does not take a jaundiced eye to see this relationship as exploitative.

Asymmetrical reciprocity grades into redistribution in the literature on the Inka and subject economies. As originally proposed by Polanyi (1957:128), redistribution referred simply to "appropriational movements towards a center and out of it again." Murra (1980 [1956]) initially posited that the Inka state economy functioned as a redistributive agency, taking in the goods produced through the labor of subject populations and reallocating them to the people who performed the labor, after a cut was taken out to support the state apparatus. Although he disavowed Garcilaso's (1960 [1609]) notion of Tawantinsuyu as a welfare state, Murra viewed the production, storage, and distribution cycle of the political economy as a substitute for a market system. In later writings (e.g., Murra 1975), he reconsidered this position, but the notion of redistribution as the organizing feature of the Inka and other political economies remains a dominant element in the Andean literature.

Evaluations of redistribution subsequent to the original postulations have shown that the term encompasses several kinds of economic relations. Smelser (1959), for example, distinguished among household-ing, share-out, pooling, and mobilization as increas-ingly comprehensive and complex kinds of redistribu-tive exchange relationships. Each type is characterized by movement of goods into a central authority and some reverse movement away from the center, but the level of the social unit involved and the scale and pur-pose of the movement differ significantly. Earle (1977, 1978) argued that mobilization is most characteristic of more-complex societies—that is, in polities ranging from chiefdoms to states, both of which may be funded through staple finance. Mobilization is essentially a political economic process whereby labor and goods are extracted from a subject populace to support the elite sector of society and its associated personnel, such as craft specialists and functionaries. Relatively few of the goods that reach the center ever find their way back down the line, and those that do are exchanged in political and ceremonial contexts. Mobilization thus does not serve as a means of providing the basic sub-sistence needs of the general populace.

Marxist analyses of the Inka economy focus on such issues as inequalities of class, social relations of pro-duction, and central control of productive resources. Godelier (1974) and Lumbreras (1978), for example, have suggested that the state itself derived from class conflict over access to the means of production. It is difficult to understand that perspective, given that Inka society may not have been class differentiated until the military conquests established the need for more-complex administrative structures. A more useful ele-ment of the Marxist approach has been the focus on control of peasant labor by the elite stratum (e.g., Espinoza Soriano 1975). A number of analysts have drawn attention to the central change in the social relations of production in the Inka economy—from the state's dependence on the general labors of the peasantry to the development of independent institu-tions of attached specialization. This transition was detailed first by Murra (1980 [1956]), in his seminal dissertation on the Inka economy, but the Marxist view offers an alternative perspective. By emphasizing the exploitative aspects of the relationship rather than the integrative aspects of traditional institutions, the Marxists draw attention to the increasing class differ-entiation that the elites were fostering within the em-pire (Patterson 1985).

These perspectives provide significant insight into the organization and development of the Inka political economy, but they downplay or avoid several critical issues. The most important of those issues derives from evaluation of the criteria underlying the shifts in in-stitutional relations developed under state auspices, particularly in latter decades of Inka rule. Given that the state developed new institutions of production that differed from existing forms, we may ask if the new economic processes or relations were extensions of ex-isting forms or if they represented significant transfor-mations. Wachtel (1977:62–75) and Murra (1980 [1956]) have argued that the Inka political economy can be seen as a local or regional economy expanded to encompass the empire. Conversely, the Inkas clearly were transforming relations of production from de-pendence on corvée to development of specialized la-bor classes. Such variables as the energetics of different forms of production, transportation costs, and the rel-ative security of differing strategies are particularly sig-nificant here. If it can be shown that the new forms of economic activity and institutions created by the state or transformed from prior models were significantly more efficient than those that preceded them, it may be reasonable to postulate that the development of the state economy resulted from a calculated interplay be-tween sociopolitical and energetic considerations.

Given the limitations of the preceding arguments, it may be more effective to conceive of the Inka economy as a nonmarket, central-place, dendritic system (Fig. 8.1).[2] This structure was characterized by strong verti-cal ties and few, if any, horizontal exchanges. Regions were integrated with one another primarily through mutual ties with higher levels in the hierarchy. The hierarchy was appropriate to a system in which eco-nomic interactions were largely structured around po-litical relationships and in which the political economy functioned to extract resources from a region whose economy it did not control directly, as was often the case in archaic empires.

This model may be envisioned as a variant of one of a series of ideal distribution models described by Carol Smith (1976), which associate specific kinds of pro-duction and distribution of goods with labor organiza-tion and the spatial distribution of elites. From the least to the most complex, the spatial models are as follows: extended network systems, bounded network systems, solar central-place systems, dendritic central-place systems, and interlocking central-place systems. Smith (1976:319) argues that political-territorial or administrative systems are always based on the solar central-place model, because administrative systems cannot afford to permit overlap of boundaries or com-petition between centers. This model is associated

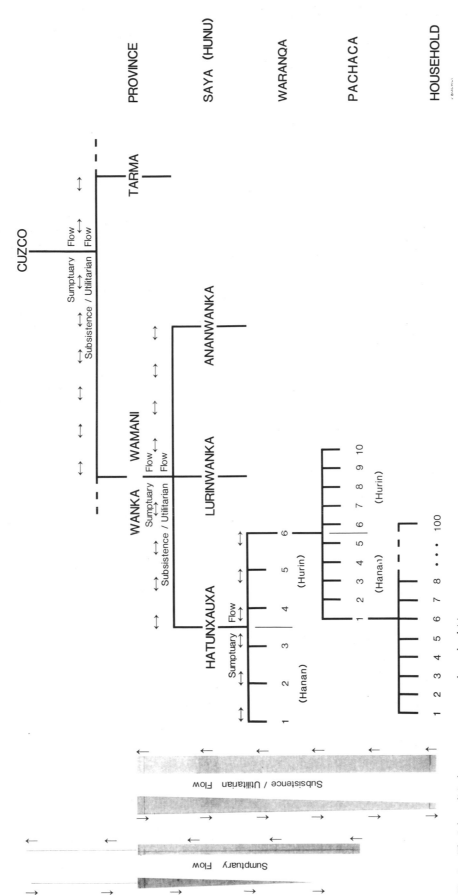

Fig. 8.1. The Inka political economy, represented as a dendritic structure.

with partially commercialized distribution systems and partially stratified social systems (Smith 1976: 338). Members of the elite and merchants invariably live in urban centers, which are several times larger than any other places in the system. Fully differentiated from the rural hinterland, the urban centers need to be supported by rural production.

Smith's assertion that administrative systems are invariably based on this spatial-distributive model appears to be founded on a series of assumptions that are not necessarily applicable to the Andean case. The most important of them is that "market trade is necessary to the operation of the economy" (Smith 1976: 340). The basis of the last three models cited above, in fact, is a market economy, in which the peasantry is bound economically to the elite stratum through elite control over one or more of the factors of production.

The Inka economy and most of the subject societies it ruled were not dependent upon on price-setting markets, however. With the partial exceptions of the north and central coasts of Peru and the highlands of Ecuador, Andean societies did not rely heavily on specialized, integrated economies. Under Inka rule, elites generally did not import basic commodities strategic to the normal operation of the provincial economy, such as tools or industrial goods, nor did they serve as middlemen for exports. The sketchy evidence available indicates that, with the exception of sumptuary goods, little was exported from any given region or flowed back down the chain from elites to commoners. Virtually all utilitarian goods were manufactured locally or were obtained through dyadic or polyadic exchanges among the peasantry. Similarly, the commoner population did not generally manufacture goods designed for export; most exported goods were produced by attached specialists. Specialized production may have been present among sierra societies, but specialization for a general-demand population appears to have operated independent of elite oversight (see Earle et al. 1987; Costin and Earle 1989; Costin et al. 1989).

Because markets did not exist in most imperial territory and because, as Smith suggests (1976:323), commercial integration would have eroded the elites' power base, the lack of market development under Inka rule is not surprising. The Inkas themselves neither were market oriented nor had the power to control or effectively tap into an economy organized along those lines among subject populations. It is noteworthy in this regard that the Inkas took little advantage of the specialized economies of the north and central coasts of Peru (Netherly 1978; Ramirez-Horton 1982) and may have suppressed market systems to some degree in the highlands of Ecuador by pooling control of regional exchange in some goods under sanctioned elites (Salomon 1986).

Under these conditions, the dendritic central-place model that Smith employs to describe monopolistic markets or peripheries of modern economic systems seems structurally most appropriate in describing the Inka economy. Among the key features of this type of economy is a linear arrangement that is inclusively vertical, with different levels linking to several smaller places but to only one major, high-level center in a region (Smith 1976:319). This organization is efficient for channeling the flow of raw materials upward to the central place and the flow of specialized goods down from the major center. The linear, hierarchical nature of the system and its central role as a means of bulking goods for consumption by higher levels are clearly appropriate to the Inka case. Given that Smith's conception of this model—like the solar central-place model—was based on a market economy, however, the model must be modified.

If the state political system is treated as a demand population, without specifying the nature of the exchange mechanism, the structure may accommodate the Inka situation.[3] The state economy was designed to channel natural resources and their products upward, mobilizing support for the elite institutions of the sociopolitical system. It did not provide a means of circulating goods among specialized subsystems of the general populace nor did it serve as a surrogate market. Because the economy was designed as an extractive system, the flow of goods was heavily weighted in the upward direction. Food and craft goods produced for the state were bulked at central places where they were either consumed by state personnel or redirected to support state activities elsewhere.

Those goods and services directed back down the hierarchy were intended to meet two needs, both of which ultimately served to maintain the upward flow. First, subsistence support was necessary for the personnel who were responsible for state production. Second, political relations with subordinate elites needed to be cemented. As was observed in Chapter 7, the Inkas' dependence on subject elites to administer state projects required that the elites be courted with perquisites of office at the same time that they be coerced into collaboration.

In archaic political economies, these needs could have been met through a variety of means, such as fixed tribute or a proportional tax on the products of the general populace. The Inkas, initially reliant on economic relations established before their ascendancy, opted for an alternate strategy based on the establishment of discrete elite or state resources from which most goods in the political economy were developed. Among these resources were agricultural and pastoral lands, mines, and undomesticated biota. The strategy left the products of resources in commoner hands largely untouched, although the alienation of peasant resources effectively amounted to removing productive potential from the hands of the general populace (see Salomon 1986:158–72).

Within this overall strategy, a series of options lay along the continuum from low control–low investment to high control–high investment. The least intensive approach was to permit producers to support themselves from their own resources while working for the state. This option was most broadly followed early in the imperial development and for the production of general subsistence and utilitarian goods throughout the empire. It may also have been applied toward some peripheries of the empire where the object of state occupation was largely the procurement of minerals, metals, or other kinds of specialized products, either within or beyond state limits. This stratagem was ineffective for close control over production and distribution, however.

In a second, more intensive approach, the state provided workers with resources that they could cultivate or exploit to support themselves. This option was most effectively used with colonists (mitmaqkuna) resettled in new territories to work specific resources for the state. The evidence for state farms suggests that they were organized primarily along these lines (e.g., Wachtel 1982; La Lone and La Lone 1987). This system afforded the state increased control over the labor rendered and the products yielded but was not significantly more efficient than the first option.

A third stratagem was the formation of enclaves of attached specialists who worked full-time for the state and were not required to produce for themselves. This intensive approach was the least fully developed by the state and was limited exclusively to specialized producers, such as the sequestered aqllakuna and craft specialists of the highest status, including the smiths producing the finest metalwork and textiles for the state (see "Specialized Labor Statuses and Craft Pro-

duction," below). Such an institution provided the elite authorities the greatest control, because the producers were under the immediate direction of the consumers. It also afforded the gains in efficiency that specialization and quality control provide. The cost of this approach was a high investment in developing resources by the state and an increase in supervisory and supportive personnel.

Although the data on the issue remain sketchy, it appears that the state was moving toward this more direct (territorial) strategy of attached specialization in the latter decades of the empire (Murra 1980 [1956]: 153–86). In this shift, one subset of state personnel produced the agricultural and utilitarian commodities required by craft specialists and service personnel. The development was uneven throughout the empire, a situation partially explicable by the varied nature of economic organization among the subject societies. In addition, the transition was only partially realized by the time of the Spanish conquest, and it is not clear to what extent the shift would have been undertaken had the Inkas been left to develop the economy more fully.

Most complex distribution systems, including the dendritic central-place system, depend on the coexistence of one or more of the other types of exchange in the broader economy (Smith 1976:314). That was certainly the case in the present instance. Murra (1980 [1956]) has shown that the success of the Inka imperial political economy was initially predicated on the existence of subordinate economies that could be intensified to support state personnel and activities. The state's continued heavy dependence on the productivity of self-sufficient producers required that the subject subsistence economies continue to function effectively at the local level. One of the most intriguing elements of the Inka economy, however, is that some of the subordinate economies were more complex than the imperial system. In Ecuador and on the Peruvian coast, the populace used monetary goods, merchants trafficked in a wide range of commodities, and the populations were far more specialized and integrated than were the highland populations from which the imperial economy first developed. In neither of these regions is there strong evidence that the state took advantage of the efficiencies of specialization by the subject communities.

With the preceding discussion setting the context for the regional focus of this study, we may now turn to the Upper Mantaro to examine how the state set up its political economy. To address this issue, I will focus on three principal aspects of the imperial economy: agricultural production, storage, and production of ceramics.

Production of Agricultural Goods

The most important transformation in the development of the Inka political economy consisted of a change in the relations of production between the imperial administration and the subject populations, from corvée toward attached specialization. The production of agricultural goods for the state provides vivid evidence that the Inkas were initiating radical changes in the political economy. In numerous areas, the Inkas appropriated and intensified lands around major state installations to support the personnel stationed at those locations. The state also increasingly developed agricultural zones set aside for specialized production, the most remarkable known example being the state farms of Cochabamba, Bolivia.[4] There the emperor Wayna Qhapaq ordered virtually all native residents removed from the valley and brought in 14,000 agricultural workers to farm the lands, both as permanent colonists and as corvée laborers (Wachtel 1982). The maize harvest was temporarily housed in 2,500 storehouses at Cotapachi before its transport to Cuzco, where it was reportedly used to feed the Inka armies. Other state agricultural farms were set up at Abancay, Yucay, and Guaiparmarca/Ocomarca, among other areas (Espinoza Soriano 1973a; La Lone and La Lone 1987). In each case, the mitmaq colonists were given usufruct rights on lands they used to support themselves.

Evidence for state agricultural production is indirect in the Upper Mantaro region, but it seems clear that the Inkas appropriated thousands of hectares of productive land and substantially increased agricultural production. To assess the nature and degree of increased production required for state needs, we may evaluate three lines of evidence: (1) the distribution of Xauxa and Wanka settlements with respect to state facilities and productive lands, (2) the productivity of lands surrounding Hatun Xauxa but minimally occupied by subject populations, and (3) the amount of food production required to maintain state stockpiles. Together, these factors provide insight into the disposable supplies produced by state farms. It must be emphasized that the figures in this section and in the section entitled "State Storage" should be taken as best estimates (Tables 8.1–8.10), not as precise representa-

tions. The figures are based on a series of explicit assumptions explained in the text; changes in these assumptions would obviously affect the calculations. Because the assumptions are based on a set of realistic conditions and concrete data, however, the figures can be taken as sound estimates.

As a first step in evaluating the productivity of state lands, it will be necessary to assess which lands were put to state use. Even though documentary evidence on this point is not available, a reasonable evaluation may be made, based on settlement distribution. Perhaps surprisingly, the state's augmentation of agricultural output seems not to have required displacement of indigenous population, alienation of much community land, or significant investments in land improvement. The Inkas apparently used lands that were either uncultivated or underused during Wanka II, when production was focused in the uplands. The location of Hatun Xauxa, the distribution of Inka storage facilities, and the settlement pattern of subject communities together suggest that the Inkas focused production on the lands immediately surrounding the provincial center. Because conflict in Wanka II put the area largely off-limits, the increase in regional production for the state would not have required alienation of many community fields, if any, even though the production would have entailed a marked increase in labor investment by the local residents.

The low Wanka III population in the productive lands around Hatun Xauxa suggests that the state maintained dominant control over the area. Under Inka rule, the native populace shifted from their nucleated ridgetop communities to dispersed settlements along the lower flanks of the valleys.[5] This change would have reduced the local military threat, would have been markedly more efficient for access to productive lands, and would have transferred most of the population from the tuber-growing zone into land better suited for the preferred maize. Most of the native populace, however, did not resettle in the immediate vicinity of Hatun Xauxa or near the major state storage facilities (see Fig. 6.1). The lack of subject population is especially notable in the southern Yanamarca Valley, in the Mantaro Valley to the northeast of Hatun Xauxa, and along the ridge between the Masma Valley and the main Mantaro Valley.

The principal Xauxa towns of Marca and Hatunmarca lay to the northwest about 6 and 10 km away, respectively, and the density of the major strip settlement on the western Mantaro Valley flanks picked up about 5 km southeast of Hatun Xauxa. Major towns up the Mantaro River—at Llocllapampa, Huacjras-marca, and Llamap Shillón—also lay 10 km or more away. The lands around Hatun Xauxa were not entirely vacant. Nine villages were situated within 5 km of the center, with a total estimated population of 6,321 (about 15 percent of the study region's population).[6] With the exception of Chucchus (J74) and Huancas de la Cruz (J59), the fertile southern Yanamarca Valley was uninhabited in Wanka III. Moreover, only a scattering of villages lined the eastern side of the valley within 10 km of the center, even though a major series of storage facilities lined the ridge between the Mantaro and Masma valleys. The area around the state center and adjacent to most of its storage facilities thus remained relatively underpopulated in comparison with adjoining areas.[7]

Present evidence suggests that the residential communities in this low-density zone specialized in agricultural production for the state. The dense concentration of agricultural tools and the lack of craft by-products in households excavated at Huancas de la Cruz and Chucchus suggest strongly that the residents of the settlements were installed to cultivate nearby lands (see "Agricultural Intensification for the State," below). These settlements also lay adjacent to the principal storage facilities at Hatun Xauxa, which were constructed on the hillslopes between the southern Yanamarca area and the Inka center. Because comparable data on productive activities are not available for the other communities within 5 km of Hatun Xauxa, it cannot be confirmed at present that their residents specialized in agricultural production.

Estimates of State Agricultural Production

Four basic agricultural production zones surrounded Hatun Xauxa: valley bottom, hillslopes, uplands, and puna (Tables 8.1–8.4; Fig. 3.4). In determining the extent of these land-use zones, some simplifying assumptions were made. First, transportation time and effort were not taken into account in determining areas of production; the calculated areas thus refer to the amount of land available at a given linear distance from the center. Such an assumption seems warranted because agricultural societies typically have a threshold of a few kilometers before intensity of use drops off (see Chisholm 1968; Dennell 1980). This method of calculation increases the proportion of uplands and hillslopes included in the estimates of productivity over what would be predicted based on a strictly energetic model. It also decreases the amount of maize lands and increases the amount of land best suited for

potatoes and other highland crops over what would otherwise be predicted. A second simplifying assumption entailed averaging production figures for each crop across all zones, because information is not currently available for the differential production of every crop in each zone under prehistoric conditions.

Catchments were determined for radii of 5 and 10 km around the center and for the zone of low population density. The catchment of 5 km was chosen because population picked up markedly just beyond that point in both the Yanamarca and the Mantaro valleys. A catchment of 10 km was calculated to assess the proportion of each type of land that would have been available had the state drawn from lands intermixed among the indigenous population. In an alternative approach, it was assumed that the paucity of settlements in certain areas around Hatun Xauxa indicated state control over the lands. A modified Thiessen polygon was therefore constructed around Hatun Xauxa that incorporated the sparsely populated lands up to the limits of dense settlement. The confines of this territory were set close to the concentrations of subject communities, under the assumption that some subject settlements would have been established as close to the edges of state territory as possible.

About 5,698 ha of arable land existed within 5 km of the center, and about 17,404 ha within 10 km; the amount of arable land within the polygon totaled 6,586 ha (Table 8.1). The majority of the arable land within 5 km (3,155 ha; 55.4 percent) and in the polygon (4,685 ha; 71.1 percent) was fertile valley bottomland, on which there was no Wanka II and little Wanka III occupation (Fig. 8.2). Even within a radius of 10 km, about 42.5 percent (7,403 ha) of the arable land was valley bottom. The hillslopes composed the second-largest productive zone within both radii, the uplands made up the third-largest zone, and the puna was not productive agriculturally.

The productivity of an averaged optimal use of these lands has been estimated (Tables 8.2–8.4); the crop cycles used in making these calculations were derived from UMARP's land-use studies (Hastorf 1983: Table 23). It has been assumed that the lands were used in crop cycles that would not have degraded the soil and would have optimized output, taking labor input and caloric output into account. Although early documentary references to indigenous foods emphasize maize, chicha, and, to a lesser extent, chuño (Murra 1980 [1956]: 13), the Inkas likely used a rotating cycle of plants on their lands in order to maintain nutrients in the soil; such maintenance would not have been possi-

Table 8.1. Areas of Agricultural Production Zones (Catchments) around Hatun Xauxa

Production zone	Catchment[a]	Total area (ha)	% of area	% of zone arable (ha)	Arable area (ha)	% of total arable area
Valley	5 km	3,505	44.6	90.0	3,155	55.4
	10 km	8,226	26.2	90.0	7,403	42.5
	Polygon	5,206	61.4	90.0	4,685	71.1
Hillslopes	5 km	2,568	32.7	60.0	1,541	27.0
	10 km	10,609	33.8	60.0	6,365	36.6
	Polygon	1,361	16.0	60.0	817	12.4
Uplands	5 km	1,671	21.3	60.0	1,003	17.6
	10 km	6,059	19.3	60.0	3,635	20.9
	Polygon	1,806	21.3	60.0	1,084	16.5
Puna	5 km	110	1.4	0.0	0	0.0
	10 km	6,522	20.8	0.0	0	0.0
	Polygon	110	1.3	0.0	0	0.0
Total	5 km	7,854	100.0	73.5	5,698	100.0
	10 km	31,416	100.1[b]	56.7	17,404	100.0
	Polygon	8,483	100.0	80.7	6,586	100.0

Source: Based on Hastorf 1983.

[a]Catchments are given as zones within a 5-km radius and a 10-km radius of Hatun Xauxa and within a Thiessen polygon around Hatun Xauxa.

[b]Total differs from 100.0% because of rounding error.

ble over the long term had a crop such as maize been cultivated to the virtual exclusion of other crops. Evidence for crop variation can be found in the flora recovered from test excavations in seven storehouses above Hatun Xauxa (D'Altroy and Hastorf 1984: 345). Carbonized botanical remains were recovered from 14 proveniences, 7 of which contained maize; 11, quinoa; 6, talwi; and 2, potatoes. Although the sample size was too small to consider these proportions as representative of a cross section of agricultural products stored in the qollqa, the presence of all major highland taxa indicated that the Inkas cultivated a range of crops.

For the valley lands, an average 10-year crop cycle would have been as follows: fallow, potato, maize, Andean tuber, quinoa, maize, quinoa, maize, bean, and quinoa. For the hillsides, the 7-year cycle used for these calculations was fallow, potato, maize, potato, maize, quinoa, and lupine. For the uplands, a 5-year cycle of fallow, fallow, potato, Andean tuber, and quinoa was used. While the crop cycle was shortened as elevation increased, the estimated amount of land assumed to be arable decreased from 95 percent (valley) to 60 percent (uplands), and the proportion of time that land was left fallow increased from 10 percent to 40 percent. As in all agricultural economies, some proportion of each harvest must be set aside as seed for subsequent plant-

ings. Werge (1977:19) reports that today about 25 percent of the potato harvest of traditional small farms (less than 2 ha in potatoes) and 23 percent of medium farms (2–10 ha) is retained for seed. Assuming a comparable retention of maize and quinoa seed, we may reduce the total food available for human consumption by about 25 percent overall.

For the present discussion, I will evaluate the production of potatoes, maize, quinoa, and mashwa—all staple crops of the region. Tables 8.2 through 8.5 contain estimates of the potential output of the lands in the region and the length of time that 10,000 adult males could have been fed from the production. The estimates are based on average modern yields produced with traditional techniques. Crop yields vary substantially, of course, depending on factors such as the variety of crop being cultivated, soil productivity, access to water and fertilizer, climatic cycles, and insect spoliation, but a series of working averages can be used for the present calculations. An average prehistoric productivity of 3.290 t/ha may be used for potatoes. For maize, an average modern yield of 0.740 t/ha, with a range of 0.180–1.600 t/ha, may be cited for traditional techniques,[8] whereas quinoa produces about 1.975 t/ha and mashwa yields about 6.525 t/ha[9] (Hastorf 1983:59, 67, 71).

Given this information, the size of population that

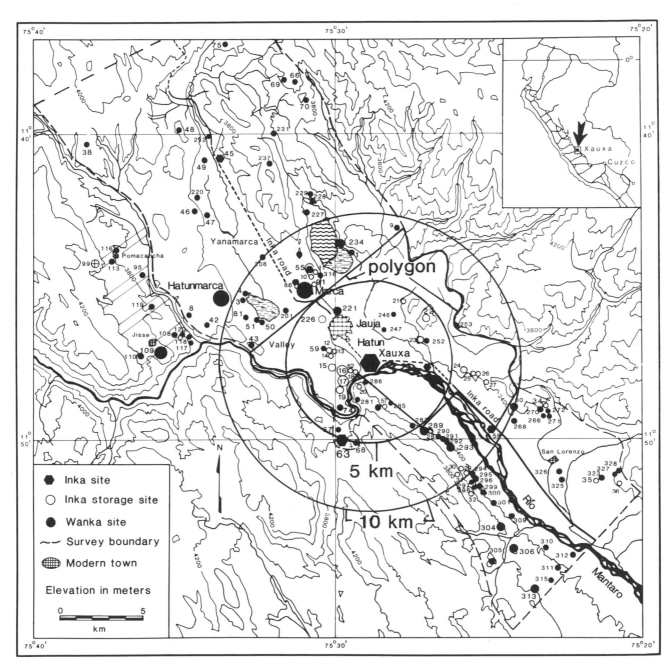

Fig. 8.2. Distribution of zones of agricultural production in the Upper Mantaro survey area: 5-km radius, 10-km radius, and Thiessen polygon.

could have been supported by the agricultural output of lands surrounding Hatun Xauxa may be estimated. If it may be taken that the principal use of the agricultural production was for state consumption, the area needed to support the population resident in the villages distributed among the fields must first be subtracted. Whether or not they were actively involved in state production, their consumption would have reduced the amount of food available to the state for

other purposes. The total populations within the polygon and the 5-km radius are estimated to have been 6,144 and 6,321, respectively, excluding Hatun Xauxa. Including Hatun Xauxa and other Inka sites, these estimates rise to 13,253 and 14,164.

For the daily caput (caloric uptake) for this population, Thomas's (1973:72) figure of 1,495 kcal/day/person will be used; this figure is based on a cross section of the highland population of Nuñoa, by sex

Table 8.2. Agricultural Productivity of 5-Kilometer Catchment around Hatun Xauxa

Production zone	Crop	Length of cycle (yr)	% of arable land in production	Area of land in production (ha)	Output rate (t/ha)	Productive output (t)	kcal × 10⁶	kcal × 10⁶ minus 25% seed storage
Valley	Fallow	10	10.0	316	0.000	0	0	0
	Potato		10.0	316	3.290	1,038	820	615
	Maize		30.0	947	0.740	700	2,528	1,896
	Tuber (mashwa)		10.0	316	6.525	2,059	1,070	803
	Quinoa		30.0	947	1.975	1,869	6,561	4,921
	Bean		10.0	316	0.315	99	36	27
							11,016	8,262
Hillslopes	Fallow	7	14.3	220	0.000	0	0	0
	Potato		28.6	440	3.290	1,449	1,144	858
	Maize		28.6	440	0.740	326	1,176	882
	Quinoa		14.3	220	1.975	435	1,526	1,145
	Lupine (talwi)		14.3	220	0.280	62	78	58
							3,924	2,943
Uplands	Fallow	5	40.0	401	0.000	0	0	0
	Potato		20.0	201	3.290	660	521	391
	Tuber (mashwa)		20.0	201	6.525	1,309	681	510
	Quinoa		20.0	201	1.975	396	1,391	1,043
							2,593	1,944
Total	Fallow			937		0		
	Potato			956		3,147		
	Maize			1,387		1,026		
	Tuber (mashwa)			516		3,368		
	Quinoa			1,367		2,700		
	Bean			316		99		
	Lupine (talwi)			220		62		
Grand total							17,533	13,150

Sources: Caloric values are calculated from those given by Leung 1961, as follows (in kcal/kg): potato (fresh), 790; maize (dried), 3,610; mashwa (fresh), 520; quinoa (dried), 3,510; bean (fresh), 360; lupine (fresh), 1,260. Other figures are calculated from Hastorf 1983.
Note: Apparent discrepancies in sums and multiplication products are due to rounding errors.

and age. To account for the populace living in nonstate villages, a total of $9.185 × 10^6$ to $9.450 × 10^6$ kcal per day (for the polygon and the 5-km radius, respectively) must therefore be subtracted to determine the calories available for state use. Thus, on an annual basis, the amount unavailable as surplus to the state would have been 3,353 to $3,449 × 10^6$ kcal, or 21.0 to 26.2 percent of the estimated useful caloric productivity of the polygon ($15,931 × 10^6$ kcal) and 5-km ($13,150 × 10^6$ kcal) catchment zones, respectively. If the maximum population estimated for Hatun Xauxa and the nearby state settlements is included as part of populace that had to be supported, the percentages of the potential outputs consumed by the resident population would have attained 45.4 percent for the polygon and 58.8 percent for the 5-km radius.

These figures indicate that the lands in the immediate vicinity of the center could have been used to support a much larger population than needed to be sustained on an annual basis, even using the maximum populations estimated for state and local settlements. After taking into account the consumption needs of the village populace, we may estimate that 10,000 additional adult males (at a daily caput of 2,500 kcal) could have been supported for a little more than a year on the agricultural output of the lands within 5 km of Hatun Xauxa, assuming the crop cycle described above (Table 8.5). Similarly a state work force of 10,000 adult males could have been supported for about 501 days on the potential surplus production of the polygon surrounding the center, if the food were consumed in the most calorically efficient manner possible.

When calculations are made for the consumption of

Table 8.3. Agricultural Productivity of 10-Kilometer Catchment around Hatun Xauxa

Production zone	Crop	Length of cycle (yr)	% of arable land in production	Area of land in production (ha)	Output rate (t/ha)	Productive output (t)	kcal × 10^6	kcal × 10^6 minus 25% seed storage
Valley	Fallow	10	10.0	740	0.000	0	0	0
	Potato		10.0	740	3.290	2,436	1,924	1,443
	Maize		30.0	2,221	0.740	1,643	5,933	4,450
	Tuber (mashwa)		10.0	740	6.525	4,830	2,512	1,884
	Quinoa		30.0	2,221	1.975	4,386	15,396	11,547
	Bean		10.0	740	0.315	233	84	63
							25,849	19,386
Hillslopes	Fallow	7	14.3	909	0.000	0	0	0
	Potato		28.6	1,819	3.290	5,983	4,727	3,545
	Maize		28.6	1,819	0.740	1,346	4,858	3,644
	Quinoa		14.3	909	1.975	1,796	6,303	4,728
	Lupine (talwi)		14.3	909	0.280	255	321	241
							16,209	12,157
Uplands	Fallow	5	40.0	1,454	0.000	0	0	0
	Potato		20.0	727	3.290	2,392	1,890	1,417
	Tuber (mashwa)		20.0	727	6.525	4,744	2,467	1,850
	Quinoa		20.0	727	1.975	1,436	5,040	3,780
							9,396	7,047
Total	Fallow			3,104		0		
	Potato			3,286		10,811		
	Maize			4,039		2,989		
	Tuber (mashwa)			1,467		9,574		
	Quinoa			3,857		7,618		
	Bean			740		233		
	Lupine (talwi)			909		255		
Grand total							51,454	38,590

Sources: See note to Table 8.2.
Note: Apparent discrepancies in sums and multiplication products are due to rounding errors.

food used in state activities, it must be taken into account that much of the state food was consumed during the agricultural off-season, when the peasantry was performing many nonagricultural labor duties for the state. This period corresponds to the time when sierra populations characteristically recoup caloric deficits incurred during the leaner agricultural season. This seasonal compression of use of state goods implies that the food grown on lands around the center could have annually provided upwards of 42,000 to 55,000 adult males with full rations for three months, not including the farmers growing the food.

Agricultural Intensification for the State
Although state administrators thus had access to nearby lands to oversee the production of significant quantities of food, questions remain concerning how much additional labor was required of the populace and how much food was actually grown. With respect to Wanka III, none of the available documents states clearly that the Inka state set aside particular lands for its use or that the local populace rendered any particular agricultural products to the state as gathered or cultivated crops. At present, only one very generalized published statement on local contributions to agriculture is available, in the testimony provided the inspector Vega (1965:169) in 1582. The witnesses reported that, following pacification, "[the emperor] sent them to tend fields of food and to make clothing."[10] Because this statement is typical of peasants' testimony on state duties and contributes little to understanding their agricultural activities, we must rely on archaeological data for insight into state-sponsored intensification.

The archaeological record in the region provides

Table 8.4. Agricultural Productivity of Polygon Catchment around Hatun Xauxa

Production zone	Crop	Length of cycle (yr)	% of arable land in production	Area of land in production (ha)	Output rate (t/ha)	Productive output (t)	kcal × 10⁶	kcal × 10⁶ minus 25% seed storage
Valley	Fallow	10	10.0	469	0.000	0	0	0
	Potato		10.0	469	3.290	1,541	1,218	913
	Maize		30.0	1,406	0.740	1,040	3,755	2,816
	Tuber (mashwa)		10.0	469	6.525	3,057	1,590	1,192
	Quinoa		30.0	1,406	1.975	2,776	9,743	7,307
	Bean		10.0	469	0.315	148	53	40
							16,358	12,269
Hillslopes	Fallow	7	14.3	117	0.000	0	0	0
	Potato		28.6	233	3.290	768	607	455
	Maize		28.6	233	0.740	173	624	468
	Quinoa		14.3	117	1.975	231	809	607
	Lupine (talwi)		14.3	117	0.280	33	41	31
							2,081	1,560
Uplands	Fallow	5	40.0	434	0.000	0	0	0
	Potato		20.0	217	3.290	713	563	423
	Tuber (mashwa)		20.0	217	6.525	1,415	736	552
	Quinoa		20.0	217	1.975	428	1,503	1,127
							2,802	2,101
Total	Fallow			1,019		0		
	Potato			919		3,023		
	Maize			1,639		1,213		
	Tuber (mashwa)			685		4,472		
	Quinoa			1,739		3,435		
	Bean			469		148		
	Lupine (talwi)			117		33		
Grand total							21,241	15,931

Sources: See note to Table 8.2.
Note: Apparent discrepancies in sums and multiplication products are due to rounding errors.

Table 8.5. Sustenance Provided by Principal Crops Grown in Vicinity of Hatun Xauxa

Crop	Productive output minus 25% for seed (t)			Days of caloric needs met for 10,000 adult males			Days of caloric needs met for 10,000 adult males minus villagers[a]	
	5 km	10 km	Polygon	5 km	10 km	Polygon	5 km	Polygon
Potatoes	2,360	8,041	2,267	75	254	72	55	57
Maize	770	2,242	910	111	324	131	82	104
Quinoa	2,025	5,714	2,576	284	802	362	210	286
Mashwa	2,526	7,181	3,354	53	149	70	39	55
Total	7,681	23,177	9,107	523	1,529	634	386	501

Note: Apparent discrepancies in sums are due to rounding errors.
[a]Estimates for the 10-km radius are not provided, because data are lacking on the size of the indigenous population for the entire radius.

surprisingly little evidence for state-developed irrigation systems, terracing, wetlands reclamation, or other forms of agricultural intensification that are found elsewhere in the Andes. Study of land use in the Upper Mantaro region suggests that some developmental schemes were undertaken during Inka rule, but as yet none can be unambiguously attributed to the imperial occupation (Hastorf and Earle 1985:591; see also Hastorf 1983, n.d.). Instead, the remnants of land improvements are concentrated in the valleys adjoining the main valley, in areas occupied intensively during Wanka II (Hastorf 1983:157–65). The principal regional irrigation systems, for example, lay in the rolling uplands west and north of Tunanmarca (Parsons and Matos Mendieta 1978). Up to 15 km long, these canals watered fields primarily used for tuber-complex crops. The intent here seems to have been to extend the growing season by irrigating crops before the onset of the rains. Canals drained an additional 195 ha in lands with very high water tables, notably adjacent to Lagunas Tragadero and Paca and in the Masma Valley. Terracing is found on hillslopes throughout the region, both in the form of lynchets on gentle slopes and in more-formal stone-faced terrace systems on steeper slopes, such as along the Río Mantaro gorge west of the main valley, but none of this is clearly Inka in origin.[11]

Despite the lack of obvious evidence for state land improvements, two kinds of archaeological data point toward specialized agricultural production for the Inkas: the previously cited regional settlement pattern and the distribution of agricultural tools at Wanka III settlements. Recall that the key point concerning settlement patterning lies in the low-density Wanka occupation surrounding Hatun Xauxa, in an agriculturally productive area. With respect to the second issue, specific types of stone tools appear to have been used to cultivate or harvest particular kinds of crops. Russell's (1988) analysis of stone hoes used in maize cultivation shows that hoe use was markedly higher at low elevations than at ridgetop settlements and that the use increased radically from Wanka II to III. The highest concentrations of these hoes occurred in Chucchus (J74, at 3,600 m elevation), a newly settled Wanka III village at the southernmost end of the Yanamarca Valley, just west of the main storage facilities above Hatun Xauxa (Fig. 8.3). In two residential compounds excavated at the site, hoes were recovered in densities of 8.07 and 8.90 per cubic meter (Table 9.3); surface collections at the site also recovered unusually high concentrations of hoes.

The excavation densities are comparable to the highest densities (up to 10.78 hoes/m³) found at Marca, a town comparably situated topographically and altitudinally. The densities are markedly higher than those from residential compounds at Wanka III Hatunmarca (0.00–0.34 hoes/m³), a ridgetop settlement (3,850 m). At Chucchus, the lack of by-products of the manufacture of other goods—such as wasters from ceramic production, debitage from stone tool production, or spindle whorls from spinning and weaving—suggests that the residents were deliberately installed to produce maize for the state and were relieved of other kinds of labor duties in their home community (Costin et al. 1989; Earle and D'Altroy 1989: 191–96).

Agricultural intensification may be evaluated from an additional perspective: the proportion of labor that the peasantry was required to invest to provide food for the state. Assuming that the state lands lay in the immediate vicinity of Hatun Xauxa and that the local population was required to undertake the bulk of the labor investment in cultivation, we may estimate the additional labor required. For simplicity's sake, the figure of 10,000 adult males supported for one year on state storage will be used here. These individuals would have increased the number of adult males fed from food grown in the region from about 6,000 to 16,000, thereby increasing the total amount of food needed by a factor of 2.7. If the stored goods were kept for two years, the increased labor investment would have been about 1.3 times that before Inka rule.

Three factors may have ameliorated the increased investment. First, the Xauxas and Wankas themselves were likely principal consumers of the food stored in state warehouses, thereby reducing the amount of food that the peasants would have had to produce for themselves. Although state activities may have been onerous, the available evidence suggests that temporary labor for the state was concentrated during the agricultural off-season, from June to September. However, cultivating state fields was a major burden during the time that farmers would have normally dedicated to their own crops (see Mitchell 1980). Moreover, even those attached specialists who ostensibly worked full-time for the state were granted plots of land on which to grow their own food. The colonist maize farmers of the Cochabamba Valley are a case in point (Wachtel 1982). Thus, the state's contribution to the food consumed annually by the peasantry may have been relatively small, although significant in its maize content.

A second ameliorating factor was that the produc-

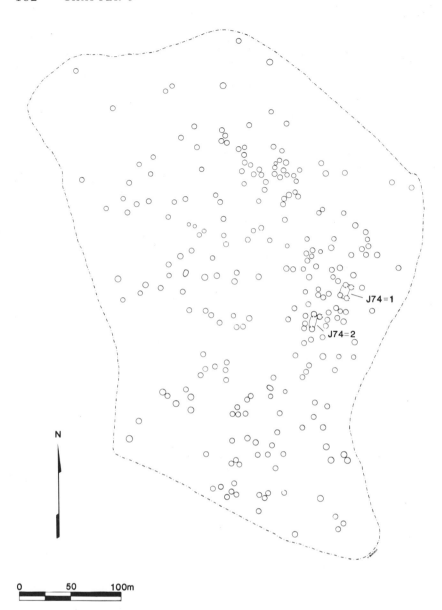

Fig. 8.3. Chucchus (J74), a Wanka III village in the southern Yanamarca Valley.

J74=1

J74=2

N

0   50   100m

tivity of lower valley lands opened up for maize production under state rule would likely have improved
the ratio of labor input to food output. However, the
high, rolling uplands surrounding the Wanka II communities are about twice as efficient for potato production as the bottomlands (Hastorf 1983:119). In addition, Hastorf (1983:195) observes that the relative
productivity and extent of each land-use zone in the
region exhibit an almost perfect inverse relationship.
The Mantaro Valley bottomlands (2,862 ha) are
the least extensive, followed by the tributary valleys
(5,750 ha), the surrounding hills (10,131 ha), the uplands (8,134 ha), and the puna and nonarable lands

(13,507 ha). The shift to lower elevations may thus
have increased the productivity of maize in the region,
but the rolling uplands and tributary valleys would
have continued to be a principal zone for cultivation of
peasant crops and perhaps state crops as well.

Third, if mitmaqkuna were brought in to farm the
lands and workers from saya other than Hatunxauxa
tilled state fields near the center, the number of workers available might have increased substantially. I am
not aware of any documentary references to mitmaqkuna farmers at Hatunxauxa, but colonists from Yauyos, Chucuito, and Huamachuco were resettled at or
near the center. The labors of such additional workers

would have both reduced the workload on the residents of the Hatunxauxa saya and decreased the amount of food left to the state after feeding its workers.

In sum, it seems highly likely that the Inkas increased agricultural production in the Mantaro region, especially in the area immediately surrounding the provincial capital. The quantities of goods needed to fill the vast storage complexes, described in the next section, would have required access to thousands of hectares of prime agricultural land for maize, quinoa, potatoes, and other crops. Because we do not know the precise balance among these foods kept in the storehouses, the above estimates of the amounts of lands dedicated to state production must be considered reasonable but provisional.

State Storage

As is apparent from the preceding discussion, state storage played a pivotal role in the management of the Inka political economy.[12] Polanyi et al. (1957) first drew attention to the systematic relationship between mass mobilization and storage in their discussion of the development of complex society and staple finance. In their argument, nonmarket state economies extract goods from the general populace through labor obligations or through production of specific goods by commoners attached to the state. Murra (1980 [1956]) adapted this argument to interpret Inka storage, contending that goods were mobilized from the local populace through corvée to finance state activities at Cuzco and in the provinces. The principal use of stored goods was to support administrative and religious personnel, the military, specialists attached to the state, and corvée laborers.

A series of factors contributed to the need for heavy investment in regional storage complexes, among them characteristics of the agricultural regime, military logistics, and variations in demand. The need for centralized storage derived initially from the seasonality of production in the Andes, as is typical of agrarian societies. The demand for goods, however, did not vary precisely with the availability of goods during the annual cycle. Permanent state personnel, such as the administrative and religious elites, had to be supported throughout the year by goods drawn from state resources. Most state-supported corvée, in contrast, was conducted during the agricultural off-season and

the planting season. Similarly, military campaigns were scheduled for the off-season, to coincide with the times when labor could be most readily mobilized and the larders were stocked. The chroniclers considered military support to be the primary use for the goods stockpiled in state storehouses (e.g., Sancho 1917 [1532–33]: 141; Cieza 1967 [1553]: ch. 44, pp. 143–44; see Murra 1980 [1956]: 42, 128). However, some campaigns lasted for years, and rebellions could not always be assumed to coincide with the agricultural off-season. These needs placed great demands on state resources, because even a moderate-sized army would have rapidly exhausted the resources available in any given region. The heavy weight of most subsistence and utilitarian goods, coupled with the inefficient modes of Andean transport, further required that support facilities be stockpiled along major routes of travel (see Chapter 5).

Under these circumstances of uneven supply, poor transportation, and partially stochastic demand, the most effective solution to ensuring support for state need was to develop resources throughout the empire for local storage in state-controlled facilities. According to one oral tradition, the Inka state storage system originated in the mid-fifteenth century, when Pachacutec ordered that facilities be built to expedite the construction of Cuzco (Betanzos 1987 [1551]: ch. 12, p. 56). Additional storehouses (qollqa) were built at provincial centers and at road stations with the expansion and consolidation of the empire over the following century. The resulting multilevel system elicited admiring comments from the Spaniards, who enthusiastically appropriated the stored goods during the early years of the conquest.

Several chroniclers affirmed the systematic association of storage complexes with provincial centers (e.g., Cobo 1956 [1653]: vol. 2, bk. 2, ch. 25, p. 114), some mentioning Hatun Xauxa specifically (e.g., Sancho 1917 [1532–33]: 141; Castro and Ortega Morejón 1974 [1558]: 101; Guaman Poma 1980 [1614]: /336 [338], p. 308; see Fig. 8.4). Cieza (1967 [1553]: ch. 12, p. 37) and Polo (1917 [1567]: 77), who visited the area about 15 years after the first Spanish arrival, expressed admiration for the storage system, which was still functioning despite the demise of Inka power in the valley. Of the documentary sources, the petitions of 1558–61 (Espinoza Soriano 1971) have been very useful for evaluating state storage, because of their detailed lists of stockpiled goods appropriated by the Spaniards.

DEPOCÍTODELÍNGA COLL CA

Fig. 8.4. Emperor Thupa Inka Yupanki and Apo Pomachaua, a khipu kamayoq (keeper of the mnemonic knot records), within an Inka storage facility. Illustration by Guaman Poma (1980 [1614]: /336 [338], p. 308).

Storehouse Architecture

Within the UMARP survey region, 1,992 storehouses, with a total estimated building capacity of 123,716 m³, have been recorded in 30 sites (Table 8.6).[13] Because of the likelihood that stored goods were packaged in some form—in bales or jars, for example—the entire volume of these buildings was probably not used for storage. As will be described shortly, the practice of packaging goods may have reduced actual storage capacity to between 10 and 75 percent of the structure volumes.

As was characteristic of many Inka facilities, there is extensive evidence of prior planning and supervised execution in construction. It is important to emphasize that the construction of this vast storage system appears to have been entirely a state venture (cf. Browman 1970). Spatial distribution, masonry, and internal layout all bear the stamp of state planning. The storehouses were systematically separated from local villages, even along the west side of the main valley, where storehouse complexes were generally associated with the strip settlement along the hilly flanks. There the storage facilities were set apart from the habitation areas by 100 to 200 m and often stood by themselves adjacent to small series of terraces. In the Yanamarca Valley, home to the large Xauxa communities of Marca and Hatunmarca, no storage facilities have been located, apart from site J19, which lay at the outer fringe of the main complexes above Hatun Xauxa (Figs. 8.5 and 8.6). Only a few structures (57 in sites J10, J11, and J91), at the north end of the main Mantaro Valley, lay immediately adjacent to Xauxa habitation; even there, the size of the local population under Inka rule is not clear.

Bearing in mind that some variations occurred within and among sites, a description may be drawn of a typical Mantaro region storehouse. The pirka masonry of the storehouses conformed to the rock that was immediately available as fieldstone (Fig. 8.7). Because of the geology of the region, most buildings were erected from limestone, although a few complexes (e.g., J25–J27, J35, J36) were built from friable metamorphics or river cobbles. Two structure plans were used: circular (Fig. 8.8) and rectangular, each containing a single room. Morris (1967) has made the reasonable suggestion that the use of two shapes of structures was in part an accounting device and has further suggested that maize was stored in the circular storehouses and tuber crops in the rectangular buildings. Exploratory excavations by UMARP in six structures at two facilities (J16 and J17) above Hatun Xauxa did not support the latter suggestion (D'Altroy and Hastorf 1984), but it seems highly probable that the Inkas organized the contents of their storehouses systematically.

The mean volume of the structures (to roofline) in the region is estimated to have been about 52 m³ for circular storehouses and 71 m³ for rectangular storehouses. The qollqa with circular plans were generally very close to round, with an exterior diameter of about 5.5 to 6.0 m and wall thicknesses of about 0.5 to 0.6 m. The maximum heights of the structures probably attained a mean of about 3.5 m or more, but wall deterioration has precluded accurate estimation. The walls of circular structures canted slightly inward (Fig. 8.8), whereas those of the rectangular buildings typically were more erect. Storehouses with rectangular floor plans ranged from about 6.0 to 8.0 m in length and from about 4.0 to 5.0 m in width. The wall thicknesses, masonry, and wall heights were comparable to

Table 8.6. Distribution of State Storage Facilities in Upper Mantaro Valley

Distance from Hatun Xauxa (km)	Sites	Frequency of structures	Volume (m³)	Cumulative total of structures		Cumulative total of volume	
				Frequency	%	(m³)	%
0–1.0	J15	93	5,251				
	J16	359	23,398				
	J17	479	27,075				
	J18	118	7,164				
	J62	20	1,730				
		1,069	64,618	1,069	53.7	64,618	52.2
1.1–2.0	J14	32	2,112				
	J19	99	7,269				
	J20	18	684				
		149	10,065	1,218	61.1	74,683	60.4
2.1–3.0	J12	60	4,048				
	J13	35	2,758				
		95	6,806	1,313	65.9	81,489	65.9
3.1–4.0	J23	66	5,610				
	J57	37	1,838				
	J226	37	1,861				
		140	9,309	1,453	72.9	90,798	73.4
4.1–5.0	J21	39	3,272				
	J22	75	6,278				
		114	9,550	1,567	78.7	100,348	81.1
5.1–6.0	J10	29	1,760				
	J11	24	1,286				
	J28	21	901				
	J91	4	183				
		78	4,130	1,645	82.6	104,478	84.4
6.1–7.0	J24	63	5,079	1,708	85.7	109,557	88.6
7.1–8.0	J25	23	1,286				
	J26	15	838				
	J27	42	3,515				
		80	5,639	1,788	89.8	115,196	93.1
8.1–9.0	J29	15	490				
	J30	8	313				
	J31	41	2,207				
		64	3,010	1,852	93.0	118,206	95.5
9.1–10.0	J32	46	2,078	1,898	95.3	120,284	97.2
10.1–11.0	J34	17	689	1,915	96.1	120,973	97.8
16.1–17.0	J35	39	1,517				
	J36	38	1,226				
		77	2,743	1,992	100.0	123,716	100.0

Note: Volumes are structure volume to the roofline, based on an estimated height of 3.5 m, and are not adjusted for packaging.

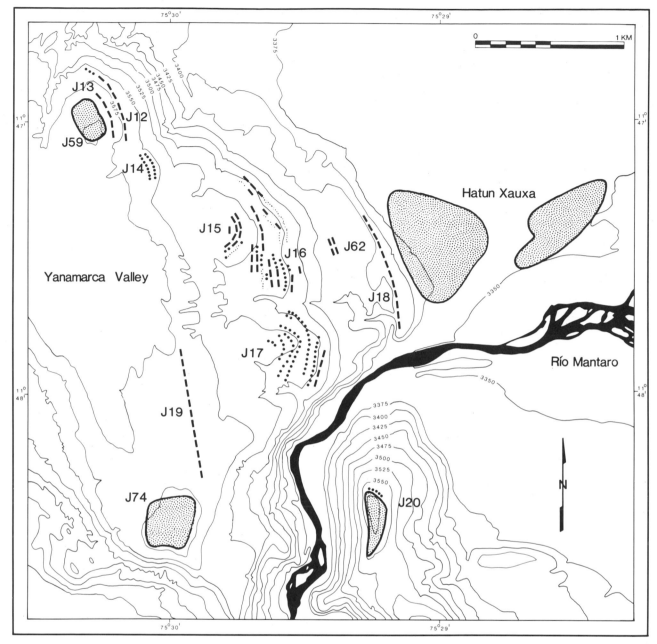

Fig. 8.5. Distribution of storage complexes above Hatun Xauxa. Dashes and dots represent areas dominated by storehouses with rectangular and circular floor plans, respectively. Shading indicates habitation areas (J59, J74, and area adjacent to storage site J20) or administrative settlements (Hatun Xauxa).

those of the circular structures. No direct evidence of roofing techniques was obtained during the field research reported here, but early documents and fieldwork elsewhere suggest that circular structures were topped by a conical or semiconical thatched roof, held up by a framework of poles (Guaman Poma 1980 [1614]: /336 [338], p. 308). The roofs of rectangular structures were most likely built of the same materials,

but were gabled (*dos aguas*) (Morris 1967; Browman 1970:263; Gasparini and Margolies 1980:303).

State storage facilities were internally highly organized. They consisted of single or multiple rows of circular or rectangular buildings, following the contours of the hills on which they were built (Figs. 8.9 and 8.10). In the larger complexes, such as J16 and J17, above Hatun Xauxa, a few structures were offset

Fig. 8.6. View north from storage site J20 across the Río Mantaro toward main storage complexes (J15, J16, and J17) west of Hatun Xauxa.

Fig. 8.7. Circular state storage structure at site J20, overlooking the main Mantaro Valley to the east.

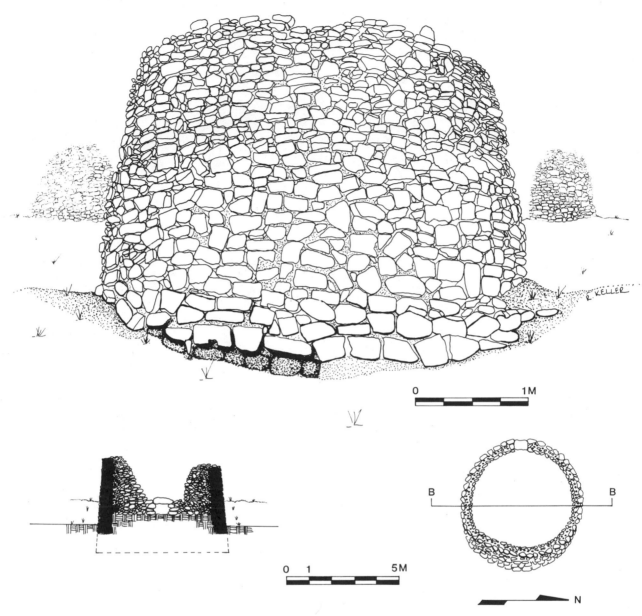

Fig. 8.8. Circular storehouse from site J10, above Laguna Paca.

from the principal rows, probably for residences or administration. The extraordinary standardization of the state structures is exemplified in the variations in the complexes extending about 7 km along the east side of the valley. The mean volumes for rectangular structures at J21 and J22 were estimated at 84 m³; at J23 and J27, 85 m³; and at J24, 81 m³. Coefficients of variation[14] for length and width measurements of structures within sites typically ranged between 5 and 10 percent, remarkably low for fieldstone buildings adjacent to croplands (D'Altroy 1981: Table I-2).

Clearly, the state planners conceived of these storage facilities as standardized units and had them built accordingly.

Regional Distribution of Storage

Storage complexes were found in three major spatial groupings in the region: (1) above Hatun Xauxa in the hills separating the Yanamarca Valley from the main Mantaro Valley, (2) north and south of Hatun Xauxa on the west side of the main valley, and (3) along the slopes and ridges on the east. Viewed from a slightly

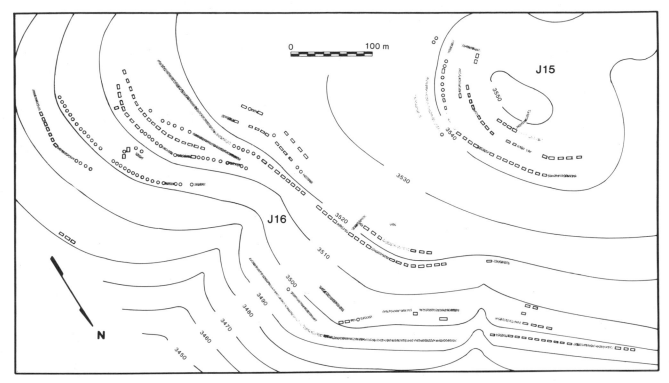

Fig. 8.9. Storage complexes J15 and J16, about 1 km west of Hatun Xauxa. Mottled areas show zones of rubble from deteriorated structures.

different perspective, the storage facilities fell into two principal contexts: adjacent to the Inka administrative center and dispersed throughout the valley.

This distribution is represented graphically in Figure 8.11. Each column represents the structure volume of a given storehouse complex, with the height of the column being proportional to the volume of the site. Two features of the regional distribution pattern should be apparent from these graphs. First, by far the greatest concentration of storehouses was located adjacent to Hatun Xauxa, the Inka provincial capital, with storage volume falling off systematically as a function of distance from the center. Second, the circular and rectangular storehouses were distributed systematically throughout the valley, but not in the same patterns. Each of these points merits brief exploration.

A little more than half of the storehouses in the survey region were concentrated within 1 km of Hatun Xauxa. Of the 1,992 structures located, 1,069 (53.7 percent) were found in five complexes on the hills west of the center (Fig. 8.5); they represented about 52.2 percent (64,618 m³) of the total structure volume in the region. The remaining storage fell off systematically as a function of distance from the administrative center. A regression of structure volume—by 1-km

concentric bands around Hatun Xauxa—against the logarithm of distance yields an R^2 of .6717 (SE$_{\hat{y}}$ = 10,443; Fig. 8.12a).[15] The relationship of decreasing volume as a function of distance from the center holds, even if the core facilities within the first kilometer from the center are discounted to eliminate the overwhelming effects of the massive storage there (R^2 = .6938; SE$_{\hat{y}}$ = 1,881; Fig. 8.12b).[16]

Two related explanations for the concentration of storage capacity around Hatun Xauxa may be suggested, one pertaining to the use of space and one pertaining to the development of state farms. First, by concentrating storage around the provincial capital, the expected location of primary consumption, the Inkas would have reduced the costs of transporting goods at the time at which they were required. This approach is concordant with a central theme of Inka planning—favoring ready access to products at the time of need, at the expense of investing labor more heavily during production and storage. Second, given that agricultural goods were reportedly stored in buildings adjacent to the lands on which they were grown, the concentration of storehouses at the center conforms to a pattern in which state farms encircled the provincial capital. Recall that the lands immedi-

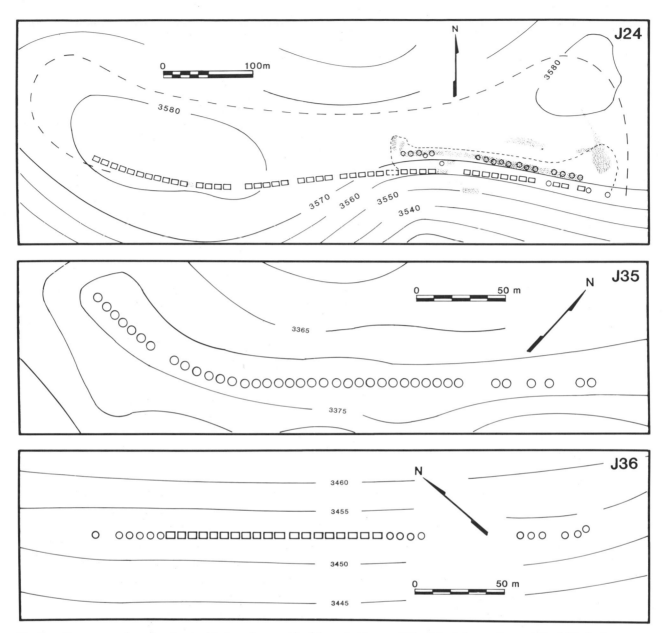

Fig. 8.10. Storage complexes J24, J35, and J36, on the east side of the main Mantaro Valley. Mottled areas show rubble. A Wanka I residential area is associated with J24; dashed lines mark surface remains of habitation.

ately surrounding Hatun Xauxa were seemingly underpopulated during Inka rule. A series of regression analyses, analogous to those just described, shows a strong inverse relationship between the storage capacity and the size of the resident population surrounding the provincial capital (D'Altroy and Earle n.d.). The local population was settled in locations that suggest that the state personnel were deliberately keeping them away from the lands that were used to produce state foods. In combination with other data reported just above, this evidence points to the development of state farms around the capital.

The distinction between the distributions of circular and rectangular storehouses further suggests patterned differences in the productivity of the microzones of the main valley (Earle and D'Altroy 1982: 286). Excluding the main complexes just above Hatun Xauxa (J15–J18, J62), the estimated structure capacity on the east (29,310 m³) and west (29,748 m³) sides of the river is virtually identical, within 17 km of the

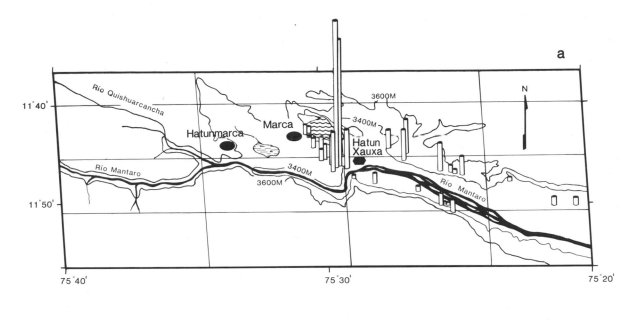

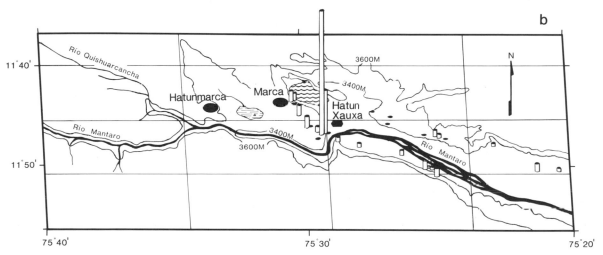

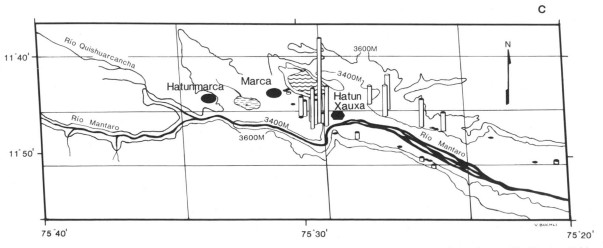

Fig. 8.11. Distribution of storehouse volumes in the Mantaro Valley. Column height is proportional to volume of facility (see Table 8.6); grids consist of square blocks 12 km on a side. *a*, All structures; *b*, structures with circular floor plans; *c*, structures with rectangular floor plans.

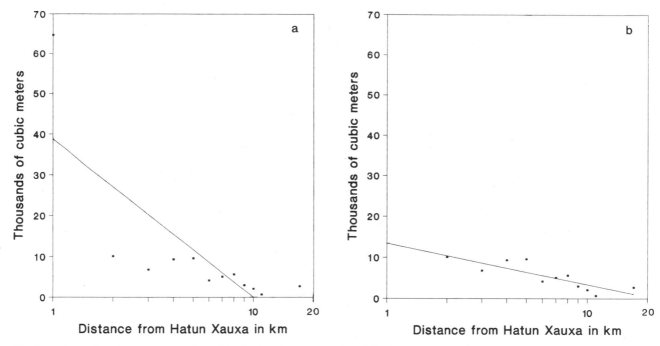

Fig. 8.12. Regression of state storage volume, by 1-km bands, against (*a*) log of the distance from Hatun Xauxa, including all bands, and (*b*) log of the distance from Hatun Xauxa, outside 1 km surrounding the center.

center.[17] However, the east-side complexes were heavily weighted in favor of structures with a rectangular floor plan (303 rectangular, 114 circular), whereas those on the west were predominantly circular (225 rectangular, 281 circular; see Table 8.7). Taking into account solely the complexes downriver from Hatun Xauxa, the structure capacity on the west is reduced to 8,511 m³, which is about one-third (1 : 2.90) that of the east-side capacity (29,310 m³). The data from Franco et al. (1979:35–39) indicate that the east side of the valley downriver from Hatun Xauxa has more-fertile soil, reduced threat of frost, and greater rainfall above the valley floor than does the west. The concentration of Inka storehouses along the eastern ridgeline, coupled with the lack of subject population in the immediate area, again suggests strongly that the Inkas reserved this land for state production.

Storehouse Contents

With present documentary information, it is difficult to estimate the proportion of the storehouses filled at any time or the proportions dedicated to particular goods. In a broad review of Spanish comments on Inka storage, Murra (1980 [1956]: 13, 25) found that out of 287 references to storage by 28 chroniclers, 86 mentioned food. The relatively low proportion that took note of food probably indicates a greater Spanish concern with exotica and military matériel than with the more mundane subsistence supplies. Of the 77 comments that Murra discusses concerning food, 9 referred to food generally; 29 dealt with maize and 7 with chicha; 1 noted a scarcity of maize and mentioned vegetables, root crops, and herbs; 7 mentioned chuño and 1, potatoes; 5 noted quinoa; 3 mentioned oca; and 12 mentioned ch'arki.[18] Because of the lack of specificity in the amounts of these goods stored at any given location and because the Spaniards often took preferential note of grain crops (Murra 1980 [1956]: 13), these figures can be used only as a means of evaluating storehouse contents in a very general sense.

A more direct means of assessing the amount of food stockpiled by the state use is through archaeological investigation. A field study of Inka storage by Morris (1967) provides some useful data to this end. Judging from the associations between known storehouse contents and architecture, he has estimated that 40 to 65 percent of the 39,700 m³ of storage space at Huánuco Pampa was used for highland tubers, and about 5 to 7 percent was probably devoted to maize. That leaves about 28 percent for unspecified goods, some of

Table 8.7. Distribution of State Storehouses in Upper Mantaro Valley, by Shape

Sites			Circular storehouses		Rectangular storehouses		Total	
Above Hatun Xauxa (within 1 km)	On west	On east	Frequency	Volume (m³)	Frequency	Volume (m³)	Frequency	Volume (m³)
		J10	29	1,760	0	0	29	1,760
		J11	24	1,286	0	0	24	1,286
		J12	9	542	51	3,506	60	4,048
		J13	0	0	35	2,758	35	2,758
		J14	32	2,112	0	0	32	2,112
J15			19	1,011	74	4,240	93	5,251
J16			128	7,898	231	15,500	359	23,398
J17			415	22,659	64	4,416	479	27,075
J18			0	0	118	7,164	118	7,164
	J19		0	0	99	7,269	99	7,269
	J20		18	684	0	0	18	684
		J21	0	0	39	3,272	39	3,272
		J22	0	0	75	6,278	75	6,278
		J23	0	0	66	5,610	66	5,610
		J24	0	0	63	5,079	63	5,079
		J25	23	1,286	0	0	23	1,286
		J26	15	838	0	0	15	838
		J27	1	30	41	3,485	42	3,515
	J28		21	901	0	0	21	901
	J29		15	490	0	0	15	490
	J30		8	313	0	0	8	313
	J31		35	1,516	6	691	41	2,207
	J32		33	1,526	13	552	46	2,078
		J34	17	689	0	0	17	689
		J35	39	1,517	0	0	39	1,517
		J36	19	681	19	545	38	1,226
	J57		21	591	16	1,247	37	1,838
J62			0	0	20	1,730	20	1,730
	J91		0	0	4	183	4	183
	J226		36	1,824	1	37	37	1,861
Total Hatun Xauxa			562	31,568	507	33,050	1,069	64,618
Total west			281	13,545	225	16,243	506	29,788
Total east			114	5,041	303	24,269	417	29,310
Grand total			957	50,154	1,035	73,562	1,992	123,716

Note: Volumes are structure volume to the roofline, based on an estimated height of 3.5 m, and are not adjusted for packaging.

which were likely the arms, sumptuaries, and craft goods mentioned by Cieza (Morris 1981:354–55). As Morris suggests, the dominance of tubers in the storehouses at Huánuco Pampa undoubtedly reflects to some degree the productive capacities of the lands in the immediate vicinity of the provincial center. However, of the 128 qollqa excavated at Huánuco Pampa, only 6 yielded macrobotanical specimens of maize and only 3 yielded potatoes (Morris 1981:333, 339). No macrobotanical remains were recovered from the 4 storehouses at Aukimarka, and only 1 of the 12 qollqa excavated at Tunsucancha yielded maize (Morris 1967:225–27). Because noncarbonized remains deteriorate rapidly in the sierra, the lack of mac-

robotanical remains is unfortunate but not surprising. Conversely, flotation samples from 3 of 6 qollqa excavated at sites J16 and J17 above Hatun Xauxa yielded maize; 3 yielded dense concentrations of quinoa; 2 yielded potatoes; and 1 yielded lupine (D'Altroy and Hastorf 1984:345). Two of the 6 qollqa yielded essentially no crop remains (a small amount of quinoa attributed to background was recovered). Until flotation samples are analyzed from more-extensive excavations, the available archaeological data may be used only with care.

As a result of the limited concrete information regarding the proportions of storehouse volume dedicated to stockpiling food, any calculations of the numbers of individuals that may be supported must encompass a range of values. The range, however, will provide a realistic means of estimating the length of time that a given number of personnel, such as a bivouacked army, could be supported at any location.

Stored goods can be measured archaeologically only through potential storage volume within warehouses, adjusted for packaging, whereas caloric values are generally determined by weight (e.g., kcal/kg). Ratios are therefore needed to convert weight of goods to storage volume. One liter of dried, shelled maize weighs about 770 g, so an active adult male, such as a soldier, would have required about 1.3 liters of maize per day to satisfy his caloric needs, and an adult woman bearer would have required about 1.0 liters.[19] Weight-to-volume ratios for whole potatoes are approximately the same as those for dried, shelled maize. About 3.0 kg, or 3.9 liters, of fresh potatoes would have been needed to supply the daily caloric needs of an adult male (see Chapter 5).[20] For chuño, the weight-to-volume ratio is more difficult to derive, but it may be estimated that the whole potatoes, when dried, would lose about 50 percent of their volume and 75 percent of their weight. These estimates yield about 385 kg/m³, or 385 g/liter, for chuño. Because the potatoes that have been recovered archaeologically from storehouses indicate that fresh potatoes were preferred over chuño (Morris 1981:340), calculations for caloric values here will be based on volumes for the former.

These figures permit estimation of the state's ability to maintain its personnel by drawing on the storage facilities in the Upper Mantaro region. To convert building volume into potential storage volume, packaging must be taken into account. The evidence available suggests that the Inkas frequently stored maize shelled, in large flared-rim jars, often called *aríbalos* or aryballoid jars (cf. Rowe 1946:243). In excavations at Huánuco Pampa, for instance, Morris (1981:333) found maize to be consistently associated with these jars, although at Hatun Xauxa, maize was only occasionally found with ceramics (D'Altroy and Hastorf 1984:347). Modern sierra farmers generally store maize on the cob or shelled in sacks, but these storage techniques are usually in a household context in which space is not at a premium. No cobs were recovered from storehouses at either Huánuco Pampa or Hatun Xauxa, but excavations in Xauxa communities have recovered carbonized cobs in household refuse (Hastorf 1983). Given the lack of solid evidence to the contrary and some evidence in favor, it will be assumed

for the present calculations that maize was stored shelled in flared-rim jars. This storage technique provided an effective means of maximizing the preservation of the shelled maize, but at a great cost of space.

The principal factors contributing to the decay of stored foods are fungi, insects, rodents, and inherent characteristics of the grain, such as a tendency to sprout (Christensen and Kaufmann 1969; Morris 1981:333–39). By housing closed containers in qollqa built at high elevations, the Inkas minimized the deleterious effects of these factors. Architectural features, such as porous subfloors and drainage canals, designed to keep the temperature and humidity low, also contributed to extending the life span of the stored maize. Packaging maize in this manner was costly, however, because it significantly reduced the proportion of the interior space of storehouses that could be used effectively.

To estimate the reduction of potential storage capacity resulting from storing maize in jars, some calculations may be made for the volume within jars and the number of jars of a given size that could be stored within qollqa for which field measurements are available. In making this estimate, the standardization of Inka ceramics is a considerable help. It will be assumed here that the jars used in qollqa were at the upper end of the size range of the form. Because there are very few large, complete Inka flared-rim jars from the Hatun Xauxa region, it will be necessary to rely on similar jars from Cuzco to make estimates of storage volume.

In a study of these jars from the archaeology museum of the Universidad Nacional del Cusco, Miller (1972:3) reports that the larger of two subcategories of the vessels stand between 0.80 and 1.01 m in height. These figures correspond well to those cited by Pardo (1939) for the same set of materials. Miller derives a standardized set of proportions for the vessels, from which it may be calculated that a jar of this shape and 1.0 m high contains about 0.15 to 0.20 m³ of storage space.[21] The variation depends on how bulbous the body is, how sharp the angle of carination is, and how high the jar was filled. For present purposes, the larger volume of 0.20 m³ will be assumed.

We may use these figures to estimate the amount of maize that could have been stored in jars in a typical Xauxa-region storehouse. The mean storage volume of jars inside the circular storehouses in the principal magazines above Hatun Xauxa (J15–J17) would have been about 6.1 m³.[22] Given the weight of the jars and their contents, it seems highly unlikely that a second layer was laid over the first. The result is that only 9.9 percent (J16) to 11.5 percent (J15) of the estimated volume of these storehouses would have been used to store maize. Circular storehouses in other complexes distributed throughout the valley have mean interior diameters as low as 3.23 m. Storage volumes have been estimated for qollqa of diameters 3.5 and 4.0 m, using jars of the same size. The smaller of these qollqa could have held 3.7 m³ of maize, and the larger would have contained about 5.5 m³.[23] If maize were stored in a similar fashion in rectangular storehouses, the typical storehouse would have contained about 9.0 m³ of maize.[24] For purposes of calculating lower-end figures for storage volumes, these quantities will be expressed as the rounded value of 10 percent of interior structure volumes (Tables 8.8–8.10).

Because potatoes were typically packaged in straw bales (Morris 1981:339; cf. Werge 1977 and D'Altroy and Hastorf 1984:343–47), they could make much more efficient use of the interior space of the qollqa in which they were stored. It is difficult to estimate precisely the proportion of volume occupied by the baled potatoes, but Morris (1981:357) suggests that about 25 percent of the space may have been left unused, to accommodate packing materials and containers and presumably to provide access and air circulation. That figure will be used here.

In the principal storage facilities above Hatun Xauxa (i.e., within 1 km) are an estimated 562 circular qollqa, with the capacity (at 6.1 m³ each) to contain about 3,428 m³ of maize stored in jars. In the same radius are an estimated 507 rectangular qollqa, with a total interior volume of 33,050 m³. Reduced by 25 percent to account for packaging, the latter figure may be lowered to 24,788 m³. Additional compensation is needed, because surely a significant proportion of these qollqa was assigned to store goods other than food. The thousands of loads of straw, firewood, sandals, blankets, and myriad other goods that the Xauxas and Wankas provided the Spaniards out of the storehouses provide testimony to that effect. Because we cannot yet estimate this proportion with confidence, calculations have been based on two proportions for nonfoods: 20 and 40 percent.

The state's capacity to store food, taking into account the space postulated to have been occupied by food packaging and storage of materials other than food, is shown in Table 8.8.[25] The figures should be taken as a reasonable bracketing of the actual quantities of foods that the state stored. These estimates

may further be used to evaluate the state's capacity to sustain workers from its stored goods (Table 8.9). For making an overall assessment, the food storage estimates have been simplified to a consideration of the four main crops of potatoes, maize, quinoa, and mashwa. Under conditions of 40 percent nonfood storage and 25 percent dedicated to packaging, the state could have sustained 10,000 adult male workers for a total of 2,412 days (6.6 years). If the grains were stored in jars, the total period of sustenance is estimated to have been 907 days (2.5 years). Even if we use the lower figure, Chalcuchima's army of 35,000 soldiers, discounting porters and camp followers, could have tapped into the region's storehouses for about 259 days.

The Inkas had thus developed the capacity to support an army of several tens of thousands for close to a year, solely from the food in its regional storehouses. Little wonder, then, that the 15,534 hanegas (878 m³) that Presidente Gasca's men consumed in 1548 made only a dent in the goods that were still being replenished in the Xauxa magazines (Guacrapáucar 1971a [1558]: 209).

Storage Capacity and Agricultural Production

The estimates of storage capacity may be used further to address the problem of state agricultural production. Using the data from Tables 8.2 through 8.4, we may calculate how much storage space would have been occupied by the crops that could be produced in the vicinity of Hatun Xauxa. For illustrative purposes, this storage volume has been calculated only for potatoes, maize, quinoa, and mashwa (Table 8.10). For example, the potatoes in the polygon catchment (919 ha) would have taken up about 3,925 m³ of storage space (at 3.29 t/ha and 0.77 t/m³), or 74 average rectangular storehouses. If the potatoes were stored as chuño for two years, as the desiccated product is today in the Mantaro (Sikkink 1988:69), the volume of potatoes stored from these areas of production would have been doubled. By inverting the estimation process, we may see that the 33,103 m³ of tuber (calculated as potato) storage estimated for the region's rectangular qollqa would have required cultivation of 3,874 ha, in a two-year replacement cycle.[26]

Comparable figures can be calculated for the other crops (Table 8.10). Following the exemplary case described at the end of the preceding section, we may see that the maize and quinoa, stored in jars, would have taken up about 1,129 circular storehouses or 827 rectangular storehouses. The four crops, stored as bales in

Table 8.8. Food Storage Capacities of State Storehouses, Adjusted for Nonfood Storage and Food Packaging

Site	Volume (m³)			Volume reduced 20% (m³)			Volume reduced 40% (m³)			Volume reduced 40% + 90% jar reduction (m³)			Volume reduced 40% + 25% bale reduction (m³)		
	Circular	Rectangular	Total	Circular	Rectangular	Total	Circular	Rectangular	Total	Circular	Rectangular	Total	Circular	Rectangular	Total
J10	1,760	0	1,760	1,408	0	1,408	1,056	0	1,056	106	0	106	792	0	792
J11	1,286	0	1,286	1,029	0	1,029	772	0	772	77	0	77	579	0	579
J12	542	3,506	4,048	434	2,805	3,238	325	2,104	2,429	33	210	243	244	1,578	1,822
J13	0	2,758	2,758	0	2,206	2,206	0	1,655	1,655	0	165	165	0	1,241	1,241
J14	2,112	0	2,112	1,690	0	1,690	1,267	0	1,267	127	0	127	950	0	950
J15	1,011	4,240	5,251	809	3,392	4,201	607	2,544	3,151	61	254	315	455	1,908	2,363
J16	7,898	15,500	23,398	6,318	12,400	18,718	4,739	9,300	14,039	474	930	1,404	3,554	6,975	10,529
J17	22,659	4,416	27,075	18,127	3,533	21,660	13,595	2,650	16,245	1,360	265	1,625	10,197	1,987	12,184
J18	0	7,164	7,164	0	5,731	5,731	0	4,298	4,298	0	430	430	0	3,224	3,224
J19	0	7,269	7,269	0	5,815	5,815	0	4,361	4,361	0	436	436	0	3,271	3,271
J20	684	0	684	547	0	547	410	0	410	41	0	41	308	0	308
J21	0	3,272	3,272	0	2,618	2,618	0	1,963	1,963	0	196	196	0	1,472	1,472
J22	0	6,278	6,278	0	5,022	5,022	0	3,767	3,767	0	377	377	0	2,825	2,825
J23	0	5,610	5,610	0	4,488	4,488	0	3,366	3,366	0	337	337	0	2,525	2,525
J24	0	5,079	5,079	0	4,063	4,063	0	3,047	3,047	0	305	305	0	2,286	2,286
J25	1,286	0	1,286	1,029	0	1,029	772	0	772	77	0	77	579	0	579
J26	838	0	838	670	0	670	503	0	503	50	0	50	377	0	377
J27	30	3,485	3,515	24	2,788	2,812	18	2,091	2,109	2	209	211	14	1,568	1,582
J28	901	0	901	721	0	721	541	0	541	54	0	54	405	0	405
J29	490	0	490	392	0	392	294	0	294	29	0	29	221	0	221
J30	313	0	313	250	0	250	188	0	188	19	0	19	141	0	141
J31	1,516	691	2,207	1,213	553	1,766	910	415	1,324	91	41	132	682	311	993
J32	1,526	552	2,078	1,221	442	1,662	916	331	1,247	92	33	125	687	248	935
J34	689	0	689	551	0	551	413	0	413	41	0	41	310	0	310
J35	1,517	0	1,517	1,214	0	1,214	910	0	910	91	0	91	683	0	683
J36	681	545	1,226	545	436	981	409	327	736	41	33	74	306	245	552
J57	591	1,247	1,838	473	998	1,470	355	748	1,103	35	75	110	266	561	827
J62	0	1,730	1,730	0	1,384	1,384	0	1,038	1,038	0	104	104	0	779	779
J91	0	183	183	0	146	146	0	110	110	0	11	11	0	82	82
J226	1,824	37	1,861	1,459	30	1,489	1,094	22	1,117	109	2	112	821	17	837
Total	50,154	73,562	123,716	40,123	58,850	98,973	30,092	44,137	74,230	3,009	4,414	7,423	22,569	33,103	55,672

Note: Volume reductions of 20 and 40 percent were made to account for storage of goods other than food; volume reductions of 90 and 25 percent were made to account for loss of space attributable to packaging. Apparent discrepancies in sums are due to rounding errors.

Table 8.9. State's Capacity to Sustain Adult Males on Stored Foods, Assuming Average Crop Mix Yields from Polygon Catchment

Crop	Storage conditions[a]	Circular storage volume (m³)[b]	Rectangular storage volume (m³)[c]	Storage volume (liters)	Volume required per day per adult male (liters)[d]	Days of caloric needs met for 10,000 adult males
Potatoes	40% nonfood, 25% packaging (bales)		13,383	13,382,678	3.9	343
Maize	Case 1: 40% nonfood, 25% packaging (sacks)	6,018		6,018,400	1.3	463
	Case 2: 40% nonfood, 90% packaging (jars)	808		807,553	1.3	62
Quinoa	Case 1: 40% nonfood, 25% packaging (sacks)	16,551		16,550,600	1.3	1,273
	Case 2: 40% nonfood, 90% packaging (jars)	2,201		2,201,447	1.3	169
Mashwa	40% nonfood, 25% packaging (bales)		19,712	19,712,322	5.9	333
Total	Potatoes, mashwa, and Case 1					2,412
	Potatoes, mashwa, and Case 2					907

[a]These calculations assume that grains were stored in circular structures, either in sacks (case 1) or in jars (case 2), and that tubers were stored in rectangular structures in straw bales.
[b]The mean storage volume of circular storehouses in the region is 52 m³.
[c]The mean storage volume of rectangular storehouses in the region is 71 m³.
[d]These volumes are based on an intake of 2,500 kcal per day.

Table 8.10. Storage Requirements for Principal Inka Crops Potentially Grown around Hatun Xauxa

Crop	Catchment	Productive output (t)	Volume (m³)[a]	Storehouses of either shape required		Storehouses required after 90% volume reduction for jars		Storehouses required after 25% volume reduction for bales	
				Circular	Rectangular	Circular	Rectangular	Circular	Rectangular
Potatoes	5 km	3,147	4,087	79	58			105	77
	10 km	10,811	13,923	268	196			357	261
	Polygon	3,023	3,925	75	55			101	74
Maize	5 km	1,026	1,332	26	19	256	188	34	25
	10 km	2,989	3,882	75	55	747	547	100	73
	Polygon	1,213	1,575	30	22	303	222	40	30
Quinoa	5 km	2,700	3,375	65	48	649	475	87	63
	10 km	7,618	9,523	183	134	1,831	1,341	244	179
	Polygon	3,435	4,294	83	60	826	605	110	81
Mashwa	5 km	3,368	4,374	84	62			112	82
	10 km	9,574	12,434	239	175			319	233
	Polygon	4,472	5,808	112	82			149	109
Total	5 km	10,241	13,169	253	185	905	663	338	247
	10 km	30,902	39,761	765	560	2,578	1,888	1,020	747
	Polygon	12,142	15,602	300	220	1,129	827	400	293

Note: Apparent discrepancies in sums and multiplication products are due to rounding errors.
[a]Weight : volume ratios are as follows: for maize, potatoes, and mashwa, 0.77 t/m³; for quinoa, 0.80 t/m³.

rectangular qollqa, would have taken up 293 buildings. These figures are concordant with the numbers of buildings actually recorded in the region: 957 circular and 1,035 rectangular, for a total of 1,992 qollqa (Table 8.7).

The Inkas would thus have not had to go far afield to keep their staple larders well stocked. It remains to be asked why such a large concentration of stored goods was deemed necessary at this location. Surely a principal need was for the population resident at Hatun Xauxa. As was discussed in Chapter 6, however, this group probably did not exceed a few thousand permanent personnel. An additional need lay in the support provided to state personnel passing through the region. All state functionaries traveling north and south along the qhapaq ñan or to and from Pachacamac would have stopped at the center, perhaps for a few days at a time. Among them was Wayna Qhapaq, who, along with his personal entourage, was lavishly entertained by the Wanka and Xauxa elites on the way to one of his major sallies into Ecuador (Cobo 1956 [1653]: vol. 2, bk. 2, ch. 16, p. 89). It seems most likely, however, that the majority of the subsistence supplies in these magazines was destined for support of the imperial armies that periodically passed through the region and the corvée laborers working on state projects.

Specialized Production for the State

The development of state agricultural settlements draws attention to the specialized labor statuses created by the state or elaborated from previously existing statuses of attached laborers. Because of the Inkas' dependence on an interlocking system of generalists and specialists of varying degrees and kinds, the incipient development of the specialized state economy merits additional examination. Costin (1991) has presented a thoughtful model of the development of economic specialization. In her discussion, she defines four parameters of specialization: context of production, concentration of production, constitution of production units, and degree of specialization. Each of these parameters varies along its own continuum: independent to attached contexts of production, dispersed to nucleated concentration, kin-based to occupationally based units, and part-time to full-time degrees of specialization. In varying combinations, these parameters define a series of kinds of specialization. Four of them are of

particular interest here: dispersed corvée, individual retainers, nucleated corvée, and retainer workshops.

These kinds of specialization would be expected to develop under conditions in which social or political considerations played a dominant role in determining economic relations. The demand crowd would be politically restricted, and principles of supply and demand, cost-efficiency, and price setting would play a lesser role than in a market economy or would be of no direct consequence. These kinds of specialization would be expected to be fostered or deliberately established by elite patrons or by the administrative stratum in a political economy. The kinds of specialization that would result depend on a number of factors, principal among them being ownership of the resources from which the state revenues were derived. In an economy in which the state owned or directly worked few resources but mobilized its support through taxation of goods or mercantile activities, little corvée would be expected. Instead, we would expect intensification of production of household or community resources by the taxpaying population, who would provide the fundamental staple finance for the state. This transition would be coupled with development of attached specialists who would work directly for the elites and be principally involved in production of the sumptuary goods that underwrote wealth or prestige finance. In an economy in which the state owned or directly controlled a large proportion of the resources from which its staple finance was derived, we would expect a much broader development of attached specialists employed to work state resources. The latter, of course, was the situation in the Inka empire, whereas the former characterized such early empires as the Aztecs.

Labor Statuses

The most important of the Inka attached specialists were the mitmaqkuna, the *yanakuna,* and the aqllakuna. The first of these have already been mentioned; they were forcibly resettled colonists set up by the state to meet military and economic needs. Forts along the eastern borders from Ecuador to Argentina, for instance, were staffed by mitmaqkuna, as were internal garrisons. These colonists were also widely employed to produce specialized agricultural goods, such as maize, coca, and peppers, and to manufacture craft items (see "Production of Imperial Ceramics," below). The yanakuna were a special status of individual, detached from their kin group and assigned to serve permanent duty for the state. Among their responsibilities were agricultural duties and house service for the elites. Although sometimes termed slaves by later commentators, yanakuna could attain positions of high status within the imperial administration. The last specialized category—the aqllakuna—consisted of young women, separated from their families and assigned to live in segregated precincts within state installations. There they wove cloth and brewed chicha, until awarded in marriage to men honored by the state.

Goods were produced for the state in several contexts, including the households of the peasantry, communities specializing in the production of certain commodities, and state installations, some of which were established as enclaves specifically to produce for the state. The extensive research into the Inka economy by Murra (e.g., 1975, 1980 [1956]) details the state's reliance on the productive capacities of the household (see also Rowe 1946). For instance, each family was given wool from state herds annually and was required to weave cloth from it; thus the household gave only its labor, the materials having been supplied. Analogous directives were given to peasants to collect undomesticated biotic resources, such as honey and feathers, and render them to the state. Murra (1975:251) has suggested that this form of taxation was comparable to working state lands or weaving for the state, in that the peasantry gave none of its own resources but simply collected that which already belonged to the state. Although this argument may have worked as a legal justification and surely reflected the state's ability to enforce its claims, the facts remain that the state received goods in the process and that the materials so rendered came from resources that had previously pertained to the subject populace. Here it may be that the peasantry's insistence to the Spanish authorities that they rendered only labor to the state and not goods at least partially reflects their recognition that their own resources were threatened by the new forms of taxation introduced by the European invaders.

Analyses of the detailed census documents from Huánuco (Helmer 1955–56 [1549]; Ortiz de Zúñiga 1967 [1562], 1972 [1562]) and Chucuito (Diez de San Miguel 1964 [1567]) show that the Inkas required specialized production of certain kinds of commodities at peasant communities especially well situated with respect to the appropriate natural resources. In the Huánuco region, for example, the distribution of artisans among Chupachu and Queros villages shows that settlements in suitable locations tended to specialize in the production of such goods as sandals, rope, or

ceramics (see LeVine 1987). Thus, although labor assignments were ostensibly to be made on the basis of population, the state clearly took into account environmental variations in making some assignments.

Among the most prominent craft enclaves set up by the state were the pottery manufacturing centers. Documentary and archaeological research has shown that the Inkas established potting centers at Cajamarca, in the Peruvian central highlands (Espinoza Soriano 1973a); at Hupi or Milliraya, near Lake Titicaca (Murra 1978; Spurling 1987); and at El Potrero-Chaquiago, in Argentina (Lorandi 1984), for example. The first of these contained members of at least 14 ethnic groups, and 100 potters were said to be settled at the second. Even if pottery manufacture was a seasonal occupation, the numbers of ceramics that these individuals produced would likely have been quite impressive.

Archaeological evidence of state-supported weaving, in the form of concentrations of spindle whorls in architectural compounds at Inka settlements, has been recovered from Huánuco Pampa (Morris and Thompson 1985:91–92) and El Potrero-Chaquiago (Williams 1983). Concentrations of state weavers have also been recorded at Lamay (outside Cuzco), where a Wanka elite headed 500 households in a colonist community (Toledo 1940b [1571]: 71), and at Hupi or Cupi (Murra 1978). Similarly, artifacts from a lapidary workshop have been recovered from the site of Pucará de Tilcara, in northern Argentina (Krapovickas 1964, 1981–82).

These specialized enclaves of craft producers working for the state were a particularly elaborated form of attached specialization often found in societies organized at the chiefdom level. The intent underlying the development of attached specialization was to control both the process of production and the distribution of the products. Other forms of forced production by the state, such as a tax on goods generally produced by the populace, would not have allowed the elite to control both the materials that went into the products and the distribution of goods made to state specifications. For many kinds of utilitarian goods, this disadvantage would have been of little consequence. For goods that were imbued with status or that served both political and utilitarian ends, monopoly control over the raw materials as well as the goods allowed the state to control the entire economic cycle, from extraction to production, distribution, and consumption.

By assigning manufacture of state goods to a limited

number of persons who could be trained and monitored, the stylistic integrity of state goods could be maintained. In a political economy in which the stamp of state manufacture conferred status, such control was likely a key element underlying the fostering of state production centers. Attached specialization, coupled with control over resources, also ensured that the quality of state goods was as high as the state supervisors could extract or chose to designate. It also must be emphasized that the specialized enclaves, which produced large quantities of state goods, gained for the Inkas the economies of scale that mass production provides. Both controlled political economies and market economies benefit from efficiency of production and from cost-benefit assessment of labor commitments.

Production of Imperial Ceramics

The clearest archaeological evidence for increased, controlled production of craft goods specifically for state purposes is found in the ceramics manufactured in the imperial Inka style. Inka pottery was a distinctive ware, readily distinguishable from the styles of subordinate populations (e.g., Meyers 1975; Alcina Franch et al. 1976; Morris 1978:321; D'Altroy 1981; Julien 1982; Costin 1986). An array of distinctive vessel shapes was decorated primarily with geometric designs in polychrome slips (see Figs. A.1–A.13, in the Appendix). The standardization of vessel form and decoration provided an unambiguous stamp of imperial manufacture and facilitated production by local potters as part of their labor obligations. Despite the standardization, regional variants can be found throughout the empire, so that the Inka pottery from Cuzco, for example, can be distinguished from that of Huánuco, Pachacamac, Lake Titicaca, or Hatun Xauxa. Along with documentary evidence cited below, this finding suggests strongly that state ceramics were produced and consumed within restricted regions.

In an extensive study of the Inka road system, however, Hyslop (1984) noted that some state personnel used ceramics of local non-Inka styles, even when residing at some installations that bore the stamp of Inka construction or that were named as Inka sites in early documentary sources. This practice appears to have occurred primarily in regions that were not intensively integrated into the empire or in settlements that were at secondary or lower levels in the regional hierarchy. Principal among them were settlements in northern Chile and northwestern Argentina. At major Inka centers in the central sierra, such as Huánuco Pampa,

Pumpu, and Hatun Xauxa, the ceramic assemblages were heavily dominated by state ceramics, to the virtual exclusion of non-Inka styles (D'Altroy 1981; Morris and Thompson 1985). It is therefore fair to say that the presence of Inka ceramics likely indicates the production and distribution of goods by the state, but that a lack of Inka ceramics at a settlement does not necessarily imply lack of a state presence. Although further research on this issue is needed, the lack of Inka pottery at some of the state settlements probably resulted from the slow process of installing production centers and training the ceramists in the manufacture of state pottery.

State control of ceramic manufacture should have produced Inka vessels that were highly standardized and distinct from those of subject production. Similarly, the political status conferred through access to these goods should have resulted in intensive labor investment. Compositional homogeneity should have resulted from reservation of sources of raw materials for state use. Stylistic and morphological standardization should have been an outcome of the use of attached specialists making ceramics to state specifications. Furthermore, state ceramics should have been consumed in a pattern that conformed to a dendritic structure of political and economic relations. That is, the flow of state goods should have followed relationships defined along vertical lines, with little evidence for horizontal exchange.

Following similar lines of reasoning, Hagstrum (1985, 1986) and Costin (1986) have argued that sumptuary ceramics should be distinguishable from utilitarian pottery on the basis of the amount of labor invested. Sumptuary goods should have been more labor-intensive and thus more costly to manufacture, particularly in their decoration. To evaluate labor investment in both modern and archaeological ceramics in the Mantaro Valley, Hagstrum devised an ordinal production task index modeled after that proposed by Feinman et al. (1981). Costin employed an analogous rank-scoring approach in analyzing late prehistoric pottery, in which points were assigned to the amount of time estimated necessary to execute each surface finishing or decoration task. Both analyses shows a consistent pattern of high labor investment in production of imperial Inka ceramics—higher than any of the other archaeological or modern wares assessed.

Both Hagstrum and Costin argue that the distinctions between Wanka and Inka pottery are largely explicable by the organization of the craft specialists who produced them. The former vessels were likely produced by independent specialists who made their wares for a general demand population. These potters should have focused on standardization of their ceramics largely to minimize costs. Because the demand population consisted of the general populace and because the vessels were utilitarian in nature, the ceramics were relatively unelaborated. In contrast, the Inka vessels were likely made by attached specialists, producing goods for a politically defined demand crowd. The consuming population in this case comprised the state personnel and the regional elites designated by the state as appropriate recipients of state goods.

To assess the evidence for manufacturing of state and subject ceramics at settlements in the study region, Costin (1986:396–420) created a measure of production called the waster index. This measure is calculated as 100 times the ratio of overfired by-products of ceramic manufacture (wasters, clinkers, vitrified sherds) to total consumed ceramics. Given appropriate sampling strategies, it may be measured on the basis of increasingly comprehensive units, from the collection unit to the household, state, or region. Costin's analyses show that ceramic production in the region was organized primarily as a community specialty. In Wanka II, Umpamalca (J41) was the principal center of potting in the Yanamarca Valley, whereas Marca (J54) became the center in Wanka III.

Surprisingly, only 1 of the 314 wasters recovered from Wanka III or Inka contexts was clearly from an Inka vessel; it was a modeled feline appliqué from a flared-rim jar recovered from Marca.[27] A second waster in the state style was also recovered from this site, but the sherd's distortion precludes complete confidence in its stylistic assignation. This evidence clearly points to production of Inka ceramics at locations other than the Inka provincial capital, the auxiliary state settlements in the region, and the subject residential communities. At present, however, we cannot determine where Inka ceramic production was carried out.

The problem of the control of resources—a central element of the development of attached specialization in the Inka political economy—has been addressed by analyzing the raw materials used in the imperial Inka ceramics from the region. In a study reported in detail elsewhere (D'Altroy and Bishop 1990), 173 sherds in the Inka and Wanka ceramic styles were analyzed through instrumental neutron activation analysis (INAA). The sherds were drawn from the Cuzco area, the Isle of the Sun in Lake Titicaca, the Mantaro Valley, and Tarmatampu. Within the Mantaro region, a range

of vessel forms and styles was analyzed from seven Inka (J4–J6, J16, J17, J45, J60) and three subject (J2, J54, J59) settlements. A series of statistical approaches was employed to determine relationships among the proveniences from which the materials were recovered, the style of the ceramics, and the ethnic affiliations of the residents (Inka or Wanka). I will summarize only the most important results here.

Figure 8.13 is an average-linkage cluster analysis dendrogram that presents global clustering tendencies in the data set.[28] In this plot, all but one of the sherds from Lake Titicaca (at the bottom of the dendrogram) are separated from the ceramics from Cuzco, which are also well separated from the Upper Mantaro samples. Among the Upper Mantaro ceramics, some clusters of Xauxa Inka and Base Roja sherds are visible, but the patterning is not well defined; further global cluster analyses did not clarify the situation. Stepwise discriminant analysis was then employed to reclassify the imperial Inka samples into regional groups based on chemical composition. In Figure 8.14, the plot of 110 sherds on the first two discriminant functions is shown, with 5 outliers removed (see D'Altroy and Bishop 1990: Fig. 3). This procedure effectively separated the Inka ceramics from the Mantaro, Cuzco, and Lake Titicaca regions, although one sherd each from Hatun Xauxa and Lake Titicaca corresponded closely to the Cuzco material.

The compositional analyses similarly showed that the Inka and non-Inka ceramics from the Upper Mantaro collections were distinguishable from one another. Moreover, at least two separate sources of raw materials could be distinguished among the Mantaro Inka ceramics.[29] The products of these two sources were distributed differentially among the region's settlements. Most Inka ceramics from Hatunmarca were distinct from those that formed the bulk of the imperial wares at Hatun Xauxa, Marca, and the road station J45, at the north end of the Yanamarca Valley. Inka ceramics from the other settlements were derived from a combination of sources.

A principal implication of these results is that ceramics in each province were made regionally; some imperial Inka pottery may have been shipped out from the capital, but production of the pottery was largely farmed out to the provinces. This evidence also shows that the distribution of Inka ceramics was structured within the Mantaro region, probably by status and by location. As present, we can only sketch out the situation, but it seems probable that the distribution of the state wares was structured along lines of political rela-

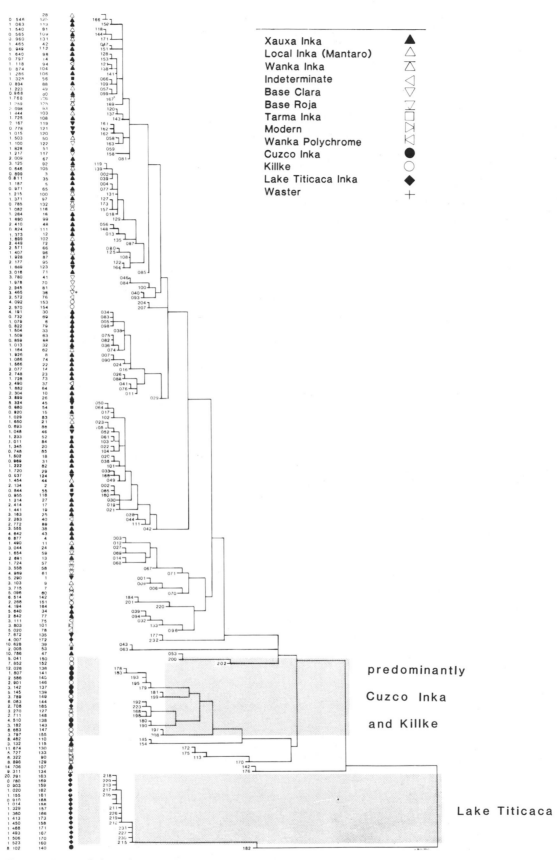

Fig. 8.13. Average-linkage cluster analysis dendrogram of 173 sherds analyzed for chemical composition by INAA (see D'Altroy and Bishop 1990).

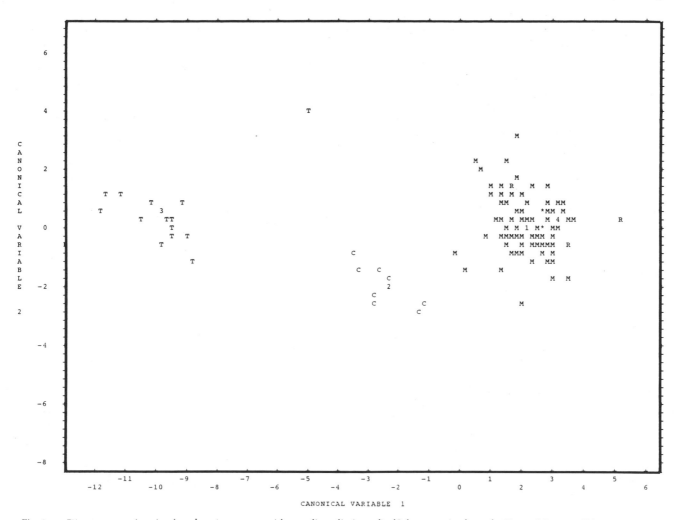

Fig. 8.14. Discriminant plot of reduced set (110 cases, with 5 outliers eliminated) of Inka ceramics from the Upper Mantaro (*M*; group centroid = 1), Cuzco (*C*; group centroid = 2), Lake Titicaca (*T*; group centroid = 3), and Tarma (*R*; group centroid = 4). Overlap of different groups is indicated by an asterisk. (See D'Altroy and Bishop 1990.)

tionships. Intrasite variations in the distribution of these ceramics, supporting this view, will be explored in Chapter 9.

The results of these analyses are consonant with a state ceramic production organization in which (1) most state pottery was made and used within limited regions, (2) the production of state ceramics and the production of subject ceramics were discrete, and (3) the state ceramics were the most labor-intensive and standardized of all pottery in the region. Localized production and consumption of state ceramics was expected, because pots break and weigh a great deal, especially in proportion to their value; they were therefore not likely to have been moved great distances. Additionally, the dendritic character of the political economy would have tended to compartmentalize

production and distribution systems. The dispersal of state production centers throughout the empire indicates that this policy was not unique to the Mantaro region (Espinoza Soriano 1973b; Murra 1980 [1956]; Lorandi 1984; Spurling 1987).

Summary

In this chapter, I have argued that the imperial political economy can be understood as a dendritic system, in which goods and services were mobilized upward through a variety of institutions. The goods that were moved down the hierarchy corresponded to support for labor rendered and to political largess. Conversely, little horizontal exchange was conducted directly under state auspices, although low-level specialized production for exchange continued among the subject populace (Earle 1985; Earle et al. 1987). A general trend toward increased control and specialization in the Inka economy can be seen in policies concerning both access to resources and organization of labor. With respect to resources, the development of state farms and ceramic production units indicates increasing state control over the goods employed in the economy, from the raw materials up.

The widespread distribution of state production enclaves indicates two key factors underlying the organization of labor. First, the presence of such facilities at numerous locations underscores the state's need to produce most goods for its personnel near the points of consumption. Although this practice may be viewed simply as a matter of convenience, the costs and difficulties of transportation in the rough Andean terrain would have made centralized production of all but the most elite, sumptuary goods prohibitively expensive. State transport efficiency was poor, and dispersed production was an absolute necessity. Second, the development of the imperial production enclaves shows that state needs could not be met by the productive capacities of general peasantry in the later decades of the empire (Murra 1980 [1956]: 153–86). The enclaves would have served the dual purposes of economies of scale and economies of control. The distribution of these enclaves throughout the empire would have ameliorated the inescapable costs of transporting bulky goods.

This distribution draws attention to three general trends in the development of the economy: the tendency to move to greater independence of production (release from reliance on subject corvée), greater control over the quality of the product, and increased efficiency of production. These three issues are not unrelated, of course, but they emphasize that Inka innovation did not consist simply of manipulating existing socioeconomic relationships. Instead, the state was changing social relations of production according to criteria that showed an awareness of the energetic costs and benefits of differing strategies—a point generally overlooked with respect to Inka economic organization.[30]

As other investigators have noted (e.g., Morris 1982; Salomon 1986) and I have argued throughout this chapter, these kinds of economic transformations were not applied equally throughout Tawantinsuyu. Although the data remain sketchy, the movement toward intensive production seems to have corresponded fairly well to the areas of most intensive political incorporation—that is, the Peruvian highlands and parts of Bolivia. Even in these regions, however, state production was spatially variable, focusing on a few areas of high productivity. State production toward the frontiers of imperial dominion appears to have been present but more limited. The immediate vicinity of state settlements in highland Ecuador was the location of some state farming (see Salomon 1986), for instance, and enclaves in Argentina and Chile were designed to extract specific localized resources (see González 1983). The progressive shift toward more-intensive production in highland Ecuador suggests that the state may have been expanding the area of territorial control. Nonetheless, the remarkably slim evidence for state production or extraction on the fertile north coast of Peru implies that the Inkas had made a deliberate strategic choice to maintain indirect rule in some regions of the empire.

9

Continuity and Change in Wanka Society

The advent of the Inka empire brought about varied changes in the subject societies incorporated into Tawantinsuyu. Studies of the impact on sierra societies frequently emphasize either of two seemingly contradictory elements of life under imperial rule. First was the apparently ubiquitous state intrusion into subject life, ranging from extraction of household labor and military service to specification of sumptuary rules. In contrast was the continuity of the traditional household and community, upon which the state built its ruling superstructure. Each view, not surprisingly, contains significant elements of truth. Murra (1975, 1980 [1956]) has partially accounted for this seeming paradox by arguing that the state drew directly from local social systems both as models for its administration and as convenient structures for implementing state policies (see also Wachtel 1977). Continuity of local socioeconomic organization was greatly to the state's benefit, especially in the early imperial decades, because the Inkas' principal source of wealth lay in the productive labor of their subjects. Even during the later development of specialized productive statuses, dissolution of the fundamental social units would have been counterproductive.

At the same time, imperial demands inexorably disrupted the fabric of subject life. Forced resettlement, alienation of resources, and extraction of labor—coupled with the loss of native autonomy—left an indelible mark on many subject groups. That imprint varied, however, across time and among the conquered polities. Even within provinces incorporated fairly intensively into the empire, including the Upper Mantaro region, the impacts of state rule varied locally. This variation draws attention to a third feature of Inka-subject relations that numerous researchers emphasize: the presumably idiosyncratic character of interaction between the rulers and particular ethnic groups. Various authors have pointed out, for example, that specific ethnic groups were often put to particular tasks. Thus, the Rucanas were favored as litter bearers, the Cañares and Chachapoyas as soldiers, and the residents of the Lake Titicaca area as stonemasons (see Rowe 1946; Murra 1980 [1956]).

In partial contrast to this view is the present work, which views many of the apparently region-specific elements of Inka rule more as systemic variations than as consequences of historical events or an Andean mind-set. Historical circumstances, such as the degree of native resistance, were certainly critical to the development of Inka policies, but the development of state-subject relations also depended fundamentally on the position and physiography of the region and on the nature of its resources in the overall scheme of the empire. It is from the perspective of combined systemic and historical circumstances that the impacts of state rule on the Wankas can be most effectively evaluated.

Within Wanka society, Inka rule produced some significant changes while other features remained remarkably stable. Chapter 7 treated the partial merging of the native authority system and the state administration, with a consequent increase in the organizational complexity and power of the Wanka elite strata. Equally striking changes in the indigenous settlement organization and in some activities pursued within subject communities contributed to intensification of state control over the region. Although the state-subject relationship was heavily weighted in favor of state interests, it was not one-sided. Some accommodations to the Inka presence enhanced the status of local elites and improved the quality of life for much of the population, notably by a reduction in local conflict and by an improvement in diet and life expectancy (see Earle et al. 1987). At the same time, basic elements of traditional society remained largely unaffected. Sociopolitical and economic organization still relied on the ayllu as the fundamental socioeconomic unit, despite the intrusion of imperial demands and bureaucracy. In addition, apart from the changes that the Inkas engineered in the political economy, there appears to have been little increase in specialization or exchange among the region's populace (Earle 1985; Earle et al. 1987; Costin and Earle 1989).

In this chapter, the archaeological evidence for continuity and transformation in native society is examined primarily for residents of the Yanamarca Valley settlements. Three aspects of local change are of special interest here: (1) the restructuring of the regional settlement system, (2) the state-related activities pursued at subject settlements, and (3) the impacts of imperial rule on the economics of subject society. The first feature draws interest because of the likely inextricable relationship between the political hierarchy and the organization of the settlement system. Equally important for the effectiveness of imperial rule was the distribution of the local populace, both with respect to productive resources and with respect to military considerations. The latter two aspects of local change, treated later in this chapter, provide insight into transformations at the household level of native society.

Settlement Pattern Change in Wanka III

The advent of Inka rule marked the inception of the Wanka III phase (A.D. 1460–1533).[1] This era witnessed four major trends in the settlement system of the indigenous populations in the main Mantaro and northern adjoining valleys: (1) truncation of the upper level of the indigenous settlement hierarchy, (2) abandonment of defensively located settlements in tuber-growing areas as the population dispersed into smaller villages, (3) reoccupation of low, valley-flank locations more conducive to maize cultivation, and (4) retention of low-density occupation within the first 5 km surrounding the provincial capital, Hatun Xauxa. In the following sections, each of these points and its implications for state-subject relations is considered.

Population Estimates for Wanka III

The various Junín Project and UMARP surveys have recorded a total of 99 sites with at least minimal evidence of Late Horizon occupation within the contiguous study region. Of these 99 sites, 75 exhibit more than just a trace of Late Horizon occupation. A trace here is generally defined as just 1 or 2 Inka or Inka-related sherds, although the 11 Inka-related sherds found scattered throughout J109 (Llamap Shillón; 31.4 ha) were considered to represent an ephemeral occupation. These 75 sites together are estimated to have housed between 27,062 and 45,103 individuals, at 60 and 100 percent occupation, respectively.[2] These estimates represent a significant drop—25.8 percent—in overall population size for the study region, from a maximal estimate for Wanka II of 60,862. Apart from the Inka provincial capital, Hatun Xauxa, the largest settlements in the region were the newly founded town of Marca (population: 2,484–4,140) and the continuously occupied Hatunmarca (population: 2,466–4,110). These figures also indicate a radical drop in population—68.8 percent—for the largest settlements of the region, from 13,259 for Wanka II's largest settlement, Tunanmarca, to Marca's 4,140. Associated with this shift was a significant transferral of the locus of power from indigenous centers to the state administrative center; this restructuring of population among Wanka III settlements will be examined below.

The apparent drop in regional population under Inka rule may be a consequence of several processes, some resulting from sociopolitical circumstances and some from the difficulties of making accurate assessments of population size. As will be described below, the Inkas appear to have maintained an area of relatively low population density in the immediate environs of the provincial center, which would have tended to keep the main valley's population density relatively low within UMARP's survey area (see also Chapter 8).

A second, more significant social process stemmed from the extensive resettlement program undertaken by the state. The Inkas employed forced resettlement of individuals or entire sociopolitical groups as a major tool in breaking up hostile political units and in effecting state economic programs (Rowe 1946:269). By 1533 the policy had fragmented numerous ethnic groups, including the Wankas, and new settlers may have outnumbered the indigenous population in some provinces (Rowe 1946:269–70). The early chroniclers unfortunately lumped together various categories of displaced peoples into two groups: mitmaqkuna, the colonists; and yanakuna, the retainers or servants (Pease 1978:99–105). The principal uses of mitmaqkuna were as craft or agricultural specialists, military garrisons, and maintenance personnel for state facilities (e.g., Espinoza Soriano 1970:14, 1973a:240; Salomon 1986:158–66; see also Chapter 8).

The effect of the resettlement program on demography in the research area can be only partially understood with present data. Cieza (1984 [1551]: ch. 54, p. 169) mentions that Wayna Qhapaq resettled nobility (*orejones*) from Cuzco in the province of Xauxa, apparently as part of a military strategy to secure control over the central sierra. An additional shift between the Ecuadorian sierra and Hatunxauxa is corroborated by documentation from both regions. It appears probable in this case that a matched exchange may have occurred between the Wankas and the Cañares and Chachapoyas. Both of the latter mitmaqkuna groups were situated in the village of La Purificación de Guacho, in the Lurinwanka saya, when Toledo (1940a:22) conducted his audiences in 1570: "[I]n said town of La Concepción an oath was taken and received according to the law from don Diego Lucana, principal of the Cañares, Chachapoyas, and Llaguas mitmaqkuna, who are in this repartimiento of the Lurinwankas in the town that is called La Purificación de Guacho."[3] Salomon (1986:159) notes that Cañares and Chachapoyas were sometimes imported together for policing actions, which may explain their presence in the area (see also Browman 1970:268; Murra 1986).

Statements, such as the following, in other documents confirm that some members of the saya of Hatunxauxa were settled in Cañare territory, near Quito:

"The lords of Xauxa did [Wayna Qhapaq] great services, and some of the captains and warriors accompanied him" (Cieza 1967 [1553]: ch. 64, p. 215).[4] Among those people was the heir apparent to the Hatunxauxa ayllu of Huacjrasmarca, whose death in Ecuador eventuated in litigation over leadership rights at home some 80 years later: ". . . in the time of the Inka Wayna Qhapaq, inasmuch as said Inka took said Guaman Misari, eldest son of said Apo Misari, with him to Quito and Tumipampa with other kurakas of said saya of Hatunxauxa" (Espinoza Soriano 1969 [1597]: doc. 3, p. 63).[5] At least some of these colonists were settled in the multiethnic enclave of El Quinche, which contained residents from at least six ethnic groups: Angaraes, Cañares, Guangas (Wankas), Ichinguis, Tacuris, and Yauyos (Aquiles Pérez 1960, cited by Salomon 1986:163). Among the Wanka elites was the kuraka of the parcialidad, don Diego Guaman Ñaupa, who petitioned the native magistrate in 1580 for return of some subjects who had fled to Quito (Salomon 1986:163). It seems probable, as noted in Chapter 7, that this Ñaupa was directly related to the kuraka don Diego Ñaupari, resident of Hatunxauxa and segunda persona to don Francisco Cusichaca, cacique principal of the saya of Hatunxauxa (Cusichaca et al. 1971 [1561]: 260). Although the function of the enclave is unclear from present documentation, the original role of the Wankas (Xauxas?) in the region was likely military support of Wayna Qhapaq's conquests.

The size of some of the mitmaq communities is exemplified by the pueblo of Lamay, near Cuzco, which minimally contained about 500 heads of household, according to its Wanka leader: "Don Francisco Vichic, who said he is a native of Ananwanka, mitmaq of Lamay, placed by the Inka Wascar, and that his father was a kuraka who governed five hundred Indians of Lamay, and that, because age and memory are failing him in governing them, a brother has succeeded him in office and that he is eighty-nine years old . . ." (Toledo 1940c [1571]: 159).[6] If all or most of the Lamay mitmaqkuna were from the Upper Mantaro Valley, this single community may have incorporated almost 2 percent of the entire region's population. Even though this settlement may have been exceptionally large, it illustrates the possible extent of state resettlement for these societies.

Additional groups of resettled Wankas have been recorded at the provincial center of Willka Wamán (Carbajal 1965 [1586]: 218) and at Cuzco (Cieza 1984 [1551]: ch. 93, p. 260). The first of them was part of the center's resident garrison, reported to have been

30,000 strong. Although no information is presented as to the function of the Cuzco residents, it seems likely that they formed part of the sacred imperial geography surrounding the capital, which replicated the distribution of ethnic groups throughout the empire.

As was described previously, the mitmaqkuna program seems to have been part of a coordinated policy to reduce threats to security and to meet state economic demands elsewhere in the empire. By moving many residents from their defensible hilltop settlements, the Inkas initially defused a threat to state security in the province. Use of the Cañares and Chachapoyas also suggests that the Inkas, by importing groups loyal to the state, were anticipating a potentially volatile political situation.

The population estimates derived from the archaeological data conform well to the information provided in early documentary sources. Recall that in the 1582 visita by Vega (1965), Hatunxauxa was described as the least populous of the three saya, with 6,000 "war Indians." This figure has been used to estimate a population of 36,000 for the entire saya, a total that falls comfortably within the population range estimated archaeologically for the area within the survey region. Although this region does not encompass the entire Hatunxauxa territory, it does contain the areas with the highest concentrations of population, especially within about 20 km of Hatun Xauxa. Examination of airphotos shows that some settlements with layouts comparable to those of Late Intermediate or Late Horizon sites were located up the Río Mantaro gorge and to the east of the main valley. They were few, however, and most were small; they would likely have constituted a relatively small proportion of the late prehistoric population.

In contrast to Hatunxauxa's archaeological data, the recorded archaeological remains of Inka-period settlements in the Lurinwanka saya are conspicuously sparse, although it must be noted that Browman's (1970) survey of the Lurinwanka and Ananwanka territories focused on the main valley sectors of their territories. The relative lack of Inka-period Lurinwanka sites does not fit the documentary estimate of 50 percent more inhabitants than in Hatunxauxa. In contrast, the territorial borders of Ananwanka reconstructed from historical toponymy and linguistic distinctions contain the remains of numerous large settlements, most notably Arhuaturo, on a hill to the southwest of modern Huancayo. The largest Lurinwanka site in the main valley is Patancoto, a settlement of perhaps 8 ha. Additional sites were located along the hill flanks or river terraces of the main valley (e.g., at Queros and Saño), but the main concentrations of Lurinwanka population have yet to be located archaeologically.

Two possibilities may be suggested for the apparent lack of congruence between the archaeological evidence and the historical evidence for population distribution south of the Hatunxauxa saya. One is that the very narrow territory ascribed historically to the Lurinwankas was actually substantially broader than that reconstructed on ethnohistorical maps (e.g., Espinoza Soriano 1971: inset map; Cerrón-Palomino 1977). Because of the continuity in place names from early Spanish documents and in regional variations in native dialects, this suggestion seems unlikely. A second possibility is that further archaeological surveys in the Lurinwanka saya, to the east and west of the main valley, would significantly expand the inventory of sites or estimates of population for the division. In addition, because no firm population figures are available for the Lurinwanka sites, the discrepancy may be more apparent than real.

Distribution of Wanka III Settlements

The introduction of imperial control into the Upper Mantaro Valley resulted in significant shifts in the structure of power and demography within the region. I have argued that the Inkas were attempting a fairly intensive exploitation of the Upper Mantaro region and that they employed native elites in the regional administration. Under these circumstances, we might expect to find a relatively smooth hierarchical relationship between Inka power and the subject society visible in the regional settlement system. This sort of a relationship may be measured through analysis of the regional rank-size settlement distribution, which will only be summarized here.[7] As the reader will recall from Chapter 4, a rank-size distribution plots the logarithm of a site's size against the log of the rank of its size. A well-integrated settlement system, in which the size of a site is proportional to its functional complexity, should yield a straight-line plot of points.

If all Late Horizon settlements in the study region are treated as part of a single settlement hierarchy, the resulting pattern is remarkably close to the log-linear model that one would expect of a well-integrated system (Fig. 9.1). The imperial center of Hatun Xauxa is estimated to have contained housing for close to 7,000 people, whereas the two largest Wanka III towns in the region had populations of about 4,140 (Marca) and 4,110 (Hatunmarca). These towns, it will be recalled,

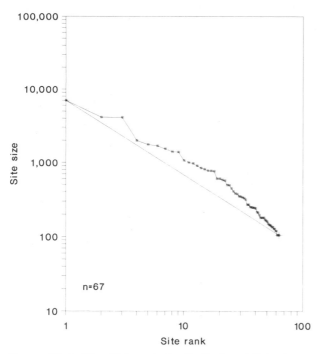

Fig. 9.1. Wanka III and Inka rank-size distribution of all sites in the Upper Mantaro survey region. Site size refers to estimated population.

were markedly reduced in size from the largest Wanka II centers, which had boasted populations of more than 13,000.

The rank-size curve is slightly convex, a form that typically results from one of two circumstances. Either the second-rank settlement is larger than would be expected, given the size of the largest settlement, or the largest settlement is smaller than would be expected, given the size of the second-rank and other sites in the region (see Johnson 1980, 1987; Paynter 1983; Schacht 1987:174). In this case, the convex deviation from the model line is primarily a result of the essentially equivalent size of the two largest subject towns, a relationship that will be explored further below.

To measure the convexity of the rank-size curve, Johnson's (1987) rank-size index (RSI) may be employed.[8] The index approaches 1.0 in highly convex systems, has a value of zero in a log-linear distribution, and produces increasingly large negative values as the distribution becomes more concave. The Late Horizon distribution, which includes the Inka center and supporting facilities (e.g., J4, J6, J45, J63; Fig. 9.1), has an RSI value of .0930. Although the form of the distribution for this index has not been fully described, treat-

ment of the Inka settlements as an integral part of the settlement system brings the regional pattern close to that expected in a log-linear model. This congruence is apparent visually in the proximity of the line of empirical rank-size relationships to the log-linear model line.

The form of the curve suggests strongly that the Inkas restructured the region's settlements into a well-integrated system. As will be shown below, the distribution of state goods provides a corroborative line of evidence that the Inkas were drawing the local populace into an articulated political and economic structure. The development of this apparently integrated settlement system required substantial reorganization of the native society. At the time of the Inka conquest, the settlement organization of Wanka II society indicated a developing hierarchical society (Chapter 4, esp. Fig. 4.11). The preceding 150 years had been a time of fractious local relations, characterized by the movement of the region's inhabitants into nucleated, defensively constructed settlements situated high on the ridgelines surrounding the valley. When the Inkas conquered the Mantaro region, they undertook a program of pacification that included abandonment of the defensive settlements and deportation of resistant groups. The northwest part of the Yanamarca Valley was effectively depopulated, and 18 new Yanamarca sites were established in easily accessible locations to the south and east, closer to Hatun Xauxa.

The rapidity and thoroughness with which the northern settlements were abandoned are startling. Radiocarbon dates from Tunanmarca and Umpamalca show that they were contemporaneous with Hatunmarca and other Wanka II communities and were apparently occupied right up to the Inka conquest circa 1460 (Earle et al. 1987:80–81). Nonetheless, extensive fieldwork at these two settlements—including systematic surface collections and excavations in 17 residential compounds—has failed to recover a single artifact attributable to the Wanka III occupation of the region. This finding may be contrasted to the widespread evidence for native access to Inka ceramics at settlements distributed throughout the region, including locations surrounding this small area.

The Yanamarca resettlement is most reasonably explained as a deliberate depopulating of the zone by state edict. Local oral histories recounted ardent resistance to the Inka conquest by the northernmost Wankas and their deportation subsequent to defeat (e.g., Toledo 1940a [1570]; Vega 1965 [1582]; see Chapter 5). On the face of it, the apparent lack of any habitation in the northern Yanamarca, even in new settlements, would be surprising, especially when the productivity of these uplands and the presence of extensive late prehistoric irrigation systems are considered. This forced dislocation of perhaps 20,000 people from one small valley, coupled with the total abandonment of the major population and political center of Tunanmarca, dramatically illustrates the impact of the Inka conquest on native societies.

The selectivity of the effect is particularly notable, if the partial continuity of indigenous residence to the south is taken into account. Of the nine Wanka II settlements in the Yanamarca, only Hatunmarca (J2), J8, J42, and J53 continued to be occupied after the Inka conquest. The Wanka III population of Hatunmarca, however, fell from about 11,055 to 4,110, as the area occupied within the residential architecture decreased about 73 percent. The abandonment is potentially explicable in terms of state security or as part of the mitmaqkuna resettlement program, for the Inkas often deported recalcitrant groups to other parts of the empire (Rowe 1946:269; Cobo 1956 [1653]: vol. 2, bk. 2, ch. 23, p. 109). In commenting on the settlement reorganization, Cieza wrote: "[T]he Indians, leaving the fortresses that they had occupied previously, organized their towns in good order, both in the valleys of the plains and in the mountains and altiplano of Collao" (Cieza 1967 [1553]: ch. 24, p. 83; see also p. 84).[9] He noted that in the Mantaro area these new settlements were supposed to have been established on the valley flanks, where a major strip of Wanka III sites is now found (Cieza 1967 [1553]: ch. 24, p. 167; Fig. 6.1).

The settlement pattern in the Jisse area, on the west side of the Río Quishuarcancha drainage, paralleled that of the Yanamarca Valley. During Wanka II the residents were clustered in fortified settlements on ridgetops. The major settlement of the region, Llamap Shillón (J109), closely resembled Tunanmarca and Hatunmarca. Protected by as many as five defensive walls, with two major internal divisions and multiple subdivisions, Llamap Shillón was typical of the densely packed centers of Wanka II. At its maximal extent, the settlement rivaled Tunanmarca and Hatunmarca in population (4,374 to 7,290), although no obvious area of comparable public architecture has been preserved. Neighboring Wanka II communities shared similar topographies and defensive characteristics. Huacjrasmarca (J108), for instance, was perched on a knoll whose nearly sheer sides fell 400 m to the east and south; even so, this small settlement (8 ha, with

4.1 ha of occupation) of 369 to 615 people was encircled by a series of ascending, fortified terraces.

Even with the establishment of eight new hamlets and villages along the lower Río Quishuarcancha and in the hills near Pomacancha and Janjaillo, the Jisse-area population appears to have decreased markedly in Wanka III. To judge from the light scatter of Inka ceramics—13 of the 1,842 sherds (1,247 diagnostics) recovered from the surface—the native populace continued to reside in Huacjrasmarca at a reduced level. Conversely, the people may have essentially abandoned Llamap Shillón, for no Inka-style architecture or imperial Inka pottery has been discovered in surface work at the latter settlement (Table 9.1). Pending more-detailed excavation data, it appears that these high, defensive settlements, like those in the northern Yanamarca Valley, were essentially abandoned under the Inkas. It remains unclear whether any of the residents of the area were forcibly deported, however, as appears likely for the Tunanmarca-associated communities.

With the partial or complete abandonment of Tunanmarca, Llamap Shillón, Umpamalca, and other high-elevation sites in Wanka III, many of the Yanamarca and Jisse residents dispersed into smaller villages in poorly defensible locations. Most settlements in both valleys were situated either on the valley floor or on the adjacent low slopes. With the possible exception of Marca, whose northeast flank was protected by a single wall, none of the new sites displayed any defensive features, such as encircling walls or moats. It may be surmised that not only did the Inka-imposed peace make vulnerable locations accessible for reoccupation, but the state also prohibited defensive construction at the new towns and villages.

In the main Mantaro Valley, the settlement pattern shift from Wanka II to III is less well described, in large part because of a lack of intensive excavation. A recent UMARP survey of the region shows that members of the indigenous society occupied a strip settlement along the west side of the valley, at an elevation of about 3,400 m, whereas the eastern side was more sparsely settled. With the exception of a few somewhat nucleated sites just west of modern Muquiyauyo, the strip occupation consisted of a dispersed series of small villages and hamlets, no more than a few hundred meters apart, along the upper edge of the low valley flanks. The architectural remains at these sites are generally in poor condition. They typically consist of a few score of circular pirka foundations at the borders of

Table 9.1. Wanka III and Inka Surface Collection Data

Site	Site area (ha)[a]	Number of collections with Inka ceramics	Number of sherds[b]				% Inka[e]	Inka or Wanka III
			Inka	Inka-related[c]	Wanka II–III[d]	Total		
J1	1.8	10/10	5,596	29	2,223	2,848	20.9	W III
J2	27.4	38/58	503	98	12,585	13,186	3.8	W III
J3[f]	1.4	0/0	0	0	0	0	0.0	W III
J4	5.9	1/1	66	0	470	536	12.3	Inka
J5	46.6	17/17	5,716	35	80	5,831	98.0	Inka
J6	0.7	0/0	73	2	4	79	92.4	Inka
J8	5.4	7/7	3	1	326	330	0.9	W III
J9	9.3	1/1	50	2	102	154	32.5	W III
J37	6.0	1/3	1	0	307	308	0.3	W III
J38	4.9	1/5	3	0	173	176	1.7	W III
J39	—[g]	0/0	4	1	477	482	0.8	W III
J42	3.3	13/13	139	5	376	520	26.7	W III
J43	1.9	6/6	20	24	797	841	2.4	W III
J45	1.2	1/1	74	3	18	95	77.9	Inka
J46	3.4	2/6	12	3	254	269	4.5	W III
J47	6.0	4/6	150	7	809	966	15.5	W III
J48	5.3	1/6	14	1	311	326	4.3	W III
J49	11.1	3/5	14	2	371	387	3.6	W III
J50	1.6	6/6	34	2	287	323	10.5	W III
J51	0.7	1/3	4	0	9	13	30.8	W III
J53	1.7	1/9	1	0	120	121	0.8	W III
J54	27.6	9/9	503	86	2,564	3,153	16.0	W III
J55	1.1	6/6	41	6	51	98	41.8	W III
J59	11.2	2/2	156	0	271	427	36.5	Inka
J60	2.3	1/1	1	1	74	76	1.3	W III
J63	2.1	4/4	173	52	378	603	28.7	Inka
J74	13.2	7/7	16	12	386	414	3.9	Inka
J75	1.0	4/4	136	30	491	657	20.7	W III
J78	4.5	0/0	0	1	23	24	0.0	W III
J105	0.6	1/1	1	0	0	1	100.0	W III
J106	0.9	1/1	1	0	13	14	7.1	W III
J108	4.1	4/5	13	6	308	327	4.0	W III
J109	31.4	0/6	0	11	406	417	0.0	W III
J110	2.2	1/1	42	7	6	55	76.4	W III
J113	10.2	2/2	4	0	16	20	20.0	W III
J116	5.6	2/2	46	2	17	65	70.8	W III
J117	12.0	1/2	1	0	12	13	7.7	W III
J118	0.5	1/1	108	7	35	150	72.0	W III
J119	7.1	2/2	18	1	63	82	22.0	W III
J120	0.9	1/1	39	7	49	95	41.1	W III
J123	—[g]	0/0	46	5	87	138	33.3	W III
J130	10.0	1/3	4	1	40	45	8.9	W III
J131	1.7	1/1	1	1	227	229	0.4	W III
J132	—[g]	0/0	2	0	23	25	8.0	W III
J137	2.6	2/3	5	0	130	135	3.7	W III
J139	7.0	1/2	12	1	59	72	16.7	W III
J140	1.1	0/0	1	0	5	6	16.7	W III
J141	5.1	0/0	1	0	9	10	10.0	W III
J142	2.8	1/2	7	0	36	43	16.3	W III
J145	1.5	0/0	1	0	27	28	3.6	W III
J201	1.5	1/2	2	0	12	14	14.3	W III
J203	5.5	0/0	2	0	18	20	10.0	W III
J205	1.0	0/0	2	0	2	4	50.0	W III
J207	1.0	0/0	2	0	67	69	2.9	W III
J208	0.8	0/1	2	0	8	10	20.0	W III
J212	1.0	1/2	4	0	13	17	23.5	W III
J213	0.5	0/0	4	0	38	42	9.5	W III
J214	0.9	0/0	1	0	0	1	100.0	W III
J218	10.2	0/0	1	0	0	1	100.0	W III
J221	10.0	1/2	3	0	11	14	21.4	W III
J223	4.3	0/0	2	0	0	2	100.0	W III

Continued on next page

Table 9.1—*Continued*

Site	Site area (ha)[a]	Number of collections with Inka ceramics	Number of sherds[b]				% Inka[e]	Inka or Wanka III
			Inka	Inka-related[c]	Wanka II–III[d]	Total		
J224	1.4	1/1	4	0	2	6	66.7	W III
J226	1.8	1/1	5	0	0	5	100.0	W III
J227	3.3	1/1	10	0	2	12	83.3	W III
J228	2.7	1/1	4	0	10	14	28.6	W III
J231	2.1	1/1	5	0	265	270	1.9	W III
J234	10.3	0/1	1	0	3	4	25.0	W III
J240	2.6	1/1	2	0	2	4	50.0	W III
J243	4.8	1/4	11	0	10	21	52.4	W III
J245	4.7	1/1	1	0	5	6	16.7	W III
J246	2.8	0/1	1	2	21	24	4.2	W III
J247	0.3	0/2	0	0	3	3	0.0	W III
J252	9.2	1/1	24	0	4	28	85.7	W III
J266	3.4	1/1	26	0	0	26	100.0	W III
J267	6.7	1/1	7	0	0	7	100.0	W III
J268	3.8	1/1	8	0	0	8	100.0	W III
J269	1.2	1/1	26	0	3	29	89.7	W III
J270	1.6	2/2	15	0	0	15	100.0	W III
J272	2.5	1/1	25	0	0	25	100.0	W III
J281	2.9	1/1	4	0	75	79	5.1	W III
J285	6.4	1/1	22	0	42	64	34.4	W III
J286	1.3	0/0	0	2	62	64	0.0	W III
J288	4.0	1/1	0	10	0	10	0.0	W III
J289	15.1	1/1	2	0	49	51	3.9	W III
J291	2.4	0/1	0	2	26	28	0.0	W III
J292	3.6	0/1	0	1	10	11	0.0	W III
J293	9.1	0/2	0	0	1	1	0.0	W III
J294	1.2	2/2	30	0	28	58	51.7	W III
J295	1.6	0/2	0	1	18	19	0.0	W III
J297	0.8	0/1	0	0	35	35	0.0	W III
J298	0.8	1/1	6	0	31	37	16.2	W III
J300	8.1	2/2	33	0	61	94	35.1	W III
J304	11.8	0/1	1	0	15	16	6.3	W III
J306	11.6	0/1	1	0	44	45	2.2	W III
J310	0.8	1/1	76	0	4	80	95.0	W III
J313	13.3	1/1	45	0	4	49	91.8	W III
J314	—[g]	1/1	0	1	17	18	0.0	W III
J323	4.0	1/1	21	1	37	59	35.6	W III
J327	1.1	0/1	2	1	17	20	10.0	W III

Note: All sites at which UMARP or Junín surveys found Inka ceramics are included.

[a]Total area of site (not just Wanka III or Inka component).

[b]Frequency of diagnostic sherds in all surface collections.

[c]Wanka-Inka and imitation Inka sherds.

[d]Base Roja, Base Clara, Wanka Red, and Micaceous Self-slip sherds.

[e]Percentage of Inka sherds in total.

[f]The chronological assignment of site J3 to Wanka III is based on data from several other surface surveys in the region.

[g]Small site for which an accurate measurement is currently unavailable.

terraced fields. The repeated construction of the structures as integral elements of the terrace buttressing system indicates that the residents built the terraces at the same time that the residential architecture was erected.

At present, it appears that only a small proportion of the main Mantaro Valley settlements occupied during Wanka III had been inhabited in the preceding century and a half. None of the Wanka III strip settlements bears the marks of defensive orientation, such as high ridgetop location, defensive walls, or moats. Instead, the sites were located primarily on hillslopes, just above the fertile agricultural lands of the valley bottom. The issue of Wanka II–III transitions in the main valley will require additional research, however, because the densities of Inka ceramics at many of these sites were substantially lower than at many sites in the Yanamarca Valley. It seems reasonable to say, at present, that the consistent presence of a few state sherds throughout the strip settlement shows that the area was occupied under Inka rule. Evidence is unfortunately insufficient to determine if the relative lack of Inka pottery can be attributed primarily to a low-density occupation or to the potentially low status of the settlements.

Some of the larger west-bank Wanka II or III towns present particular chronological dilemmas. Some sites appear to have been abandoned under Inka rule (e.g., J289, J306), only small Inka ceramic components were recovered from others (e.g., J221, J304), and still others cannot be clearly assigned to either phase (e.g., J218, J234). An example of the first situation may be found in J289, which was established on a low knoll elevated about 50 m above the surrounding terrain but retains no evidence of defensive walls. Considering the striking efforts made to fortify Wanka II settlements no more than 15 km away, it would have been remarkable had J289 and nearby settlements been occupied during the troubled fourteenth century. Because only two Inka sherds have been recovered from surface collections at J289, however, it is difficult to assign a Wanka III occupation to the settlement; thus the site has been classified as having both Wanka II and Wanka III occupations. It is hoped that excavation at these sites in the main valley will clarify their chronological placement at some point in the future (see Parsons and Earle n.d. for further discussion).

Nonsystematic estimates of the density of surface architecture at these Wanka III settlements suggest that habitation was comparable to that of Marca and Hatunmarca, that is, about 50 structures per hectare. This density is substantially lower than densities at definitive Wanka II sites in the Yanamarca and Jisse areas, which were as high as 174 structures per hectare. The interior organization of the main-valley settlements was also comparable to that of the northern Wanka III towns. Virtually all space was given over to loosely clustered residential architecture, consisting of household compounds, most of which appear to have contained one or two buildings.

Some of the strip sites lay adjacent to sets of storehouses, generally separated from the habitation architecture by 100 to 200 m. In Chapter 8, I suggested that the architectural characteristics of the storage structures marked them as Incaic facilities, although the composition of the associated ceramics was equivocal (cf. Browman 1985). Few Inka ceramics were found associated with the qollqa, but the overall surface ceramic density was very low. Although extensive excavation will be required to resolve satisfactorily the chronological assignment of these facilities and the associated settlements, factors such as the location, the lack of defensive characteristics, and the presence of a few Inka sherds indicate that most of the strip settlements were occupied, at least in part, under Inka rule.

Accompanying the abandonment of most high-elevation defensive sites and the dispersal of the populace was a general shift from a zone of rolling uplands primarily suited for highland crops, such as tubers, to valley floors and margins, better suited for maize-complex agriculture (Earle et al. 1980:35–43; LeBlanc 1981:286–87; Hastorf 1983). The location of many of the new settlements, just above the fertile valley bottom and adjacent gentle slopes, suggests that the population was reclaiming lands conducive to growing maize, as Cieza (1967 [1553]: ch. 49, p. 164) reported.[10]

The occupation of lower elevations is illustrated in Figure 9.2, in which the distribution of Wanka III population is given, by elevation, for the areas with the most secure population estimates. When the Wanka III distribution is compared with that of Wanka II (Fig. 4.3), it can be seen that the overall movement resulted in a shift from lands on which maize crops would have failed to lands on which the grain could be grown quite successfully. Hastorf (1983) has shown that this shift in microenvironments was accompanied by a proportional change in the composition of plant foods recovered from household middens. Wanka III households yielded substantially more maize and fewer tubers than did Wanka II households, indicating that the residents of the later communities were taking advantage of the land in the immediate vicinity of the new settlements. Of the maximal Wanka II population of 60,862, only 15,195 residents (25.0 percent) were located at 3,600 m or below (Fig. 4.9). In Wanka III, excluding the Inka settlements, 25,106 (68.8 percent) of the maximal 36,484 inhabitants of the region lived at 3,600 m or below. If the Inka settlements are included, these figures rise to 33,560 (74.4 percent) of 45,103.

If we shift to a somewhat broader spatial perspective, the general resettlement to lower elevations and dispersed villages is supported by Browman's (1970: 247) conclusion that the Wankas in the main valley moved down from hilltops and upper slopes into loca-

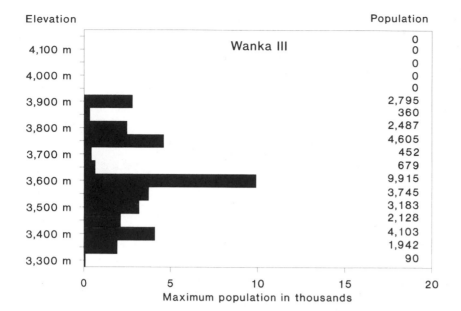

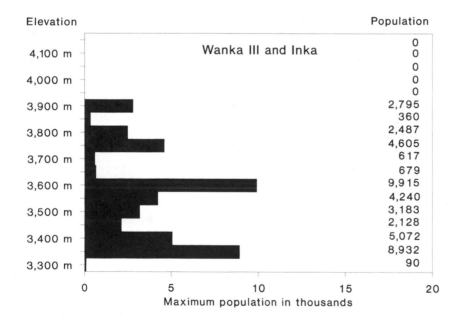

Fig. 9.2. Wanka III population and Wanka III and Inka population, by altitude.

tions at or near the valley floor. Hyslop (1979:58), who has noted a similar downward shift of local populations in the Lupaqa region, suggests that the attraction of Inka centers and interaction with the state may have also contributed to this type of resettlement. It therefore appears that the detailed pattern reconstructed for the Upper Mantaro region may have been only a small segment of a larger process occurring throughout the highlands (see also Rowe 1946:272; Lavallée and Julien 1983).

An additional, more minor settlement trend during Wanka III was the establishment of a few villages in the Huaricolca puna to the north and west of the Yanamarca Valley. UMARP has briefly investigated a cluster of three of these sites—J66, J69, and J70—but they are not included in the population estimates here because of a lack of spatial continuity in surface survey in the area. All three villages were situated in saddles adjacent to peaks in the rolling grasslands, at elevations of about 4,200 m. Each village comprised several score of household compounds, intermixed with and surrounded by a complex of stone corrals. Little of the land in the immediate vicinity of the settlements is currently under cultivation, although some nearby spring-watered fields produce tubers. Excavations in households in each of these settlements yielded surprisingly well-preserved organics, mostly potatoes. The Wanka III occupation of these settlements was established by the presence of poor-quality ceramics in the Inka style, mostly flared-rim jar fragments, within household trash. Whether these herding villages were state-run or were peopled by Wankas who had access to state ceramics cannot be established with present data. Nonetheless, the Wanka III settlement in this zone indicates a broad use of environmental zones in the region under Inka rule.

The spatial relationship between the Wanka III population and Hatun Xauxa provides intriguing insights into the interaction between the state and its subjects. Rather than serve as a magnet for local population, attracting a series of satellite communities, the center lay in the midst of a relatively underpopulated zone. Within 5 km of Hatun Xauxa were 9 small communities, boasting an aggregate population of only about 6,321. Outside this zone, the population density increased rapidly. Because the lands in this zone are among the most fertile in the region, the relative lack of subject population merits closer evaluation.

In Chapter 8, I suggested that the state had probably alienated nearby lands for production of its own crops. This zone included the southern Yanamarca Valley, the northern main Mantaro Valley on both sides of the river, and perhaps the Masma Valley. The lack of native population on the east side of the Mantaro Valley is especially striking, because some of the region's best maize lands were located there (Franco et al. 1979: inset map; Hastorf 1983). The string of state storehouses along the ridge separating the main valley from the Masma subvalley (Fig. 6.1) provides a strong clue that the lands were set aside for state production and were not available for settlement by the indigenous peoples.

Evidence supporting this proposition may be found in the artifactual remains recovered from villages within the zone. Only two of these villages have been studied in any detail: Chucchus (J74) and Huancas de la Cruz (J59) (Earle et al. 1987:74–78). Both sites were newly settled in Wanka III and were closely associated with the major concentration of state storage facilities to the west of Hatun Xauxa. As was described in Chapter 8, surface collections and excavations have shown the two villages to be highly specialized in maize agriculture, to the virtual exclusion of other kinds of productive activities typically found in Wanka households. The two residential compounds exca-

vated at Chucchus, for instance, yielded no evidence of stone tool production, spinning, or ceramic manufacture, but they did yield unusually high concentrations of the stone hoes thought to have been used in maize agriculture. This finding contrasts with the distribution of evidence for household production at other contemporaneous towns, such as Hatunmarca and Marca, in which virtually all domestic compounds examined yielded by-products of all four craft activities.

Taken together with the location of the settlement adjacent to the main storage facilities above Hatun Xauxa, and the relative lack of other habitation within 5 km of the capital, the artifactual assemblage indicates strongly that Chucchus was founded by the state as a specialized farming village. Such villages have been recorded historically in numerous regions of the empire, generally for specialty crops such as maize and coca.[11] In each recorded case, the settlers were allocated lands adjacent to the state fields for growing food for their households. Under these circumstances, the lack of Inka ceramics is understandable. The farmers were attached specialists, but their subsidy by the state consisted of a guaranteed opportunity to resources, not a direct allocation of the products of those resources. It thus appears that, even at settlements whose existence depended on state order, access to state goods was defined by hierarchical status, not simply by affiliation.

Changes in the Subject Economy

The Inka political economy was developed as an extractive system superimposed over the domestic and political economies of the native populace. Because the Inka economy drew directly from the resources and labor previously at the disposal of the native societies, while creating new social relations of production and exchange, the subject economies were necessarily affected, although the significance and nature of the effects undoubtedly varied. Conversely, the state depended heavily on the locally constituted subject labor forces as self-supporting productive units, even when specialized productive communities were set up. Because of this dependence, maintaining continuity in the local economies was very much to the state's benefit. These apparently contradictory elements of the state's use of local groups in its political economy raise questions as to the effects of state rule on subject production, consumption, and exchange.

In this section, I will examine some of the principal

effects on the subject economy produced by the imposition of state rule. My concerns lie with changes in household and community labor organization, shifts in subjects' access to resources, and the intrusion of state-related activities into economic life at indigenous communities. These topics have been chosen to illustrate, not exhaust, the kinds of changes induced and imposed by state demands on labor and resources.[12]

In Chapter 2, I suggested that the degree of imperial penetration into local affairs should have varied systematically, in large part according to the degree to which the labor, natural resources, and security of the region were critical to imperial interests. We have already seen how the strategic importance of the Upper Mantaro region contributed to an intensive political integration of the native elites into the imperial administration. This change should have been accompanied by an equally intensive economic integration of the region, part of which has already been described for the state political economy.

The nature and degree of economic effects on the subject population by the imperial system can be evaluated archaeologically in several ways. Analysis of changes in settlement patterns has already provided one means of recognizing the impacts of imperial rule. The shift of much of the population to lower elevations, the relative lack of residence around the provincial capital, and the founding of specialized farming villages at Chucchus (J74) and Huancas de la Cruz (J59) indicate some of the effects of Inka rule on agricultural practices. More-direct means of assessing the economic interaction, however, can be found by examining the activities performed for or underwritten by the state at subject communities.

I have previously noted the surprising lack of archaeological evidence for craft production at Hatun Xauxa, suggesting that the state parceled out production of various kinds of goods to subjects residing in their home communities. If this argument is to hold, we would expect to find changes in production at local communities—primarily associated with the political economy—and relatively wide distribution of state goods employed in support of economic activity and political relations. The integration of elites into the state administration has already given reason to suspect that the latter should have been the case. Conversely, because the state ostensibly interfered minimally in the domestic economy of its subjects, we should find little evidence of fundamental change in the economic activities of the householders intended to support the Wankas themselves.

This section evaluates the appropriateness of these expectations. The provisioning of goods supplied by the state will be assessed by examining the regional distribution of Inka ceramics. The hierarchical nature of the distribution of state goods within subject communities will be evaluated by examining access to state ceramics at Hatunmarca. Changes in household productive activities at settlements will then be evaluated to determine the effects of Inka rule on domestic labor.

Regional Distribution of Inka Ceramics

The Inka political economy has been characterized here as a dendritic system, tied into the local economies primarily through exploitation of labor. Virtually all movement of goods was vertical, and the majority of that effort consisted of the mobilization of bulk subsistence and utilitarian goods upward from the producer populace to the more elite strata. A significant proportion of the goods produced in the system was also transformed into wealth or sumptuary items by craft specialists attached to the elite. Much of this wealth was used as a kind of political or ceremonial currency, in which the unequal bonds tying the state and subject populace together were reinforced.

Within the political economy, there should have been a significant transfer of subsistence and, to a lesser extent, utilitarian goods back down from the elite to the lower elite strata and to the commoner population. The more prestigious goods (e.g., qompi cloth, crafted metal objects, fancy ceramics) were transferred short distances down the hierarchy, whereas subsistence and utilitarian goods (e.g., sandals, awasqa cloth) were provided to a wider range of the subject populace. Because production of these goods by corvée was exchanged in part for subsistence support, much of the produce was consumed by the peasantry—not in their roles as peasants but in state-defined capacities, such as military service, rotating labor on state projects, and specialized production.

The intensity of the movement of goods back down the hierarchy should have been proportional to the extent to which the subject population was integrated into the imperial administration. State policies in the Upper Mantaro region suggest that imperial goods would have reached the hands of the subject population through at least two mechanisms: gifts or payments for status and services, and support for state activities conducted at local communities. The direct incorporation of native elites into the provincial bureaucracy would have necessitated sanction of their status with gifts of state manufacture. By assuming the role of provider of goods for politically related activities, the state effectively undercut the independent prestige of the local elites and reinforced their need to rely on the state for their status. The complementary side of this state provisioning entailed the intervention of the state into production and consumption within Wanka communities.

Early written sources recount that elites at various levels of the provincial bureaucracy were entitled to a variety of material perquisites, including cloth and other craft objects (e.g., Toledo 1940a [1570], 1940b [1571]; Diez de San Miguel 1964 [1567]; Ortiz de Zúñiga 1967 [1562]). These goods served as means of status legitimation and perhaps as political currency in elite-elite relations. Textiles probably played the most significant material role in solidifying that relationship (Murra 1962), but other goods, such as metal and wooden drinking cups, were also typically used to cement the unequal bonds between ruler and subject. Additionally, the local lords conducted ceremonial hospitality as part of their obligations to the populations that supported them. In some areas, such as the Huánuco region, the state at least partially underwrote these political festivities by supplying the jars in which the chicha was brewed (Morris and Thompson 1985). In the Upper Mantaro Valley, Inka flared-rim jars supplanted local jars and deep basins in the Wanka domestic assemblages, particularly in elite households (Costin 1986:305; Earle et al. 1987:89; Costin and Earle 1989:700–701). The distribution of these vessels suggests that the Inkas assumed the role of sponsoring ceremonial hospitality within subject communities.

The question remains, however, as to whether systematic gradations existed in the kinds of ceramics to which various members of the subject populations and the imperial staff had access. Settlement studies on the Late Horizon in the central highlands suggest that interaction between the state and local groups was largely limited to administrative centers or other locations designated by the state (see Morris 1972b). Studies by Thompson (1968a, 1972a,b) of the Yacha, Chupachu, and Wamalí villages in the Huánuco area, for instance, recovered almost no Inka ceramics from local sites. The Inka vessels that were recovered were primarily large jars, heavily concentrated in elite households, such as in the Yacha village of Ichu (see Morris 1972a). The Junín Project's survey showed a similar paucity of state wares at villages in the Junín, Tarma, and Huasahuasi areas (Parsons and Hastings 1977:44–49; Hastings 1985). The generally low proportion (less than

2 percent) of Inka-style ceramics at high-elevation (greater than 4,000 m) Asto settlements to the south of the study region paralleled these findings, although at 6 of the 11 lower-elevation sites, Inka ceramics constituted between 10 and 17 percent of the assemblages (Lavallée and Julien 1983:37–39). These archaeological studies tend to confirm historical reports that the Inkas prescribed the nature and selectively limited the extent of interaction between themselves and subject groups.

In the Upper Mantaro region, present data show that access to Inka ceramics was not a perquisite just of imperial or paramount local personnel. As was noted above, 99 sites within the survey zone have yielded Inka-related ceramics in surface collections, and Browman (1970:126) found Inka pottery at 126 sites in his survey of the main Mantaro Valley, which partially overlapped the UMARP and Junín study regions.[13] Although Hyslop (pers. com. 1988) has observed that a few scattered Inka sherds can be found at subject settlements throughout many provinces, these findings suggest strongly that the state maintained closer relations with the Wankas than with numerous groups farther north or immediately to the south.

The dendritic model of state-local relations suggests that the mediating role played by the region's elites should have systematically affected the distribution of state goods. More specifically, the occurrence of Inka ceramics and architecture within and among communities should have resulted directly from the residents' differential interaction with the state. Several state policies would have contributed to this pattern: control over physical access to administrative centers, farming out of economic activities, use of material goods manufactured to state specifications on state projects (Morris 1974; but see Hyslop 1985), and a concomitant lack of direct, barter exchange with provincial groups (Morris 1974; Murra 1980 [1956]).

If the distribution of state goods followed this sort of structure, some expectations for the archaeological record may be sketched out. Assuming that the largest subject sites or those with the greatest architectural sophistication (e.g., greatest size, finest masonry, highest number of buildings per residential compound) were the residences of the elites, as indicated by the settlement hierarchy and the architectural data, the size of the site and the quantities of Inka pottery present should have been directly related. Within sites showing internal architectural stratification, state pottery should have been differentially distributed in favor of elite architectural districts. Furthermore, the range

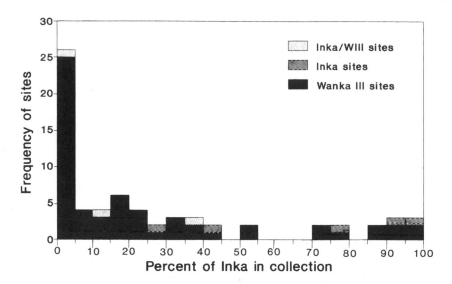

Fig. 9.3. Percentages of Inka ceramics in surface collections from the 67 sites with 20 or more Inka and/or Wanka III diagnostic sherds.

of Inka pottery forms found at these communities should have been restricted in comparison with those found at the administrative center. For example, a local lord conducting political hospitality on behalf of the state may have been provided with state storage and serving vessels, but the domestic ceramics associated with them may have been purely local. In addition, if the state were delegating specific tasks to particular villages, the range of state vessels should have differed from site to site, to the degree that different vessel forms or proportions within assemblages were employed in the tasks.

To assess the appropriateness of these propositions, we may first evaluate the distribution of Inka ceramics among settlements during the Inka occupation.[14] The present analysis will treat only the 67 sites with at least 20 Inka or Wanka III sherds in their collections, to minimize the number of ephemeral occupations being evaluated. This eliminated 32 settlements from which at least 1 Inka or Wanka III sherd was recovered. As can be seen in Table 9.1 and Figure 9.3, these 67 remaining sites have been classed into three categories: Inka (state), Wanka III (subject habitation), and Inka–Wanka III (mixed Inka and subject features). Second, we may analyze the distribution of Inka ceramics within major local settlements to gain insight into hierarchical access to state goods among residents of specific settlements. The distribution of Inka ceramics at Hatunmarca will be examined here, because of the importance of the settlement and the extensiveness of the surface material recovered.

The distribution of Inka ceramics in the region indicates that state-subject relations in the area were complex and pervasive and that access to state ceramics differed significantly among villages. At many settlements, Inka ceramics constituted a small proportion of the surface diagnostic pottery assemblages, even at settlements with imitation Inka architecture. Perhaps surprisingly, the percentage of Inka ceramics recovered from a number of small villages exceeded that from the towns of Hatunmarca and Marca, but the total number of Inka vessels that were consumed was weighted heavily in favor of the large communities. As will be shown below, the probable mixing of Wanka II and III collections at Hatunmarca undoubtedly contributed to the relatively low percentage of state pottery at the settlement. An additional significant trend is that virtually the entire range of the basic vessel shapes was found at local settlements, but Hatunmarca and Marca were the only ones with a wide range of vessel types.

The percentage of Inka sherds found in surface collections from Wanka III sites in the survey zone ranged from 0.0 to 100.0 percent (Table 9.1). Eleven sites not otherwise identified as of state origin had more than 50 percent Inka ceramics in their diagnostic surface collections, and an additional 6 such sites had more than 30 percent. These results suggest the ubiquity of the Inka presence in the region, but they must be accepted with care. Only 1 of these sites (J116) yielded Inka ceramics in more than one collection, and the sites also had one or more of the following characteristics: They were small (less than 10 ha), the total number of diagnostics attributable to the Inka-period occupation was less than 100 (in 14 of the sites), or the extent of the

Wanka III surface occupation remains to be defined securely. It should also be kept in mind that an additional 32 contemporaneous sites have been held out of the analysis for lack of adequate collection sizes or well-defined Inka presence. Nonetheless, the number of sites with proportionally large Inka ceramic assemblages may be taken to indicate extensive distribution of state pottery, even to tiny hamlets.

Among the sites graphed in Figure 9.3 were Huancas de la Cruz (J59; 36.5 percent Inka) and Chucchus (J74; 3.9 percent Inka), likely farming villages adjacent to the main sets of state storage structures above Hatun Xauxa. The general lack of Inka ceramics in the residences of Chucchus, despite its proximity to the capital, suggests that the state did not always provide a basic subsistence assemblage even to inhabitants of its specialized farming settlements. This possibility conforms to the historical documentation for state farms elsewhere in the empire, where the farmers were expected to support themselves in addition to laboring for the state (e.g., Wachtel 1982; La Lone and La Lone 1987). Other Wanka III communities whose ceramic assemblages were dominated by local types and whose architecture was typically Wanka in style yielded Inka components approaching 25 percent of the diagnostic assemblage. Most of the local settlements in the Mantaro Valley, however, yielded Inka components of less than 10 percent and often less than 5 percent.

The proportion of Inka pottery at Wanka settlements overlaps the proportion of state pottery at sites assumed here to be state posts, on the basis of architecture and location: Hatun Xauxa (J5), J6, J45, and J63. The four sites yielded from 28.7 percent (J63) to 98.0 percent (Hatun Xauxa) Inka ceramics in their diagnostic assemblages (Table 9.1). Hatun Xauxa is clearly the distinctive settlement in the group, in ceramics and architecture. The similar compositions of some state and local assemblages suggest that the distinction between the activities at small state sites and some local villages may not have been clear-cut. As will be argued below (see "Changes in the Wanka III Domestic Economy"), the performance of state tasks at local settlements may account for some of this similarity.

Considering only the sites at which normal surface collecting techniques were used, the two largest Wanka sites were clearly dominant in the number of Inka sherds estimated for the whole site.[15] Hatunmarca and Marca are estimated to have had maximally about 111,079 and 86,792 Inka sherds, respectively, on their ground surfaces, whereas no other site is estimated to have had more than 10,000 state sherds. The two biggest sites therefore received a highly disproportionate number of Inka vessels, even though some of the smaller sites had higher surface densities of state ceramics. As is described below with reference to Hatunmarca, this dominance by the large sites is primarily attributable to the residence of native elites and to the performance of state tasks at these towns, not simply to the size of the residential population.

All 10 basic rim types recovered from the provincial center, Hatun Xauxa, were recovered from the Wanka towns in the Yanamarca Valley. The dominant form was the flared-rim jar, which constituted 72.0 percent of the rim sherds collected, a figure somewhat larger than the 52.8 percent found for the same rim form at Hatun Xauxa. The Inka ceramic assemblages at the larger sites were more complete than those at the smaller villages, but this result may have been largely a function of the sizes of the collections. Because of the low numbers of rims recovered at many sites, I could not determine if access to particular vessel forms was limited among villages.

It was possible to compare the sizes of flared-rim jars that were surface-collected from the Inka center of Hatun Xauxa (J5) and the subject town of Hatunmarca (J2). The evidence surprisingly indicated that the Hatunmarca residents receiving state ceramics had access to storage vessels comparable in size to those of the state elites at Hatun Xauxa. The mean exterior diameter of vessels of this shape from the state center was 25.0 cm, and that of the town was 22.9 cm.[16] Although residential areas in neither the state center nor the subject communities were likely to have been the location of major concentrations of storage, the similarity of vessel sizes suggests that the elites of the town enjoyed some perquisites appropriate to those of favored status.

From these data, we may conclude that the Inkas did not exclude the Wankas from access to state pottery. On the contrary, Inka ceramics were widespread among settlements, and residents of the largest towns were provided with thousands of vessels. The question of whether particular forms were destined for specific villages, in association with performance of state tasks, cannot be addressed with present data. It is nevertheless clear that the greatest proportion of the Inka pottery went to the subject settlements that housed both the largest populations and the local elites.

Distribution of Inka Ceramics at Hatunmarca

The compositional analysis described in Chapter 8 draws attention to an intriguing feature of the distribution of Inka ceramics at Wanka settlements. The analysis indicated at least two sources of production of state wares. One source provided most of the pottery to Hatun Xauxa, Marca, and some small state settlements, such as J45. The other source supplied most of the ceramics consumed at Hatunmarca (see D'Altroy and Bishop 1990: Fig. 5). The separation of Hatunmarca from Marca and the affiliation of Marca with the state provincial center likely imply distinct kinds of interaction between the residents of the towns and the state. Because the two towns were close to one another, the energetic cost of transporting vessels probably had little impact on the distribution of state wares. A more likely explanation is that the elites residing in Marca were politically elevated and received goods that were accorded the highest status in the region.

In any hierarchy, the goods associated with status legitimation and with elite activities will be disbursed according to the status of the individuals or groups involved. The Inka provincial administration, however, was distinctive in a way that would have produced specific consequences for state-supported activity at subject towns. First, the higher levels in the political system were increasingly comprehensive functionally and symbolically, in part because an elite at any level simultaneously held each lower position in the hierarchy. A waranqa kuraka (lord of 1,000 households), for example, was also ostensibly a pachaca kuraka for 1 of the 10 units of 100 households in his waranqa. To the extent that each position was associated with specific functions, such as hospitality, or with specific symbols of status, the material goods associated with each higher position should have been more additive than discrete. In comparison with the elites of higher levels, an elite occupying any given level in the political hierarchy should have had access to a more restricted range of goods.

At a settlement as important as Hatunmarca (Fig. 4.4), multiple levels of the state political hierarchy should have been represented. To judge from the population that we have estimated to be resident at the settlement, an individual occupying a position at least as elevated as waranqa kuraka, and perhaps pichqawaranqa kuraka (head of 5,000 households or, more realistically, 3,000 households in the Hatunxauxa saya), should have lived in the town. By extension, several lower-status individuals integrated into the state hierarchy were also likely resident.

One's place of residence within towns such as Hatunmarca was likely determined by status and kinship affiliation. Study of the architectural layout of other late prehistoric but better-preserved communities, such as Tunanmarca (J7), Chawín (J40), and Llamap Shillón (J109), has shown that settlements were subdivided into numerous architectural sectors by stone walls. These sectors, which contained scores of residential compounds, likely corresponded to barrios or neighborhoods. It seems probable, to judge from historical data on the composition of sierra communities, that residence in such barrios depended on kin affiliation and status.

Each of the two major architectural sectors at Hatunmarca contained a central area with unusually large and finely built structures and broad, open plazas (Fig. 9.4). The buildings in these sections often incorporated the most elaborate masonry found at the site. The central area of the southern residential sector was especially notable for the investment of labor in large buildings imitative of the Inka architectural style (Fig. 9.5). The largest, most centrally located structures in that area exhibited rectangular floor plans, gables, and trapezoidal niches. Similar imitation of Inka-style architecture is preserved in numerous buildings at Marca (Figs. 9.6 and 9.7). Two of the architectural compounds that were excavated at Hatunmarca (J2=1 and J2=3; Figs. 3.14 and 9.8, respectively) yielded some of the highest quantities of Inka ceramics, metals, and exotics recovered at any compounds in the region. The two compounds also contained high proportions of burned camelid bone and maize, both of which likely indicate high-status feasting (Sandefur 1988; Hastorf n.d.). These areas thus give every indication—fancy architecture, open plazas, high-quality artifactual and ecofactual assemblages—of having been the locus of public activity and elite residence (see Earle et al. 1987:44–58).

The sociopolitical hierarchy and the status-associated uses of space within Hatunmarca should therefore have produced a strong spatial trend in the distribution of state goods. The greatest concentrations of Inka ceramics at Hatunmarca should have been found in the central sectors of each of the major architectural divisions, because those were the areas of public activity and elite residence. Similarly, the greatest diversity of both Inka vessel form and style should have been found in these areas.

Before evaluating patterning in the distribution of Inka ceramics at the town through inferential statistics, it will be useful to examine the distribution graphically. Fifty-five surface collections were taken here, consisting of 5 collections from each of 11 strata defined by variations in surface architecture. Figure 9.9a

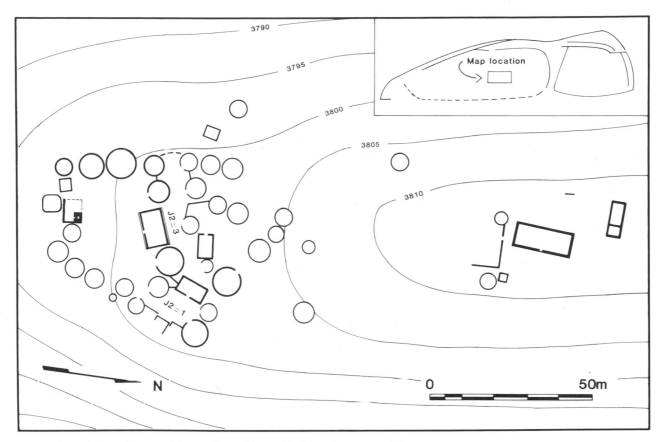

Fig. 9.4. Area of elite residence and fine-quality architecture in the southern sector of Hatunmarca.

Fig. 9.5. Wall niches on the interior of a rectangular central public-ceremonial structure at Hatunmarca, imitative of Inka architectural canons.

Fig. 9.6. Architecture in elite residential compound J54=1 at Wanka III–IV Marca. The rectangular structure is imitative of the imperial Inka style.

Fig. 9.7. Wall niches on the interior of a circular elite residential structure in compound J54=7 at Marca.

illustrates the distribution of all 61,017 sherds recovered from these collections ($\bar{X}$ = 1,129.9; SD = 1,149.8; range = 60–6,535).[17] Column height in Figures 9.9a–c is proportional to the value of the collection; in Figure 9.9a the value represents the frequency of sherds recovered. This illustration shows that the northern sector of the site was far more heavily occupied than the far south and that the central areas of each of the two major architectural sectors were generally more heavily occupied than the peripheries.[18]

Although the sherd densities are generally positively correlated with the distribution of standing architecture and concentrated rubble, farmers' destruction of buildings during field clearing for crops has made a precise correlation difficult to assess.

Two lines of evidence suggest that the frequencies of sherds illustrated in Figure 9.9 combine materials from Wanka II and III. First, both the frequencies of Inka ceramics and percentages of collections represented by the Inka sherds fall off markedly away from

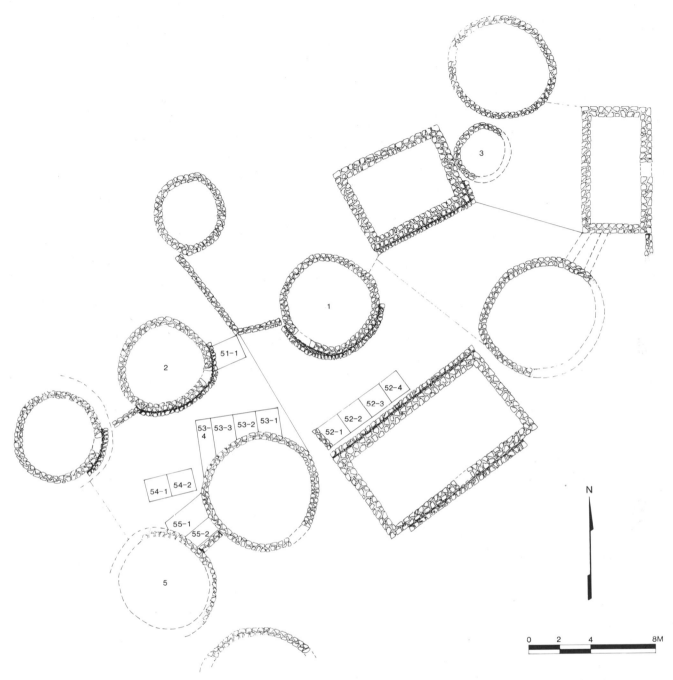

Fig. 9.8. Elite residential compound J2=3 in the central southern area of Wanka III town of Hatunmarca (see Fig. 9.4). Numbered sectors indicate excavated areas.

the more elegant architectural zones. Second, excavation of a residential compound (J2=4; Fig. 9.10) in a peripheral area with no surface Inka sherds yielded a Wanka II ceramic assemblage. This trend may indicate either a distinction between centrally located elites with access to Inka ceramics and peripheral commoners without access or a contraction of population

to the centers of each architectural sector in Wanka III. The latter interpretation seems most reasonable at present, because excavations from commoner compounds in Wanka III often yielded significant percentages of Inka pottery, sometimes as high as 40 percent (Earle et al. 1987:44–45).

Because of the apparent contraction of the popula-

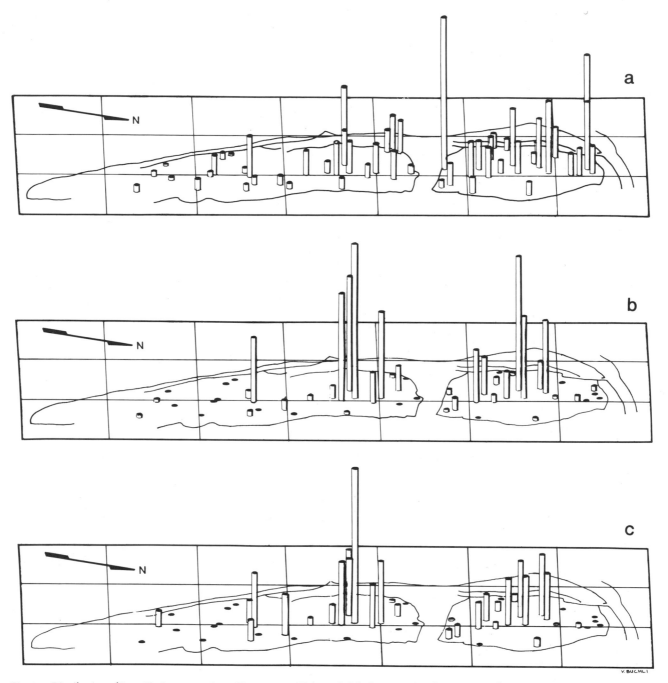

Fig. 9.9. Distribution of Late Horizon ceramics at Hatunmarca. Column height is proportional to quantity of ceramics present. *a*, Frequency of all ceramics in all 55 surface collections; *b*, frequency of Inka ceramics in 55 collections; *c*, percentage of diagnostic pottery represented by Inka ceramics.

tion from 6,633–11,055 in Wanka II to an estimated 2,466–4,110 in Wanka III, an evaluation of the distribution of Inka ceramics should focus on areas most clearly occupied during the latter period. To accommodate the population shrinkage, the 28 surface collections with fewer than two Inka sherds were removed from the analysis, leaving 27 samples. In using this criterion, I have assumed that the presence of two or more Inka sherds in a collection indicates that the area was actively occupied during Wanka III.

Figures 9.11a and 9.11b illustrate the frequency of Inka sherds and the percentage of diagnostic sherds

Provincial Power in the Inka Empire

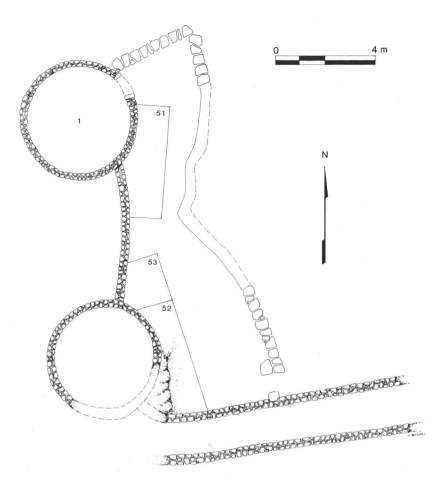

Fig. 9.10. Wanka II residential compound
J2=4, from southwest edge of
Hatunmarca.

represented by the Inka ceramics, respectively. These two measures should reflect two related aspects of state-subject relations. The frequency of Inka ceramics should roughly indicate the intensity of activity supported by the state at the settlement, whereas the percentage of Inka diagnostics should more closely indicate the proportion of activities supported by the state. Although these measures of state-supported activity are not precise, because some meaningful activities most likely did not entail the use of ceramics, the distribution of imperial ceramics should generally be proportional to the intensity of state activity throughout the settlement.

Whether calculated by frequency or percentage of diagnostics, the highest concentrations of Inka pottery were found in the two central sectors of the settlement, in the areas with high-quality, imitation Inka architecture. Both the highest frequency (62 sherds) and the highest percentage of diagnostics (29.4 percent) were found in a collection taken from within the most elaborate architectural complex in the town, in the

southern sector. Comparable frequencies were found in collections in the northern sector of the settlement. Overall, the percentage of assemblages consisting of Inka ceramics tended to be somewhat lower in the north than in the south, probably because of the more intensive use of the north in Wanka II. The heavy Wanka II occupation would have tended to overwhelm the Wanka III ceramics in the surface collections, thereby reducing the apparent proportion of Inka ceramics in the collections.

This distribution ought to be a classic case of spatial autocorrelation, in which the value of a variable at any given location is systematically related to the value of that variable at nearby locations. In this instance, a location exhibiting a given frequency of Inka ceramics should have been near other locations with comparable frequencies. The social assumption underlying this statistical expectation is that residential neighborhoods were likely differentiated at least in part by status. Because lineages were ranked within ayllu and because it can reasonably be expected that most mem-

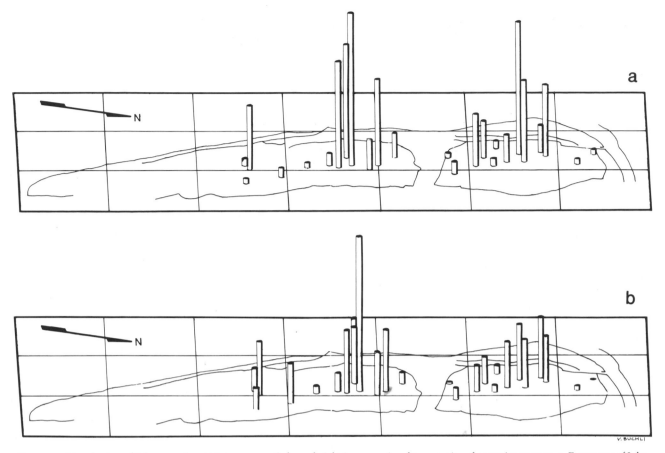

Fig. 9.11. Distribution of Inka ceramics at Hatunmarca. Column height is proportional to quantity of ceramics present. *a*, Frequency of Inka ceramics in 27 surface collections corresponding to principal area occupied under Inka rule; *b*, percentage of diagnostic pottery represented by Inka ceramics.

bers of any lineage would have tended to reside near one another, the ranking should show up on the ground in terms of differential access to the goods signifying status.

To determine if this pattern differed systematically from what would be expected if the collection values obtained were distributed randomly across the settlement, spatial autocorrelation statistics (Moran's *I*) were calculated for two variables (Table 9.2). The frequency of Inka sherds, as noted above, should provide a measure of intensity of Inka-supported activity. Spatial autocorrelation was also measured for the percentage of diagnostics consisting of Inka ceramics, to control for the decrease in residential and artifactual density toward the periphery of the site.

Moran's *I* is a measure of spatial autocovariance, standardized by the variance of the data series and a weighting term.[19] To calculate this statistic, Wanka III Hatunmarca was divided into 27 Thiessen polygons,

each surrounding one of the surface collections yielding more than one Inka sherd (Fig. 9.12). It is likely that passage from one area of the site to any other was channeled by pathways, traces of which remain today. Lacking precise information as to the locations of these paths of travel, I have assumed that a ready means could be found to move from any area of the site to an adjacent one. A weight of 1 was therefore assigned to each pair of adjoining polygons, on the premise that areas unoccupied during Wanka III could have readily been traversed by residents of the community. A weight of zero was assigned to all nonadjoining pairs.

The probabilities of obtaining the values of Moran's *I* calculated for both the frequency and the percentage distributions of Inka ceramics at Hatunmarca are less than .05 (Table 9.2; Fig. 9.13). The probability of obtaining the value of *I* for the percentage data is greater than that for the frequency data, which may be attributed to the compensation for lower ceramic den-

Table 9.2. Test for Spatial Autocorrelation of Inka Surface Ceramics at Hatunmarca

	Model 1	Model 2
Calculated I	.2503	.2189
Expected value	−.0385	−.0385
Variance[a]	.0109	.0147
Z-score[b]	2.77	2.12

Note: Model 1 assumes that the spatial distribution of the frequency of Inka ceramics does not differ from that expected from a randomized distribution of the values obtained. Model 2 assumes that the spatial distribution of the percentage of diagnostic sherds consisting of Inka ceramics does not differ from that expected from a randomized distribution of the values obtained.

[a]Calculated from 1,000 randomized permutations.

[b]Significant at $p = .05$.

sities introduced by standardization (taking percentages). Clearly, there is a strong a spatial trend to the distribution of surface Inka ceramics at this town, including both public and residential zones. These results confirm the expectation that preferred access to state ceramics was closely related to location within the settlement. Because the most elegant architecture and many objects of elite status (e.g., metals, marine shells, tropical flora) were concentrated in the same central zones of the settlement (Earle et al. 1987; D'Altroy and Hastorf n.d.), it may be fairly concluded that this spatial trend in distribution of state ceramics indicates an analogous trend in social status.

The apparent concentration of Inka ceramics in the two central architectural sectors conforms to the expectations laid out above for status-related residential location and access to state goods. Access to certain goods, in this case Inka ceramics, was closely associated with the location of one's residence, which, in turn, was based on one's position in the sociopolitical hierarchy. The spatial trend found here—concentration of high frequencies in the central areas of the two architectural sectors and decreasing frequencies near the site peripheries—is marked. It is tempting to suggest that the two zones of relatively high status corresponded to the hanan and hurin social divisions characteristic of sierra societies, but the more-detailed examination of the distribution of symbolically encoded information (e.g., designs on ceramics, forms of sumptuary goods) that could potentially provide insight into this problem remains a subject for future work (cf. Dillehay 1977a).

Changes in the Wanka III Domestic Economy

The most notable transitions in subject economic life ushered in by the Inka conquest occurred in the political economy, as the local elites were drawn into the regional imperial economy. In the household economy, shifts occurred, but they were more subtle. The organization of most domestic economic activities did not change markedly, but the activities themselves and the associated material culture did undergo some transitions. These changes can be recognized in a number of areas, including diet, specialization in the organization of subsistence and craft labor, access to craft goods, architectural differentiation, and burial treatment (Earle et al. 1987:100). In this section, I will outline major lines of change in household labor and will present exemplary material that summarizes the shifts.

The general Wanka II pattern, in which the residential household comprised both the fundamental pro-

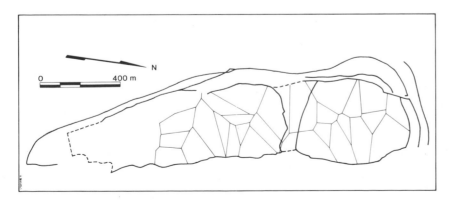

Fig. 9.12. Thiessen polygons surrounding surface collections with two or more Inka sherds at Wanka III town of Hatunmarca.

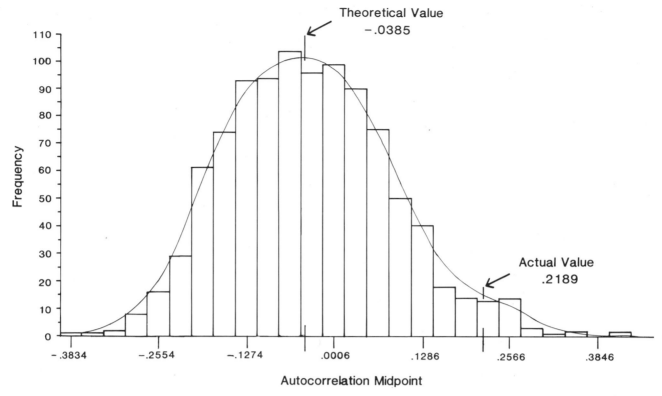

Fig. 9.13. Empirical distribution curve for values of Moran's *I*, calculated from 1,000 permutations, for frequency distribution of Inka ceramics at Hatunmarca.

ductive and consumptive units, continued to hold for the Wanka III domestic economy in the Yanamarca Valley (Earle et al. 1987:100–105). Regardless of status or residence in continuously occupied settlements (e.g., Hatunmarca) or newly founded settlements (e.g., Marca), residents of virtually all households continued to carry out their own household maintenance and casual manufacturing tasks. These activities included agriculture, food preparation and storage, and casual stone-tool manufacture. As was noted above, however, residents of some communities—especially Chucchus —were heavily involved in specialized economic activities, such as maize agriculture and ceramic manufacture, to the virtual exclusion of other productive activities.

The overall organization of household productive activities may be represented in a manner analogous to that used to summarize the Wanka II household data (Chapter 4). For Wanka III, a total of 12 households were excavated, from the towns of Hatunmarca (J2) and Marca (J54; Fig. 9.14) and the villages of Huancas de la Cruz (J59) and Chucchus (J74). Elite resi-

dential compounds were found only at the two larger settlements. It should be noted, however, before the following examination of patterning in the data, that the two villages had been greatly disturbed; only one compound was excavated at Huancas de la Cruz and two at Chucchus. Although the small size of the excavated sample renders interpretations provisional, surface collections from the latter site in particular were found to be comparable in composition to the excavated materials.

Exemplary evidence for variations in household production is presented in Table 9.3. The same four indexes of production calculated for the 17 Wanka II households (Chapter 4) were also determined for the 12 Wanka III compounds: hoe density, waster index, blade production index, and whorl density (cf. Earle and D'Altroy 1989). As a group, these indexes provided a general measure of the range and intensity of productive activities pursued within the households. The relationships among households with respect to these measures of production are represented in Figures 9.15 through 9.17. Here, as in the plots for

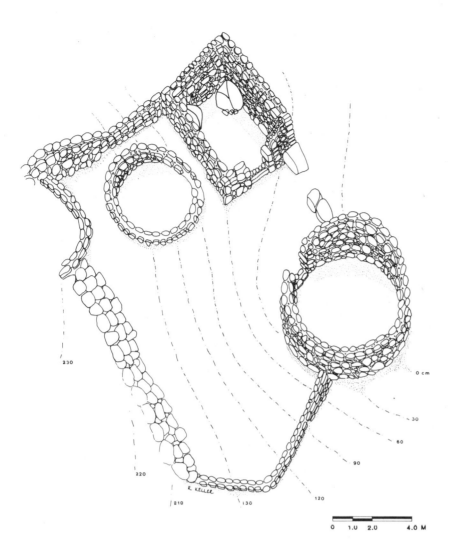

Fig. 9.14. Elite residential compound J54=1, at the northeast end of the Wanka III–IV town of Marca. The rectangular structure is imitative of Inka architectural canons but may have been built postcontact.

Table 9.3. Production Indexes for Wanka III Residential Compounds

Site	Residential compound	Status	Hoe density	Waster index	Blade production index	Whorl density
Hatunmarca (J2)	J2=1	Elite	0.25	0.09	2.74	7.64
	J2=2	Commoner	0.00	0.17	1.62	2.97
	J2=3	Elite	0.34	0.06	2.20	6.60
	J2=5III	Elite	0.17	0.17	0.71	8.59
Marca (J54)	J54=2	Commoner	4.72	0.51	0.06	8.76
	J54=4	Elite	5.83	0.76	0.31	6.19
	J54=7	Elite	0.91	2.30	0.20	1.18
	J54=9	Commoner	10.78	0.68	1.05	21.98
	J54=10	Commoner	5.64	1.22	0.60	7.92
Huancas de la Cruz (J59)	J59=1	Commoner	1.70	0.07	1.00	0.85
Chucchus (J74)	J74=1	Commoner	8.90	0.00	0.00	3.42
	J74=2	Commoner	8.07	0.00	0.00	0.00

Source: After Earle and D'Altroy 1989: Table 1.

Note: For definitions of indexes, see notes to Table 4.1.

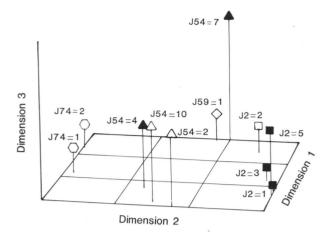

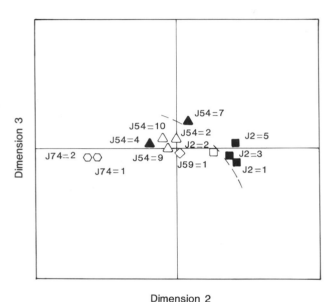

Fig. 9.15. Plots of similarities among Wanka III residential compounds at Hatunmarca (J2), Marca (J54), Huancas de la Cruz (J59), and Chucchus (J74), based on production indexes. *Top,* three-dimensional plot; *bottom,* second and third dimensions of top plot, rotated around dimension 3. Solid symbols indicate elite compounds; open symbols, commoner compounds. J54=9 is such a remarkable outlier with respect to hoe density and whorl density that including it in the top plot would have compressed all other points on the plot into a tiny sector.

the Wanka II compounds, the more similar the compounds were in terms of productive activities, the closer were their representative points in the plots.[20]

In Figures 9.15a and 9.15b, the households from each site clustered together, separated primarily along dimension 2 (cf. Earle and D'Altroy 1989: Figs. 4 and 5). The site clusters graded from Chucchus (J74)

through Marca (J54) and Huancas de la Cruz (J59) to Hatunmarca (J2). Inspection of the raw index values in Table 9.3 shows that the values for hoe density, whorl density, and blade production were jointly responsible for the gradation. Along dimension 2, the sites graded (1) from those at the lowest elevations to those at the highest and (2) from those nearest Hatun Xauxa to those farthest away; the implications of these trends will be examined shortly. The high values of the Marca households on dimension 3 result from a high level of ceramic production. Overall, this plot illustrates that households within communities were generally engaged in the same proportions of productive activities and that these activities differed systematically among communities.

In Figure 9.15b, only the second and third dimensions are shown, permitting a fairly reasonable separation between the elite and commoner households, crosscutting sites. With the exception of household J54=4, from Marca, the households classified a priori as elite on the basis of architecture and location clustered together on the right side of the plot. This separation of statuses was clearly a reflection of the relative participation of the members of the two statuses in maize agriculture, as measured by hoe density. The location of household J54=4 among the commoner households may have resulted from an error in the pre-excavation architectural classification. Alternatively, the residents of this compound may have just been unusually heavily involved in maize production.

Our ability to distinguish Wanka III residential households by site, on the basis of agricultural, cloth, stone tool, and ceramic production parallels the situation found in Wanka II. A related question of interest is whether the Wanka II compounds can be distinguished from those of the succeeding period, on similar grounds. Put in economic terms, the question is whether the activities pursued in Wanka III households differed in some regular way from those of the Wanka II households. This is perhaps the central economic question concerning the Inka impacts on the daily life of the imperial subjects.

The answer to this question is a qualified yes. Domestic activities changed in systematic ways under Inka rule. As will be demonstrated below, the subject diet, the kinds of agriculture pursued, the labor invested in spinning, and the balance of agricultural labor carried out by elites and commoners, among other things, shifted at the household level. We cannot, however, simply ascribe these changes to state mandate. Some changes appear to have been an indirect consequence of state policy, such as the reduction in local hostilities, which opened up lands for use that had previously been off-limits.

To address the problem of Wanka II–III shifts, all 29 excavated compounds were plotted in a three-dimensional scaling solution comparable to those created for each period. In this plot (Fig. 9.16a; Kruskal's stress 1 = .118; R^2 = .882), a gradation existed along dimension 1 from the Umpamalca households through Tunanmarca, Hatunmarca (II and III), Chucchus, and Huancas de la Cruz to Marca. The compound clusters of the various settlements overlap considerably, suggesting that Wanka II and III would not sort out neatly. Inspection of the scatterplot of dimensions 1 and 3, however, provided a clue as to how to clarify this relationship. The overlap among the settlements from the two periods was entirely a function of the location of the Hatunmarca compounds. It will be recalled that Hatunmarca was located at a relatively high elevation (3,800 m) but was intermediary between the Wanka II settlements (Umpamalca and Tunanmarca) and the Wanka III settlements (Marca, Chucchus, and Huancas de la Cruz). It therefore appears that the spatial or microenvironmental placement of Hatunmarca was reflected in the combined emphases on the four activities measured by the production indexes.

A further three-dimensional solution (stress 1 = .104; R^2 = .908) was therefore produced, with all Hatunmarca (II and III) households removed, leaving 22 compounds to be evaluated. In this configuration, the Wanka III households could be grouped by site, although the two remaining Wanka II site clusters overlapped extensively. Of greater interest was that the households belonging to each phase could be separated by a plane in three dimensions or by a single line across the plot of dimensions 1 and 3 (Fig. 9.16b). The removal of the Hatunmarca households thus permitted complete separation of the remaining pre-Inka and Inka-period residential compounds from one another, based on four household activities. Hoe density made the principal contribution to the separation, although the Wanka III increase in spindle whorl concentration was also important.

An alternative rotation of the combined Wanka II–III data in Fig. 9.16a permitted a partial separation of the elite and commoner compounds across the two periods. A cluster of elite compounds is visible in the lower left corner of the plot (Fig. 9.17). This cluster includes all elite compounds from Hatunmarca (II and III) and Umpamalca (II) and one from Tunanmarca (II). The Marca (III) elite compounds lie to the right.

This pattern, in which the Hatunmarca elites grouped with the Wanka II elites, suggests that there was interaction between status and environmental location in determining the mix of household labor.

What is to be made of this patterning? An initial conclusion is that the nature of household economic organization shifted significantly as a direct consequence of the Inka conquest. To a certain extent, that shift did occur. The density of spindle whorls per cubic meter essentially doubled from Wanka II to III, a change that may be partially attributed to an increased demand for cloth production imposed by the Inka state (Costin 1986; see also Earle et al. 1987). Similarly, the village of Chucchus (J74) seems to have been established as a maize-producing settlement, as reflected in an extremely high density of hoes.

It is equally significant that environmental location was the common variable separating the sites from one another both between periods and within Wanka III. In each case the lower-elevation sites, with a higher proportion of maize lands in their catchments, were separated from the higher-elevation sites, with a high proportion of tuber and grazing lands in their catchments. Also recall that the high-elevation sites were those closest to the principal source of chert for the fine stone tools used widely for cutting and harvesting (Russell 1988). Not surprisingly, then, the intensity of maize agriculture was inversely related to the intensity of chert tool manufacture.

The shifts in household production from Wanka II to III at the site level thus exhibit three basic trends. First, the higher-elevation sites can be distinguished from the lower sites between Wanka II and III and within Wanka III, by their agricultural tools and stone-tool debris. This finding clearly indicates that household economic activities were focused within very short distances of the settlements—a matter of a few kilometers at most. As was argued in Chapter 4 (see also LeBlanc 1981; Hastorf 1983), the focus on nearby lands probably resulted from a concern for security in Wanka II and, during both phases, the increase in cost of economic activities at greater distances from the home settlements. Second, the similarities among Wanka III sites may be graded by distance from Hatun Xauxa. The evidence suggests strongly that settlements close to the capital were more highly specialized than those farther away, perhaps indicating greater state interest in controlling the productive activities of the nearby settlements. Third, Hatunmarca, the sole major settlement occupied both before and under the Inkas as well as the environmentally central settle-

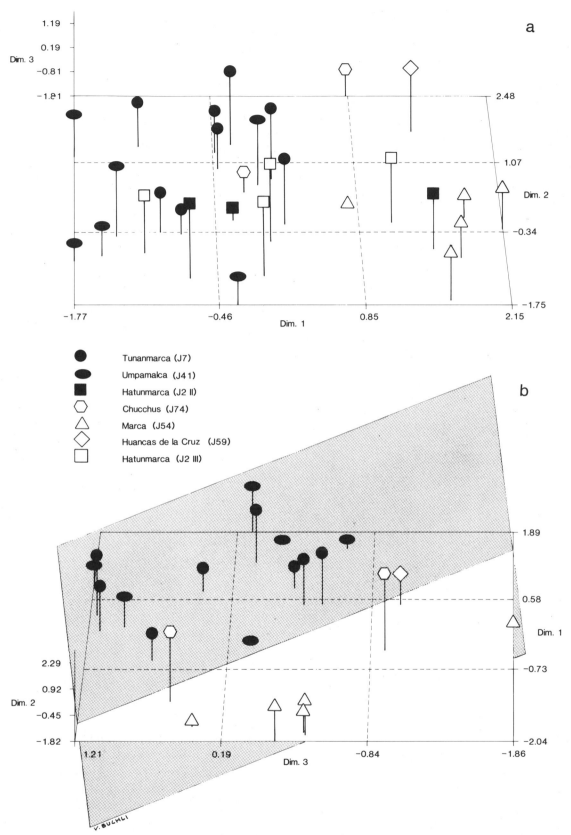

Fig. 9.16. Plots of similarities among Wanka II and III residential compounds, based on production indexes. *a*, All 29 residential compounds excavated; *b*, with Hatunmarca compounds removed. Solid symbols indicate Wanka II compounds; open symbols, Wanka III compounds.

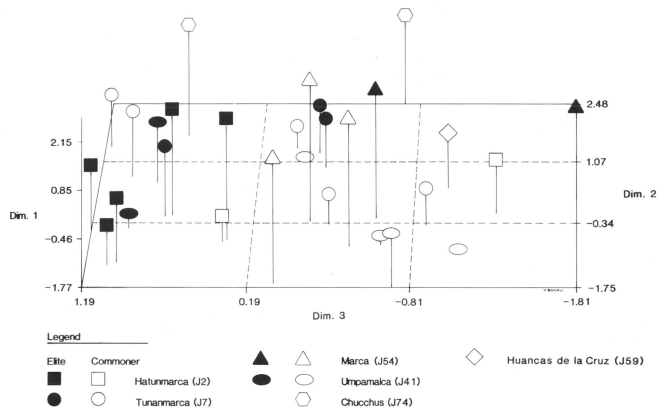

Fig. 9.17. Plot of similarities among all 29 Wanka II and III excavated residential compounds, based on production indexes and rotated to display status. Solid symbols indicate Wanka II compounds; open symbols, Wanka III compounds.

ment, provided a link between the settlements at high and low elevations and from Wanka II to III. This link may have represented both temporal and spatial continuity in domestic economics within the settlement.

The elite-commoner distinction in production may be summarized as follows (see also Costin and Earle 1989; D'Altroy and Hastorf n.d.). During Wanka II the households classified as elites and commoners under the UMARP sampling scheme were involved in comparable sorts and intensities of productive activities at the household level. With the advent of the Inkas, the proportional contribution of households at the elite end of the spectrum decreased in agricultural and textile production, to the extent that elite and commoner compounds can be distinguished from one another more readily. This finding implies that status distinctions in household labor—absent or poorly developed in Wanka II—were gelling under Inka rule (cf. Costin and Earle 1989). If we consider that Wanka II elite and commoner households could be distinguished on the basis of residential location, access to exotic materials and labor-intensive prestige goods, and architectural

complexity, size, and elegance, then the lack of class separation on the basis of categories of household labor is especially notable.

The implication is that elite access to resources and prestige products preceded elite control over labor, or at least the specialized labor institutions introduced by the Inkas. The concentration of labor-intensive goods in elite compounds implies a degree of elite control over intensified subsistence and sumptuary production. However, the lack of differential economic activities at the household level implies that general labor reorganization lagged behind control over resources and the production and distribution of sumptuary goods. Put another way, certain kinds of labor (e.g., attached specialization) were intensified before the institutional relations were changed.

These trends may be used collectively to assess the extent to which the state directly intervened in the household activities of its subjects. The Inka conquest clearly had an impact on the nature of subsistence and utilitarian production pursued within households. Much of the change, however, may have been more a voluntary shift resulting from effective use of new environmental locations than an enforced shift resulting from imperial mandate. Areas in which state intervention appears to have had a more direct effect may be found in (1) the increased production of cloth in Wanka households, (2) the apparent specialization of maize production at Chucchus, to the exclusion of other productive activities, and (3) the proportional decrease in agricultural labor invested by elites.

Summary

The impact of the Inka conquest of the Upper Mantaro Valley was clearly visible in the redistribution of the native populace in Wanka III, both within the region and between Wanka Wamaní and other provinces of the empire. Several major shifts in resettlement occurred, focused on the abandonment of high-elevation, fortified settlements and the founding of smaller, lower-elevation, unfortified villages. The reduction of hostilities, which opened up highly productive pastoral and agricultural territories that were inaccessible in Wanka II, resulted in a more dispersed settlement distribution and a broader economy. Although the state appears to have taken an active hand in setting up some agriculturally specialized settlements and in reducing the concentration of the populace in defensive centers, the shift to lower elevations likely provided an attractive opportunity for the indigenous populace to exploit a wider variety of ecozones, especially valley-floor lands that could be used to grow maize.

The marked settlement hierarchy that had existed among native settlements in Wanka II was truncated at the top, as Hatunmarca and Tunanmarca were, respectively, significantly reduced in size and entirely abandoned. The upper echelon of regional power, previously focused at these centers, was taken over by the state at Hatun Xauxa. The continued hierarchical relationship between the elite and commoner segments of the native population, however, remained visible in the settlement pattern.

The settlement changes described here for Wanka III sites provided the context within which the central transformations of indigenous society occurred. These changes lay in the restructuring of power and in the activities pursued within subject communities. The analysis here has shown that the Wanka elites were extensively drawn into the state hierarchy. To judge from the patterns elicited from the distribution of Inka ceramics, state goods were accessible to a broad spectrum of the local populace, but access was hierarchically defined. The coupled effects of state ties and demands were recognizable all the way down to the household level. The nature of some activities pursued within domestic contexts was altered, in part as an effort to meet the demands of state production and in part as a consequence of perquisites granted to the elites. This change, of course, returns us to a central element of imperial rule—the simultaneous need to court the compliance of subjects and to command production for state-defined consumption.

10

Conclusion

This chapter returns to some of the issues discussed in the first two chapters, in an effort to bridge several themes running through this work. The central goal of this book has been to examine the relationships among various types of power in the formation and development of the Inka empire, as an example of the evolution of the most complex premodern societies. I have argued here that the use of models of empires provides an effective means of examining this problem for three basic reasons (see Luttwak 1976; Hassig 1985).

First, using models invites us to be explicit about theory and to specify the assumptions underlying our explanations of culture change. The hegemonic-territorial model, in particular, facilitates analysis of imperial development as a combined outcome of the organized use of material and energetic resources, and of the organization of decision-making. Second, this approach focuses on the strategic aspect of imperial expansion and on the varying relationships between the core polity and its subject groups. The range of polities subsumed within the premodern empires would have made distinct policies effective for imperial rule at different locations and times. This situation suggests that the broad patterns and internal variation in, for example, political organization need to be examined concurrently to understand imperial formation. A central question therefore concerns the degree to which variation is truly idiosyncratic or is an expectable instance of trends found elsewhere. Third, the model provides a common conceptual and analytical vocabulary that is useful for cross-cultural comparison. The overwhelming majority of the literature on the Inkas in the last couple of decades has used analytical concepts or terminology tailored explicitly to Andean cultures. Part of the intent of this volume has been to move away from an explanation of the Inka empire in its own terms and toward an explanation that provides common ground for comparison.

Throughout the remainder of this chapter, I will briefly draw out some comparisons with other early empires, in an effort to appraise the comparability of rule among them. The present discussion is intended only to highlight a limited number of areas of similarity and distinction and is not remotely exhaustive. Far more thorough comparisons of the Inka empire with others have been drawn elsewhere (esp. Katz 1972; see also Carrasco 1982, Wolf 1982, and Mann 1986), and the reader is referred to them for greater detail.

Military Power

In Chapter 2, I suggested that three essential elements of imperial rule consisted of military, political, and economic power, coupled with judicious assertion of imperial ideology. This work has treated the application of Inka military power as comprising two broad stages: conquest and consolidation. The first stage combined pitched battle, siege, and diplomacy as means of taking new territories. In this effort, the Inkas appear to have economized the use of force, as Luttwak (1976) has argued is appropriate for any effective military strategy. Several circumstances would have led to this approach, apart from a self-interest in minimizing potential losses. The numerical limitations of Inka personnel required that allied and newly conquered subjects be used to man the armies. The unreliability of some of these detachments, the logistical demands of maintaining large contingents in the field, and some disastrous campaigns would collectively have contributed to a considered use of diplomacy, backed up by massive force. The preservation of productive human and natural resources would also have been a strong incentive to take new lands intact, because, after all, the acquisition of resources was a central intent of the imperial endeavor. In a complementary fashion, the storied Inka massacres of besieged strongholds and rebellious subjects undoubtedly served the dual purposes of eliminating intransigent enemies and dissuading others from such actions.

Each of these approaches has obvious parallels in other early empires. The hard-point defensive strategy employed to secure Inka territories, for instance, was broadly comparable to that of the Romans of the third century A.D. (Luttwak 1976), although the Inka use of hard points occurred in a stage of development, not retrenchment (Rawls 1979). The Roman razing of Carthage and methodical investiture of Masada and the Mongol butchery in Persia (Morgan 1986) also served the dual ends of retribution and dissuasion. Similarly, the Romans, the Mongols, and Alexander depended heavily on allied or conscripted armies to conduct much of their fighting, but they consistently maintained a core military leadership composed of ethnic elites. The seasonality of Inka campaigns, required because of difficulties of transportation and heavy reliance on conscripted peasants, also had a direct parallel in Aztec campaign strategy (Hassig 1988) and was virtually a universal feature of early imperial expansion. The Roman approach to militarism differed radically from the Inka in two important ways,

however. First, the Inkas never effected a true territorial military strategy, designed to form a hardened perimeter around the empire. Second, Roman army service was transformed from a citizen duty to a career. It is in the lack of a truly professional army, apart from a very limited core, that the military organization of the Inkas differed most notably from that of other major empires. Even here, however, there are indications that the Inkas were setting up specialized, full-time military entities (Murra 1986). In broad strokes, then, Inka military strategy fell between that of the Aztecs and the Romans. The development of an infrastructure of roads, garrisons, and supply depots was far more intensive than the Aztec approach, but not nearly so professionalized as the Roman.

The conquest of the Upper Mantaro Valley occurred relatively early in the Inka imperial expansion, only a score or so years after the first emergence of the Inkas as a power in the southern highlands. The rapid capitulation of much of the region without resistance emphasizes the efficacy of military persuasion even in the most populous region of the central sierra. Those northerners who put up a concerted fight were overrun and deported en masse, their settlements forever vacated. The failure of the Wankas to withstand the Inka assault may have stemmed initially from their lack of coordinated leadership. In a region beset by chronic local conflicts, the Wankas may have found it difficult to form an effective alliance against the invaders. The scale of warfare conducted by the Inkas also appears to have been far beyond anything previously undertaken in the highlands. This factor may have led to misapprehension of the potential threat and to ready capitulation once the armies presented themselves.

Three policies were significant in reducing the possibility of rebellion in the region. First, an undetermined number of residents were used for long-term campaigns in the north, especially under the emperor Wayna Qhapaq. Second, most of the populace shifted downslope from the fortified redoubts of the fourteenth century into dispersed villages, probably as a combined consequence of imperial demands and the residents' desire to take advantage of the lower valley lands. Third, enclaves of military mitmaqkuna were established in the valley. That these included Cañares and Chachapoyas, who were subdued only in the last decade or so of Inka rule and who generally served as internal garrisons, suggests strongly that the Upper Mantaro was not considered entirely pacified even in the 1520s.

The location of the Upper Mantaro region made it

pivotal for Inka military strategy. As concerns shifted from assertion of dominion to assimilation of populations, the region became a prime candidate for imperial development because of its agricultural productivity and its placement along the spine of the Andes at points with good east-west passage. Some aspects of the Inka occupation may be used to appraise the shift in military strategy here. The positioning of the provincial center, Hatun Xauxa, at a point better suited for interregional travel than for local administration implies broad-scale planning in situating nodes of imperial control. The poorly defensible position and the lack of fortification at the center further indicate that it was visualized neither as a hard point in perimeter defense nor as a frontier settlement in the vanguard of a slowly expanding empire. Instead, its role lay in providing personnel, resources, and infrastructural support for campaigns conducted elsewhere.

The erection of the extensive storage facilities draws attention to the need for logistical support for the armies. The initial development of the physical infrastructure can be seen most clearly in these terms, because the difficulties imposed by terrain and technology required construction of facilities throughout the empire. The military nature of centers such as Hatun Xauxa may have diminished in comparison with political, economic, or religious features, as threats to state security diminished. Even with the consolidation of military control in the central sierra, however, the necessity for maintaining military readiness is written throughout the valley and at each provincial center along the main highway.

In its military role, the Upper Mantaro Valley appears to have been comparable to most of the other major points of Inka control between Cuzco and Quito. Each of the provincial centers along the sierra road—Willka Wamán, Hatun Xauxa, Pumpu, Huánuco Pampa, Cajamarca, and Tumipampa—served primarily as a location for logistical support. None was notably fortified with cordons of forts like those surrounding Quito, along the eastern frontiers of Peru, Bolivia, and Argentina, or along the south Chilean frontier. Instead, the imperial facilities appear to have bivouacked traveling armies and supported garrisons temporarily. This approach is in keeping with a strategy in which the overarching goal was to maintain security among the provinces and in which the regional investment of resources was designed for campaigns elsewhere or for support of perimeter defenses breached by intruders.

In sum, although the data on perimeter regions are sketchy, Inka military strategy appears to have been weighted toward territorial control in the central part and northern reaches of the empire, with a more hegemonic approach still being used on the north Peruvian coast and toward the southern peripheries at the time of the empire's collapse. The development of internal garrisons, a logistical infrastructure, and forts at the limits of imperial lands collectively afforded an effective means of securing peace throughout Tawantinsuyu. The occupation of subject lands, especially throughout the sierra, yielded direct control of imperial territory, without the constant reconquest or extensive subvention of peripheral client polities that typically underwrite hegemonic control. The choice of this strategy does not imply that Inka rule was internally uncontested or that emperors were not plagued by rebellions, but it does indicate that the Inkas were promoting a relatively even degree of security throughout their territory.

Political Power

The second aspect of imperial rule discussed in this work was political power. The Inka political strategy for incorporating subject territories is a complicated issue, but some general trends can be suggested. It has been argued here that interaction among a relatively limited number of considerations had a major impact on the choice of policy for a region: (1) the resources potentially available for exploitation, (2) the extant political complexity of the subject group, (3) proximity to Cuzco and the main lines of transit through the Andes, and (4) the security threat posed by an independent polity. The broad outcomes of these factors entailed a territorial approach throughout the Andean highlands from Bolivia to southern Ecuador and perhaps on the central Peruvian coast, with a more indirect approach applied in northern Ecuador, northwest Argentina, Chile, and the north coast of Peru.

The material remains of imperial administration, especially the large provincial centers, were concentrated most heavily in the first area. Most state investment in land and water intensification, public works, and the administrative and logistical infrastructure was also found here. These regions were the ones for which the documentary sources record the most intensive use of ethnic elites in the imperial administration and in which the decimal hierarchy was most thoroughly applied (see, e.g., Murra 1968; Julien 1982, 1988). The territorial approach to the occupation of the area makes sense because of its productivity, its location surrounding Cuzco, its initial political similarities to Inka society, and its importance for security. That assertion should not be taken to imply an equivalent degree of control throughout the sierra, however, because the degree of exploitation of an area is generally proportional to the potential imperial gain and to the costs involved in overseeing the dominated regions (see Hassig 1985:100). Thus the populous and highly productive Upper Mantaro Valley and perhaps the similar Willka Wamán and Cajamarca regions appear to have been more intensively integrated than, say, the Huasahuasi, Acos, Carahuarazo, and Yauyos areas that lay among them (see Schreiber 1987). The Pumpu and Huánuco regions presented a slightly different situation, in that the relative lack of nearby local population combined with the regions' strategic importance to make construction of largely self-contained imperial centers an effective solution to attaining direct control.

It was suggested in Chapter 7 that the relative lack of intensive incorporation of the southern sectors of the empire and the north coast of Peru derived from fundamentally different considerations. In the south, the populations were relatively small and politically simple, and the resources extracted were primarily raw materials, such as ores and precious stones. Under these circumstances, indirect rule may have been sufficient to attain imperial goals, without substantial investment of an administrative overlay. The north coast of Peru presented radically distinct problems: a higher degree of political and economic complexity than characterized the Inkas themselves, and a significant threat to imperial security. It likely would not have been cost-effective, or perhaps even practicable, for the Inkas to have undertaken a highly integrated political approach there, and a policy of decentralization and indirect control appears to have made more sense.

Both centralizing and centrifugal tendencies are visible in Inka political strategy. The centralizing forces derived in part from the efficiency and control provided by an increasingly unified political organization. By drawing subject elites into a swelling administration, the Inkas would have started to drive a wedge between the native elites and their traditional constituencies. The shift of elites' sources of power from community allocation to state delegation would have resulted in their serving two masters, perhaps neither one particularly well. The proportion of the native elites actually replaced by the Inkas is unclear, but the requirement of state sanction for succession and the threat of removal would have provided the elites with a strong incentive to pay close heed to the state's interests. As traditional rights to office shifted toward Inka appointment, some subject elites may have seen their constituents' support erode. At the same time, the abilities of the rulers to keep tabs on provincial matters would have increased, thus reducing the potential threat of rebellion. Assertion of political power within subject territories would therefore have been of considerable value to the Inkas in attaining provincial control.

The spatial and structural dispersal of political and economic power derived from a number of sources. First, the sheer size of the empire, coupled with the patchy distribution of population and the limitations of transportation and communication, required that the Inkas conduct much of their governance according to provincial needs, not core needs. A significant element can be found in the density and distribution of Andean populations. In contrast to the urbanization that frequently accompanied the development of other empires, the formation of large urban settlements was not a significant element under Inka rule. Large urban populations comparable to those of central Mexico, Rome, China, and Mesopotamia were not found in Tawantinsuyu, which boasted few, if any, settlements that exceeded 100,000 inhabitants and little important bulk exchange between areas of concentrated population. Cuzco itself probably housed around 100,000 or fewer inhabitants and was not a major marketing center. In this sense, the Inka empire appears to have been most comparable to that of the Mongols, for whom even the imperial capital of Qaraqorum was exceedingly modest. The ecological complexity of the Andes and the concentration of agriculturally productive lands in compartmentalized valleys, separated by desert or mountains, also contributed to a situation in which no single location could readily vacuum up the empire's resources. Instead, the Inkas reinvested the resources of their conquests, both human and natural, throughout the empire in an increasingly territorial strategy of occupation.

The location of the Upper Mantaro region, the requirements of intensive agricultural and craft production, and the maintenance of security in a populous valley would have combined to make direct integration more effective than indirect rule through clients. The political system installed by the Inkas relied heavily on Xauxa and Wanka elites who were appointed to state offices while retaining status as locally sanctioned leaders. Before the conquest, the region had been politically fragmented, so the Inkas created three political divisions within the province and appointed local elites as paramounts. Succession to office was determined according to locally acceptable rules for the most part, but the state reserved the right to appoint and remove officials. To make the state decimal and local kin-based political structures correspond, some state units were apparently declared congruent with the local units. Because the Inka government seems to have been founded on similar kin principles, this policy may have been a simple but effective means of drawing the local political systems into an increasingly centralized state hierarchy.

Conversely, the local units may have been partially restructured when state divisions were installed or when local units were grouped for state purposes, such as labor or military exactions. Certain introduced political features—notably the centralization into saya (said to correspond to hunu, or 10,000 heads of household) and the division into pachaca (100 heads of household)—became sufficiently entrenched that they persisted in that form into the Colonial Period, without benefit of the Inka superstructure. This system continued to be used directly to mobilize goods and manpower for political purposes, such as in the prestations to the Spaniards that continued through 1554.

Comparisons between the Inka approaches to political incorporation and the methods of other early empires underscore both fundamental parallels and differences. The indirect rule that the Mongols applied to the occupation of the great civilizations of China and Persia appears to be similar to the Inka policy on the Peruvian north coast, as does the Mongols' adoption of a decimal administrative hierarchy from a subject polity. The latter point is pertinent, of course, not because of the decimal character of the system but because of the parallel appropriation of organizational principles from politically more complex, conquered societies. The use of subject ethnic elites both in the provincial bureaucracy and as clients, while maintaining ethnic solidarity at the highest levels, was similarly widespread among early empires, such as in the Roman and Mongol polities. The Inkas differed significantly from the Aztec hegemonic approach, however, by extending political control extensively throughout their territory (Litvak King 1971; Carrasco 1982). Conversely, although the Inkas developed a structured bureaucracy, they never approached the Roman, Chinese, or Sasanian degree of administrative development. Neither was a civil bureaucracy set against the

wealthy families, as appears to have been case in the Sasanian polity (Wenke 1987:259). The Inka empire was not sufficiently differentiated for such developments, and it is not clear how long it might have taken, if ever, for this kind of segmentation of secular and religious groups and of civil and private groups within society to occur.

Economic Power

The application of economic power in early empires was attained through a variety of means, among them labor mobilization, direct levies on output, taxation on commerce, and establishment of separate production systems. The political economy is an area in which the Inkas differed in a number of significant ways from other early empires. Having developed in a region mostly lacking monetary and market systems, the Inkas opted for two approaches: a rotating corvée tax and the late formation of enclaves of attached specialists who produced the state's subsistence and sumptuary goods (Murra 1980 [1956]). The Inkas did not have the option of mobilizing resources through taxation on large-scale commerce and generally did not have an economic infrastructure of specialized regions, producing for a broad market, from which goods could be mobilized directly. Even in those areas in which the more specialized regional economies were found, the Inkas appear to have taken a hands-off approach and may have even discouraged regional exchange (see Salomon 1986:143–86).

The Inka use of a labor tax, as is often argued, preserved certain important principles of elite-commoner relations that were common in the Andes. The most important of these principles was preservation of the self-sufficiency of the peasantry. The Inka adoption of attached specialization may be seen in part, however, as recognition that the labor tax was an inefficient way to fund state activities. Under the economic and transport conditions present in the Andes, development of state productive resources and personnel in a regionally focused system was an effective solution. It remains unclear to what extent this program had crystallized by the Spanish invasion, but the extraordinary resettlement program indicates strongly that the Inkas realized the need to control production closely, both for security and for efficiency. The cost of administration, of course, rose proportionally.

The need for regional elites to administer production for the Inka state favored the development of a managerial stratum. Both the producers and the managers—apart from the provincial governor, his immediate entourage, and some specialists—were drawn from the subject populace. The evidence shows that the Wankas were drawn into the Inka state political economy at least in general corvée duties, craft production, specialized farming communities, management of centralized storage, and perhaps local administration of labor. It seems probable that two or more as yet unidentified settlements produced pottery for the state and that the region's inhabitants were among the attached metalsmiths recorded historically at Hatun Xauxa. An extensive role for Wanka elites in the administration of state storage also seems assured. The entrenchment of these elites in administrative positions, with preferential hereditary access, thus appears to reflect the consolidation of political and economic control in the hands of a limited kin.

An additional dramatic change can be found in the settlement shift from the high-elevation, defensive, nucleated settlements of Wanka II to the lower, more dispersed communities of Wanka III. Even the brief analysis of the new population distribution presented in Chapter 9 shows that aspects of the reorganization were systematic. The area around the Inka provincial center, Hatun Xauxa, was markedly underpopulated but contained some new, specialized, agricultural villages and most of the state storage facilities. It seems most likely that this spatial pattern was a direct consequence of planned Inka use of lands as a function of distance from the administrative center. The radical drop in population from the largest Wanka II centers to Wanka III towns—on the order of two-thirds—also resulted in a rank-size settlement structure that accorded well with an integrated state-local system. This physical pattern fit what would be expected in a society in which the residents of subject communities were drawn extensively into the state political organization and political economy at their home settlements as well as at the provincial center.

The imperial conquest had much less marked consequences for the Wanka domestic economy. Householding remained essentially stable, whether household- or community-based production was involved. The principal changes occurred in activities resulting from household members' participation in the political economy. Here the Inkas intervened substantially, providing goods used in political and ceremonial relations and extracting resources, such as silver, that previously had been at the disposal of the native elites. The establishment of maize-farming villages is most

appropriately viewed in this context as well. Because so much of the state's material support came from the capacities of a self-sufficient peasantry, continuity in domestic economics was to be expected, but the modest amount of change was surprising (see Earle et al. 1987; D'Altroy and Hastorf n.d.).

The Inka political economy thus clearly differed from the economies of the Aztecs, Chinese, and Romans, for example, in which markets and money were central to imperial finance. A total lack of comparability in economy is not implied, however. The limitations of archaic transport systems, for instance, fed into a regional focus for most subsistence and utilitarian activities in early empires, whether conducted by the state or by subject populations. The limited ranges of bulk goods implied that virtually all long-distance exchange was conducted in prestige goods in both Mesopotamia and the Aztec empire (Adams 1974; Schneider 1977; Hassig 1985), as well as in the Inka polity. In this, the Inkas differed from the Roman provinces surrounding the Mediterranean, which provided the markedly more efficient option of water transport. The much heavier proportion of entrepreneurs in other empires also distinguished those polities from the Inka empire, but administered traders provided a characteristic means of procuring long-distance goods for core elites of the Inka, Aztec, and Early Dynastic empires, among others.

In a related note of economic comparison, it can be observed that the scale of operation generally plays an important role in economic organization. In expanding empires, in which administrative personnel, other elites, and the military, for example, swelled more rapidly than population size, there would have been a demand for intensified production. This demand, whether political or market-oriented, would have created a stimulus for increased efficiency. The economy did not have to be monetized, nor did the production of goods have to be motivated by supply and demand (e.g., in a political economy with an increasing bureaucracy), for economic managers to be prompted to shift toward increasingly efficient, specialized production (cf. Champion [1989b], who argues implicitly that scale is not relevant). Thus, the shift toward greater labor specialization in the Inka political economy, as in other empires, was likely partially a function of the increased demand for output, whether in raw materials, subsistence or craft goods, or services.

Given the dual advantages of increased efficiency and control, it is not surprising that the use of a resettlement program for establishing specialized productive enclaves was not unique to the Inkas. The Sasanians, for example, moved tens of thousands of people as part of an intensive effort to reshape the human and natural environment for imperial exploitation (Wenke 1987:259). The Romans also set up state establishments for extraction of mineral resources and craft production, such as in Moesia Superior (Bartel 1989: 180–83). State-sponsored land and water improvement projects, to be staffed by specialized farmers for ultimate state benefit, were similarly characteristic of a number of early empires, among them the Aztecs and the Sasanians.

The spatial distribution of intensified state production appears to fit the general pattern described here. Those regions in which large-scale state production was undertaken, primarily in highland Peru and parts of Bolivia, often corresponded to the areas in which the most intensive political incorporation was undertaken. Conversely, those areas in which political incorporation appears to have been more indirect, such as the north coast of Peru and the most southerly parts of the empire, frequently coincided with zones in which economic exploitation was small-scale or focused on spatially restricted resources, such as mineral wealth. That relationship does not imply a precise coincidence between areas of intense political occupation and economic exploitation. It does suggest, however, that the policies underlying both elements of imperial rule were coordinated and that regional differences were variations on general themes of imperial rule.

Although these few points of comparison could be expanded, they are not intended to make an argument for great similarity between the Inka approach to political economy and the approaches of other early empires. They are raised here to emphasize that, for purposes of comparison, economic strategy can profitably be distinguished from the structural features of the political economy.

Concluding Comments

This study has been intended to contribute to the literature on complex premodern political and economic formations. At the inception of the work, I argued that the evolutionary significance of archaic empires lies in the changes that resulted from the integration of diverse societies into polities, unified along a variety of dimensions. I have suggested that various models of empires offer tangible insights but tend to obscure the nature of imperial systems on a number of counts. The

dominant core-periphery approach, for instance, effectively underscores the transformation of labor relations that occurs in both the core and peripheral sectors of the empire, but it tends to dichotomize regions into populations of the exploiters and the exploited. Because core-periphery analyses emphasize ties constituted through the core and periphery elites, the dynamics of regional politics and nonimperial economics are generally lost. Wolf's (1982) notion of tributary empires partially redresses the latter problem but takes little account of internal variation among the early and non-Western empires.

The hegemonic-territorial model has been applied here to focus attention on the strategic dimension of imperial formation and organization. It directs us to variations in imperial relations with subject populations and to the ties among varying kinds of imperial power. In particular, it evaluates imperial development as the outcome of a series of basic considerations, such as security and varying demands on and opportunities for extracting imperial resources, as applied to particular circumstances. As other authors have shown for the Romans (Luttwak 1976), the Aztecs (Hassig 1985), and the late Chinese (Skinner 1977), imperial strategy and relations with subject populations have real spatial dimensions. This view contrasts with the often unrealistic evaluation by some authors of the ability of archaic transportation systems to move bulk goods, resulting in a misapprehension of the nature of ties between the core and subject populations. Paradoxically, the recognition by many authors that core-periphery is a structural relationship rather than a spatial one has led them to ignore the very real constraints resulting from geography and simple transportation technology.

The various studies cited throughout this work have shown that although there is no one kind of empire, there are reasons that particular kinds of military, political, and economic approaches should have been coupled in similar ways under comparable circumstances. The present work has emphasized that Inka rule and local transformations in the Upper Mantaro region were, to a large degree, the outcomes of systematic approaches to a complex web of conditions. Historical circumstances set the stage for the imperial conquests, and the characteristics of Andean societies constrained the options initially available to the Inkas. Nonetheless, the effectiveness of imperial strategies was delimited by variables basic in important ways to all early empires. Most fundamentally, a balance had to be struck between the acquisitive, expansionist directions of imperial development and the resources and capacities of subject territories. The expansionist goals of the imperial elites may have been grandiose, but the human and natural features of conquered territories provided both opportunities and limitations for imperial development.

In Tawantinsuyu the outcomes of these situations produced a diverse polity that was still fashioning its basic institutions when the Spaniards invaded. Because imperial goals and conditions were in flux throughout the century that the empire endured, it has been useful to analyze Inka rule as a set of flexible strategies, guided by considerations of control and efficiency, with respect to politics, economics, and security. These strategies had to be played out in the context of widely varying subordinate societies and were directed, at least initially, by the organization of subject groups at the time of conquest. Military policies, the direction of restructured economics, and the nature of administrative innovations all suggest, however, that the Inkas were not so heavily constrained by convention as is often implied. Instead, they put convention to work within the context of new arrangements.

In closing, I return to a theme that has been a central feature of most modern treatments of the Inka empire: the remarkable diversity of the Andean societies drawn under the imperial aegis. My efforts here have been intended partly to subsume this diversity under a general explanation of Inka policies and partly to examine the specific nature of imperial rule in one small section of the vast polity. Balancing the particular and socially general aspects of imperial polities remains a daunting task, and it is likely that any given characterization will quickly be superseded. As we analyze the nature of the Inkas and other early empires further, however, it is in this balance that we will attain a clearer understanding.

Appendix:
Inka-Style
Ceramics
from the
Upper
Mantaro
Valley

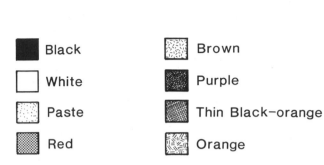

■ Black		▨ Brown	
□ White		▦ Purple	
▫ Paste		▨ Thin Black–orange	
▨ Red		▨ Orange	

Fig. A.1. Legend for Figures A.2 through A.13.

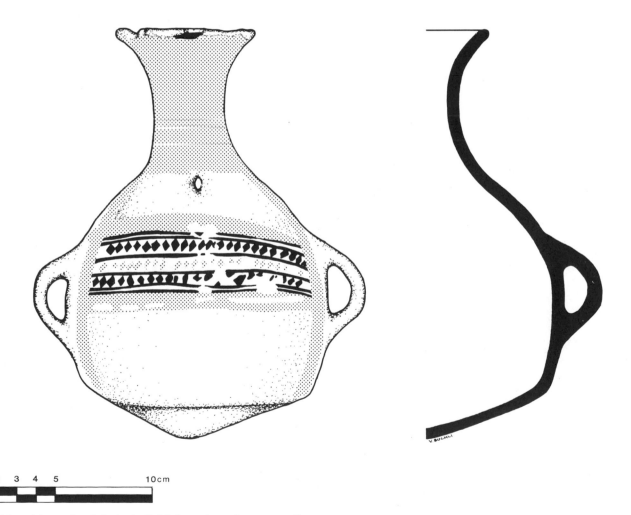

0 1 2 3 4 5   10cm

Fig. A.2. Inka miniature flared-rim jar (*aríbalo*). Provenience: J2=1-1-3-5-6/10.

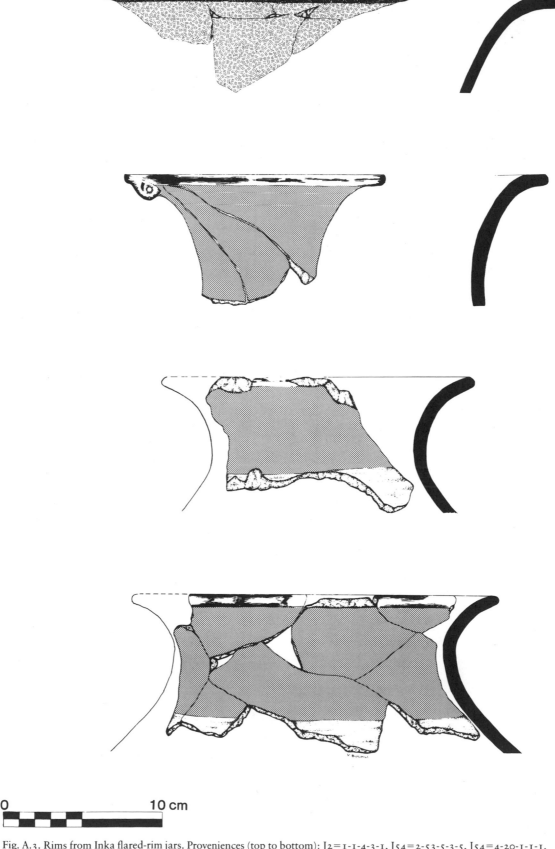

Fig. A.3. Rims from Inka flared-rim jars. Proveniences (top to bottom): J2=1-1-4-3-1, J54=2-53-5-3-5, J54=4-20-1-1-1, J2=1-1-2-3-3.

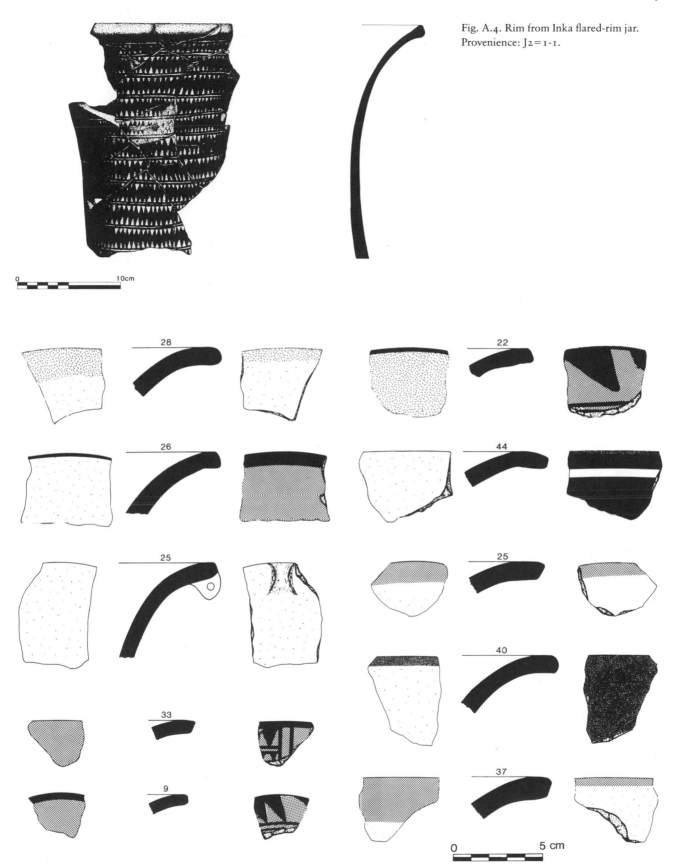

Fig. A.4. Rim from Inka flared-rim jar. Provenience: J2=1-1.

Fig. A.5. Inka flared-rim jars. Rim diameters (cm) appear above profiles. Proveniences (left to right): (first row) J5=13, J5=5; (second row) J5=4, J2=32; (third row) J5=2, J54=1; (fourth row) J5=7, J54=3; (fifth row) J5=3, J54=4.

Provincial Power in the Inka Empire

Fig. A.6. Geometric polychrome motifs from Inka flared-rim jars. Proveniences (left to right): (first row) J5=2, J63=4, J6=1, J5=10; (second row) J5=3, J5=4, J5=4, J2=T1; (third row) J5=2, J16=F1, J5=13, J5=13.

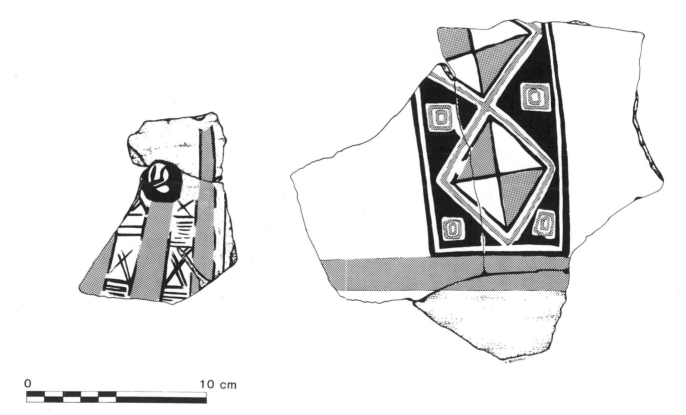

Fig. A.7. Geometric polychrome motifs from Inka flared-rim jars. A modeled feline motif is present in left figure. Proveniences: J2=3-54-2-3-1, J2=3-1-3-3-3-1/42.

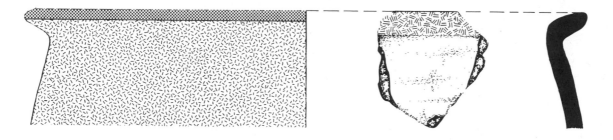

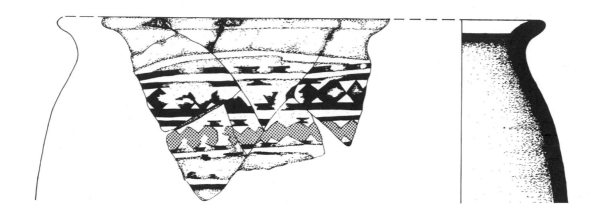

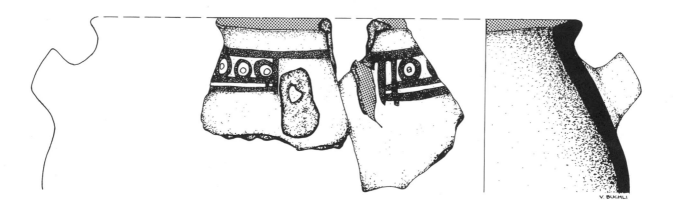

0   10cm

Fig. A.8. Inka closed bowls. Proveniences (top to bottom): J2=1-54-1-3-1, J2=1-55-1-3-2, J2=3-53-1-5-1.

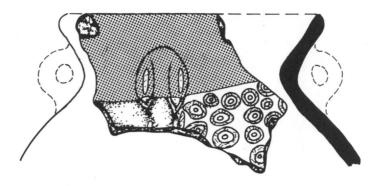

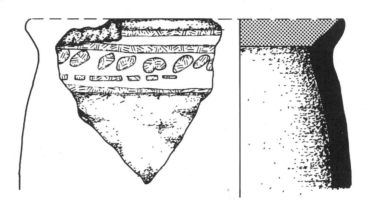

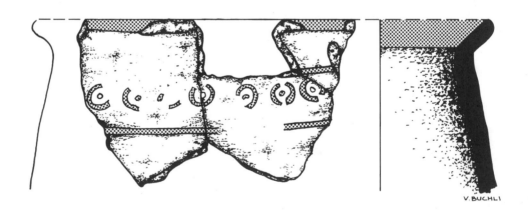

0   10cm

Fig. A.9. Inka open-mouth jar (top) and closed bowls. Proveniences (top to bottom): J2=1-55-1-4-2, J2=1-54-1-3-1, J2=1-54-1-3-1.

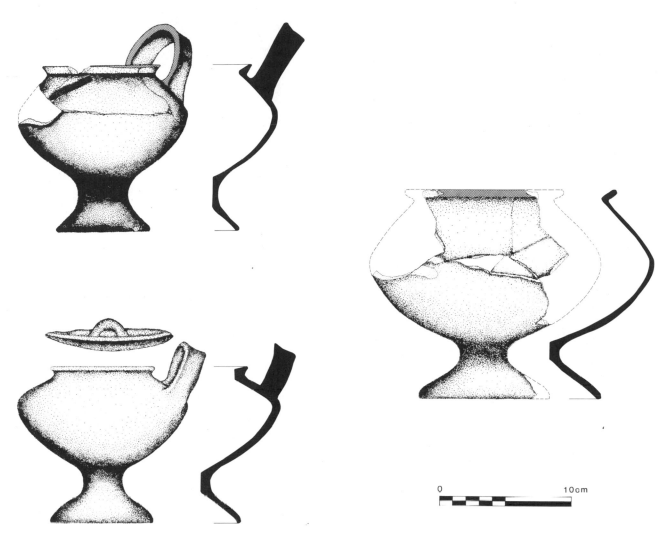

Fig. A.10. Reduced-fired Inka pedestal cooking vessels in micaceous paste. Proveniences: J54=8-51-1-1-1 (upper left), J2=F1-3-1 (lower left), J2=F1-3-1/4 (right).

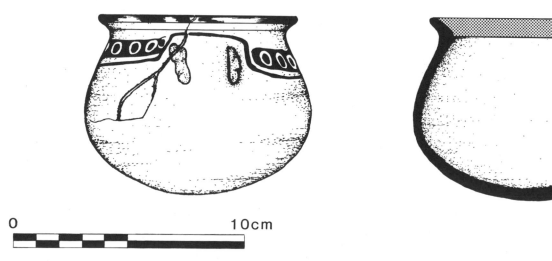

Fig. A.11. Small Inka closed bowl. Provenience: J2=3-1-4-3-1/47.

Provincial Power in the Inka Empire

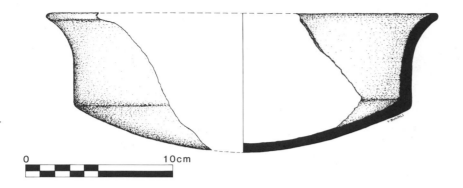

Fig. A.12. Carinated bowl. Provenience unavailable.

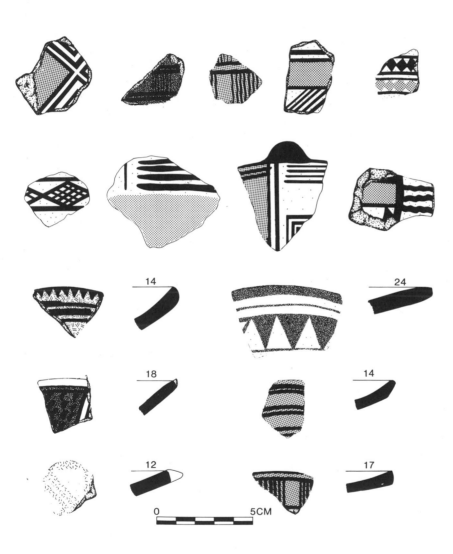

Fig. A.13. Inka polychrome plates. Rim diameters (cm) appear above profiles. Proveniences (left to right): (first row) J5=11, J5=2, J5=2, J5=9, J5=5; (second row) J1=T2, J54=2, J45=1, J5=13; (third row) J5=3, J5=5; (fourth row) J5=2, J5=7; (fifth row) J5=10, J5=10.

Notes

Chapter 1

1. See Luttwak's (1976) examination of the strategy of the Roman empire for a discussion of this issue.

Chapter 2

1. The means by which the Inkas implemented political power on the ground will be considered in detail later in Chapter 2 and in Chapter 7.

2. This approach assumes that explanations for human behavior must be sought in abstract, arbitrary, culture-specific notions of reality (Hodder 1982a; Shanks and Tilley 1984) and that modern interpretations of the past are fundamentally biased by the analyst's membership in a given society.

3. A related epistemological issue concerns the appropriateness of positivism as a method (Hodder 1982a; Wylie 1982, 1985). Although an extended discussion of positivism as the basis for explaining change in human society is inappropriate at this point, I do wish to underscore that I share the view that conclusions about causes of change in human society must be subject to verification. On this basis, explanations of systemic change based on recourse to the content of ideology are ultimately unsatisfactory (Price 1982). See Earle and Preucel (1987) for a review of and debate among adherents to various positions on this issue.

4. This appears to be a paraphrase of Sahlins and Service's thesis in *Evolution and Culture* (1960), in which simpler societies were seen as deriving from and building on more-complex ones.

5. The literature critical of world-systems theory is extensive and cannot be reasonably reviewed here. For summary views, see Schneider (1977), Nash (1981), Wolf (1982:22–23), Ragin and Chirot (1984), Kohl (1987a,b), Schortman and Urban (1987), Shannon (1989), and Chase-Dunn and Hall (1991).

6. For an excellent review of Marxist theories of imperialism, see Attewell (1984:207–51).

Chapter 3

1. Temperatures for Huancayo (3,150 m) from 1952 through 1960 show little annual variation, with the coldest temperatures occurring in the winter months of June and July, which had mean temperatures of 9.9° and 9.8° C, respectively. In the warmest months, January and February, the mean temperatures were 12.2° and 12.0° C, respectively (World Weather Records 1966:15). These temperatures are for a point about 150 m below the minimum elevation of the archaeological study area, but well within Wanka territory. Browman (1970:6) observes that the mean annual tempera-

ture for Jauja is only 0.5° C lower than that of Huancayo, but the higher reaches of the study have significantly lower temperatures. An averaged linear lapse rate of 0.65° per 100 m gain in elevation has been reported for the central Andes (Hastorf 1983:40). For the main Mantaro Valley, Franco et al. (1979:36) report that the likelihood of frost at 3,900 m is 10 percent and 21 percent during the critical agricultural months of October and November, respectively.

Peak rainfall occurs during January and February, with 90 percent of the annual precipitation falling between September and April (Franco et al. 1979:33). Jauja has a mean annual precipitation of 635 mm, and Huancayo 740 mm (Browman 1970:6). Annual variations in monthly precipitation of up to 40 percent can occur, creating further problems in the predictability of agriculture (World Weather Records 1966:145; see also Hastorf 1983:40). All microvariations in rainfall affect agricultural potential within the valley, because rain tends to fall in localized storms.

2. The principal investigator of UMARP in 1977–81 was Timothy Earle (University of California, Los Angeles). Terence D'Altroy, Christine Hastorf, and Catherine Scott (UCLA) served as graduate codirectors for this phase of research. In 1982–83 this same personnel constituted a team of co–principal investigators. Since 1983 Earle, D'Altroy (Columbia University), and Hastorf (University of Minnesota) have directed the project.

3. These documents have also been analyzed by Murra (1975:243–54), who focused on the organization of the mnemonic system itself. LeVine (1979) has additionally used the records to examine features of economic specialization of the two political groups Hatunxauxa and Lurinwanka.

Chapter 4

1. More-extensive treatments of pre-Inka Wanka society may be found in Espinoza Soriano (1969, 1971, 1973b), LeVine (1979), Earle et al. (1980, 1987), and LeBlanc (1981).

2. A number of problems in defining territory arose from the *mitmaqkuna* policy, in which massive numbers of subjects were resettled in a program of internal colonization. Under Spanish rule, displaced social groups tried to reassert control over lands traditionally held within their communities. The colonists, on their part, frequently tried to hold on to what were often prime resources (e.g., Espinoza Soriano 1969). Other native elites readily grasped the potential of the Spanish legal system to exploit the confusion after the Inka collapse and sometimes asserted specious claims to resources. The resulting litigation, of course, provides much of the useful information on territories and traditional rights of access to resources among indigenous groups. An example of the use of Spanish courts to settle conflicting claims among Xauxa elites is cited in Chapter 7 in a discussion of sociopolitical organization.

3. "[H]ay tres cabeceras de tres repartimientos en él, según se ha dicho, que el uno se llama *Santa Fee de Hátun Xauxa,* que fue el dicho nombre puesto por el Inca; porque antes del Inga se llamó *Xauxa,* y porque asentó allí algunos días, la llamó *Hátun Xauxa,* que quiere decir *Xauxa la grande;* y la otra cabecera de Hurin Guanca era antiguamente el pueblo de (*así*) que agora es de *San Jerónimo de Tunnan,* y al presente lo es el pueblo de la *Concepcíon de Achi* . . . y la cabecera del otro repartimiento de *Hanan Guanca* era el pueblo que agora se nombra *Santa Domingo de Cicaya"* (Vega 1965 [1582]: 168–69).

4. None of the linguistic divisions discussed here corresponds precisely to the borders of modern political territories, but for the purposes of this presentation the lack of correspondence is insignificant.

5. "Poco se difería esta lengua de los guancas a la común: como la de portugueses a la de los castellanos, digo la destos xauxas y la de los guancas" (Pizarro 1986 [1571]: ch. 13, p. 75). This edition of Pizarro's memoir has interpolated the words *"la de los"* before *"guancas,"* implying that the Xauxas and the Wankas spoke different languages, an idea that is not indicated in the original.

6. "Cada repartimiento de los tres deste valle tiene su lenguaje diferente uno de otro aunque todos se entienden y hablan la lengua general del de los Quichuas, ques la una de las tres lenguas generales deste reino" (Vega 1965 [1582]: 168).

7. Ethnic identity was commonly signaled in the Andes by distinctive dress. Such means of displaying ethnicity were given legal status by the Inka administration. Whether in military service or living in resettled colonies, members of subject groups were required to wear the clothing typical of their ethnic affiliation (Cobo 1956 [1653]: vol. 2, bk. 2, ch. 24, p. 113).

8. "Estos naturales de Xauxa son de dos parcialidades: unos que se llaman xauxas, y otros guancas. . . . Los Xauxas traen unas faxas coloradas alrededor de las caueças, de anchor de una mano; los guancas las traen negras. Su habla es la común que llaman quechuasimi" (Pizarro 1986 [1571]: ch. 13, p. 75).

9. "Estauan todos repartidos en tres parcialidades: aunques todos tenían y tienen por nombre los Guancas" (Cieza 1984 [1551]: ch. 84, p. 242).

10. See Chapter 7 for a more extended discussion of the decimal hierarchy and its correlation with other, native political structures.

11. "[The valley] was so populous: that at the time that the Spaniards entered it, they said and it is certain that there were more than thirty thousand Indians: and now I doubt there to be ten thousand" (Cieza 1984 [1551]: ch. 84, p. 242). ("Fue todo tan poblado: que al tiempo que los Españoles entraron en él, dizen y se tiene por cierto, que auía más de treynta mill Indios: y agora dubdo auer diez mill.")

12. "[E]n tiempos pasados del Inca eran mucho mas; porque el repartimiento de Hatun Xauxa se contaba tener entonces seis mill indios de guerra, y el repartimiento de

Hurin Guanca doce mill indios de guerra, y los Hanan Guancas nueve mill indios de guerra" (Vega 1965 [1582]: 167).

13. "[N]o paró hasta el valle de Xauxa, donde había alguna controversia y división sobre los límites y campos del valle, entre los mismos que dél eran señores. . . . Guayna Capac . . . mandó juntar los señores Alaya, Cucichaca, Guacaropa y entre ellos con equidad repartío los campos de la manera que hoy día lo tienen" (Cieza 1967 [1553]: ch. 64, p. 215).

14. Such consideration was not always the case. Salomon (1986) shows that the Inkas respected some existing borders in the Quito area while restructuring others.

15. There seems to be little evidence for the ayllu's existence in the northern or southern reaches of the empires, however (e.g., Salomon 1986; Lorandi and Boixadós 1987–88).

16. Salomon (1986:122) sounds a cautionary note concerning the Spaniards' tendency to adopt native terms into their legal jargon and retroactively to apply them to prehistoric societies. *Ayllu,* the Nahuatlism *tianguiz* (market), and the Arawak *cacique* (chief) are only three of the most prominent of the terms to appear in inappropriate contexts. Because of this, Salomon warns against assuming that the colonial documentation of native ayllu is sufficient evidence to conclude that the unit existed in any particular region in prehistory. Salomon's justifiable concerns are specifically raised with respect to the highlands of Ecuador, however, and probably do not apply in the Xauxa region. To judge from litigated claims to political authority and economic rights made in Spanish courts in the sixteenth century (Espinoza Soriano 1969, 1971; Cusichaca et al. 1971 [1561]), the term seems to be appropriate for the late prehistoric and early colonial Xauxas and Wankas.

17. For more-detailed evaluation of this material, see Espinoza Soriano (1971), LeVine (1979), LeBlanc (1981:356–73), and D'Altroy (1987).

18. "[A]ntes del Inca, nunca fueron sujetos a nadie, más de que en cada uno destos repartimientos tuvieron y conocieron por sus señores a los indios más valientes que hubo; como fueron; en *Hátun Xauxa,* a Auquiszapari y a Yaloparin, indios valientes; y en *Hurin Guanca* a Canchac Huyca y a Tacuri y a Añana, indios valientes; y en *Hanan Guanca,* a Patan Llocllachin y a Chavin [o Chauin]; y en los *Chongos,* Patan Cochache, indios valientes" (Vega 1965 [1582]: 169).

19. Because of the apparent standardization in reports of Late Intermediate sociopolitical organization in the Toledan visitas, it has been observed that the apparent pre-imperial disorder may have been exaggerated. The motivation behind the misleading representations may lie in the desire, on the part of both the Inkas and the Spaniards, to legitimize their rights to rule by bringing order to society. Considering the archaeological evidence to be discussed shortly, my inclination is to believe that the oral history describing societies in a state of flux fairly represented the situation.

20. ". . . cada parcialidad tenya un cinchecona y que en este valle de Xauxa hasta la mitad de los anaguancas los guardaua" (Toledo 1940a [1570]: 18).

21. Murra (1970:462) has observed that there was only a rough agreement between calendar age and the status of hatun runa and has cautioned that we should not conflate the European and Andean concepts of age and status. This point is well taken. Across the population, however, making the rough correlation serves the useful purpose of allowing us to examine changing relationships between taxpayers and dependents.

22. "[A]ntes del Inca, . . . no salían fuera deste valle a pelear, sino era, dentro del valle, los de la una banda del río que por él pasa con los indios de la otra" (Vega 1965 [1582]: 169).

23. This section only summarizes the major trends of the Late Intermediate Period occupation of the region. The reader is referred to Earle et al. (1980, 1987), LeBlanc (1981), and Hastorf (1983) for more-extended treatments of the archaeology of the Wanka I and II phases.

24. The methods used to estimate population size from archaeological evidence are too complex to explain in detail here (see Earle et al. 1987:8–10; Parsons and Earle n.d.). In brief, however, each residential compound (containing two structures, estimated from archaeological data) was assumed to house one household of about six individuals; the density of residential compounds for each site was estimated archaeologically; and an occupation figure ranging from 60 to 100 percent was assumed for residential compounds at each site, depending on the site's length of occupation.

25. It should be observed, however, that the Wanka I settlement area at Hatunmarca is not yet well defined. Neither can we be sure that public architecture was absent at the site, because the Wanka II and III construction activities have buried the evidence. For present purposes, the Wanka I component at Hatunmarca has been taken to be comparable to the other known contemporaneous sites, for lack of definitive information to the contrary.

26. See Earle et al. (1987:7–10) for a discussion of the procedures used to derive these estimates. The figures presented here differ somewhat from those presented in earlier publications, because of reassessment of residential site sizes.

27. LeBlanc (1981:271) has estimated that at least 20 to 40 percent of the Yanamarca Valley population must have immigrated to have achieved a population 4.7 times that of Wanka I.

28. A series of other papers and publications examines the domestic and political economies before and under Inka rule. Among them are Costin (1985, 1986), Costin et al. (1989), D'Altroy (1986), D'Altroy and Earle (1985), Earle (1985), Earle and D'Altroy (1982, 1989), Earle et al. (1987), Hastorf (1983, 1985, 1986), Hastorf and DeNiro (1985), Hastorf and Earle (1985), Russell (1988), and Sandefur (1988).

29. The statuses of *elite* and *commoner* were initially sam-

pling categories of residential compounds, defined on the basis of compound location, quality of masonry, size of buildings, size of compound, and number of buildings per compound. Subsequent analyses have shown that these two may represent parts of a continuum with clear differences between the upper and lower ends (e.g., Costin and Earle 1989; D'Altroy and Hastorf n.d.).

30. Dean Arnold (1975, 1985) has suggested that the development of community-based cottage industries in ceramic manufacture tend to be concentrated in locations that are simultaneously rich in clay resources and agriculturally marginal. Although the details of the argument are outside the present study, these two basic features do describe the location of a number of ceramic-producing settlements in the Upper Mantaro region (see Hagstrum 1985, 1986; Costin 1986).

31. To create these plots, the matrix of raw values of indexes for the households was transformed into a matrix of rank dissimilarities, using the Brainerd-Robinson correlation coefficient modified to be calculated on rank values (LeBlanc 1981:187). This calculation was made using the SAS procedure PROX; the Minkowski metric power and root values were set at 1. The resulting matrix was then used as input into the SAS multidimensional scaling procedure ALSCAL, which uses Kruskal's (1964) least-squares monotonic transformation (Joyner 1983). A Euclidean distance model was used to generate the distances between points for the plots. The three-dimensional plot was created using SAS PROC G3D.

The choice of a rank-dissimilarity coefficient was intended to be a conservative approach to compensate for three features of the data set. First, it is not clear if the values produced by the indexes follow normal or other well-understood distributions, especially because two of them are based on ratios. A second, associated problem stems from the very high values for some household compounds for some indexes; an example may be found in the blade production index value for J41=7. Third, because the sample that was used for these calculations included only the securely defined occupation contexts (excluding, e.g., construction fill and disturbed contexts), some index values were based on a very few artifacts. Ranking the households within each index reduced the effects of these problems.

Chapter 5

1. In this analysis, I draw in part on previous studies of the Inka military (e.g., Bram 1941; Rowe 1946:203–9, 274–82; Rawls 1979:116–74; Murra 1986; Hyslop 1990:146–90). Summary accounts of the sequence of Inka conquests are provided by Rowe (1946), Brundage (1963), and Katz (1972). The best original sources are Cabello Valboa (1951 [1586]), Cobo (1956 [1653]), Sarmiento (1960 [1572]), Murúa (1962 [1590–1600]), Cieza (1967 [1533]), and

Betanzos (1987 [1551]). The military tactics used by the Inkas to conquer the Andes have been ably described elsewhere (e.g., Bram 1941; Rowe 1946:203–9, 274–82; Rawls 1979:116–56) and need not be reviewed here.

2. The disruptive wars of succession following the death of an Inka ruler posed an additional problem, one that increased the potential damage of other threats (see Conrad and Demarest 1984; Murra 1986).

3. See Van Creveld (1977:5–39) for parallels in European siege warfare of the seventeenth century.

4. Rawls (1979:123) has observed that the smaller estimates were often reported by witnesses describing events that occurred in their lifetimes.

5. Among the early sources that include accounts of the conquest are Cabello Valboa (1951 [1586]: 319), Cobo (1956 [1653]: vol. 2, bk. 2, ch. 13, p. 81), Sarmiento (1960 [1572]: ch. 44, p. 249), Murúa (1962: vol. 1, ch. 21, p. 51), Cieza (1967 [1553]: ch. 49, pp. 162–64; 1984 [1551]: ch. 84, p. 243), Garcilaso (1960 [1609]), and the visita of Toledo (1940a [1570]: 18–36). Care needs to be taken not to treat all accounts as though they independently corroborate one another, because of the chroniclers' penchant for borrowing freely without acknowledgment. Rowe (1985), for example, has published a 1569 deposition, filed in Cuzco by the descendants of Thupa Yupanki, that may well have been a principal source of information for at least the first three of the authors cited above. Nonetheless, the accounts that drew from Cuzco-based informants (e.g., Sarmiento, Murúa) and from Mantaro Valley informants (e.g., Cieza, Toledo, and Vega 1965 [1582]) arose from separate oral traditions and may be treated as essentially independent of one another. Where they corroborate one another, we may be reasonably sure that the accounts are as close a representation of the truth as one might expect, given the chronic problems with translation and codification of history.

6. "[A] la onzena pregunta dixo queste testigo oyo dezir al dicho su padre e aguelo que quando vino el dicho ynga a conquistar y señorear esta tierra se puso en un cerro en este rrepartimyento con la gente que traya que serian diez myll yndios de guerra que en su lengua se llama este número uno y que ally se fue su visaguelo deste testigo que se llamaua apoguala el qual le dio la obediencia y lo mochó y que auia lleuado consigo diez yndios soldados por quel hera uno de los cincheconas deste valle y auia dicho a los yndios que le rrespetauan por ser su sinchecona que se estuuiesen ascondidos por quel queria ver sy el ynga les hazya algun mal tratamyento o le mataua e que ansy oyo dezir a los que dicho tiene que el dicho visaguelo llego a hablar al dicho ynga y a subjetarsele y que los demas yndios que llebaua consigo llegaron con el y los otros se quedaron ascondidos y el dicho topa ynga oyo dezir este testigo que auia dado al dicho su visaguelo unas camysetas y mantas galanas y unos vasos en que bebiese que llaman entrellos aquilla e que con esto auia vuelto a los yndios questaban escondidos los quales su auian holgado mucho de ver lo quel dicho ynga auia dado el dicho

su visaguelo e que quando le vieron uenir entendieron que hera el ynga que los venya a matar e quando le conoscieron que hera su cinchecona se holgaron mucho e como les hallo comyendo [sic] [¿con miedo?] les dixo que no temyesen e que fuesen con él a darle obidencia al ynga por que le auia preguntado por ellos e ansy el dicho cinchecona su visaguelo deste testigo lleuo consigo todos sus yndios al dicho ynga y le dixo qué queria que hiziese dellos y el dicho ynga le dixo que fuese con el hasta quito e que oyo dezir que allí le dieron la obidencia e que a otros que no le obedescian ny le uenian a mochar les hazia guerra e les subjetaua matando a algunos dellos e tomandoles sus tierras e a otros que uenyan a darle la obidencia los rescibia e questo es lo que oyo dezir de lo contenido en la dicha pregunta" (Toledo 1940a [1570]: 19–20).

7. "Los del valle de Xauxa, sabida la venida de los enemigos, mostraron temor y procuraron favor de sus parientes y amigos y en el templo suyo de Guarivilca hicieron grandes sacrificios al demonio que allí respondía. Venídoles los socorros, como ellos fuesen muchos, porque dicen que había más de cuarenta mill hombres a donde agora no sé si hay doce mill, los capitanes del Inca llegaron hasta ponerse encima del valle y deseaba sin guerra ganar las gracias de los Guancas y que quisiesen ir al Cuzco a reconocer al rey por Señor; y así, es público que les enviaron mensajeros. Mas, no aprovechando nada, vinieron a las manos y se dio una gran batalla en que dicen que murieron muchos de una parte y otra, mas que los del Cuzco quedaron por vencedores; y que siendo de gran prudencia Lloque Yupanqui no consintió hacer daño en el valle, evitando el robo, mandando soltar los cativos; tanto, que los Guancas, conocido el beneficio y con la clemencia que usaban teniéndolos vencidos, vinieron a hablar y prometieron de vivir dende en adelante por la ordenanza de los reyes del Cuzco y tributar con lo que hobiese en su valle; y pasando sus pueblos por las laderas, los sembraron, sin lo repartir, hasta que el rey Guayna Capac señaló a cada parcialidad lo que había de tener" (Cieza 1967 [1553]: ch. 49, pp. 163–64).

8. Whether the "Guancas" were from the Mantaro Valley or from Guancabamba, in the northern Andes, is open to question, given the current evidence.

9. ". . . puso guarniciones ordinarias con soldados mitimaes, para que estuviesen por frontera" (Cieza 1967 [1553]: ch. 64, p. 216).

10. Rawls (1979:122) suggests that only 10 to 20 percent of the available manpower would have been mobilized at any given time, but there is some evidence that the service could be more burdensome (Murra 1986).

11. See Van Creveld (1977), Engels (1978), and Ferrill (1985) for a more exhaustive consideration of these issues. A more thorough examination of Inka logistical problems and strategies may be found in D'Altroy (n.d.).

12. At least 10 estimates of the size of the Inka army are available, ranging from 50,000 to 400,000 (Hemming 1970:190, 572–73).

13. Murra (1980 [1956]: 53) suggests that Zárate may have exaggerated the number of llamas present, but that it must have far exceeded the number of soldiers. This conclusion is apparently unwarranted, however. Given the haste with which the Quiteñans retired—they burned the excess cloth that could not be carried—it is unclear whether they salvaged many of their animals or left most of them behind.

14. Haggard and McClean (1941:79) set 1 libra to equal 0.46006272 kg for Mexico and Spain.

15. Weights for porters were standardized at 59 kg (Greska et al. 1982:7), which is higher than the 55 kg average weight for adult males of the Nuñoa district, Department of Puno (Thomas 1973:44). Both weights are likely higher than the weights of late prehistoric males.

16. These distances conform fairly well to a variety of estimates of the distances that armies can travel on a daily basis. Crown (1974:265, n. 117) cites Clines (1973) for the following estimates: Egyptian army under Thutmose III, 24 km/day, and under Ramses II, 21.6 km/day; Babylonian army, 29.8 km/day; and Roman army, 23.4–31.2 km/day. He also cites Saggs (1963) as estimating 48 km/day for Assyrian infantry. Hassig (1988:56–66) provides a comparable range of estimates from various sources, and estimates 19-32 km/day for Aztec armies. Engels (1978:20) estimates 31.2 km/day for the fastest march executed by Alexander's Macedonian army, which was noted for its speed of movement. Most of Alexander's marches were considerably less rapid.

17. Engels (1978:131–34) evaluates a comparable problem for Alexander's army and discusses the consequent difficulties introduced into the battle of Issus.

18. Thomas's detailed evaluation of caloric consumption permits a breakdown by numerous variables, among them age, sex, and levels of exertion (see also Leonard 1987). These values have been modified here to account for various kinds of activities (Durnin and Passmore 1967; Leslie et al. 1984; D'Altroy n.d.). Thomas's mean yearly consumption estimate of 2,094 kcal/day for adult Nuñoa males is considerably below that suggested for premodern armies from other parts of the world. If the additional expenditures are added on for armies on the march or for porters carrying substantial loads (Leatherman et al. 1983), the values are closer but still not precisely comparable. Hassig (1985:20–21, 1988:64), for example, estimates 3,800 kcal/day for Aztec soldiers, a value that is comparable to the 3,600 kcal/day estimated by Engels (1978:123) for Alexander the Great's men, based on U.S. Army figures. Van Creveld (1977:21, 24) reports a basic ration of 2 pounds/day of bread supplemented by meat, beans, or other foods containing protein for the soldiers in Napoleon's army. He also cites a total ration of 3 pounds/day for the French soldier under Louvois in the mid-seventeenth century. As will be shown shortly, Hassig's and Van Creveld's figures are essentially identical. Some of the difference between the Andean figures and those of other situations (e.g., Europe, modern U.S. Army) is at-

tributable to lower body weight for the Andean peoples, but it is difficult to ascertain why the other estimates are higher than the empirically measured Nuñoa values. The detail and nature of Thomas's study make it the most appropriate source for the exercise here. The conformity of the empirical values and the model values calculated by Leslie et al. (1984) for this same population provides support for acceptance of the values derived here.

19. Whether these loads corresponded to the load that an individual animal or human porter could carry is unclear.

Chapter 6

1. See Hassig (1985:100–101) and Chapter 2 for discussions of this strategic approach.

2. Hyslop's (1984) intensive study of long sections of the road system provides a detailed description of its organization and construction and of the support facilities built along it (see also Regal 1936, 1972; Rowe 1946:229–33; Salomon 1986:151–58).

3. The issue of the distribution of state lands and storage facilities in the Upper Mantaro will be explored further in Chapter 8.

4. Because the features of Inka settlements in this region are described in detail elsewhere, I will summarize only their principal characteristics here. The information is drawn mainly from studies by Rowe (1944), Morris (1972b), Gasparini and Margolies (1980), González Carré et al. (1981), Hyslop (1984, 1985:275–93), and Morris and Thompson (1985). Readers are referred to other sources for information on other kinds of imperial facilities known from elsewhere in the empire, such as the military installations found throughout the highlands of Ecuador (Meyers 1976; Salomon 1986: 148–51); royal rural retreats, such as Chinchero, outside Cuzco (Alcina Franch 1976); or religious facilities, such as that at Raqchi (Gasparini and Margolies 1980:234–54; La Lone and La Lone 1987).

5. The complexities of this conceptual system are sometimes obscure and subject to debate, but it seems that the spatial arrangement can be viewed from at least two perspectives, in accordance with varying concepts of Inka social structure (Wachtel 1973:71–94). See Morris (1990) for a detailed elaboration of the relationship between the zeque system and the layout of Huánuco Pampa.

6. Gasparini and Margolies (1980:103) have alternatively suggested that the dimensions of the plazas were proportioned to represent symbolically the power that had conquered the territory. It is not clear what the data are that support their argument.

7. Garcilaso (1960 [1609]: vol. 2, bk. 6, ch. 10, p. 207), who most likely copied from Cieza, used the term *Llacsapallanca*. See Chapter 4 for a discussion of the possible pre-imperial relationships between Laxapalanga and other subregions within the Wanka domain.

8. ". . . le daban indios para poner por mitimaes en Jauja y en Llajapallanga" (Diez de San Miguel 1964 [1567]: 81).

9. "[C]uentan que fueron hechos grandes sacrificios en Pachacama por Tupac Inca Yupanqui y grandes fiestas, las cuales pasadas dio la vuelta al Cuzco por un camino que se le hizo, que va a salir al valle de Xauxa, que atraviesa por la nevada sierra de Pariacaca, que no es poco de ver y notar su grandeza y cuán grandes escaleras tiene" (Cieza 1967 [1553]: ch. 59, p. 196).

Cieza (1967 [1553]: ch. 15, p. 46) also comments as follows: "Those people who may read this book and who have been in Peru [may] behold the road that goes from Lima to Xauxa through the rugged mountains of Huarochirí and through the snowy mountains of Pariacaca, and those who listen to them will understand if what they saw is not what I describe." ("Los que leyeran este libro y hobieren estado en el Perú miren el camino que va desde Lima a Xauxa por las sierras tan ásperas de Huarochiri y por la montaña nevada de Pariacaca y entenderán, los que a ellos lo oyeren, si es más lo ellos vieron que no lo que yo escribo.")

10. Each of the tampu in Guaman Poma's list is accompanied by a symbol designating the status and activities of the installation. Translations of the symbols provided by Guaman Poma may be found in Murra and Adorno (1980 [1614]). See Hyslop (1984:279) for illustration and interpretation of the symbols.

11. A more recent archaeological survey in the area of Xulcatambo indicates that the area of the Inka site is substantially larger than that recorded by LeVine (Bruce Owen, pers. com. 1987).

12. "Este inga tenía dos gobernantes generales en toda la tierra, llamados *suyoyoc apo,* el uno residía en Xauxa y el otro en Tiaguanaco, pueblo de Collasuyo" (Sarmiento 1960 [1572]: ch. 52, p. 257).

13. "Desde el ualle de Xauxa, yndios Guancas, gouernó y rreynó este dicho *Ynga*" (Guaman Poma 1980 [1614]: /116 [116], p. 94).

14. "El pueblo de Xauxa es grande y está en un valle muy hermoso, y es tierra templada: passa un rio poderoso por la una parte del pueblo. Es abundoso de bastimentos e ganados; está hecho a manera de pueblo de Espana, muy junto e sus calles bien traçadas. Hay a vista del otros uchos pueblos sus subjetos, y era tanta la gente que paresció allí de la del mesmo pueblo e sus comaracas, que otra semejante en un solo pueblo no se ha visto en Indias, porque al parescer de quantos españoles lo vieron se juntaban cada día de la plaça principal mas de cient mill animas, y estaban los mercados e otras plaças e calles del mesmo pueblo tan llenos de gente, que parescia cosa de maravilla su grandissima moltitud. Avía hombres que tenían cargo de contar aquella gente cada día, para saber los que venían a servir a la gente de guerra: otros tenian cargo de mirar todo lo que entraba en el dicho pueblo" (Estete 1917 [1532–33]: 96–97).

15. "La plaza es grande e tien un cuarto de legua. . . . [E]s verdad que había sobre cient mill animas. . . . Este pueblo

de Xauxa es muy bueno e muy vistoso e de muy buenas salidas llanas" (Pizarro 1959 [1533]: 90).

16. "En todas estas partes auían grandes aposentos de los Ingas: aunque los más principales estauan en el principio del valle en la parte que llaman Xauxa: porque auía vn grande cercado, donde estauan fuertes aposentos y muy primos de piedra: y casa de mugeres del sol: y templo muy riquíssimo: y muchos depósitos llenos de todas las cosas que podían ser auias. Sin lo qual auía grande número de plateros, que labrauan vasos y vasijas de plata y de oro para el servicio de los Ingas y ornamentos del templo. Estauan estantes más de ocho mill Indios para el servicio del templo, y de los palacios de los señores. Los edificios todos eran de piedra. Lo alto de las casas y aposentos eran grandíssimas vigas, y por cobertura paja larga" (Cieza 1984 [1551]: ch. 84, pp. 242–43).

17. "Les ruines de la plaine, au milieu desquelles s'élèvent aujourd'hui les huttes du hameau de *Tambo*, sont des constructions, probablement plus grandes que n'ont jamais été celles de Tarmatambo. Par leur disposition générales, elles appartiennent pourtant au même ordre architectural. Là on remarque, non seulement les restes d'une résidence royale, de palais à grandes galeries, à vastes cours, mais encore des monuments constituant un important sanctuaire. Le centre était formé par un terre-plein semblable à celui que nous avons vu à Huamachuco, et sur lequel les Espagnols ont établi, comme on devait s'y entendre, une chapelle plus délabrée que les ruines du sanctuaire auquel ce temple minuscule a succédé" (Wiener 1880:242–43).

18. See, for example, the studies of Huánuco Pampa (Morris and Thompson 1985), Pumpu (LeVine 1985), Chucuito (Alcina Franch 1976), and Inkawasi (Hyslop 1985). It is regrettable that a project that was funded to undertake extensive excavations at Hatun Xauxa in 1988 had to be suspended. It is our hope that conditions will permit this work to be conducted in the near future.

19. "[H]abían enviado aquellos seiscientos hombres para acabar de quemar la ciudad de Xauxa, habiendo quemado ya la otra mitad ya siete u ocho dias, y entonces quemaron un edificio grande que estaba en la plaza y otras cosas a vista de la gente de la ciudad con muchas ropas y maiz, para que los españoles no lo aprovecharon" (Sancho 1917 [1532–33]: 141).

20. ". . . terraplén sostenido por gruesos muros de piedras poligonales y esquinas de granito" (García 1942:97).

21. See Menzel (1959) and Gasparini and Margolies (1980) for a description of usnu at coastal centers.

22. These expectations have been slightly modified from the original propositions laid out at the inception of research (D'Altroy 1981). The principal changes have been the rephrasing of some statements concerning the expected relationships between architecture and ceramic deposits. In particular, the lack of ceramics recovered archaeologically from kallanka at other state installations (e.g., Huánuco Pampa; see Morris and Thompson 1985) has caused a reconsideration of the use of some sectors of Hatun Xauxa.

23. Sherds attributable to the Wankas were 1.3 percent, or 78 of 5,831 diagnostic sherds.

24. An additional issue, which has not yet been resolved, concerns the Inka practices of disposing of waste products. If the Inkas systematically kept certain sectors of the settlement relatively free of debris, as appears to have been the case with kallanka, that practice raises problems with respect to interpreting the activities conducted. However, the concentrations of pottery in the zones of best architectural preservation alleviate some of these problems.

25. See Chapter 9 for a comparison of the size distribution of flared-rim jars at Hatun Xauxa with that of similar vessels from the Wanka III town of Hatunmarca.

26. Recall that surface collections were taken as circles of 10 m in diameter. Sample size is thus a direct measure of surface density. It should be noted that this regression procedure does not rigorously separate the principal elements of diversity measures: evenness, richness, and heterogeneity (see Bobrowsky and Ball 1989). The regression is most appropriate to assessing richness in the set of samples.

27. Analysis of the additive nature—with respect to vessel types—of the increasingly large collections is presented elsewhere (D'Altroy n.d.). In brief, however, flared-rim jars were consistently present in any collection, followed by simple plates and low-necked ollas.

28. "[S]e había ido con la gente de guerra, e había pasado un río que estaba junto cabe el pueblo, de una puente de red" (Pizarro 1959 [1533]: 90).

29. "Puentes de crisnejas grandes que abía en tienpo del Ynga, como es de Bombom, Xauxa . . . y otros puentes de palos y balsas que los yndios balseros lo lleuan, como en los llanos y en el Collau y Cangallo y Uancayo. . . . Y después el señor bizorrey marqués de Cañete el biejo mandó hazer de cal y canto la puente de Lima y la puente de Xauxa y la puente de Ango Yaco" (Guaman Poma 1980 [1614]: /357 [359], p. 329).

30. "Caminó el Gobernador dos días por un valle muy abajo, a la orilla del río de Xauxa que era muy deleitable y poblada de muchos lugares, y al tercer día llegó a un puente de redes que está sobre el dicho río, el cual habían quemado los soldados indios después que hubieron pasado" (Sancho 1917 [1532–33]: 147).

31. See note 16, above.

Chapter 7

1. For reviews of early commentators, see Rowe (1946), Moore (1958), Pease (1978), Murra (1980 [1956]), and Porras Barrenechea (1986).

2. I thank Brian Bauer for providing me a copy of his dissertation (1990) immediately upon its conclusion. It has enlightened me considerably on the nature of the Cuzco and Paruro regions just before and during the imperial era.

3. For lengthy treatments of the overall administrative

strategies, see Rowe (1946), Moore (1958), Zuidema (1964), Wachtel (1977), Schaedel (1978), and Rostworowski (1988).

4. This sort of dilemma has been described previously for the Roman empire (Luttwak 1976), in which support of client kings created powerful border polities that were transformed into threats to the empire's stability. The readiest solution, in the Roman situation, was to convert the clients into provinces and its residents into potential imperial citizens. This gave the imperial core greater control over the clients at the same time that the new provinces gained a greater interest in imperial stability. The principal cost of the conversion, from the Roman perspective, was an increased demand on core resources to ensure the peace.

5. Silverblatt (1988) makes the intriguing argument that the use of kin terms in the imperial administration can be seen as an effort by the Inkas to assert a cultural sanction for their imposed leadership.

6. It has been observed that these quarters corresponded generally to major ecological zones—Antisuyu being the tropical forest and montaña, Chinchasuyu the north coast and highlands, Kollasuyu the altiplano, and Cuntisuyu the south coast and highlands (see Schaedel 1978). The Xauxa region fell in Chinchasuyu, although some affiliated montaña villages could conceivably have been located in Antisuyu.

7. Rowe (1946:262) proposes that the ideal division of a province would have included two saya, based on the Inka pattern of dual divisions. He also suggests that a highly populous province, such as Wanka Wamaní, could be divided into three saya if each of two divisions would exceed 10,000 taxpayers. Wedin (1965:55–61) has strongly attacked this proposal, arguing that the divisions of 10,000 were military, not civil.

8. See Wachtel (1977:75–81) for a shortened, more accessible discussion.

9. See also Cock (1977), Netherly (1978), and Salomon (1986) for examples of duality in the southern Peruvian highlands, the north coast of Peru, and the central highlands of Ecuador, respectively.

10. The possibility that the decimal system was borrowed from Chimor, the last major polity to fall to the Inkas (ca. 1470), suggests that shortness of time may have also prevented the installation of the system in many areas (see Zuidema 1964:221).

11. Several other important functions were delegated to decimal or other local elites on the state's behalf elsewhere, for which there is no corroborative evidence for the Xauxa area. Among them are the collection of foodstuffs for the army and state officials. Parallel to this function was the production of support required for the corvée laborers working on state projects (Murra 1975:33–34). On occasion the decimal system also supervised specialized activities, such as weaving and mining (Morris 1974; Murra 1975:145–70). Finally, these elites administered justice to the local populace.

12. Numerous other variations on Inka-subject political relations have been described in other regions of the empire. Among the more important are those of the semi-autonomous highland kingdoms of the Lake Titicaca region, the Lupaqa being the best-understood of these (see Murra 1968).

13. See Moore (1958) for a detailed discussion of Inka law and subject rights.

14. The principal source of information on political organization is the 1570 visita (Toledo 1940a). Supplementary data are available in a 1563 Wanka petition submitted in 1571 to Toledo (1940b) and petitions to the Audiencia Real in 1558–61 (Espinoza Soriano 1971), as well as in a brief synthetic inspection of 1582 (Vega 1965).

15. "Esto dicho repartimiento de Hurin Guanca tiene hacia la montaña que llaman Andes, un pueblo nombrado San Juan Bautista de Uchubamba. . . . [E]n éste están reducidos otros pocos indios del repartimiento de Hátun Xauxa y del repartimiento de Hanan Guanca" (Vega 1965 [1582]: 173).

16. "Mango Inca . . . con muchos indios de guerra que trajo de Losandes vino a unos pueblos subjetos al dicho Valle de Xauxa en especial Andamarca que es donde tiene sus chacaras de ají el dicho don Jeronimo el cual Mango Inca le robó la tierra le quemó los pueblos e le mató muchos indios los mas valientes del dicho Valle" (Guacrapáucar 1971c [1560]: 223).

17. "[Thupa Inka] hizo los caciques que llaman de uno que son diez myll indios y de piscaguaranga que son de cinco myll yndios e de guarangas que son de myll yndios e de piscapachaca que son quinyentos yndios y de pachaca que son cien yndios para que los gobernasen" (Toledo 1940a [1570]: 36).

18. "[S]uplicaua que en continuación de la costumbre quel dicho ynga tenía le hiziese merced de le dar el dúho e vestidos que por insignias de señorío el dicho ynga solía dar a semejantes caciques de diez myll indios como el hera e auia de ser" (Toledo 1940b [1571]: 96).

19. ". . . don felipe pomacao prencipal de la pachaca del pueblo de santana ques en este dicho rrepartimyento de los luringuancas" (Toledo 1940a [1570]: 26).

20. "[D]ejieron que nunca estos testigos que el dicho don Cristobal Cargua Alaya, fuese cacique del dicho aillo, sobre que se litiga, sino que fueron caciques de cien indios del dicho aillo, sus antepasados del dicho don Cristobal" (Espinoza Soriano 1969 [1598]: doc. 4, p. 68).

21. ". . . el duho e vestidos que por insignias de señorío el dicho ynga solia dar a semejantes caciques de diez myll yndios como el lo hera e auia de ser . . . y su Excelencia dio al dicho don Carlos y don hernando de su mano dos pares de ropas de la que los dichos yndios suelen traer para que las tuuiesen por insignias del dicho cargo e ymbistitura" (Toledo 1940b [1571]: 96–98).

22. "[E]l dicho topa ynga . . . auia dado al dicho su visaguelo unas camysetas y mantas galanas y unos vasos en que bebiese" (Toledo 1940a [1570]: 20).

23. The possibility also exists that Surichaca took on this appellation as a way of promoting his status in the eyes of the Spaniards—an occasional practice among native nobility.

24. ". . . e que mandaua e mandó a los dichos yndios que presente estaban e a los demas de la dicho prouincia de hanaguanca que oviesen e tuuiesen al dicho don carlos por cacique principal y le guardasen y hiziesen guardar todas las onrras preheminencias franquezas y ecensiones e otras cosas que por rrazon del dicho cargo deuia y le deuen ser guardadas y que no le pusiesen en ello impedimiento alguno porque Su Excelencia lo rrescibía desde luego al uso y exercicio del dicho oficio y le mandaua e mandó que hiziese todo buen tratamyento a los dichos naturales e no les lleuase mas tributos de los que fueron obligados a dar" (Toledo 1940b [1571]: 97).

25. "[Q]uando algunos cincheconas yuan con los yndios que le rrespetauan a dar la obedencia al dicho topa ynga yupanqui, les hazía caciques y señores de los yndios y que a los que no querían venir de paz y los conquistaua los ponía caciques de su mano que hera a los quel quería y a los capitanes que mejor le seruían y entre otros indios los ponía caciques y señores como quería de los capitanes que le servían y de otros allegados asy syn otro respecto" (Toledo 1940a [1570]: 25–26).

26. "[N]o les suscedían sus hijos en estos cacicazgos ny otros parientes mas de que quando alguno moría sy los yngas vían que tenía abilidad algun hijo suyo le nombraua en el cacicazgo" (Toledo 1940a [1570]: 29).

27. "[A] la segunda pregunta dixo queste testigo no se acuerda de los que pasaua antes que el ynga gouernase por que no lo vio mas de auerlo oydo dezir a su padre guamachiguala y a su aguelo Xaxaguaman que fueron caciques nombrados por el ynga que conquisto esta tierra" (Toledo 1940a [1570]: 17–18).

28. "A la primera pregunta dixo ques de hedad de nouenta e tres o nouenta e quatro años e que deciende de linaje de caciques que hizo topa ynga yupanqui" (Toledo 1940a [1570]: 30).

29. Similar organization has been documented for many other places, such as Jequetepeque, on the north coast (Netherly 1978:120–21); the Lupaqa region (Espinoza Soriano 1975; Julien 1982); and Huánuco (Diez de San Miguel 1964 [1567]: 323–32).

30. Dunbar Temple (1942) has reconstructed the genealogy of this family from the Inka era into the eighteenth century. The account provides an excellent example of the maintenance of traditional status positions by native elites under colonial rule.

31. ". . . que el dicho don Francisco Sulichaque es cacique principal deste tiempo e que el dicho don Cristobal es su pariente e lo mismo el dicho don Diego Ñaupari" (Cusichaca et al. 1971 [1561]: 345).

32. The attribution of the name *Guanca* to the El Quinche mitmaqkuna raises questions as to whether the last individual was actually related to the others. One possibility is that the use of the ethnic group's name was an example of the application of the term *Wanka* to all peoples from the Upper Mantaro Valley—a circumstance that occurred repeatedly in the early documentary sources.

33. "E vido este testigo que el dicho Sulichac cacique principal que a la sazon era del dicho repartimiento envió a Caxamarca todo lo susodicho con el dicho don Diego Ñaupari con trescientos indios poco mas o menos para que lo diesen al dicho marques" (Cusichaca et al. 1971 [1561]: 345).

34. "A Vuestra Alteza pedimos y suplicamos en los dichos nombres y de los demás principales e indios del dicho Valle lo mande ver y tasar y que se nos pague sobre que pedimos justicia y costas" (Guacrapáucar 1971 [1558]: 201).

35. The nature of the accounting system and the role of the native population in managing imperial stores are examined in Chapter 8.

36. "[D]espués de salidos, juntos los señores, iban los quipos de las cuentas y por ellos, si uno había gastado más que otro, los que menos habían proveído lo pagaban, de tal suerte que iguales quedasen todos" (Cieza 1967 [1553]: ch. 12, p. 37).

37. Rowe (1946:254) describes the ayllu as a theoretically endogamous kin group with descent in the male line, holding a communal territory (cf. Moore 1958:22). Murra (1980 [1956]: 29, 191), citing González Holguín (1952 [1608]: 48), underscores the variable extent of the ayllu and notes that although "a settlement controlling certain fields was a llacta," land "was owned and cultivated 'ayllu by ayllu.'" In the view of Zuidema (1964:26–27), the ayllu "was the group of all people who were [bilaterally] descended from one particular ancestor." Zuidema's argument extends beyond the limits of the Xauxa area data, but the perception of the ayllu as a corporate, territorial, kin-based group with patrilateral inheritance seems to describe the Wankas, as is shown later in Chapter 7.

38. Most of the ayllu affiliations can be seen in the following listing of informants in the earliest of the litigation published by Espinoza Soriano (1969 [1571]: doc. 1, p. 54): "(1) Don Juan Turimaya, del ayllo de Jauja-Collana, que dijo tener setenta años, y tal pareció por su aspecto. (2) Alonso Huari Tolla, del dicho ayllo, que dijo tener ochenta y seis años, y tal pareció por su aspecto. (3) Alonso Astomanga, del ayllo de Marco, dijo tener sesenta años, y así pareció por su aspecto. (4) Don Cristóbal Pularimachi, del ayllo de Paca, que dijo tener sesenta años. Y tal pareció por su aspecto. (5) Alonso Curo, del ayllo de Paca, dijo tener sesenta años. Y tal pareció por su aspecto. (6) Felipe Yupari, del ayllo de Ichoca, dijo tener setenta años. Y tal pareció por su aspecto. (7) Anton Cancalcuri, del ayllo de Huarancayo, dijo tener sesenta años. Y tal pareció por su aspecto. (8) Don Francisco Colque Sulca, del ayllo de los Mitines de Guamachuco, que dijo tener ochenta años. Y tal pareció por su aspecto. (9) Don Martín Carbanampa, del ayllo de Llocllapampa, que pareció tener más de cincuenta años. (10) Pedro Carva Sule,

del ayllo de Guacras, que dijo tener sesenta y siete años. Y tal pareció por su aspecto. (11) Luis Topara, del ayllu de Guaillas, dijo tener setenta y ocho años. Y tal pareció por su aspecto."

"(1) Don Juan Turimaya, of the ayllu of Jauja-Collana, who said he is seventy, and he seemed to be so from his appearance. (2) Alonso Huari Tolla, of said ayllu, who said he is eighty-six, and he seemed to be so from his appearance. (3) Alonso Astomanga, of the ayllu of Marco, who said he is sixty, and he seemed to be so from his appearance. (4) Don Cristóbal Pularimachi, of the ayllu of Paca, who said he is sixty. And he seemed to be so from his appearance. (5) Alonso Curo, of the ayllu of Paca, who said he is sixty. And he seemed to be so from his appearance. (6) Felipe Yupari, of the ayllu of Ichoca, who said he is seventy. And he seemed to be so from his appearance. (7) Anton Cancalcuri, of the ayllu of Huarancayo, who said he is sixty. And he seemed to be so from his appearance. (8) Don Francisco Colque Sulca, of the ayllu of the mitmaqkuna of Guamachuco, who said he is eighty. And he seemed to be so from his appearance. (9) Don Martín Carbanampa, of the ayllu of Llocllapampa, who seemed to be more than fifty. (10) Pedro Carva Sule, of the ayllu of Guacras, who said he is sixty-seven. And he seemed to be so from his appearance. (11) Luis Topara, of the ayllu of Guaillas, who said he is seventy-eight. And he seemed to be so from his appearance."

39. "[D]ejieron que nunca estos testigos que el dicho don Cristobal Cargua Alaya, fuese cacique del dicho aillo, sobre que se litiga, sino que fueron caciques de cien indios del dicho aillo, sus antepasadaos del dicho don Cristobal. Y que la parte del dicho don Juan eran los que fueron caciques principales del dicho aillo" (Espinoza Soriano 1969 [1598]: doc. 4, p. 68).

40. "¿Después de la muerte del dicho Mango Misari, quien fue principal del dicho pueblo de Guacras, y entró a gobernar los indios de el?" (Espinoza Soriano 1969 [1571]: doc. 1, p. 56).

41. "Juan Manco Misari, principal que al presente es del dicho pueblo de Guacras" (Espinoza Soriano 1969 [1571]: doc. 1, p. 53).

42. "Hernando Guaman Alaya, que es del ayllo de Sacras y no del Guacras que es conjunto al ayllo de Luringuaillas" (Espinoza Soriano 1969 [1599]: doc. 3, p. 106).

43. "Don Martín Carbanampa, del ayllo de Llocllapampa, que pareció tener más de cincuenta años" (Espinoza Soriano 1969 [1571]: doc. 1, p. 54).

44. "Indios del ayllo y parcialidad de Llampray Cacras y Purac, de que es principal Hernando Carua Arannia, que están poblados en el pueblo de Llocllapampa, sujetos al dicho don Hernando Pascual Riquira, cacique" (Espinoza Soriano 1969 [1599]: 30).

45. A project intended to address this problem had to be suspended in 1988, because the political climate precluded field research (see note 18 for Chapter 6).

Chapter 8

1. Some evidence exists that the term *ayllu* has been applied to kin groups that varied substantially in internal complexity, size, lineality, and kin structure. The Spanish application of the term to groups in regions in which other languages were dominant has also obscured the picture.

2. See Schaedel (1978) for an analogous argument for the Inka political structure.

3. In an analogous argument, Santley (1986:234) has suggested that the Aztec central-place system was probably organized as a dendritic political economy.

4. In contrast, the evidence for private estates of the royalty or nobility remains limited, despite the suggestions by Conrad and Demarest (1984) that privatization of the best lands required territorial expansion by each successive emperor. One good example of such an estate, however, may be found at Chinchero (Alcina Franch et al. 1976).

5. See Chapter 9 for a fuller discussion of Wanka settlement patterns under Inka rule.

6. These villages were J59, J67, J68, J74, J221, J246, J252, J285, and J286.

7. The principal exceptions to this pattern occurred in two locations on the west side of the Mantaro Valley: just north of Marca, and about 9 km south of Hatun Xauxa. The amount of state storage in these locations was relatively small, and as is discussed later in Chapter 8, the state storage was spatially segregated from the Wanka residential areas.

8. Salera et al. (1954, cited in Hastorf 1983:71) provide an average estimate of 1,400 kg/ha for maize production in the Mantaro Valley proper.

9. Other modern studies cite contemporary mashwa yields ranging from 1.2 t/ha on the least productive small farms to 100.0 t/ha on extraordinarily productive cooperatives (Werge 1977:18). The small farms, which average about 4.3 t/ha, are probably far more representative of the mashwa yields obtained in late prehistory. Even these small farms, which generally do not have access to irrigation, depend heavily on dung, guano, and synthetic fertilizers to maintain productivity. For 1976, a year with a relatively poor mashwa harvest, Franco et al. (1979: Table A-28) report figures ranging from about 2.8 to 6.6 t/ha for fields in fallow in the preceding year, and 2.3 to 2.9 t/ha for fields in cultivation in the preceding year. These figures correspond well to the 4.0 t/ha that Thomas (1973:108) reports for the high-altitude Nuñoa yields in the Puno region.

10. ". . . les mandó que le hiciesen chácaras de comidas, y ropa" (Vega 1965 [1582]: 169).

11. Hastorf and Earle (1985:591) suggest that the development of these lands in Wanka II resulted from two processes associated with the emergence of political ranking. First, the concentration of population in the higher elevations during a time of intense regional conflict would have limited the productive, low-valley agricultural resources

available to the population. Second, the concomitant development of political hierarchies apparently resulted in the development of a surplus economy. The leadership of the native communities appears to have been exploiting intra-regional conflict as a means of expanding its control of human and natural resources (see Chapter 4). The products of the intensified economic activities were differentially available to the members of the society, with the elites gaining an increasing proportion of the subsistence, utilitarian, and prestige goods that resulted from the increased labor investment. Under these circumstances of sociopolitical restrictions on land resources, intensification appears to have been employed as a means of producing the surplus needed to support the increasing agriculturally nonproductive sector.

12. Because the state storage system and the organization of storage in the Upper Mantaro have been explored in detail elsewhere, this section is intended to summarize only some of the most salient characteristics of the state storage system in the region (see Morris 1967, 1972b, 1981; D'Altroy 1981; Earle and D'Altroy 1982; D'Altroy and Hastorf 1984; D'Altroy and Earle 1985; LeVine n.d.).

13. The reader who has used storehouse data from previous publications may notice slight discrepancies between the present figures and those published earlier (e.g., Earle and D'Altroy 1982; D'Altroy and Hastorf 1984). The modifications presented here result from additional fieldwork, which has allowed us to refine our estimates of the makeup of storage complexes. To those for whom the modifications will cause inconvenience, I offer my apologies.

14. CV $=(SD \times 100)/\bar{X}$.

15. t test for significance of slope: $t = -4.52$; df = 10; $p < .05$ (one-tailed). The values for the calculations in this paragraph differ slightly from those reported in Earle and D'Altroy (1982), because of additional data collected on storage facilities since the 1982 article was written.

16. t test for significance of slope: $t = -4.52$; df = 9; $p < .05$ (one-tailed).

17. This includes all state storage facilities within the UMARP study region but does not include the facilities farther to the south recorded by Browman (1970).

18. Murra (1980 [1956]: 25, n. 104) notes that three additional references to "seeds" and "bread" probably actually refer to maize.

19. The U.S. standard weight for dried, shelled South American flint maize is 58 pounds per bushel, which may be rounded to 60 pounds for convenience (D. Fetherston, U.S. Feed Grains Council, pers. com. 1987). On the cob, the ratio is 70 lb/bu. In metric measurements, these values are roughly 770 kg/m³ and 870 kg/bu (using figures of 27.3 kg/bu and 28.3 bu/m³).

20. The U.S. standard weight for whole potatoes is 60 lb/bu (G. Porter, Potato Association of America, pers. com. 1987), from which a conversion may be made to the same figure of 770 kg/m³ (or 770 g/liter) derived for the maize.

21. The more important of these proportions are the following: (1) rim diameter, approximately 35 percent the height of the vessel; (2) average jar body height, 95 percent the maximum body width (range = 90–103 percent); and (3) jar body height, two-thirds the height of the entire vessel. Judging from a nonrigorous sampling of illustrations of Inka ceramics in other publications (e.g., Alcina Franch et al. 1976; Meyers 1976; Morris and Thompson 1985), these ratios were fairly standard throughout the empire, although some regional variations undoubtedly occurred.

22. The mean interior diameters of the circular storehouses in the principal magazines above Hatun Xauxa (J15–J17) lie between 4.4 and 4.7 m. The estimated total interior volume of these qollqa, as derived from Table 8.6 data, lies between 53.2 and 61.7 m³ (based on an estimated height of 3.5 m). Using an average qollqa diameter of 4.5 m, and a jar body diameter of 0.70 m (derived from Miller's proportions), a storehouse could have held 30 large jars, plus 1 of slightly smaller size, in a single layer.

23. The smaller of these qollqa could have held 17 jars of this size in a layer with 2 additional, slightly smaller jars, yielding a total storage volume of 3.7 m³. Twenty-three large jars and 1 slightly smaller jar could have been packed into the larger structures, for a total volume of about 5.5 m³. For the smaller storehouses, 11.0 percent of the estimated 33.7 m³ building volume would have been used; for the larger qollqa, 12.5 percent of the estimated 44.0 m³ would have been used.

24. As is the case with the circular qollqa, rectangular storehouses vary somewhat in dimensions, so rough average dimensions of 6.5 by 3.5 m will be used for interior floor space. Forty-five jars could have been close-packed in a structure of these dimensions. These figures imply that about 11.3 percent of the 79.6 m³ of volume in a building of this size would have been used.

25. The figure of 90 percent reduction for storage in jars is an average around which structures at individual sites vary. This figure is used here for ease of calculation.

26. This estimate is based on 40 percent of storage volume dedicated to other materials and 25 percent taken up by packaging (see Table 8.8, next-to-last column).

27. The lack of other vitrified sherds in the Inka style is not attributable to technological characteristics of the ceramics, because refiring experiments have shown that the Inka pottery will vitrify at temperatures well within the range attainable by the region's potters (Costin, pers. com. 1989).

28. This analysis was originally run by Ronald A. Bishop, who has graciously consented to its publication here. In this and all other analyses, log-transformed values for the elemental components were used.

29. The separation of the sources was determined on the basis of Th : Ba ratios, which may indicate the proportion of volcanic glass in the sample.

30. The strong substantivist emphasis in the literature

consistently denies that the Inkas made decisions concerning the trajectory of economic institutions based on such considerations as the relative costs and benefits of localized production and consumption in comparison with more-centralized production, with its concomitant increases in transport costs.

Chapter 9

1. For the information on regional settlement systems, I have relied on the results of several complementary surveys, which are reported at far greater length elsewhere. Among them are the extensive Junín Project survey undertaken by Parsons, Matos Mendieta, and Hastings (e.g., Parsons 1976; Parsons and Hastings 1977; Parsons and Matos Mendieta 1978; Matos Mendieta and Parsons 1979; cf. Browman 1970) and three surveys performed under the umbrella UMARP field research: LeBlanc's (1981) intensive resurvey of the Yanamarca Valley settlements, Earle's 1986 resurvey of the main Mantaro Valley settlements (Parsons and Earle n.d.), and my own 1983 survey (D'Altroy 1983, n.d.) of the Jisse-Pomacancha valley to the west of the Yanamarca Valley.

2. The methods used to derive these estimates have been described in Earle et al. (1987) and will not be presented here. In subsequent discussions, the higher of these estimates will be used, primarily because many of the Wanka III settlements were newly settled and were likely fully occupied throughout the 70-year period.

3. "[E]n el dicho pueblo de la concepción fue tomado y rrecibido juramento en forma de derecho de don diego lucana principal de los mitimaes cañaris y de chachapoyas y llaguas questan en este rrepartymiento de los luringuancas en el pueblo que se llama de la purificación de guacho" (Toledo 1940a [1570]: 22).

4. "Los señores de Xauxa le hicieron grandes servicios y algunos de los capitanes y gente de guerra le fueron acompanado" (Cieza 1967 [1553]: ch. 64, p. 215).

5. ". . . en tiempo de Inga Guayna Capac, por cuanto el dicho inga llevó consigo a Quito y Tomebamba al susodicho Guaman Misari, hijo mayor del dicho Apo Misari, con otros curacas del dicho repartimiento de Atunjauja" (Espinoza Soriano 1969 [1597]: doc. 4, p. 63).

6. "Don Francisco Vichic, que dijo ser natural de Hananguanca, mitmaq de Lamay, puesto por el Inga Huascar, y que su padre fue curaca que mandaba quinientos indios de Lamay, y que por faltarle de edad y memoria de los gobernar ha suscedido un hermano suyo en el cargo y que es de edad de ochenta y nueve anos . . ." (Toledo 1940c [1571]: 159).

7. A more detailed discussion will be presented in Parsons and Earle (n.d.).

8.

$$RSI = \frac{\sum_1^n (\log P_{obs} - \log P_{rs})}{\sum_1^n (\log P_{cmax} - \log P_{rs})}$$

where n = number of settlements in the analysis; P_{obs} = observed settlement size; P_{rs} = expected settlement size—log-linear model; and P_{cmax} = expected settlement distribution —maximum convex distribution (Johnson 1987:109).

9. "[L]os indios, dejados los pucaraes que primeramente tenían, ordenaron sus pueblos de buena manera, así en los valles de los llanos como en la serranía y llanura de Collao" (Cieza 1967 [1553]: ch. 24, p. 83).

10. The possibility should also be considered that some of the residents of the northern Upper Mantaro were forcibly resettled or induced to move into the southern part of the valley near Huancayo, an area containing rich soils and the only land low enough for secure cultivation of maize (Franco et al. 1979: inset map; Earle et al. 1980:12–13).

11. The most notable state farms have been recorded at Cochabamba (Wachtel 1982) and at Abancay (Espinoza Soriano 1973a; see also La Lone and La Lone 1987). As was described in Chapter 8, to judge from the area of land left relatively unoccupied by subject communities and the size of the storage facilities, the farms in the Hatun Xauxa region must have fallen at the upper end of the agricultural projects undertaken by the state.

12. A fuller explication of the organization of the domestic economy may be found in Hastorf (1983, 1985), Costin (1986), Earle et al. (1987), Costin and Earle (1989), Costin et al. (1989), and D'Altroy and Hastorf (n.d.).

13. Parsons and Hastings (1977:45) recorded Inka ceramics, usually in small amounts, at 49 sites in the Jauja study area. LeBlanc's (1981:244) research confirmed that state wares were present at 21 sites in the Yanamarca Valley, and surveys of about 30 percent of the Jisse area recovered imperial pottery from an additional 10 settlements (D'Altroy n.d.).

14. The discussion of the distribution of Inka and Wanka III settlements here is necessarily cursory. Full treatment will be presented in a book on the domestic economy (D'Altroy and Hastorf n.d.) and in a monograph about settlement patterns (Parsons and Earle n.d.).

15. Because two different techniques were used to recover ceramics from the Yanamarca Valley sites, it is difficult to compare densities of ceramics or total counts of Inka sherds among all sites. The grassy overgrowth and lack of cultivation at many of the small sites required that collections be taken by screening the top 15 to 20 cm of the ground in limited areas (e.g., 5 by 5 m). This method produced reasonable collections for estimating percentages of various ceramic types on the site and for dating the occupations, but it also

produced much higher quantities of ceramics per square meter of ground surface than did the normal surface-collecting technique.

16. A *t*-test yielded .05 < *p* < .10 for the mean diameters of flared-rim jars from the two sites. For J2, $\bar{X}$ = 22.9 cm, SD = 9.49 cm, and N = 36; for J5, $\bar{X}$ = 25.0 cm, SD = 8.27 cm, N = 190; df = 224; *t* = 1.348.

17. One collection, at the far southwest edge of the site, was eliminated from the sample because of disparities in frequencies of sherds recovered.

18. The surface collection with the highest ceramic density, anomalously located at the southern edge of the northern sector, was likely a dump, for it was situated in a large field with little rubble or standing architecture.

19.

$$I = \frac{N}{\Sigma\Sigma w_{ij}} \frac{\Sigma\Sigma w_{ij}(x_i - \bar{x})(x_j - \bar{x})}{\Sigma(x_i - \bar{x})^2}$$

where N is the number of regions; the double summation indicates summation over all pairs of regions; w_{ij} is the spatial weight for the pair of regions *i* and *j*; x_i and x_j are their data values; and $\bar{x}$ is the mean for the entire sequence.

20. To create these plots, a matrix of Brainerd-Robinson rank dissimilarities among compounds was plotted in three dimensions, using a Euclidean distance model. The SAS procedures PROX and ALSCAL were used to perform the calculations and plotting; see Chapter 4 for a more detailed explanation.

Glossary

This glossary contains most of the non-English terms and terms of non-English origin that are used in the text, with the preferred definition for this book listed first. Because translations and meanings of terms vary, a range of definitions is provided in some cases to exemplify the range of meaning, but this glossary should not be taken as an exhaustive survey. Specific quoted definitions, attributed in brackets, are derived from Cerrón-Palomino 1976a [CP]; González Holguín 1952 [1608] [DGH]; Urioste's glossary-index in Guaman Poma 1980:1075–1108 [GP]; Haggard and McClean 1941 [HM]; Hornberger and Hornberger 1983 [HH]; Hyslop 1990:333–34 [JH]; and Murra 1980 [1956]: 191–94 [JVM]. Cerrón-Palomino's dictionary refers to the modern Quechua of the Junín region; the Hornbergers' dictionary is based on the modern Quechua from the Cuzco region. Languages are Arawak (A), Quechua (Q), and Spanish (S). Words in brackets in the definitions are this author's insertions.

allauca (Q; also *allawqa* [CP:26]): right.

altiplano (S): high-elevation plain (Bolivia).

Ananwanka (Q): upper (moiety) division of Wanka ethnic group; southernmost of three political divisions of Inka province of Wanka Wamaní, populated principally by Wanka and Xauxa ethnic groups.

Antisuyu (Q): northeastern part of Inka empire.

aqlla (Q; plural *aqllakuna*): "woman chosen for state and religious service" [JH:333]; "hidden" [GP:1076].

awasqa (Q): rough cloth; "common, thick cloth" [GP: 1077].

ayllu (Q): localized descent group, varying in inclusiveness, frequently subdivided into moieties, lineages, or both; "division, genealogy, lineage, or kinship" [GP:1078, after DGH:39]; "kinsman, family relation" [CP:33].

cacicazgo (A-S): domain of a cacique.

cacique (A): leader; frequently applied by Spaniards to anyone in position of indigenous authority.

cacique principal (A-S): paramount leader of sociopolitical unit.

ceja de la montaña (S): upper forested area on eastern slopes of Andes.

ceja de selva (S): upper fringe of jungle.

chala (Q): coastal environmental zone.

ch'arki (Q): freeze-dried (jerked) meat.

chaski (Q): "postal messenger" [GP:1079].

chicha (A): "a fermented beverage, generally of maize, originally a Caribbean word" [JH:333]. In Quechua: *aqha, aswa* [GP:1079].

Chinchasuyu (Q): northwestern part of Inka empire.

chullpa (Q): (aboveground) tomb.

chunka kamayoq (Q): official at head of 10-household census unit.

chuño (Q): freeze-dried potatoes.

cinche (Q; plural *cinchecona*): valiant man, native elite; generally applied with reference to pre-Inka era.

Cuntisuyu (Q; also **Condesuyu, Kuntisuyu**): southwestern part of Inka empire.

dos aguas (S): gabled (roof).

gobernador (S): governor; used by Spaniards to refer to regent temporarily holding office in native authority hierarchies.

hanan (Q): upper half or moiety of dual units characterizing Inka sociopolitical organization.

hanega (S): dry measure approximating 1.60 bushels [HM: 76], 56.6 liters, or—for shelled maize—43.6 kg.

hatun (Q): big, great.

hatun runa (Q): "adult, married male" [GP:1081]; " 'Male peasant,' DGH, p. 154. An adult male, married and enumerated in the Inca census. Literally 'big man' " [JVM: 192].

hunu (Q): unit of 10,000; often used to refer to census or sociopolitical unit ostensibly consisting of 10,000 households.

hunu kuraka (Q): official at head of 10,000-household census unit.

hurin (Q): lower half or moiety of dual units characterizing Inka sociopolitical organization.

ichoca (Q; also *ichuq* [CP:56], *lloq'e* [HH:386]): left.

indios (S): generally, the indigenous commoner population.

janca (Q): highest-elevation environmental zone, without permanent human occupation, characterized by glaciers and sparse biota.

kallanka (Q): "a long hall, often with a gabled roof" [JH: 333].

kancha (Q): "an enclosure; several rooms placed around a patio, generally within a rectangular perimeter wall" [JH:333].

kayao (Q): one of three divisions, *qollana-payan-kayao*, found in Cuzco-area sociopolitical organization.

khipu (Q; also *quipu*): "cords with knots used [as a mnemonic device] in Inka accounting" [GP:1086]; "knot, ancient Andean recording system" [HH:89]; from *oquipuni*, "to count by [use of] knots" [DGH:309].

khipu kamayoq (Q): official responsible for keeping records on knotted strings.

Kollasuyu (Q; also **Qollasuyu** [HH:188]): southeastern part of Inka empire.

kuraka (Q; also *curaca, kuraqka* [JVM:192]): native elite; "local ethnic authority" [GP:1085]; "representative of the local god" [HH:84].

libra (S): measure of weight equal to about 0.46 kg, for Peru and Mexico (HM:79).

llaqta (Q; also *llacta*): "town" [GP:1087]); " 'Pueblo.' DGH, p. 207. A town, a nucleated settlement" [JVM: 192]; "town, city, fatherland, nation, country, community" [HH:111].

marca (Q; also *malka* [CP:85]): "people [town], population" [CP:85].

mit'a (Q): "A period, one's turn. . . . Prestations to one's ethnic group, [to] one's lord and to the Inca state" [JVM:

192]; "period [season]; that which returns cyclically, and the turn in which to undertake something [task]" [GP: 1090].

mitmaq (Q; plural *mitmaqkuna*): "a settler from some other place; an Inka state colonist" [JH:333]; "from *mit'iy:* to send; sent by one's ethnic group of origin to attend to outside interests" [GP:1090].

montaña (S): upper, humid, forested environmental zone on eastern side of Andes; source of fruit and wild biota.

orejón (S): long-ear; Inka nobility, distinguished by large ear spools.

pachaca (Q; also *pachaqa* [GP:1090], *pachak* [HH:151]): unit of 100; often used to refer to census or sociopolitical unit ostensibly consisting of 100 households.

pachaca kuraka (Q): official at head of 100-household census unit.

parcialidad (S): sociopolitical subdivision of unspecified scope.

payan (Q): one of three divisions, *qollana-payan-kayao*, found in Cuzco-area sociopolitical organization.

pichqachunka (Q; also *pisqachunka* [GP:1090]): unit of 50; often used to refer to census or sociopolitical unit ostensibly consisting of 50 households.

pichqachunka kamayoq (Q): official at head of 50-household census unit.

pichqapachaca (Q): unit of 500; often used to refer to census or sociopolitical unit ostensibly consisting of 500 households.

pichqapachaca kuraka (Q): official at head of 500-household census unit.

pichqawaranqa (Q): unit of 5,000; often used to refer to census or sociopolitical unit ostensibly consisting of 5,000 households.

pichqawaranqa kuraka (Q): official at head of 5,000-household census unit.

pirka (Q): rustic or fieldstone masonry.

pueblo (S): town, people.

puna (Q): high-elevation environmental zone, generally characterized by rolling grasslands; principal zone for camelid herding.

qhapaq ñan (Q; also *capac ñan*): powerful road, i.e., imperial Inka highway [see GP:1096].

qollana (Q): one of three divisions, *qollana-payan-kayao*, found in Cuzco-area sociopolitical organization.

qollqa (Q; also *qullqa* [GP:1095], *qolqa* [HH:187]): storehouse.

qompi (Q; also *qumpi* [GP:1095]): fine cloth.

quechua (Q; also *qheshwa, qheswa* [HH:109]): mid-elevation environmental zone, found on eastern and western slopes of Andes, as well as in intermontane valleys; principal highland zone for maize-complex crops.

Quechua (Q): dominant language group in central Andean highlands; ethnic group on northwest side of Lake Titicaca.

relación (S): account, report.

repartimiento (S): Spanish grant of administrative control over and access to labor of group of native inhabitants.

runakhipu (Q): state officials responsible for census taking.

runasimi (Q): human speech, i.e., Quechua.

saya (Q): a sociopolitical subdivision; "the upper or lower, the right or left moiety, in Andean dual organization" [JVM:193].

segunda persona (S): position in sociopolitical hierarchy, immediately subordinate to *cacique principal* and paramount of lower moiety or half of sociopolitical unit.

selva alta (S): upper jungle.

selva baja (S): lower jungle.

suni (Q): moderately high-elevation environmental zone, above *quechua* and below *puna;* principal highland zone for tuber-complex crops.

suyu (Q): "territory, region" [HH:242].

suyuyoc apo (Q): lord of great political unit, sometimes specifically meaning half of empire. *suyuyuq:* "administration of a subdivision" [GP:1101]. *apu:* "great lord or superior judge" [GP:1076].

tampu (Q; also *tanpu* [GP:1101]): "Inka state lodging on the road system" [JH:333].

Tawantinsuyu (Q): "the Inka empire; land of the four (*tawa*) parts or provinces (*suyu*)" [JH:333].

tokrikoq (Q; also *toricoq* [JH:333], *t'oqrikuq* [JVM:193]): Inka provincial governor.

tupu (Q): "a measure of any kind, a league" [DGH:347]; "agricultural measure" [GP:1102]; "general measure" [CP:136]; "measure (volume), measure of land" [HH:253]. Not to be confused with an alternative meaning of *tupu*—"fastening pin" [HH:253].

usnu (Q; also *ushnu* [JH:334]): pyramid platform in a ceremonial complex; "a centrally located ritual complex consisting of a drain with a stone, basin, and platform within Inka settlements" [JH:334]; "ceremonial or administrative construction" [GP:1103]; "a niche, usually in a wall, used for placing idols or other venerated or sacred objects" [HH:274].

waka (Q; also *waqa* [JH:334]): shrine, sacred place, object, or power; "tutelary divinity, at the local level" [GP:1104].

wamani (Q): "Incaic administrative district" [GP:1104].

waranqa (Q): unit of 1,000; often used to refer to census or sociopolitical unit ostensibly consisting of 1,000 households.

waranqa kuraka (Q): official at head of 1,000-household census unit.

yana (Q; plural *yanakuna*): " 'a servant, a young man in service.' DGH p. 363, from *yanapa*, reciprocal services given without accounts being kept" [JVM:194].

yunga (Q): low-elevation environmental zone, above the coastal plain on the west and the jungle on the east; principal zone for coca and fruits.

zeque (Q): "a radial line or path; a radial system of forty-one lines in Cuzco that integrated Inka kinship, cosmology, and calendrics" [JH:334].

Bibliography

Adams, Richard N.

1976   *Energy and Structure.* Austin: University of Texas Press.

1978   Man, Energy, and Anthropology. *American Anthropologist* 80:297–309.

Adams, Robert McC.

1974   Anthropological Perspectives on Ancient Trade. *Current Anthropology* 15:239–58.

1979a   Common Concerns but Different Standpoints: A Commentary. In *Power and Propaganda,* ed. Mogens T. Larsen, 393–404. Copenhagen: Akademisk Forlag.

1979b   Late Prehispanic Empires of the New World. In *Power and Propaganda,* ed. Mogens T. Larsen, 59–73. Copenhagen: Akademisk Forlag.

1981   *Heartland of Cities.* Chicago: University of Chicago Press.

1984   Mesopotamian Social Evolution: Old Outlooks, New Goals. In *On the Evolution of Complex Societies,* ed. Timothy K. Earle, 79–129. Malibu, Calif.: Undena Press.

Alaya, don Cristóbal

1971   Memoria de las cosas que don Cristóbal Alaya
[1558]   cacique e indios dieron a los capitanes y gente de Su Majestad para la guerra contra Francisco Hernández Girón. In "Los Huancas, aliados de la conquista: Tres informaciones inéditas sobre la participación indígena en la conquista del Perú, 1558–1560–1561," by Waldemar Espinoza Soriano, 210–12. *Anales Científicos de la Universidad del Centro del Perú* 1:3–407. Huancayo.

Alcina Franch, José

1976   *Arqueología de Chinchero, 1: La arquitectura.* Memorias de la Misión Científica Española en Hispanoamérica, vol. 2. Madrid: Ministerio de Asuntos Exteriores.

Alcina Franch, José, Miguel Rivera, Jesús Galván, M.ª Carmen García Palacios, Mercedes Guinea, Balbina Martínez-Caviró, Luis J. Ramos, and Tito Varela

1976   *Arqueología de Chinchero, 2: Cerámica y otros materiales.* Memorias de la Misión Científica Española en Hispanoamérica, vol. 3. Madrid: Ministerio de Asuntos Exteriores.

Alvaro, don

1971   Memoria y relación de lo que yo don Alvaro
[1558]   cacique de los indios de Caravantes gasté con los capitanes de Su Majestad en la guerra de Francisco Hernández y diferente della. In "Los Huancas, aliados de la conquista: Tres informaciones inéditas sobre la participación indígena en la conquista del Perú, 1558–1560–1561," by Waldemar Espinoza Soriano, 212–13. *Anales Científicos de la Universidad del Centro del Perú* 1:3–407. Huancayo.

Anónimo Sevillano
1937   La conquista del Perú. In *Las Relaciones Primi-*
[1534]   *tivas de la Conquista del Perú,* ed. Raúl Porras
         Barrenechea. Cuadernos de Historia, no. 2. Los
         Cronistas de la Conquista, no. 1. Paris: Les
         Presses Modernes.

Arnold, Dean
1975   Ceramic ecology of the Ayacucho Basin, Peru:
        Implications for prehistory. *Current Anthropol-*
        ogy 16:183–205.
1985   *Ceramic Theory and Cultural Process.* Cam-
        bridge: Cambridge University Press.

Attewell, Paul
1984   *Radical Political Economy since the Sixties: A*
        Sociology of Knowledge Analysis. New Bruns-
        wick, N.J.: Rutgers University Press.

Badian, Ernst
1967   *Roman Imperialism in the Late Republic.* Wit-
        watersrand: University of South Africa Press.

Bartel, Brad
1989   Acculturation and Ethnicity in Roman Moesia
        Superior. In *Centre and Periphery: Comparative*
        Studies in Archaeology, ed. Timothy C. Cham-
        pion, 173–85. London: Unwin, Hyman.

Bauden, Louis
1928   *L'empire socialiste des Inkas.* Paris: Institut
        d'Ethnologie.

Bauer, Brian
1990   State Development in the Cusco Region: Archae-
        ological Research on the Incas in the Province of
        Paruro. Ph.D. dissertation, Department of An-
        thropology, University of Chicago.

Betanzos, Juan de
1987   *Suma y narración de los Incas.* Transcrip-
[1551] tion, notes, and prologue by María del Carmen
        Martín Rubio. Madrid: Ediciones Atlas.

Blanton, Richard
1978   *Monte Albán: Settlement Patterns at the An-*
        cient Zapotec Capital. New York: Academic
        Press.

Bobrowsky, Peter T., and Bruce F. Ball
1989   The Theory and Mechanics of Ecological Diver-
        sity in Archaeology. In *Quantifying Diversity in*
        Archaeology, ed. Robert D. Leonard and George
        T. Jones, 4–12. Cambridge: Cambridge Univer-
        sity Press.

Bram, Joseph
1941   *An Analysis of Inca Militarism.* Monographs of
        the American Ethnological Society, no. 4. New
        York.

Browman, David L.
1970   Early Peruvian Peasants: The Culture History of
        a Central Highlands Valley. Ph.D. dissertation,
        Department of Anthropology, Harvard Univer-
        sity, Cambridge.

1975   Trade Patterns in the Central Highlands of Peru
        in the First Millennium, B.C. *World Archaeology*
        6 (3): 322–29.
1985   Comment on Terence N. D'Altroy and Timothy
        K. Earle, "Staple Finance, Wealth Finance, and
        Storage in the Inka Political Economy." *Current*
        Anthropology 26:197–99.

Brumfiel, Elizabeth
1987   Elite and Utilitarian Crafts in the Aztec State. In
        Specialization, Exchange, and Complex Soci-
        eties, ed. Elizabeth Brumfiel and Timothy K.
        Earle, 102–18. Cambridge: Cambridge Univer-
        sity Press.

Brundage, Burr Cartwright
1963   *Empire of the Inca.* Norman: University of
        Oklahoma Press.

Burchard, Roderick E.
1974   Coca y trueque de alimentos. In *Reciprocidad e*
        Intercambio en los Andes Peruanos, ed. Giorgio
        Alberti and Alberto Meyers, 209–51. Lima: In-
        stituto de Estudios Peruanos.

Burling, Robbins
1974   *The Passage of Power: Studies in Political Succes-*
        sion. New York: Academic Press.

Cabello Valboa, Miguel
1951   *Miscelanea antártica.* Lima: Universidad Nacio-
[1586] nal Mayor de San Marcos.

Carbajal, Pedro de
1965   Descripción fecha de la Provincia de Vilcas Gua-
[1586] man. In *Relaciones Geográficas de Indias,* tomo
        1, 205–19. Biblioteca de Autores Españoles, vol.
        183. Madrid: Ediciones Atlas.

Carneiro, Robert L.
1970   A Theory of the Origin of the State. *Science*
        169:733–38.

Carrasco, Pedro
1982   The Political Economy of the Aztec and Inca
        States. In *The Inca and Aztec States 1400–1800:*
        Anthropology and History, ed. George A. Col-
        lier, Renato I. Rosaldo, and John D. Wirth, 23–
        40. New York: Academic Press.

Castro, Cristóbal de, and Diego de Ortega Morejón
1974   Relación y declaración del modo que este valle de
[1558] Chincha y sus comarcanos se governaven antes
        que oviese Ingas y despues q(ue) los vuo hasta
        q(ue) los Cristianos entraron en esta tierra. In-
        troduction by Juan Carlos Crespo. *Historia y*
        Cultura 8:91–104. Lima.

Cerrón-Palomino, Rodolfo
1972   *Apuntes sobre lingüística Wanka.* Centro de In-
        vestigación Lingüística de Amazonía, Docu-
        mento de Trabajo no. 5. Lima: Universidad Na-
        cional Mayor de San Marcos.
1976a   *Diccionario Quechua Junín-Huanca.* Lima: In-
        stituto de Estudios Peruanos.

1976b   *Gramática Quechua Junín-Huanca.* Lima: Instituto de Estudios Peruanos.

1977   *Huanca-Quechua Dialectology.* Ph.D. dissertation, University of Illinois, Urbana-Champaign. Ann Arbor, Mich.: University Microfilms.

Champion, Timothy C., ed.

1989a   *Centre and Periphery: Comparative Studies in Archaeology.* London: Unwin, Hyman.

Champion, Timothy C.

1989b   Introduction. In *Centre and Periphery: Comparative Studies in Archaeology,* ed. Timothy C. Champion, 1–21. London: Unwin, Hyman.

Chase-Dunn, Christopher, and Thomas D. Hall, eds.

1991   *Core/Periphery Relations in Precapitalist Worlds.* Boulder, Colo.: Westview Press.

Chisholm, Michael

1968   *Rural Settlement and Land Use.* 2d ed. London: Hutchinson and Co.

Christensen, Clyde M., and H. H. Kaufman

1969   *Grain Storage: The Role of Fungi in Quality Loss.* Minneapolis: University of Minnesota Press.

Cieza de León, Pedro de

1967   *El señorio de los Incas: Segunda parte de la*
[1553]   *crónica del Perú.* Lima: Instituto de Estudios Peruanos.

1984   *La crónica del Perú: Primera parte.* Lima: Pon-
[1551]   tificia Universidad Católica del Perú, Fondo Editorial.

Cobo, Bernabé

1956   *Obras.* 2 vols. Biblioteca de Autores Españoles,
[1653]   vols. 91 and 92. Madrid: Ediciones Atlas.

Cock C., Guillermo

1977   Los kurakas de los Collaguas: Poder político y poder económico. *Historia y Cultura* 10:95–119. Lima.

Cohen, Ronald, and Elman R. Service, eds.

1978   *Origins of the State: The Anthropology of Political Evolution.* Philadelphia: Ishi.

Collazos, Carlos Ch., P. H. White, H. S. White, E. T. Viñas, E. J. Alvistur, R. A. Urquieta, J. G. Vasquez, C. T. Dias, A. M. Quiroz, A. N. Roca, D. M. Hegsted, and R. B. Bradfield

1957   *La composición de los alimentos peruanos.* Lima: Ministerio de Salud Pública y Asistencia Social, Servicio Cooperativo Interamericano de Salud Pública, Instituto de Nutrición.

Conrad, Geoffrey W.

1977   Chuquitoy Viejo: An Inca Administrative Center in the Chicama Valley, Peru. *Journal of Field Archaeology* 4 (1): 1–18.

Conrad, Geoffrey W., and Arthur Demarest

1984   *Religion and Empire.* Cambridge: Cambridge University Press.

Cook, Noble David

1981   *Demographic Collapse: Indian Peru, 1520–1620.* Cambridge: Cambridge University Press.

Costin, Cathy L.

1986   *From Chiefdom to Empire State: Ceramic Economy among the Prehispanic Wanka of Highland Peru.* Ph.D. dissertation, University of California, Los Angeles. Ann Arbor, Mich.: University Microfilms.

1991   Craft Specialization: Issues in Defining, Documenting, and Explaining the Organization of Production. In *Archaeological Method and Theory,* ed. Michael B. Schiffer, vol. 3, 1–56. Tucson: University of Arizona Press.

n.d.   Textile Production. In *Empire and Domestic Economy,* ed. Terence N. D'Altroy and Christine A. Hastorf. Washington, D.C.: Smithsonian Institution Press. In press.

Costin, Cathy L., and Timothy K. Earle

1989   Status Distinction and Legitimation of Power as Reflected in Changing Patterns of Consumption in Late Prehispanic Peru. *American Antiquity* 54:691–714.

Costin, Cathy L., Timothy K. Earle, Bruce Owen, and Glenn S. Russell

1989   Impact of Inka Conquest on Local Technology in the Upper Mantaro Valley, Peru. In *What's New?: A Closer Look at the Process of Innovation,* ed. Sander E. van der Leeuw and Robin Torrance, 107–39. One World Archaeology Series, vol. 14. London: Unwin and Allen.

Crown, Alan D.

1974   Tidings and Instructions: How News Travelled in the Ancient Near East. *Journal of the Economic and Social History of the Orient* 17 (pt. 3): 244–71.

Crumley, Carole L., William H. Marquardt, and Thomas L. Leatherman

1987   Certain Factors Influencing Settlement during the Later Iron Age and Gallo-Roman Periods: The Analysis of Intensive Survey Data. In *Regional Dynamics: Burgundian Landscapes in Historical Perspective,* ed. Carole L. Crumley and William H. Marquardt, 121–72. San Diego: Academic Press.

Cusichaca, don Francisco, don Diego Eneupari [Ñaupari], and don Cristóbal Canchaya

1971   Probanza de servicios fecha en la real audiencia
[1561]   que por mandado de Su Majestad reside en esta ciudad de los Reyes destos reinos e prouincias del Pirú, a pedimento de don Francisco Cusichaca e don Diego Eneupari y don Cristóbal Canchaya, cacique del repartimiento de Atunxauxa, de lo que a Su Majestad han servido en el tiempo de

la alteraciones causadas en estos reinos y conquistas y descubrimientos dellos; Lima, 5 de
septiembre–13 de octubre de 1561. In "Los
Huancas, aliados de la conquista: Tres informaciones inéditas sobre la participación indígena
en la conquista del Perú, 1558–1560–1561," by
Waldemar Espinoza Soriano, 260–387. *Anales
Científicos de la Universidad del Centro del Perú*
1:3–407. Huancayo.

Dahl, Robert A.
1972   Power. In *International Encyclopedia of the Social Sciences,* ed. David L. Sills, 405–15. New
York: Macmillan and the Free Press.

D'Altroy, Terence N.
1981   *Empire Growth and Consolidation: The Xauxa
Region of Peru under the Incas.* Ph.D. dissertation, University of California, Los Angeles. Ann
Arbor, Mich.: University Microfilms.

1983   Field Notes: Jisse-Pomacancha Survey. Manuscript.

1986   Los efectos de la conquista inka en la organización de la economía doméstica wanka. In *Actas
y Trabajos del VI Congreso Peruano: Hombre y
Cultura Andina,* ed. Francisco Iriarte, vol. 1,
52–64. Lima: Universidad Inca Garcilaso de
la Vega.

1987   Transitions in Power: Centralization of Wanka
Political Organization under Inka Rule. *Ethnohistory* 34:78–102.

n.d.   Site Survey in the Jisse-Pomacancha Drainage.
Manuscript.

D'Altroy, Terence N., and Ronald A. Bishop
1990   The Provincial Organization of Inka Ceramic
Production. *American Antiquity* 55:120–38.

D'Altroy, Terence N., and Timothy K. Earle
1985   Staple Finance, Wealth Finance, and Storage in
the Inka Political Economy (with Comment and
Reply). *Current Anthropology* 26:187–206.

n.d.   Inka Storage Facilities in the Upper Mantaro
Valley, Peru. In *Storage Systems in the Inka Em-
pire,* ed. Terry Y. LeVine. Norman: University of
Oklahoma Press. In press.

D'Altroy, Terence N., and Christine A. Hastorf
1984   The Distribution and Contents of Inca State
Storehouses in the Xauxa Region of Peru. *American Antiquity* 49:334–49.

D'Altroy, Terence N., and Christine A. Hastorf, eds.
n.d.   *Empire and Domestic Economy.* Washington,
D.C.: Smithsonian Institution Press. In press.

Dávila Brizeño, Diego
1965   Descripción y relación de la Provincia de los Yau-
[1586] yos toda, Anan Yauyos y Lorin Yauyos, Hecha
por Diego Dávila Brizeño, Corregidor de Gua-
rocheri. In *Relaciones Geográficas de Indias,*
tomo 1, 155–65. Biblioteca de Autores Españoles, vol. 183. Madrid: Ediciones Atlas.

DeNiro, Michael J., and Christine A. Hastorf
1985   Alteration of $^{15}N/^{14}N$ and $^{13}C/^{12}C$ Ratios
of Plant Matter during the Initial Stages of Dia-
genesis: Studies Utilizing Archaeological Specimens from Peru. *Geochimica et Cosmochimica
Acta* 49:47–115.

DeNiro, Michael J., Margaret J. Schoeninger, and Christine
A. Hastorf
1985   Effect of Heating on the Stable Carbon and Ni-
trogen Isotope Ratios of Bone Collagen. *Journal
of Archaeological Science* 12:1–7.

Dennell, Robin
1980   The Use, Abuse, and Potential of Site Catchment
Analysis. In *Catchment Analysis: Essays on Prehistoric Resource Space,* ed. Frank J. Findlow
and Jonathan E. Ericson, 1–20. Anthropology
UCLA, vol. 10, nos. 1 and 2. Department
of Anthropology, University of California, Los
Angeles.

Diez de San Miguel, Garci
1964   *Visita hecha a la Provincia de Chucuito por
[1567] Garci Diez de San Miguel en al año 1567.* Lima:
Casa de Cultura.

Dillehay, Tom D.
1977a   Un estudio de almacenamiento, redistribución,
y dualismo socio-político prehispánico en la
Chaupiyunga del valle de Chillón. *Cuadernos*
24–25: 25–37.

1977b   Tawantinsuyu Integration of the Chillon Valley,
Peru: A Case of Inca Geo-political Mastery. *Journal of Field Archaeology* 4:397–405.

Dillehay, Tom D., and Américo Gordon
1988   La actividad prehispánica de los Incas y su in-
fluencia en la Araucania. In *La Frontera del Estado Inca,* ed. Tom D. Dillehay and Patricia J.
Netherly, 215–34. Proceedings, 45 Congreso Internacional de Americanistas, Bogotá, Colombia, 1985. British Archaeological Reports, International Series, no. 442. Oxford.

Dillehay, Tom D., and Patricia J. Netherly
1988a   Epílogo. In *La Frontera del Estado Inca,* ed. Tom
D. Dillehay and Patricia J. Netherly, 273–75.
Proceedings, 45 Congreso Internacional de
Americanistas, Bogotá, Colombia, 1985. British
Archaeological Reports, International Series,
no. 442. Oxford.

1988b   Introducción. In *La Frontera del Estado Inca,*
ed. Tom D. Dillehay and Patricia J. Netherly, 1–
33. Proceedings, 45 Congreso Internacional de
Americanistas, Bogotá, Colombia, 1985. British
Archaeological Reports, International Series,
no. 442. Oxford.

Dillehay, Tom D., and Patricia J. Netherly, eds.

1988c   *La frontera del estado inca.* Proceedings, 45 Congreso Internacional de Americanistas, Bogotá, Colombia, 1985. British Archaeological Reports, International Series, no. 442. Oxford.

Dowdle, Jason E.

1987   Road Networks and Exchange Systems in the Aeduan *Civitas,* 300 B.C.–A.D. 300. In *Regional Dynamics: Burgundian Landscapes in Historical Perspective,* ed. Carole L. Crumley and William H. Marquardt, 265–94. San Diego: Academic Press.

Doyle, Michael W.

1986   *Empires.* Ithaca: Cornell University Press.

Dunbar Temple, Ella

1942   Los caciques Apoalaya. *Revista del Museo Nacional* 11:147–78. Lima.

Durnin, J. V. G. A., and R. Passmore

1967   *Energy, Work, and Leisure.* London: Heinemann.

Dwyer, Edward B.

1971   The Early Inca Occupation of the Valley of Cuzco, Peru. Ph.D. dissertation, Department of Anthropology, University of California, Berkeley.

Earle, Timothy K.

1977   A Reappraisal of Redistribution: Complex Hawaiian Chiefdoms. In *Exchange Systems in Prehistory,* ed. Timothy K. Earle and Jonathan E. Ericson, 213–32. New York: Academic Press.

1978   *Economic and Social Organization of a Complex Chiefdom: The Halelea District, Kaua'i, Hawaii.* Anthropological Papers of the Museum of Anthropology, University of Michigan, no. 63. Ann Arbor.

1985   Commodity Exchange and Markets in the Inca State: Recent Archaeological Evidence. In *Markets and Exchange,* ed. Stuart Plattner, 369–97. Latham, Md.: University Press of America.

1989   The Evolution of Chiefdoms. *Current Anthropology* 30:84–88.

Earle, Timothy K., and Terence N. D'Altroy

1982   Storage Facilities and State Finance in the Upper Mantaro Valley, Peru. In *Contexts for Prehistoric Exchange,* ed. Jonathan E. Ericson and Timothy K. Earle, 265–90. New York: Academic Press.

1989   The Political Economy of the Inka Empire: The Archaeology of Power and Finance. In *Archaeological Thought in America,* ed. Carl C. Lamberg-Karlovsky, 183–204. Cambridge: Cambridge University Press.

Earle, Timothy K., and Robert W. Preucel

1987   Processual Archaeology and the Radical Critique (with Comment). *Current Anthropology* 28:501–38.

Earle, Timothy K., Terence N. D'Altroy, and Catherine J. LeBlanc

1978   Arqueología regional de los períodos prehispánicos tardíos en el Mantaro. In *III Congreso Peruano: El Hombre y la Cultura Andina,* ed. Ramiro Matos Mendieta, vol. 2, 641–66. Lima: Universidad Nacional Mayor de San Marcos.

Earle, Timothy K., Terence N. D'Altroy, Catherine J. LeBlanc, Christine A. Hastorf, and Terry Y. LeVine

1980   Changing Settlement Patterns in the Upper Mantaro Valley, Peru. *Journal of New World Archaeology* 4 (1): 1–49.

Earle, Timothy K., Terence N. D'Altroy, Christine A. Hastorf, Catherine J. Scott, Cathy L. Costin, Glenn S. Russell, and Elsie Sandefur

1987   *Archaeological Field Research in the Upper Mantaro, Peru, 1982–1983: Investigations of Inka Expansion and Exchange.* Monograph 28. Institute of Archaeology, University of California, Los Angeles.

Earls, John

1981   Patrones de jurisdicción y organización entre los Qaracha Wankas: Una reconstrucción arqueológica y etnohistórica de una época fluida. In *Etnohistoria y Antropología Andina,* comp. Amalia Castelli, Marcia Koth de Paredes, and Mariana Mould de Pease, 55–91. Lima: Museo Nacional de Historia.

Eisenstadt, Shmuel

1963   *The Political Systems of Empires.* Glencoe, Ill.: Free Press.

Ekholm, Kasja, and Jonathan Friedman

1979   Capital Imperialism and Exploitation in Ancient World Systems. In *Power and Propaganda,* ed. Mogens T. Larsen, 41–58. Copenhagen: Akademisk Forlag.

1982   'Capital' Imperialism and Exploitation in Ancient World-Systems. *Review* 6 (1): 1–51.

Engels, Donald W.

1978   *Alexander the Great and the Logistics of the Macedonian Army.* Berkeley and Los Angeles: University of California Press.

Engels, Frederick

1972   *The Origins of the Family, Private Property, and* [1891]   *the State.* 4th ed. Ed. Eleanor Burke Leacock. New York: International Publishers.

Espinoza Soriano, Waldemar

1963   La guaranga y la reducción de Huancayo: Tres documentos inéditos de 1571 para la etnohistoria del Perú. *Revista del Museo Nacional* 32:8–80. Lima.

1969   *Lurinhuaila de Huacjra: Un ayllu y un curacazgo huanca.* Lima: Casa de Cultura.

1970   Los mitmas yungas de Collique en Cajamarca,

siglos XV, XVI, y XVII. *Revista del Museo Nacional* 36:9–57. Lima.

1971   Los Huancas, aliados de la conquista: Tres informaciones inéditas sobre la participación indígena en la conquista del Perú, 1558–1560–1561. *Anales Científicos de la Universidad de Centro del Perú* 1:3–407. Huancayo.

1973a   Las colonias de mitmas múltiples en Abancay, siglos XV y XVI. *Revista del Museo Nacional* 39:225–99. Lima.

1973b   *La destrucción del imperio de los Incas.* Lima: Retablo de Papel Ediciones.

1975   Los mitmas huayacuntu en Quito o guarniciones para la represión armada, siglos XV y XVI. *Revista del Museo Nacional* 41:351–94. Lima.

1983   Los mitmas plateros de Ishma en le país de los Ayamarca, siglos XV–XIX. *Boletín de Lima* 30 (5): 38–52. Lima.

1987   Migraciones internas en el Reino Colla: Tejedores, plumeros, y alfareros del estado imperial inca. *Chungará* 19:243–89.

Espinoza Soriano, Waldemar, ed.
1978   *Los modos de producción en el imperio de los Incas.* Lima: Editorial Mantaro-Gratifal.

Estete, Miguel de
1917   La relación que hizo el señor Capitán Hernando
[1532–33] Pizarro por mandado del señor Gobernador, su hermano, desde el pueblo de Caxamalca a Pachacamac y de allí a Jauja. In *Verdadera Relación de la Conquista del Perú,* by Francisco de Xérez, ed. Horacio H. Urteaga, 77–102. Lima: Sanmartí.

Feinman, Gary M., and Jill Neitzel
1984   Too Many Types: An Overview of Sedentary Prestate Societies in the Americas. In *Advances in Archaeological Method and Theory,* ed. Michael B. Schiffer, vol. 7, 39–102. New York: Academic Press.

Feinman, Gary M., Steadman Upham, and Kent G. Lightfoot
1981   The Production Step Measure: An Ordinal Index of Labor in Ceramic Manufacture. *American Antiquity* 46:871–84.

Ferrill, Arthur
1985   *The Origins of War from the Stone Age to Alexander the Great.* London: Thames and Hudson.

Flannery, Kent V.
1972   The Cultural Ecology of Civilizations. *Annual Review of Ecology and Systematics* 3:399–426.

Flores Espinoza, Isabel
1959   El sitio arqueológico de Wari Willca, Huancayo. In *Actas y Trabajos del II Congreso Nacional de Historia del Perú: Epoca Prehispánica,* vol. 1, 177–86. Lima.

Fock, Nils
1961   Inka Imperialism in Northwest Argentina, and Chaco Burial Forms. *Folk* 3:67–90. Copenhagen.

Food and Agriculture Organization of the United Nations
1957   *Calorie Requirements.* Second Committee on Calorie Requirements, FAO Nutrition Studies, no. 15. Rome.

Franco, Efrain, Douglas Horton, and Francois Tardieu
1979   *Producción y utilización de la papa en el valle del Mantaro—Perú.* Centro Internacional de la Papa, Unidad de Ciencias Sociales, Documento de Trabajo no. 1979-1. Lima.

Frank, Andre Gunder
1966   The Development of Underdevelopment. *Monthly Review* 18:17–31.

Fried, Morton
1967   *The Evolution of Political Society.* New York: Random House.

Friedman, Jonathan, and Michael J. Rowlands
1978   Toward an Epigenetic Model of the Evolution of Civilisation. In *On the Evolution of Civilisations,* ed. Jonathan Friedman and Michael J. Rowlands, 201–76. London: Duckworth.

Fung Pineda, Rosa
1959   Informe preliminar de las excavaciones efectuadas en al abrigo Rocos No. 1 de Tschopik. In *Actas y Trabajos del II Congreso Nacional de Historia del Perú: Epoca Prehispánica,* vol. 1, 253–73. Lima.

García Rosell, César
1942   *Los monumentos arqueológicos del Perú.* Lima: [La Cotera?].

Garcilaso de la Vega (el Inca)
1960   *Comentarios reales de los Incas.* Biblioteca
[1609]   de Autores Españoles, vols. 133–35. Madrid: Ediciones Atlas.

Gasparini, Graziano, and Luise Margolies
1980   *Inca Architecture.* Trans. Patricia J. Lyon. Bloomington: Indiana University Press.

Gilman, Antonio
1981   The Development of Social Stratification in Bronze Age Europe. *Current Anthropology* 22:1–23.

Godelier, Maurice
1974   The Concept of 'Social and Economic Formation': The Inca Example. In *Perspectives in Marxist Anthropology,* 63–69. Cambridge: Cambridge University Press.

González, Alberto Rex
1983   Inca Settlement Patterns in a Marginal Province of the Empire: Sociocultural Implications. In *Prehistoric Settlement Patterns: Essays in Honor of Gordon R. Willey,* ed. Evon Z. Vogt and

Richard M. Leventhal, 337–60. Cambridge: Harvard University.

González Carré, Enrique, Jorge Cosmopolis A., and Jorge Lévano P.

1981   *La ciudad inca de Vilcashuaman.* Ayacucho, Peru: Universidad Nacional de San Cristóbal de Huamanga.

González Holguín, Diego

1952   *Vocabulario de la lengua general de todo el Perú,*
[1608]   *llamada lengua Qquichua o del Inca.* New ed. Prologue by Raúl Porras Barrenechea. Instituto de Historia, Universidad Nacional Mayor de San Marcos. Lima: Imprenta Santa María.

Greksa, L. P., J. D. Haas, Thomas L. Leatherman, R. Brooke Thomas, H. Spielvogel, and M. Paz Zamora

1982   Maximal Aerobic Power, Nutritional Status, and Activity Levels of Bolivian Aparapitas. Paper presented at the 51st Annual Meeting of the American Association of Physical Anthropologists, Eugene, Oreg.

Guacrapáucar, don Jerónimo

1971a   Memoria de los indios que yo don Jerónimo
[1558]   Guacrapáucar di al marqués don Francisco Pizarro desde que salió de Caxamarca. In "Los Huancas, aliados de la conquista: Tres informaciones inéditas sobre la participación indígena en la conquista del Perú, 1558–1560–1561," by Waldemar Espinoza Soriano, 201–10. *Anales Científicos de la Universidad del Centro del Perú* 1:3–407. Huancayo.

1971b   Memoria y relación de lo que con los capitanes
[1558]   de Su Majestad gasté yo don Jerónimo en la guerra de Francisco Hernández y diferente della. In "Los Huancas, aliados de la conquista: Tres informaciones inéditas sobre la participación indígena en la conquista del Perú, 1558–1560–1561," by Waldemar Espinoza Soriano, 213–15. *Anales Científicos de la Universidad del Centro del Perú* 1:3–407. Huancayo.

1971c   Información hecha en la audiencia [de Lima] a
[1560]   pedimento de Don Jerónimo [Guacrapáucar sobre los servicios de su parcialidad de Lurinhuanca y propios desde que llegó Francisco Pizarro]. In "Los Huancas, aliados de la conquista: Tres informaciones inéditas sobre la participación indígena en la conquista del Perú, 1558–1560–1561," by Waldemar Espinoza Soriano, 216–59. *Anales Científicos de la Universidad del Centro del Perú* 1:3–407. Huancayo.

Guaman Poma de Ayala, Felipe

1980   *El primer nueva corónica y buen gobierno.* Ed.
[1614]   John V. Murra and Rolena Adorno; translation and textual analysis of the Quechua by Jorge I. Urioste. 3 vols. Mexico: Siglo Veintiuno.

Guzmán Ladrón de Guevara, Carlos

1959   Algunos establecimientos incas en la sierra central: Hoyas del Mantaro y del Pampas. In *Actas y Trabajos del II Congreso Nacional de Historia del Perú: Epoca Prehispánica,* vol. 1, 243–53. Lima.

Haas, Jonathan D.

1982   *The Evolution of the Prehistoric State.* New York: Columbia University Press.

Haggard, J. Villasana, and Malcolm D. McClean

1941   *Handbook for Translators of Spanish Historical Documents.* Archives Collections, University of Texas. Oklahoma City: Semco Color Press.

Haggett, Peter, Andrew D. Cliff, and Allan Frey

1977   *Locational Analysis in Human Geography.* 2d ed. New York: Wiley.

Hagstrum, Melissa

1985   Measuring Prehistoric Ceramic Craft Specialization: A Test Case in the American Southwest. *Journal of Field Archaeology* 12:65–76.

1986   *The Technology of Ceramic Production of Wanka and Inka Wares from the Yanamarca Valley, Peru.* Ceramic Notes, no. 3. Gainesville: Ceramic Technology Laboratory, Florida State Museum.

Harris, William

1989   *War and Imperialism in Republican Rome, 327–*
[1979]   *70 B.C.* Reprint with corrections. Oxford: Clarendon.

Hassig, Ross

1985   *Trade, Tribute, and Transportation: The Sixteenth-Century Political Economy of the Valley of Mexico.* Norman: University of Oklahoma Press.

1988   *Aztec Warfare: Imperial Expansion and Political Control.* Norman: University of Oklahoma Press.

Hastings, Charles M.

1985   The Eastern Frontier: Settlement and Subsistence in Andean Margins of Central Peru. Ph.D. dissertation, University of Michigan, Ann Arbor.

Hastorf, Christine A.

1983   *Prehistoric Agricultural Intensification and Political Development in the Jauja Region of Central Peru.* Ph.D. dissertation, University of California, Los Angeles. Ann Arbor, Mich.: University Microfilms.

1985   New Methods for Prehistoric Economic and Political Research. *Anthropology Today* 1 (6): 19–21.

1986   Agricultura, alimentación, y economía de los Wanka durante la época inka. In *Actas y Trabajos del VI Congreso Peruano: Hombre y Cultura Andina,* ed. Francisco Iriarte, vol. 1, 168–85. Lima: Universidad Inca Garcilaso de la Vega.

n.d.   *Resources in Power: Agriculture and the Onset of Political Inequality before the Inka.* Cambridge: Cambridge University Press. In press.

Hastorf, Christine A., and Michael J. DeNiro

1985   Reconstruction of Prehistoric Plant Production and Cooking Practices by a New Isotopic Method. *Nature* 315:489–91.

Hastorf, Christine A., and Timothy K. Earle

1985   Intensive Agriculture and the Geography of Political Change in the Upper Mantaro Region of Central Peru. In *Prehistoric Intensive Agriculture in the Tropics,* ed. Ian Farrington, 569–95. British Archaeological Reports, International Series, no. 232. Oxford.

Hastorf, Christine A., Timothy K. Earle, Herbert E. Wright, Jr., Lisa LeCount, Glenn S. Russell, and Elsie Sandefur

1989   Settlement Archaeology in the Jauja Region of Peru: Evidence from the Early Intermediate Period through the Late Intermediate Period: A Report on the 1986 Field Season. *Andean Past* 2:81–129.

Helmer, Marie

1955–56   "La visitación de los Yndios Chupachos" Inka et
[1549]   encomendero 1549. *Travaux de L'Institut Français d'Etudes Andines* 5:3–50. Lima and Paris.

Hemming, John

1970   *The Conquest of the Incas.* London: Macmillan.

Hodder, Ian, ed.

1982a   *Symbolic and Structural Archaeology.* Cambridge: Cambridge University Press.

Hodder, Ian

1982b   *Symbols in Action.* Cambridge: Cambridge University Press.

1986   *Reading the Past: Current Approaches to Interpretation in Archaeology.* Cambridge: Cambridge University Press.

Hodge, Mary

1984   *Aztec City-states.* Memoirs of the Museum of Anthropology, University of Michigan, no. 18. Studies in Latin American Ethnohistory and Archaeology, vol. 3. Ann Arbor.

Horkheimer, Hans

1951   En la región de los Huancas. *Boletín de la Sociedad Geográfica de Lima* 68:3–29. Lima.

Hornberger, Esteban, and Nancy Hornberger

1983   *Diccionario tri-lingüe Quechua de Cusco:* Quechua, English, Castellano. 2d ed. La Paz, Bolivia: Qoya Raymi.

Hyslop, John

1979   El area Lupaqa bajo del dominio incaico: Un reconocimiento arqueológico. *Histórica* 3 (1): 53–81. Lima.

1984   *The Inka Road System.* New York: Academic Press.

1985   *Inkawasi: The New Cuzco.* British Archaeological Reports, International Series, no. 234. Oxford.

1988   Las fronteras estatales extremas del Tawantinsuyu. In *La Frontera del Estado Inca,* ed. Tom D. Dillehay and Patricia J. Netherly, 35–57. Proceedings, 45 Congreso Internacional de Americanistas, Bogotá, Colombia, 1985. British Archaeological Reports, International Series, no. 442. Oxford.

1990   *Inka Settlement Planning.* Austin: University of Texas Press.

Idrovo, Jaime

1988   Tomebamba: Primera fase de conquista incaica en los Andes septentrionales: Los Cañaris y la conquista incasica del austro ecuatoriano. In *La Frontera del Estado Inca,* ed. Tom D. Dillehay and Patricia J. Netherly, 87–104. Proceedings, 45 Congreso Internacional de Americanistas, Bogotá, Colombia, 1985. British Archaeological Reports, International Series, no. 442. Oxford.

Isbell, Billie Jean

1978   *To Defend Ourselves: Ecology and Ritual in an Andean Village.* Austin: Institute of Latin American Studies, University of Texas.

Isbell, William H., and Katharina J. Schreiber

1978   Was Huari a State? *American Antiquity* 43: 372–89.

Johnson, Allen, and Timothy K. Earle

1987   *The Evolution of Human Societies: From Foraging Group to Agrarian State.* Stanford, Calif.: Stanford University Press.

Johnson, Gregory

1973   *Local Exchange and Early State Development.* Anthropological Papers of the Museum of Anthropology, University of Michigan, no. 51. Ann Arbor.

1977   Aspects of Regional Analysis in Archaeology. *Annual Review of Anthropology* 6:479–508.

1980   Rank-Size Convexity and System Integration. *Economic Geography* 56:234–47.

1982   Organizational Structure and Scalar Stress. In *Theory and Explanation in Archaeology,* ed. Colin Renfrew, Michael J. Rowlands, and Barbara A. Seagraves, 389–421. New York: Academic Press.

1983   Decision-making Organization and Pastoral Nomad Camp Size. *Human Ecology* 11 (2): 175–99.

1987   The Changing Organization of the Uruk Administration on the Susiana Plain. In *The Archaeology of Western Iran,* ed. Frank Hole, 107–39. Washington, D.C.: Smithsonian Institution Press.

Jones, George T., Donald K. Grayson, and Charlotte Beck

1983   Artifact Class Richness and Sample Size in Archaeological Surface Assemblages. In *Lulu Linear Punctated: Essays in Honor of George Irving Quimby,* ed. Robert C. Dunnell and Donald K. Grayson, 55–73. Anthropological Papers of the Museum of Anthropology, University of Michigan, no. 72. Ann Arbor.

Joyner, Stephenie P., ed.
1983   *SUGI Supplemental Library User's Guide.* Cary, N.C.: SAS Institute, Inc.

Julien, Catherine J.
1982   Inca Decimal Administration in the Lake Titicaca Region. In *The Inca and Aztec States 1400–1800: Anthropology and History,* ed. George A. Collier, Renato I. Rosaldo, and John D. Wirth, 119–51. New York: Academic Press.
1983   *Hatunqolla: A View of Inca Rule from the Lake Titicaca Region.* Publications in Anthropology, vol. 15. Berkeley and Los Angeles: University of California Press.
1988   How Inca Decimal Administration Worked. *Ethnohistory* 35:257–79.

Katz, Friedrich
1972   *The Ancient American Civilizations.* New York: Praeger.

Keesing, Roger M.
1975   *Kin Groups and Social Structure.* New York: Holt, Rinehart, and Winston.

Kendall, Ann
1974   Architecture and Planning at the Inca Sites in the Cusichaca Area. *Baessler Archiv,* n.F., vol. 22, 73–137. Berlin.
1976   Descripción e inventario de las formas arquitectónicas inca: Patrones de distribución e inferencias cronológicas. *Revista del Museo Nacional* 42:13–96. Lima.
1985   *Aspects of Inca Architecture—Description, Function, and Chronology.* 2 vols. British Archaeological Reports, International Series, no. 242. Oxford.

Kennedy, David, and Derrick Riley
1990   *Rome's Desert Frontier from the Air.* Austin: University of Texas Press.

Kohl, Philip
1987a   The Ancient Economy, Transferable Technologies, and the Bronze Age World-System: A View from the Northeastern Frontier of the Ancient Near East. In *Centre and Periphery in the Ancient World,* ed. Michael J. Rowlands, Mogens T. Larsen, and Kristian Kristiansen, 13–24. Cambridge: Cambridge University Press.
1987b   The Use and Abuse of World Systems Theory: The Case of the Pristine West Asian State. In *Advances in Archaeological Method and Theory,* ed. Michael B. Schiffer, vol. 11, 1–35. New York: Academic Press.

Kolata, Alan
1986   The Agricultural Foundations of the Tiwanaku State. *American Antiquity* 51:748–62.

Krapovickas, Pedro
1964   Un taller de lapidario en el Pucará de Tilcara.
[1958–59] *Runa* 9 (pts. 1 and 2): 137–51. Buenos Aires.
1981–82   Hallazgos incaicos en Tilcara y Yacoraite (una reinterpretación). *Relaciones de la Sociedad Argentina de Antropología,* tomo 14, no. 2, 67–80. Buenos Aires.

Kroeber, Alfred
1944   *Peruvian Archaeology in 1942.* Viking Fund Publications in Anthropology, no. 4. New York.

Kruskal, Joseph B.
1964   Nonmetric Multidimensional Scaling. *Psychometrika* 29:1–27, 115–29.

Krzanowski, Andresz
1977   Yuraccama, the Settlement Complex in the Alto Chicama Region (Northern Peru). In *Polish Contributions in New World Archaeology,* ed. Janusz K. Kozlowski, 29–58. Krakow: Zaklad Narodowy im Ossolinskich.

La Lone, Darrell E.
1982   The Inca as a Nonmarket Economy: Supply on Command versus Supply and Demand. In *Contexts for Prehistoric Exchange,* ed. Jonathan E. Ericson and Timothy K. Earle, 291–316. New York: Academic Press.

La Lone, Mary B., and Darrell E. La Lone
1987   The Inka State in the Southern Highlands: State Administrative and Production Enclaves. *Ethnohistory* 34:47–62.

Larsen, Mogens T., ed.
1979a   *Power and Propaganda: A Symposium on Ancient Empires.* Mesopotamia, vol. 7. Copenhagen: Akademisk Forlag.

Larsen, Mogens T.
1979b   The Tradition of Empire in Mesopotamia. In *Power and Propaganda: A Symposium on Ancient Empires,* 75–103. Mesopotamia, vol. 7. Copenhagen: Akademisk Forlag.

Lattimore, Owen
1962   *Studies in Frontier History: Collected Papers, 1928–1958.* London: Oxford University Press.

Lavallée, Daniele
1967   Types ceramiques des Andes centrales du Perou. *Journale de la Société des Americanistes* 56: 411–48. Paris.

Lavallée, Daniele, and Michele Julien
1983   *Asto: Curacazgo Prehispánico de los Andes Centrales.* Lima: Instituto de Estudios Peruanos.

Leatherman, Thomas L., R. Brooke Thomas, L. P. Greksa, and J. D. Haas
1983   Work and Caloric Stress among Bolivian Porters. Paper presented at the Annual Meeting

of the American Association of Physical Anthropologists.

LeBlanc, Catherine J.

1981   *Late Prehispanic Huanca Settlement Patterns in the Yanamarca Valley, Peru.* Ph.D. dissertation, Department of Anthropology, University of California, Los Angeles. Ann Arbor, Mich.: University Microfilms.

Lechtman, Heather

1984   Andean Value Systems and the Development of Prehistoric Metallurgy. *Technology and Culture* 25:1–36.

Leonard, William R.

1987   *Nutritional Adaptation and Dietary Change in the Southern Peruvian Andes.* Ph.D. dissertation, University of Michigan. Ann Arbor, Mich.: University Microfilms.

Leone, Mark P.

1982   Some Opinions about Recovering Mind. *American Antiquity* 47:742–60.

Leslie, Paul W., James R. Bindon, and Paul T. Baker

1984   Caloric Requirements of Human Populations: A Model. *Human Ecology* 12 (2): 137–62.

Leung, Woot-Tsuen Wu

1961   *Food Composition Table for Use in Latin America.* Guatemala City: Institute of Nutrition of Central America & Panama.

Levillier, Roberto, ed.

1940   *Don Francisco de Toledo, supremo organizador del Peru: Su vida, su obra [1515–1582].* Vol. 2. Buenos Aires: Espasa-Calpe.

LeVine, Terry Y.

1979   Prehispanic Political and Economic Change in Highlands Peru: An Ethnohistorical Study of the Mantaro Valley. Master's thesis, Institute of Archaeology, University of California, Los Angeles.

1985   *Inka Administration in the Central Highlands: A Comparative Study.* Ph.D. dissertation, University of California, Los Angeles. Ann Arbor, Mich.: University Microfilms.

1987   Inka Labor Service at the Regional Level: The Functional Reality. *Ethnohistory* 34:14–46.

n.d.   *Storage Systems in the Inka Empire.* Norman: University of Oklahoma Press.

Levins, Richard

1966   The Strategy of Model Building in Population Biology. *American Scientist* 54 (4): 421–31.

Litvak King, Jaime

1971   *Cihuatlán y Tepecoacuilco: Provincias tributarias de México en el siglo XVI.* Mexico: Universidad Nacional Autónoma de México.

Lorandi, Ana María

1984   Soñocamayoc: Los olleros del Inka en los centros manufactureros del Tucumán. *Revista del Museo de la Plata,* tomo 7, 303–27. Sección Antro-

pología, no. 62. La Plata, Argentina: Universidad Nacional de la Plata, Facultad de Ciencias Naturales y Museo.

1988   Los Diaguitas y el Tawantinsuyu: Una hipótesis de conflicto. In *La Frontera del Estado Inca,* ed. Tom D. Dillehay and Patricia J. Netherly, 235–59. Proceedings, 45 Congreso Internacional de Americanistas, Bogotá, Colombia, 1985. British Archaeological Reports, International Series, no. 442. Oxford.

Lorandi, Ana María, and Roxana Boixadós

1987–88   Etnohistoria de los valles calchaquíes en los siglos XVI y XVII. *Runa* 17–18: 263–420. Buenos Aires.

Lumbreras, Luis G.

1957   La cultura wanka. In *Ondas Isabelinas, Organo Cultural de la Gran Unidad Escolar Santa Isabel de Huancayo,* 15–18. Huancayo, Peru.

1959   Esquema arqueológico de la sierra central del Perú. *Revista del Museo Nacional* 28:64–117. Lima.

1974   *The Peoples and Cultures of Ancient Peru.* Trans. Betty J. Meggers. Washington, D.C.: Smithsonian Institution Press.

1978   Acerca de la aparación del estado inka. In *III Congreso Peruano: El Hombre y la Cultura Andina,* ed. Ramiro Matos Mendieta, vol. 1, 101–9. Lima: Universidad Nacional Mayor de San Marcos.

Luttwak, Edward N.

1976   *The Grand Strategy of the Roman Empire from the First Century A.D. to the Third.* Baltimore: Johns Hopkins University Press.

MacKendrick, Paul

1987   The Romans in Burgundy. In *Regional Dynamics: Burgundian Landscapes in Historical Perspective,* ed. Carole L. Crumley and William H. Marquardt, 431–46. San Diego: Academic Press.

Mackey, Carol J., and Alexandra M. Ulana Klymyshyn

n.d.   Political Integration in Prehispanic Peru. Final project report submitted to the U.S. National Science Foundation, 1981–82. Manuscript.

Mann, Michael

1986   *The Sources of Social Power.* Vol. 1, *A History of Power to A.D. 1760.* Cambridge: Cambridge University Press.

Mannheim, Bruce

1985   Southern Peruvian Quechua. In *South American Indian Languages: Retrospect and Prospect,* ed. Harriet E. Manelis Klein and Louisa R. Stark, 481–515. Austin: University of Texas Press.

Martínez Rengifo, Juan

1963   La visita de Guancayo, Maca y Guaravni. In "La
[1571]   guaranga y la reducción de Huancayo: Tres do-

cumentos inéditos de 1571 para la etnohistoria del Perú," by Waldemar Espinoza Soriano, 58–69. *Revista del Museo Nacional* 32:8–80. Lima.

Matos Mendieta, Ramiro

1959 Los Wankas, datos históricos y arqueológicos. In *Actas y Trabajos del II Congreso Nacional de Historia del Perú: Epoca Prehispánica,* vol. 1, 187–210. Lima.

1966 La cconomía durante el Período de Reinos y Confederaciones en Mantaro, Perú. *Actas y Memorias del XXXVI Congreso Internacional de Americanistas,* vol. 2, 95–99. Seville.

1971 El Período Formativo en el Valle del Mantaro. *Revista del Museo Nacional* 37:41–51. Lima.

1972 Ataura: Un centro chavín en el Valle del Mantaro. *Revista del Museo Nacional* 38:93–108. Lima.

1975 Prehistoria y ecología humana en las punas de Junín. *Revista del Museo Nacional* 41:37–80. Lima.

Matos Mendieta, Ramiro, and Jeffrey R. Parsons

1979 Poblamiento prehispánico en la Cuenca del Mantaro. In *Arqueología Peruana,* ed. Ramiro Matos Mendieta, 157–71. Lima: Universidad Nacional Mayor de San Marcos.

McGuire, Randall H.

1989 The Greater Southwest as a Periphery of Mesoamerica. In *Centre and Periphery: Comparative Studies in Archaeology,* ed. Timothy C. Champion, 40–66. London: Unwin, Hyman.

Means, Philip A.

1928 Biblioteca Andina. *Transactions of the Connecticut Academy of Arts and Sciences* 29:271–525.

Menzel, Dorothy

1959 The Inca Conquest of the South Coast of Peru. *Southwestern Journal of Anthropology* 15:125–42.

Métraux, Alfred

1969 *The History of the Incas.* New York: Schocken.

Meyers, Albert

1975 Algunos problemas en la clasificación del estilo incaico. *Pumapunku* 8:7–25. La Paz.

1976 *Die Inka in Ekuador: Untersuchungen anhand ihrer materiellen.* Bonner Amerikanistische Studien, no. 8. Bonn: Seminar für Völkerkunde, Universität Bonn.

Miller, Daniel, and Christopher Tilley, eds.

1984 *Ideology, Power, and Prehistory.* Cambridge: Cambridge University Press.

Miller, George

1972 An Investigation into the Rules of Style of Cuzco Ceramics. Manuscript.

Miranda, Christóbal de

1925 Relación de los corregimientos y otras oficios que [1583] se proveen en los reynos e provincias del Pirú, en el distrito e gobernación del visorrey dellos. In *El Virrey Martín Enriquez 1581–1583,* 128–230. Vol. 9 of *Gobernantes del Perú: Cartas y Papeles,* ed. Roberto Levillier. Madrid: Imprento de Juan Pueyo.

Mitchell, William

1980 Local Ecology and the State: Implications of Contemporary Quechua Land Use for the Inca Sequence of Agricultural Work. In *Beyond the Myths of Culture: Essays in Cultural Materialism,* ed. Eric B. Ross, 139–54. New York: Academic Press.

Moore, Sally F.

1958 *Power and Property in Inca Peru.* Westport, Conn.: Greenwood Press.

Morgan, David

1986 *The Mongols.* Oxford: Basil Blackwell.

Morris, Craig

1966 El tampu real de Tunsucancha. *Cuadernos de Investigación* 1:95–107. Huánuco, Peru.

1967 Storage in Tawantinsuyu. Ph.D. dissertation, Department of Anthropology, University of Chicago.

1971 The Identification of Function in Inca Architecture and Ceramics. In *Actas y Memorias del XXXIX Congreso Internacional de Americanistas,* vol. 3, 135–44. Lima.

1972a El almacenaje en dos aldeas de los Chupaychu. In *Visita de la Provincia de León de Huánuco en 1562, Iñigo Ortiz de Zúñiga, Visitador,* ed. John V. Murra, vol. 2, 385–404. Huánuco, Peru: Universidad Nacional Hermilio Valdızán.

1972b State Settlements in Tawantinsuyu: A Strategy of Compulsory Urbanism. In *Contemporary Archaeology,* ed. Mark P. Leone, 393–401. Carbondale: Southern Illinois University Press.

1974 Reconstructing Patterns of Nonagricultural Production in the Inca Economy: Archaeology and Documents in Instituted Analysis. In *Reconstructing Complex Societies,* ed. Carol Moore, 49–68. Supplement to *Bulletin of the American Schools of Oriental Research* 20.

1978 The Archeological Study of Andean Exchange Systems. In *Social Archeology: Beyond Subsistence and Dating,* ed. Charles L. Redman, Mary Jane Berman, Edward V. Curtin, William T. Langhorne, Jr., Nina M. Versaggi, and Jeffrey C. Wanser, 303–27. New York: Academic Press.

1981 Tecnología y organización inca del almacenimiento de víveres en la sierra. In *La Tecnología en el Mundo Andino,* ed. Heather Lechtman and Ann Maria Soldi, 327–75. Mexico: Universidad Nacional Autónoma de México.

1982 The Infrastructure of Inka Control in the Peruvian Central Highlands. In *The Inca and Aztec*

States, 1400–1800: Anthropology and History, ed. George A. Collier, Renato I. Rosaldo, and John D. Wirth, 153–71. New York: Academic Press.

1988   Mas allá de las fronteras de Chincha. In *La Frontera del Estado Inca,* ed. Tom D. Dillehay and Patricia J. Netherly, 131–40. Proceedings, 45 Congreso Internacional de Americanistas, Bogotá, Colombia, 1985. British Archaeological Reports, International Series, no. 442. Oxford.

1990   Arquitectura y estructura del espacio en Huá-
[1987]   nuco Pampa. *Cuadernos* 12:27–45. Buenos Aires: Instituto Nacional de Antropología.

Morris, Craig, and Donald E. Thompson

1970   Huánuco Viejo: An Inca Administrative Center. *American Antiquity* 35:344–62.

1985   *Huánuco Pampa: An Inca City and Its Hinterland.* London: Thames and Hudson.

Moseley, Michael E.

1975   Chan Chan: Andean Alternative of the Prein-dustrial City. *Science* 187:219–25.

1983   Central Andean Civilization. In *Ancient South Americans,* ed. Jesse Jennings, 179–239. San Francisco: Freeman.

Moseley, Michael E., and Kent C. Day, eds.

1982   *Chan Chan: Andean Desert City.* Albuquerque: University of New Mexico Press.

Murra, John V.

1958   On Inca Political Structure. In *Proceedings of the Annual Spring Meeting of the American Eth-nological Society,* 30–41. Seattle: University of Washington.

1962   Cloth and Its Functions in the Inca State. *American Anthropologist* 64:710–28.

1968   An Aymara Kingdom in 1567. *Ethnohistory* 15: 115–51.

1970   Comment on Clifford T. Smith, "The Depopula-tion of the Central Andes in the Sixteenth Cen-tury." *Current Anthropology* 11:461–62.

1972   El 'control vertical' de un máximo de pisos eco-lógicos en la economía de las sociedades andi-nas. In *Visita de la Provincia de León de Huá-nuco en 1562, Iñigo Ortiz de Zúñiga, Visitador,* ed. John V. Murra, vol. 2, 427–76. Huánuco, Peru: Universidad Nacional Hermilio Valdizán.

1975   *Formaciones económicas y políticas del mundo andino.* Lima: Instituto de Estudios Peruanos.

1978   Los olleros del Inka: Hacia una historia y ar-queología del Qollasuyu. In *Historia, Problema, y Promesa: Homenaje a Jorge Basadre,* ed. F. Miro Quesada, Franklin Pease G. Y., and Daniel Sobrevilla, 415–23. Lima: Pontificia Univer-sidad Católica del Perú.

1980   *The Economic Organization of the Inka State.*
[1956]   Greenwich, Conn.: JAI Press.

1986   The Expansion of the Inka State: Armies, War, and Rebellions. In *Anthropological History of Andean Polities,* ed. John V. Murra, Nathan Wachtel, and Jacques Revel, 49–58. Cambridge: Cambridge University Press.

Murra, John V., and Rolena Adorno, eds.

1980   *El primer nueva corónica y buen gobierno.* By
[1614]   Felipe Guaman Poma de Ayala. 3 vols. Trans. Jorge I. Urioste. Mexico: Siglo Veintiuno.

Murúa, Fray Martín

1962   *Historia general del Perú, origen y descendencia*
[1590–   *de los Incas.* Colección Joyas Bibliográficas.
1600]   Madrid: Bibliotheca Americana Vetus.

Nash, Daphne

1987   Imperial Expansion under the Roman Republic. In *Centre and Periphery in the Ancient World,* ed. Michael J. Rowlands, Mogens T. Larsen, and Kristian Kristiansen, 87–103. Cambridge: Cambridge University Press.

Nash, June

1981   Ethnographic Aspects of the World Capitalist System. *Annual Review of Anthropology* 10: 393–423.

Netherly, Patricia J.

1978   Local Level Lords on the North Coast of Peru. Ph.D. dissertation, Department of Anthropol-ogy, Cornell University, Ithaca, N.Y.

1988   El reino de Chimor y el Tawantinsuyu. In *La Frontera del Estado Inca,* ed. Tom D. Dillehay and Patricia J. Netherly, 105–40. Proceedings, 45 Congreso Internacional de Americanistas, Bogotá, Colombia, 1985. British Archaeolog-ical Reports, International Series, no. 442. Oxford.

Niemeyer F., Hans, and Virgilio Schiappacasse F.

1988   Patrones de asentamiento incaicos en el Norte Grande de Chile. In *La Frontera del Estado Inca,* ed. Tom D. Dillehay and Patricia J. Netherly, 141–80. Proceedings, 45 Congreso Internacio-nal de Americanistas, Bogotá, Colombia, 1985. British Archaeological Reports, International Series, no. 442. Oxford.

Niles, Susan A.

1987   *Callachaca: Style and Status in an Inca Com-munity.* Iowa City: University of Iowa Press.

Nordenskiöld, Erland von

1924   *Forschungen und Abenteur in Südamerica.* Stuttgart: Strecker und Schröder.

Oberem, Udo

1968   Die Berfestung Quitoloma im Nördlichen Hoch-land Ecuadors. *Baessler Archiv,* n.F., vol. 16, 331–54. Berlin.

Ortiz de Zúñiga, Iñigo

1967   *Visita de la Provincia de León de Huánuco en*
[1562]   *1562, Iñigo Ortiz de Zúñiga, visitador.* Ed. John

V. Murra. Vol. 1. Huánuco, Peru: Universidad Nacional Hermilio Valdizán.

1972   *Visita de la Provincia de León de Huánuco en*
[1562]   *1562, Iñigo Ortiz de Zúñiga, visitador.* Ed. John V. Murra. Vol. 2. Huánuco, Peru: Universidad Nacional Hermilio Valdizán.

Pardo, Luis A.

1939   Hacia una nueva clasificación de la cerámica cuzqueña del antiguo Imperio de los Incas. *Revista del Instituto Arqueológico del Cusco* 4–5: 3–22. Cuzco.

Parsons, Jeffrey R.

1976   Prehispanic Settlement Patterns in the Upper Mantaro, Peru: A Preliminary Report of the 1975 Field Season. Progress report submitted to the U.S. National Science Foundation. Manuscript.

Parsons, Jeffrey R., and Timothy K. Earle, eds.

n.d.   *Settlement Patterns in the Jauja Region, Peru* [tentative title]. Monograph. Museum of Anthropology, University of Michigan, Ann Arbor. In preparation.

Parsons, Jeffrey R., and Charles M. Hastings

1977   Prehispanic Settlement Patterns in the Upper Mantaro, Peru: A Progress Report for the 1976 Field Season. Progress report submitted to the Instituto Nacional de Cultura, Lima, Peru, and the National Science Foundation, Washington, D.C.

n.d.   Field Notes: Prehispanic Settlement Patterns in
[1975–76]   the Upper Mantaro, Peru. Manuscript.

Parsons, Jeffrey R., and Ramiro Matos Mendieta

1978   Asentamientos prehispánicos en el Mantaro, Perú: Informe preliminar. In *III Congreso Peruano: El Hombre y la Cultura Andina,* ed. Ramiro Matos Mendieta, vol. 2, 540–55. Lima: Universidad Nacional Mayor de San Marcos.

Patterson, Thomas

1985   Exploitation and Class Formation in the Inca State. *Culture* 1 (1): 35–42. Montreal.

1986   Ideology, Class Formation, and Resistance in the Inca State. *Critique of Anthropology* 6 (1): 75–85. Amsterdam.

Paynter, Robert W.

1982   *Models of Spatial Inequality: Settlement Patterns in Historical Archeology.* New York: Academic Press.

1983   Expanding the Scope of Settlement Analysis. In *Archaeological Hammers and Theories,* ed. James A. Moore and Arthur S. Keene, 233–75. New York: Academic Press.

Pease G. Y., Franklin, ed.

1977   *Collaguas I.* Lima: Pontificia Universidad Católica del Perú, Fondo Editorial.

Pease G. Y., Franklin

1978   *Del Tawantinsuyu a la historia del Perú.* Lima: Instituto de Estudios Peruanos.

Peebles, Christopher S., and Susan M. Kus

1977   Some Archaeological Correlates of Ranked Societies. *American Antiquity* 42:421–48.

Pizarro, Hernando

1959   Carta a Oidores de Santo Domingo, Panama. In
[1533]   *La Historia General y Natural de las Indias* [1550], by Gonzalo Fernández de Oviedo y Valdés, 84–90. Biblioteca de Autores Españoles, vol. 121. Madrid: Ediciones Atlas.

Pizarro, Pedro

1986   *Relación del descubrimiento y conquista de los*
[1571]   *reinos del Perú.* 2d ed. Ed. Guillermo Lohmann Villena. Lima: Pontificia Universidad Católica del Perú, Fondo Editorial.

Plaza Schuller, Fernando

1980   *La incursión inca en el septentrión andino ecuatoriano.* Instituto Otavaleño de Antropología, Serie Arqueología, no. 2. Otavalo, Ecuador.

Polanyi, Karl

1957   The Economy as Instituted Process. In *Trade and Market in the Early Empires,* ed. Karl Polanyi, Conrad Arensberg, and Harry Pearson, 243–70. New York: Free Press.

1966   *Dahomey and the Slave Trade: An Analysis of an Archaic Economy.* In collaboration with Abraham Rotstein. Seattle: University of Washington Press.

Polanyi, Karl, Conrad Arensberg, and Harry Pearson, eds.

1957   *Trade and Market in the Early Empires.* New York: Free Press.

Polo de Ondegardo, Juan

1917   La relación del linaje de los Incas y cómo exten-
[1567]   dieron ellos sus conquistas. In *Colección de Libros y Documentos Referentes a la Historia del Perú,* ed. Horacio H. Urteaga, tomo 4, 45–94. Lima: Sanmartí.

1940   Informe del Licenciado Juan Polo de Ondegardo
[1561]   al Licenciado Briviesca de Muñatones sobre la perpetuidad de las encomiendas en el Perú. *Revista Histórica* 13:128–96. Lima.

Porras Barrenechea, Raúl

1950   Jauja, Capital Mítica. *Revista Histórica* 18 (2): 117–48.

1986   *Los cronistas del Perú.* Biblioteca Clásicos del Perú, no. 2. Lima: Banco de Crédito del Perú.

Price, Barbara J.

1978   Secondary State Formation: An Explanatory Model. In *Origins of the State: The Anthropology of Political Evolution,* ed. Ronald Cohen and Elman R. Service, 161–86. Philadelphia: Ishi.

1982 Cultural Materialism: A Theoretical Review. *American Antiquity* 47:709–41.

Pulgar Vidal, Javier

1964 *Geografía del Perú.* 8th ed. Lima: Textos Universitarios.

Raffino, Rodolfo

1983 *Los Inkas del Kollasuyu.* 2d ed. La Plata, Argentina: Ramos Americana Editora.

Ragin, Charles C., and Daniel Chirot

1984 The World System of Immanuel Wallerstein: Sociology and Politics as History. In *Vision and Method in Historical Sociology,* ed. Theda Skocpol, 276–312. Cambridge: Cambridge University Press.

Ramirez, Susan E.

1990 The Inca Conquest of the North Coast: A Historian's View. In *The Northern Dynasties: Kingship and Statecraft in Chimor,* ed. Michael E. Moseley and Alana Cordy-Collins, 507–37. Washington, D.C.: Dumbarton Oaks.

Ramirez-Horton, Susan E.

1982 Retainers of the Lords or Merchants: A Case of Mistaken Identity? In *El Hombre y su Ambiente en los Andes Centrales,* ed. Luis Millones and Hiroyasu Tomoeda, 123–36. Senri Ethnological Studies, vol. 10. Osaka: National Museum of Ethnology.

Randsborg, Klavs

1989 The town, the power, and the land: Denmark and Europe during the first millennium A.D. In *Centre and Periphery: Comparative Studies in Archaeology,* ed. Timothy C. Champion, 207–26. London: Unwin, Hyman.

Rawls, Joseph

1979 *An Analysis of Prehispanic Andean Warfare.* Ph.D. dissertation, University of California, Los Angeles. Ann Arbor, Mich.: University Microfilms.

Redman, Charles L.

1973 Multistage Fieldwork and Analytical Techniques. *American Antiquity* 38:61–79.

Regal Matienzo, Alberto

1936 *Los caminos del Inca en el antiguo Perú.* Lima: Sanmartí.

1972 *Los puentes del Inca en el antiguo Perú.* Lima: Imprenta Gráfica Industrial.

Rostworowski de Diez Canseco, María

1961 *Curacas y sucesiones costa norte.* Miraflores, Peru: Imprenta Minerva.

1975 La "Visita" a Chinchacocha de 1549. *Anales Científicos de la Universidad del Centro del Perú* 4:73–88. Huancayo.

1977a La estratificación social y el Hatun Curaca en el mundo andino. *Histórica* 1 (2): 249–86. Lima.

1977b *Etnía y sociedad costa peruana prehispánica.* Lima: Instituto de Estudios Peruanos.

1978 *Señorios indígenas de Lima y Canta.* Lima: Instituto de Estudios Peruanos.

1981 *Recursos naturales renovables y pesca, siglos XVI y XVII.* Lima: Instituto de Estudios Peruanos.

1983 *Estructuras andinas del poder.* Lima: Instituto de Estudios Peruanos.

1988 *Historia del Tahuantinsuyu.* 2d ed. Lima: Instituto de Estudios Peruanos.

Rowe, John H.

1944 *An Introduction to the Archaeology of Cuzco.* Papers of the Peabody Museum of American Archaeology and Ethnology, vol. 27, no. 2. Cambridge, Mass.

1946 Inca Culture at the Time of the Spanish Conquest. In *Handbook of South American Indians,* vol. 2, ed. Julian Steward, 183–330. Bureau of American Ethnology Bulletin 143. Washington, D.C.

1948 The Kingdom of Chimor. *Acta Americana* 6: 26–59.

1982 Inca Policies and Institutions Relating to the Cultural Unification of the Empire. In *The Inca and Aztec States, 1400–1800: Anthropology and History,* ed. George A. Collier, Renato I. Rosaldo, and John D. Wirth, 93–118. New York: Academic Press.

1985 Probanza de los Incas nietos de conquistadores. *Histórica* 9 (2): 193–245. Lima.

Rowlands, Michael J.

1987 Centre and Periphery: A Review of a Concept. In *Centre and Periphery in the Ancient World,* ed. Michael J. Rowlands, Mogens T. Larsen, and Kristian Kristiansen, 1–11. Cambridge: Cambridge University Press.

Rowlands, Michael J., Mogens T. Larsen, and Kristian Kristiansen, eds.

1987 *Centre and Periphery in the Ancient World.* Cambridge: Cambridge University Press.

Russell, Glenn S.

1988 *The Effect of Inka Administrative Policy on the Domestic Economy of the Wanka, Peru: The Production and Use of Stone Tools.* Ph.D. dissertation, University of California, Los Angeles. Ann Arbor, Mich.: University Microfilms.

Sahlins, Marshal, and Elman R. Service, eds.

1960 *Evolution and Culture.* Ann Arbor: University of Michigan Press.

Salomon, Frank

1986 *Native Lords of Quito in the Age of the Incas.* Cambridge: Cambridge University Press.

1987 A North Andean Status Trader Complex under Inka Rule. *Ethnohistory* 34:63–77.

Sancho de la Hoz, Pedro
1917   Relación. In *Colección de Libros y Documentos*
[1532–33]   *Referentes a la Historia del Perú,* ed. Horacio H.
            Urteaga, vol. 5, 122–202. Lima: Sanmartí.

Sandefur, Elsie
1988   *Andean Zooarchaeology: Animal Use and the
            Inka Conquest of the Upper Mantaro Valley.*
            Ph.D. dissertation, University of California,
            Los Angeles. Ann Arbor, Mich.: University
            Microfilms.

Sanders, William T., and Barbara J. Price
1968   *Mesoamerica: The Evolution of a Civilization.*
            New York: Random House.

Sanders, William T., Jeffrey R. Parsons, and Robert S. Santley
1978   *The Basin of Mexico: Evolution of a Civiliza-
            tion.* New York: Academic Press.

Santley, Robert S.
1986   Prehispanic Roadways, Transport Network Ge-
            ometry, and Aztec Politico-economic Organi-
            zation in the Basin of Mexico. In *Research in
            Economic Anthropology, Supplement 2: Eco-
            nomic Aspects of Prehispanic Highland Mexico,*
            ed. Barry Isaac, 223–44. Greenwich, Conn.:
            JAI Press.

Sarmiento de Gamboa, Pedro
1960   *Historia de los Incas.* Biblioteca de Autores Es-
[1572]   pañoles, vol. 135, 193–297. Madrid: Ediciones
            Atlas.

Schacht, Robert
1987   Early Historic Cultures. In *The Archaeology of
            Western Iran,* ed. Frank Hole, 171–203. Wash-
            ington, D.C.: Smithsonian Institution Press.

Schaedel, Richard P.
1978   Early State of the Incas. In *The Early State,* ed.
            Henri M. Claessen and Peter Skalnik, 289–320.
            The Hague: Mouton.

Schneider, Jane
1977   Was There a Pre-capitalist World System? *Peas-
            ant Studies* 6 (1): 20–29.

Schortman, Edward M., and Patricia A. Urban
1987   Modeling Interregional Interaction in Prehis-
            tory. In *Advances in Archaeological Method and
            Theory,* ed. Michael B. Schiffer, vol. 11, 37–95.
            New York: Academic Press.

Schreiber, Katharina J.
1987   Conquest and Consolidation: A Comparison
            of the Wari and Inka Occupations of a High-
            land Peruvian Valley. *American Antiquity* 52:
            266–84.
n.d.   *The Archaeology of Imperialism: Ecology, Set-
            tlement Patterns, and Political Expansion in
            Middle Horizon Peru.* Memoirs of the Museum
            of Anthropology, University of Michigan. Stud-
            ies in Latin American Ethnohistory and Archae-
            ology. Ann Arbor. In press.

Service, Elman R.
1975   *Origins of the State and Civilization: The Pro-
            cess of Cultural Evolution.* New York: W. W.
            Norton and Co.

Shanks, Michael, and Christopher Tilley
1982   Ideology, Symbolic Power, and Ritual Com-
            munication: A Reinterpretation of Neolithic
            Mortuary Practices. In *Symbolic and Structural
            Archaeology,* ed. Ian Hodder, 129–54. Cam-
            bridge: Cambridge University Press.
1984   *Re-Constructing Archaeology: Theory and
            Practice.* Cambridge: Cambridge University
            Press.

Shannon, Thomas R.
1989   *An Introduction to the World-System Perspec-
            tive.* Boulder, Colo.: Westview Press.

Sikkink, Lynn L.
1988   Traditional Crop-processing in Central Andean
            Households: An Ethnoarchaeological Perspec-
            tive. In *Multidisciplinary Studies in Andean An-
            thropology,* ed. Virginia J. Vitzthum, 65–85.
            Michigan Discussions in Anthropology, vol. 8.
            Ann Arbor: Museum of Anthropology, Univer-
            sity of Michigan.

Silverblatt, Irene
1988   Imperial Dilemmas, the Politics of Kinship, and
            Inca Reconstructions of History. *Comparative
            Studies in Society and History* 30 (1): 83–102.
            Cambridge.

Skinner, G. William
1977   Cities and the Hierarchy of Local Systems. In
            The City in Late Imperial China, ed. G. William
            Skinner, 275–351. Stanford, Calif.: Stanford
            University Press.

Skinner, G. William, and Edwin A. Winckler
1969   Compliance Succession in Rural Communist
            China. In *A Sociological Reader on Com-
            plex Organizations,* 2d ed., ed. Amitai Etzio-
            ni, 410–38. New York: Holt, Rinehart, and
            Winston.

Smelser, Neil J.
1959   A Comparative View of Exchange Systems. *Eco-
            nomic Development* 7:173–82.

Smith, Carol A.
1976   Exchange Systems and the Spatial Distribution
            of Elites. In *Regional Analysis,* ed. Carol A.
            Smith, vol. 2, 309–74. New York: Academic
            Press.

Smith, Clifford T.
1970   The Depopulation of the Central Andes in the
            Sixteenth Century. *Current Anthropology* 11:
            453–64.

Smith, Michael A.
1987a   The Expansion of the Aztec Empire: A Case
            Study in the Correlation of Diachronic and Eth-

nohistorical Data. *American Antiquity* 52: 37–54.

1987b   Household Possessions and Wealth in Agrarian States: Implications for Archaeology. *Journal of Anthropological Archaeology* 6:297–335.

Snedecor, George W., and William G. Cochran
1980   *Statistical Methods.* 7th ed. Ames: Iowa State University Press.

Spalding, Karen
1985   *Huarochirí.* Stanford, Calif.: Stanford University Press.

Spurling, Geoffrey
1987   Qolla Potters Making Inka Pottery: Ceramic Production at Milliraya. Paper presented at the 52d Annual Meeting of the Society for American Archaeology, Toronto.

Stehberg, Rubén, and Nazareno Carvajal
1988   Red vial incaica en los términos meridionales del imperio: Tramo valle del Limarí–valle del Maipo. In *La Frontera del Estado Inca,* ed. Tom D. Dillehay and Patricia J. Netherly, 181–214. Proceedings, 45 Congreso Internacional de Americanistas, Bogotá, Colombia, 1985. British Archaeological Reports, International Series, no. 442. Oxford.

Stern, Steven
1982   *Peru's Indian Peoples and the Challenge of Spanish Conquest.* Madison: University of Wisconsin Press.

Steward, Julian H.
1955   *Theory of Culture Change: The Methodology of Multilinear Evolution.* Urbana: University of Illinois Press.

Thomas, David H.
1983   *The Archaeology of Monitor Valley, 2: Gatecliff Shelter.* Anthropological Papers of the American Museum of Natural History, vol. 59, pt. 1. New York.

1986   *Refiguring Anthropology.* Prospect Heights, Ill.: Waveland Press.

Thomas, R. Brooke
1973   *Human Adaptation to a High Andean Energy Flow System.* Occasional Papers in Anthropology, no. 7. University Park: Department of Anthropology, Pennsylvania State University.

Thompson, Donald E.
1967a   La alferería inca de Huánuco. *Boletín del Museo Nacional de Antropología y Arqueología.* Lima.

1967b   Investigaciones arqueológicas en las aldeas chupachu de Ichu y Auquimarka. In *Visita de la Provincia de León de Huánuco en 1562, Iñigo Ortiz de Zúñiga, Visitador,* ed. John V. Murra, vol. 1, 357–62. Huánuco, Peru: Universidad Nacional Hermilio Valdizán.

1968a   An Archaeological Evaluation of Ethnohistoric Evidence on Inca Culture. In *Anthropological Archaeology in the Americas,* ed. Betty J. Meggers, 108–20. Washington, D.C.: Anthropological Society of Washington.

1968b   Incaic Installations at Huánuco and Pumpu. *Actas y Memorias del XXXVII Congreso Internacional de Americanistas, 1966,* vol. 1, 67–74. Buenos Aires.

1972a   Etnías y grupos locales tardíos. In *Pueblos y Culturas de la Sierra Central del Perú,* ed. Duccio Bonavia and Rogger Ravines, 67–89. Lima: Cerro de Pasco Corp.

1972b   Peasant Inca Villages in the Huánuco Region. *Proceedings of the XXXVIII International Congress of Americanists, 1968,* vol. 4, 61–66. Stuttgart-München.

Thompson, Donald E., and John V. Murra
1966   The Inca Bridges in the Huánuco Region. *American Antiquity* 31:632–39.

Tilley, Christopher
1981   Conceptual Frameworks for the Explanation of Sociocultural Change. In *Pattern of the Past: Studies in Honor of David Clarke,* ed. Ian Hodder, Glyn Isaac, and Norman Hammond. Cambridge: Cambridge University Press.

1984   Ideology and the Legitimation of Power in the Middle Neolithic of Southern Sweden. In *Ideology, Power, and Prehistory,* ed. Daniel Miller and Christopher Tilley, 111–46. Cambridge: Cambridge University Press.

Toledo, Francisco de
1940a   Información hecha por orden de Don Francisco
[1570]   de Toledo en su visita de las Provincias del Perú, en la que declaran indios ancianos sobre el derecho de los caciques y sobre el gobierno que tenían aquellos pueblos antes que los Incas los conquistasen. Concepción de Xauxa, 20 Noviembre 1570. In *Don Francisco de Toledo, Supremo Organizador del Peru: Su Vida, Su Obra (1515–1582),* ed. Roberto Levillier, vol. 2, 14–37. Buenos Aires: Espasa-Calpe.

1940b   Información hecha en el Cuzco por orden del
[1571]   Virrey Toledo, con respuestas al mismo interrogatorio utilizado en las cuatro informaciones anteriores: Añádese un auto del año 1563 del Conde de Nieva, en el cual otorga ese Virrey investidura a un cacique en la misma forma en que antes la daban los incas a los curacas. Cuzco, 13–18 marzo, 1571. In *Don Francisco de Toledo, Supremo Organizador del Peru: Su Vida, Su Obra (1515–1582),* ed. Roberto Levillier, vol. 2, 65–98. Buenos Aires: Espasa-Calpe.

1940c   Información comenzada en el Valle de Yucay el 2
[1571]   de Junio y proseguida en el Cuzco desde el 19 de

ese mes hasta el 5 de septiembre, ante el Secretario Alvaro Ruiz de Navamuel, acerca de las costumbres religiosas, sacrificios e idolatrías y manera de enterrarse de los Incas, y del modo que tenían éstos de gobernar, aplicando a los indios al trabajo para que no se hiciesen ociosos. Ratificación de la misma por los 95 testigos en el Cuzco, ante el Doctor Loarte. Junio 2–Septiembre 6 de 1571. In *Don Francisco de Toledo, Supremo Organizador del Peru: Su Vida, Su Obra (1515–1582),* ed. Roberto Levillier, vol. 2, 122–77. Buenos Aires: Espasa-Calpe.

Topic, John

1982   Lower-class Social and Economic Organization at Chan Chan. In *Chan Chan: Andean Desert City,* ed. Michael E. Moseley and Kent C. Day, 145–76. Albuquerque: University of New Mexico Press.

1985   Comment on Terence N. D'Altroy and Timothy K. Earle, "Staple Finance, Wealth Finance, and Storage in the Inka Political Economy," *Current Anthropology* 26:201–2.

Torero, Alfredo

1964   Los dialectos quechuas. *Anales Científicos* 2: 446–78. Lima: Universidad Agraria.

1974   *El quechua y la historia social andina.* Lima: Universidad Ricardo Palma.

Tosi, Joseph A., Jr.

1960   *Zonas de vida natural en el Perú.* Instituto Interamericano de Ciencias Agrícolas, Boletín Técnico no. 5. [Lima?].

Urton, Gary

1981   *At the Crossroads of the Earth and the Sky: An Andean Cosmology.* Latin American Monographs, no. 55. Austin: University of Texas Press.

1990   *The History of a Myth: Pacariqtambo and the Origin of the Inkas.* Austin: University of Texas Press.

Vaca de Castro Cavellero, Cristóbal

1908   Ordenanzas de tambos. *Revista Histórica* 3:
[1543]   427–92. Lima.

van Creveld, Martin

1977   *Supplying War: Logistics from Wallenstein to Patton.* Cambridge: Cambridge University Press.

1985   *Command in War.* Cambridge: Harvard University Press.

Vega, Andrés de

1965   La descripción que se hizo en la Provincia de
[1582]   Xauxa por la instrucción de Su Majestad que a la dicha provincia se invio de molde. In *Relaciones Geográficas de Indias,* tomo 1, 166–75. Biblioteca de Autores Españoles, vol. 183. Madrid: Ediciones Atlas.

von Hagen, Victor W.

1955   *Highway of the Sun.* New York: Duell, Sloan and Pearce.

Wachtel, Nathan

1973   *Sociedad e ideología: Ensayos de historia y antropología andinas.* Lima: Instituto de Estudios Peruanos.

1977   *The Vision of the Vanquished.* Trans. Ben and Sian Reynolds. New York: Barnes and Noble.

1982   The *Mitimas* of the Cochabamba Valley: The Colonization Policy of Huayna Capac. In *The Inca and Aztec States, 1400–1800: Anthropology and History,* ed. George A. Collier, Renato I. Rosaldo, and John D. Wirth, 199–235. New York: Academic Press.

Wallerstein, Immanuel

1974   *The Modern World-System I.* New York: Academic Press.

Wedin, Ake

1965   *El sistema decimal en el imperio incaico.* Madrid: Insula.

Wenke, Robert J.

1987   Western Iran in the Partho-Sasanian Period: The Imperial Transformation. In *The Archaeology of Western Iran,* ed. Frank Hole, 251–81. Washington, D.C.: Smithsonian Institution Press.

Werge, Robert W.

1977   *Potato Storage Systems in the Mantaro Valley Region of Peru.* Lima: International Potato Center, Socioeconomic Unit.

West, Terry L.

1981   Llama Caravans of the Andes. *Natural History* 90 (12): 62–73.

White, Leslie

1959   *The Evolution of Culture.* New York: McGraw-Hill.

Wiener, Charles

1880   *Perou et Bolivie.* Paris: Librarie Hachette.

Williams, Verónica I.

1983   Evidencia de actividad textil en el establecimiento incaico Potrero Chaquiago (Provincia de Catamarca). *Relaciones de la Sociedad Argentina de Antropología,* tomo 15, 49–59.

Wolf, Eric R.

1982   *Europe and the People without History.* Berkeley and Los Angeles: University of California Press.

World Weather Records 1951–60

1966   *South America, Central America, West Indies, and Caribbean and Bermuda.* Vol. 3 of *United States Department of Commerce, Environmental Science Service Administration, Environmental Data Services.* Washington, D.C.: U.S. Government Printing Office.

Wright, Henry T.

1977   Recent Research on the Origin of the State. *Annual Review of Anthropology* 6:379–97.

1978   Toward an Explanation of the Origin of the State. In *Origins of the State: The Anthropology of Political Evolution,* ed. Ronald Cohen and Elman R. Service, 49–68. Philadelphia: Ishi.

1984   Prehistoric Political Formations. In *On the Evolution of Complex Societies,* ed. Timothy K. Earle, 41–77. Malibu, Calif.: Undena Press.

Wright, Henry, and Gregory Johnson

1975   Population, Exchange, and Early State Formation in Southwestern Iran. *American Anthropologist* 77:267–89.

Wylie, Alison

1982   Epistemological Issues Raised by a Structural Archaeologist. In *Symbolic and Structural Archaeology,* ed. Ian Hodder, 39–46. Cambridge: Cambridge University Press.

1985   The Reaction against Analogy. In *Advances in Archaeological Method and Theory,* ed. Michael B. Schiffer, vol. 8, 63–111. New York: Academic Press.

Xérez, Francisco de

1917   *Verdadera relación de la conquista del Perú y*
[1534] *provincia del Cuzco llamada la Nueva Castilla.* Ed. Horacio H. Urteaga. Lima: Sanmartí.

Yoffee, Norman

1979   The Decline and Rise of Mesopotamian Civilization: An Ethnoarchaeological Perspective on the Evolution of Social Complexity. *American Antiquity* 44:5–35.

Zárate, Augustín de

1862   *Historia del descubrimiento y conquista de la*
[1555] *Provincia del Perú.* Biblioteca de Autores Españoles, vol. 26, 459–574. Madrid: Ediciones Atlas.

Zuidema, R. Tom

1964   *The Ceque System of Cuzco.* Leiden, Netherlands: E. J. Brill.

1977   The Inca Kinship System: A New Theoretical View. In *Andean Kinship and Marriage,* ed. Ralph Bolton and Enrique Mayer, 240–81. American Anthropological Association Special Publication no. 7. Washington, D.C.

1983   Hierarchy and Space in Incaic Social Organization. *Ethnohistory* 30:49–75.

1990   *Inca Civilization in Cuzco.* Trans. Jean-Jacques Decoster. Austin: University of Texas Press.

Zuidema, R. Tom, and D. Poole

1982   Los límites de los cuatro suyus incaicos en el Cuzco. *Bulletin de L'Institut Français d'Etudes Andines* 11 (1–2): 83–89. Lima.

Index